Better Safe Than Sorry

Better Safe Than Sorry

THE IRONIES OF LIVING WITH THE BOMB

Michael Krepon

STANFORD SECURITY STUDIES
An Imprint of Stanford University Press
Stanford, California
A HENRY L. STIMSON CENTER BOOK

Stanford University Press
Stanford, California

Printed in the United States of America on acid-free, archival-quality paper

Library of Congress Cataloging-in-Publication Data

Krepon, Michael, 1946–
  Better safe than sorry : the ironies of living with the bomb / Michael Krepon.
    p. cm.
  "A Henry L. Stimson Center Book."
  Includes bibliographical references and index.
  ISBN 978-0-8047-6063-8 (hbk. : alk. paper)
    1. Nuclear weapons—Government policy—United States.   2. Nuclear
nonproliferation.   3. United States—Military policy. I. Title.
  UA23.K77695 2008
  355.02'170973—dc22

                              2008024573

Typeset by Bruce Lundquist in 10/14 Minion

Special discounts for bulk quantities of Stanford Security Studies are available to
corporations, professional associations, and other organizations. For details and
discount information, contact the special sales department of Stanford University Press.
Tel: (650) 736-1783, Fax: (650) 736-1784

For two casualties of war: My father, Harry, who worked at the Watertown, Massachusetts, Arsenal during World War II, and the uncle I am named after, Mickey, who died at Anzio.

Midway this way of life we're bound upon,
  I woke to find myself in a dark wood,
  Where the right road was wholly lost and gone.

**Dante, *The Divine Comedy*,
Canto I (translated by Dorothy L. Sayers)**

The future, which has so many elements of high promise,
is yet only a stone's throw from despair.

J. Robert Oppenheimer, letter to Herbert Smith

When the gods punish us, they make us believe in our own
advertising.

**Daniel Boorstin, paraphrasing Oscar Wilde,
in *The Image: Or What Happened to the American Dream***

And how can we enlarge our opportunities? Can we
transmute what appears to be an immediate crisis into
a long-term problem, which presumably would permit
the application of more varied and better considered
correctives than the pitifully few and inadequate measures
that seem available at present?

Bernard Brodie, *The Absolute Weapon*

A pessimist sees the difficulty in every opportunity; an
optimist sees the opportunity in every difficulty.

Winston Churchill, origin unclear

CONTENTS

PREFACE

THE GENESIS OF THIS BOOK occurred in June 2006, when I was shivering on the spine of the Andes Mountains at a place called Tres Cruces d'Oro. Thirteen thousand feet below, at the end of a windy dirt road, lay the headwaters of the Amazon. I was sitting on this ridgetop because I was told that there was no better place to watch the sun rise.

The dark cobalt sky was already streaked with shafts of light playing off against the cloud bank below me. Then, amazingly, the sun's upward rays of white light turned the cloud tops into icebergs floating in a sea of blue. Mesmerized, I felt that I had been transported to Glacier Bay above the Amazon. The focus of this light show then shifted to a ripe orange slit that appeared between the folds of the clouds. The classic half-dome shape began to emerge below, but this time, I was watching the sun emerge in an incredibly beautiful natural setting, backed by sacred mountains and fronted by torrents of water and a well-ordered riot of plant life. From this high perch, the life-giving force of the sun was overwhelming.

Then the sun's rising dome triggered another image that is indelibly printed on my brain, the outline of a hydrogen bomb that arcs from ground zero and rises to become a monstrous, mutating mushroom cloud. Physicists learned from and borrowed the fiery processes of the sun to create the H-bomb, and with it, the limitless means to incinerate cities and turn all forms of life into ashes. My mind then flashed to Hiroshima's Genbaku Dome, the skeletal arc atop an old commercial exhibition hall that has been left in ruins, a public reminder of what happened in August 1945—and what must not happen again.

The magnificent sun had now risen above me and was too bright to observe. I was bathed in its warmth, shedding layers of protection against the bone-chilling cold. The focus of my life's work and the gift of travel came together that morning, when the life-giving and life-taking forces of the sun were juxtaposed. What would we humans make of the sun's powers?

It was time to write another book about the Bomb.

My professional work has long revolved around trying to prevent big explosions. I've worked on Capitol Hill and in the executive branch for President Jimmy Carter. But most of the time, I've worked as an outsider who tries to nudge insiders to push the envelope of what's possible. This is where I have felt most comfortable, working on projects that I believe in, speaking and writing in my own voice, and feeling grateful when I hear echoes of ideas and initiatives that I had tried to midwife. My base of operations has been the Henry L. Stimson Center, a nongovernmental organization in Washington that I co-founded in 1989.

I have been gifted many times over by foundations that have shared my enthusiasms and backed my projects. In recent years, I have been working to prevent the testing and use of space weapons, trying to promote a settlement of the Kashmir dispute, and developing nuclear risk-reduction measures that the governments of India and Pakistan might consider adopting.

None of my projects take me too far from the Bomb. Satellites, for example, provide life-giving services by guiding ambulances and police cars to their destinations as quickly as possible with global positioning systems. Satellites enable emergency calls on cell phones. Without satellites, pagers don't work and disaster relief and emergency rescue teams are handicapped. Satellites monitor the health of the planet, and they help protect soldiers who have been placed in harm's way.

Satellites are also connected to the nuclear forces of major powers, providing early warning of an impending attack, targeting information, and communicating up and down the chain of command. If satellites are attacked and if space becomes a shooting gallery, nations might feel threatened enough to consider using their nuclear weapons. Even if they don't, space warfare can produce lethal debris that kills satellites indiscriminately. Marble-size pieces of debris in low earth orbit travel at ten times the speed of a rifle bullet. They can remain a lethal hazard for many decades.

I have been working to promote a code of conduct for responsible space-faring nations that would help keep space a sanctuary free of weapons. This idea has gained traction, particularly after the Chinese test of an antisatellite weapon in January 2007, which demonstrated how much lasting damage could result from using satellites as target practice.

India and Pakistan have come a long way since they acquired nuclear bombs. They have had a series of hair-raising crises and one border war. Pakistan also became a hub of nuclear proliferation, facilitating the nuclear programs of North Korea and Iran. India and Pakistan have refused to place limits on their nuclear capabilities. In recent years, however, they have been working to demonstrate responsible nuclear stewardship. They have negotiated and properly implemented a series of confidence-building and nuclear risk-reduction measures, such as improving their means of communication in crises and providing warning of missile tests and military exercises.

Without much notice, the Kashmir dispute has become much less intractable. This dispute used to be about territory, sovereignty, religion, and inheritance—the worst causes of warfare. But in recent years, Indian and Pakistani leaders have begun to give priority to the well-being of Kashmiris. They have allowed divided families to meet, opened trade and transit routes across the Kashmir divide, and allowed cultural exchanges and religious pilgrimages to proceed.

As a consequence, India and Pakistan have come closer than ever before to resolving the Kashmir dispute. Now the biggest impediment to a settlement is domestic politics in both countries. This is a significant roadblock, but it is a huge improvement over the earlier roadblocks that led to wars. Enlightened leadership in Pakistan and India deserves the credit for progress toward nuclear stabilization and a Kashmir settlement, which would be the ultimate nuclear risk-reduction measure. I am proud to have nurtured these confidence-building measures through Stimson Center programming and publications.

There have been many success stories related to the Bomb, including quiet successes every day to lock down dangerous weapons and materials. Everything is not going to hell in a handbasket. Nuclear anxieties are well founded, but anyone over the age of 25 has lived through tougher times. A wise man once told me that problems couldn't be solved at the level of the problem. The more I've thought about this advice, the more I have come to accept it. In this book I try to take a more elevated view of hard problems.

It's also hard to make headway on difficult problems from a place of deep anxiety. Pessimism doesn't help in troubled times. Neither does naïve optimism. The Stimson Center's motto is "Pragmatic steps toward ideal objectives."

This is my philosophy as well. I believe in the value of optimism tempered by realism. Optimism is realism put to good use.

I also believe that a sense of irony helps when working on nuclear problems. Good intentions can produce terrible results, and good outcomes can sometimes result from nefarious plans. The law of unintended consequences works both ways, for good and for ill. The philosophy of "better safe than sorry" has helped keep the cold war from becoming hot—but to be on the safe side, both nuclear superpowers produced more than 125,000 nuclear weapons. The U.S. nuclear stockpile peaked in 1966 at approximately 31,700 weapons; the USSR stockpile topped off at about 41,000 weapons in 1986.[1]

The economic costs of nuclear preparedness were considerable—by 1998, the tab for the United States had risen to $5.5 trillion.[2] Spending priorities were badly skewed by public anxieties and poor choices. In recent years, the United States has spent ten times more on missile defenses that serve as the last line of defense against nuclear danger than on safeguarding the most deadly weapons and materials, which is the nation's first line of national defense. Congress appropriates approximately $1 billion annually to prevent the most dangerous weapons and materials from falling into the most dangerous hands. In 2007, Congress appropriated $286 billion in a subsidy-laden farm bill.[3] President George W. Bush sincerely believed that a war to topple Saddam Hussein was necessary in order to be safe rather than sorry. The United States spends as much money in Iraq in three days as it spends in one year locking down nuclear bombs and bomb-making materials.[4]

The nuclear dilemmas of the digital age are not carbon copies of the past. New threats appear, and old ones fade away. The threat of a surprise Soviet attack is gone, as are approximately 39,000 vintage nuclear weapons from the Soviet arsenal.[5] Americans no longer live under the specter of a massive, bolt-from-the-blue attack orchestrated by the Kremlin and the Soviet Strategic Rocket Forces. The Red Army is not poised to carry out a blitzkrieg attack across central Europe, accompanied by the detonations of hundreds of tactical nuclear weapons.

The shedding of old worries and the accumulation of new ones is a natural process, whether or not they are related to the Bomb. Because nuclear anxieties are often characterized as existential, they can override reality—even when rational analysis can demonstrate that anxieties are overdrawn. Many Americans are not old enough to compare contemporary nuclear anxieties to those faced by their parents. When everything is a crisis, yardsticks aren't necessary.

So how do the old nuclear dangers compare to the new ones? The threats of nuclear terrorism and proliferation are real and worth worrying about. But they cannot hold a candle to the nuclear threats and crises that defined the cold war. The old nuclear threats were indeed existential. They could obliterate the United States and create a planetary environmental crisis far, far worse than extreme scenarios of global warming. Contemporary threats of nuclear terrorism and proliferation are serious, but Americans have been through much worse times.

Predictions of maximum danger during the cold war were overdrawn, as were many of the proposed remedies. Today, warnings of maximum danger and many proposed remedies are also overdrawn. During the cold war, national leaders managed to navigate through dangerous waters by keeping their powder dry and their defenses up. Safe passage was secured by means of containing and deterring dangerous foes, by maintaining strong military capabilities, and by reducing dangers and maintaining domestic and alliance cohesion though diplomatic engagement. Patient and persistent engagement eventually produced diplomatic breakthroughs that were codified in arms control and reduction agreements. During previous hard times, American leaders did not denigrate treaties. Back then, reassurance was as essential as deterrence in keeping the peace.

These tools worked best when they worked together. They provided safe passage through far greater nuclear threats than what we face today. These tools can also work against new threats of nuclear terrorism and proliferation, but they will have to be adapted to meet new challenges.

One day a week I teach in the Department of Politics at the University of Virginia, where I am struck every semester by how strange and new the story of the Bomb is to my students. Episodes that are fresh and vital to me occurred before they were born. My sense is that my students and others might benefit from an impressionistic account highlighting themes rather than offering a historical narrative of the Bomb. My account includes episodes that may not be familiar to readers and some that do not merit inclusion in diplomatic histories, but these episodes might speak volumes about how we dealt with the Bomb and how the Bomb dealt with us.

Nuclear fears run much deeper at present, not just because of the 9/11 attacks but also because the George W. Bush administration as well as its harshest critics have tapped into public anxieties to promote favored policies. My approach is different. Yes, there are serious nuclear dangers, and yes, the Bush administration has acted unwisely. Remedial steps are required, and I talk about them. I also believe that nuclear dangers have been overblown and that the echo chamber of anxiety in our public square is part of the problem. The United States has been through far worse periods of nuclear peril, and we have found safe passage. We can get through this mess as well. This is a hopeful book.

There is no shortage of books or articles on the episodes highlighted in these pages. In this book I do not cover many aspects of our nuclear history, but I do draw on wonderful journalistic accounts of nuclear negotiations and superb, detailed diplomatic histories of U.S.-Soviet relations. If one episode or another in these pages beckons readers, they can turn to my endnotes to learn more. There are also many contemporary accounts in this field from strongly held points of view. Books that are deeply pessimistic or simplistic do not, in my view, help to chart our nuclear future.

I have tried to write an accessible book about dense subjects because I wish to reach general readers in addition to students and professionals in this field. Those who have worked on various aspects of the Bomb share a common language—bomb-speak—but they congregate into tribes that tend to get lost in detail and mired in ancient debates. The time is ripe for the tribes to reconnect with their fellow citizens. The way forward will require joint effort.

Henry L. Stimson once wrote, "We cannot take refuge in the folly of black and white solutions."[6] Stimson was a cabinet-level adviser for American presidents from Taft to Truman. He wrote this warning in 1947—a black-and-white time if there ever was one—when the world was dividing into the great historical face-off between Communism and the free world. Stimson was then thinking hard about the nuclear dilemma, a danger that, in his mind, dwarfed the others he wrestled with, including the defeat of Nazi Germany and Imperial Japan. As secretary of war, he oversaw and authorized the use of the Bomb to end World War II as quickly as possible, and then he resolved that no other national leader should ever have to make a similar decision. Stimson was convinced that the path to nuclear safety lay in accepting complexity and taking risk. He was prepared to take the hard path toward nuclear abolition.

I can understand why. We have memorabilia at the Stimson Center, including a copy of the briefing Stimson received about the Bomb from General Leslie Groves, the man who ran the Manhattan Project. The copy was given to Harvey Bundy, Stimson's close confidante at the War Department. Harvey Bundy passed the briefing along to his son, McGeorge, who served as President John F. Kennedy's national security adviser during the Cuban missile crisis. McGeorge Bundy gave the briefing to the Stimson Center for safekeeping before he died.

Back then, briefings were given on easels. The briefing consisted of large photographs pasted on 2 by 3 foot slabs of cardboard. These folios were the first portraits of the Bomb. The opening folio was a picture of the mushroom cloud from the first nuclear test at Alamogordo, New Mexico. The next folios consisted of aerial photographs of Hiroshima and Nagasaki before and after the atomic bomb drops. Staring at these black-and-white photographs, I can understand why Stimson warned against taking refuge in black-and-white solutions.

I begin this book with a snapshot of where we are and then move back in time to snapshots of previous periods of presumed maximum nuclear danger. The purpose of these vignettes is to place contemporary anxieties into historical context. In Chapters 3 and 4 I look at the first and second nuclear ages. My dividing point is 1991, the year that the Soviet Union collapsed and when victorious U.S. troops discovered Saddam Hussein's surprisingly advanced nuclear weapon program. The nuclear dangers and proposed remedies of the first and second nuclear ages have been quite different. These chapters provide context for my assessment of alternative nuclear futures that follows (Chapter 5). Here I suggest key drivers that can shape what lies ahead. By focusing on the events that can do the most damage, my intention is to clarify and reinforce useful preventive measures.

One lesson that will hopefully become apparent from the pages that follow is that pessimism serves no useful purpose in dealing with the dangers of nuclear proliferation and terrorism. Nuclear dangers are real and must be recognized, but overhyping the threat invites paralysis or missteps. The United States has stumbled before, but America has also made it through hard times and rebounded. With wisdom, persistence, and luck, another dark passage can be successfully navigated.

ACKNOWLEDGMENTS

THIS BOOK REFLECTS the contributions of many friends and colleagues. I am especially grateful to funders who have entrusted me with their resources. My sincere thanks go to Jonathan Fanton, Amy Gordon, and Matthew Stumpf at the John D. and Catherine T. MacArthur Foundation; Vartan Gregorian and Stephen Del Rosso at the Carnegie Corporation of New York; Naila Bolus, Paul Carroll, and Sally Lilienthal, bless her soul, at the Ploughshares Fund; Renee Schwartz and the Board of Directors at the New-Land Foundation, and Cynda and Marcel Arsenault at the Secure World Foundation.

Without the support of the Rockefeller Foundation, which provided a month-long residency at Rockefeller's Bellagio Center in Italy, this book would still be a work in progress. My thanks go to Pilar Palacia and the staff of Villa Serbelloni, where creativity and kindness reign. My colleagues at the Bellagio Center, Mary Jo Bang, Neil Fligstein, Mildred Howard, Mary Jo Salter, and Martha Sandweiss, provided helpful guidance and support.

The book cover is the work of Mildred Howard, Donald Farnsworth, and Magnolia Editions. Their creative passion and wizardry with pixels produced this depiction of the Baker shot, an underwater explosion at the Bikini Atoll in 1946.

I am thankful to Geoffrey Burn, Jessica Walsh, Carolyn Brown, Mimi Braverman, and their associates at Stanford University Press for believing in this book and for shepherding it to print.

I received research help from many quarters, especially from two of the ablest research assistants I have ever worked with at the Henry L. Stimson Center: Michael Katz-Hyman and Alex Stolar. Sam Black, Lee Dunbar, and

Adam Stern, found answers to countless questions. I am indebted to Hans M. Kristensen and Robert S. Norris, who collect and analyze data that so many others and I draw on. My thanks also go to Neyla Arnas, Hans Binnendijk, Bruce Blair, William Burns, P. R. Chari, Patrick Clawson, Lewis Dunn, Alton Frye, Adam Garfinkle, Rose Goettemoeller, Max Kampelman, Mark Kramer, Jeff Laurenti, Roger Leeds, Jeffrey Legro, Jeffrey Lewis, Clay Moltz, Michael Moodie, Polly Nayak, Richard Pierce, Paul Richards, Carl Robichaud, Peter Roman, Scott Sagan, Stephen Schwartz, Strobe Talbott, Jonathan Tucker, Elizabeth Turpen, and Jonathan M. Weisgall.

Brian Finlay, Raymond Garthoff, Edward Ifft, Ellen Laipson, Richard Rhodes, and Brad Roberts read, commented on, and suggested improvements to specific chapters. Michael Nacht, Lawrence Korb, and David Holloway were kind enough to read and comment on all chapters. My friend of forty years, Len Ackland, applied his wide-ranging knowledge of nuclear issues to scrub and edit the entire manuscript with his usual care and precision. I am thankful to these readers for pointing out factual errors and weaknesses in my analysis. The remaining shortfalls are my responsibility.

Working at the Stimson Center and helping it grow have been a privilege. To the Board of Directors, under the guidance of its Founding Chairman, Barry Blechman, and now Lincoln Bloomfield, to my co-workers, and especially to the Center's leadership, Ellen Laipson and Cheryl Ramp, I extend my sincere thanks.

The University of Virginia provides me with enriching opportunities for teaching and mentoring. I am thankful to the Vice Provost for International Affairs, Dr. Leigh Grossman, for opening a path for me to become a Diplomat Scholar at the university. It has been a pleasure to teach in the Department of Politics, where I work with dedicated colleagues.

In the final stages of writing this book, I received immense support from Dr. Christopher Thomas, Patricia Redmond, and the dedicated caregivers at the University of Virginia's Hospital and Cancer Center.

Most important of all, I am thankful for my home base. The love of my life, Alessandra, continues to be my wisest teacher. We have been fortunate in many ways, and we have received no greater gifts than our daughter, Misha, our son, Joshua, and his wife, Sarah.

Michael Krepon
North Garden, Virginia
January 2008

Better Safe Than Sorry

1 MASTER BUILDERS AND DECONSTRUCTIONISTS

THE GLOBAL SYSTEM created over many decades to prevent nuclear proliferation can be likened to a construction project. The construction is only as sturdy as the common resolve of the five nations with nuclear weapons that also enjoy permanent seats on the United Nations Security Council. As the world's strongest power, the United States has the most responsibility for building maintenance. If Washington walks away from this job, the construction site will become unsafe. But even if the United States does its job properly, Russia, China, France, and Great Britain still have to support the structure. When the five permanent members of the Security Council work in concert against the perils of proliferation, the construction provides reliable shelter. When they place other national security and commercial interests ahead of proliferation concerns, the construction becomes wobbly.

The building's load-bearing walls consist of agreements, rules, and norms designed to prevent proliferation. Treaties that set legally binding obligations constitute the steel beams that keep this structure erect. The most important rules are set by the Treaty on the Nonproliferation of Nuclear Weapons (or Nonproliferation Treaty), which was negotiated in 1968. The Nonproliferation Treaty is built around two central bargains: States that possess the Bomb promise to disarm, and states without the Bomb promise continued abstinence—so long as they can reap the benefits of the peaceful uses of the atom. The Nonproliferation Treaty initially had only forty-three signatories. Adherence grew slowly. Two of the five permanent members of the Security Council, China and France, did not join until 1992. The Nonproliferation Treaty is now the most inclusive treaty of all—every state has joined, except Israel, India, and Pakistan.

This construction project continues to grow with the addition of new tenants, export controls, additional treaties, and administrative rules and regulations designed to prevent proliferation. The building managers are based in Vienna, where the International Atomic Energy Agency is based. The agency is overseen by a board of governors representing thirty-five countries. Important decisions require a two-thirds majority on the board. Enforcement decisions require the backing of the United Nations Security Council. National leaders provide the brick for this immense construction project, and international civil servants supply the mortar.

The creation of this global system to prevent proliferation was one of the great achievements of the cold war. It was not easy to convince nations to abstain from obtaining the most powerful weapons of all—weapons that many states had the capacity to build. Throughout recorded history, humans have sought clubs to use against enemies. When humans banded together to form tribes, they sought bigger clubs. And when tribes banded together to form nations, this impulse became stronger still. Nuclear weapons are the ultimate club, but this weapon is so powerful that abstinence became conceivable— under certain protections.

Abstinence needed to be a rational calculation and not an act of faith. The rational calculation was that, if more nations sought the Bomb, others would follow, and the net effect would be great insecurity. This rational calculation, in turn, depended on intrusive monitoring and the backup provided by states possessing the Bomb, especially the United States and the Soviet Union. Without their common resolve, this construction project would never have gotten off the ground.

Early construction included the first treaty limiting nuclear testing, new regulations dealing with nuclear exports, and rudimentary inspections and safeguards at nuclear facilities. To stabilize their nuclear competition and to shore up their end of the Nonproliferation Treaty bargain, Washington and Moscow agreed to modest limits on their nuclear forces and significant limits on missile defenses. By the end of the cold war, treaties mandating deep cuts and the abolition of entire categories of nuclear forces were negotiated, which also helped shore up the Nonproliferation Treaty.

Some construction on the first floor was only partly completed. One room for a treaty that would end nuclear tests for all time was built but never occupied; this treaty was negotiated in 1996 but remains in limbo because the United States, China, India, Pakistan, and others are balking at its terms. Other planned construction was never undertaken, especially a treaty banning the production of fissile material for weapons.

Constructing the first floor of this edifice required consensus, not only between the superpowers but also between weapon possessors and abstainers. During the first nuclear age, this foundation remained strong. Even though the nuclear arsenals of both superpowers rose to absurd levels, new additions to the nuclear club were kept reasonably in check. One country (Israel) covertly acquired the Bomb, and two more (India and Pakistan) positioned themselves on this threshold. But many more countries that seriously considered the nuclear option decided to throw their lot in with the Nonproliferation Treaty.

The second nuclear age began in 1991 with the demise of the Soviet Union and the surprise discovery in Iraq of an advanced bomb program. Although U.S. and Soviet nuclear arsenals declined significantly, concerns grew over horizontal proliferation, especially in India, Pakistan, North Korea, and Iran. The scope of the proliferation problem also expanded to include extremist groups, profiteering middlemen, and transactions between outlier states.

The structure built to prevent proliferation during the first nuclear age was not designed to deal with new members of the nuclear club or the threat of nuclear terrorism. Some expected it to fall down. North Korea declared its withdrawal from the treaty in 2003, and Iran could be headed for the same exit. At the same time, none of the five permanent members of the Security Council acted like strong stakeholders during the second nuclear age. At best, they paid lip service to their commitment to eliminate the Bomb, and they had difficulties forming a common front to stop the Iranian nuclear program. The other central bargain of the Nonproliferation Treaty—that abstainers deserved help in acquiring the peaceful uses of nuclear energy—was misused. Nuclear commerce helped North Korea build nuclear weapons, a path that Iran is following.

The Nonproliferation Treaty was designed for an earlier era, before the advent of a single dominant military power, underground networks of nuclear commerce, and terrorist cells seeking nuclear weapons and fissile material. The Nonproliferation Treaty was far sturdier in a bipolar world when the superpowers could impose discipline when they agreed with each other. The first nuclear age was an exercise in establishing norms against proliferation. The norms helped to apply leverage on states that were fence-sitters. The norms did not prevent rule breaking, but they did make it easier to isolate or sanction rule breakers. During the second nuclear age, these norms were weakened, and there was less discipline to reinforce them.

The structural weaknesses of the first floor were exposed by the self-described "father" of Pakistan's bomb, A. Q. Khan, whose network supplied bomb-making equipment to Iran, North Korea, Libya, and perhaps other procurers. Other veterans of Pakistan's nuclear establishment had traveled to Afghanistan to meet with Osama bin Laden and other senior al Qaeda and Taliban operatives. The paramount threats of nuclear proliferation and terrorism were clear for all to see when al Qaeda struck on September 11, 2001. Compensating for the weaknesses of the Nonproliferation Treaty's structure required exceptional measures.

The inner circle of the George W. Bush administration held jaundiced views about the effectiveness of global nonproliferation norms and the utility of treaties. They wanted to build a second floor to address new proliferation challenges, using different tools. Rooms on the second floor would not require consensual building permits, because the second floor required the coercive instruments that the first floor lacked.

Some of this construction worked reasonably well. The Bush administration placed new emphasis on codes of conduct in combating proliferation. These codes took the form of political agreements among like-minded states to band together to prevent dangerous activities. President Bush launched the Proliferation Security Initiative in May 2003 with the declared goal of seizing weapons of mass destruction or their components when in transit. A core group of states, eleven in number, agreed to a statement of interdiction principles four months later. The core group then invited other nations to associate themselves, with varying degrees of attachment, to these principles.[1]

Another one of the Bush administration's accomplishments has been to establish a global norm criminalizing proliferation. The criminalization statute is embedded in United Nations Security Council Resolution 1540, which was unanimously approved in April 2004. This resolution imposes binding obligations on all member states "to take additional effective measures to prevent the proliferation of nuclear, chemical or biological weapons and their means of delivery." It also calls on all nations to establish effective domestic controls, including criminal statutes, to prevent proliferation.[2] The administration also supported The Hague Code of Conduct to strengthen a global norm against the proliferation of ballistic missiles capable of carrying weapons of mass destruction. Completed in 2002, The Hague Code of Conduct calls on states to exercise restraint in ballistic missile testing and development.[3] Most countries have signed on to these principles; China, Pakistan, India, North Korea, Syria, and Iran have not.

In addition, the Bush administration took essential steps to increase the geographic scope of programs to provide training and equipment to prevent proliferation. In June 2002, the United States and other industrialized countries announced the Global Partnership Against the Spread of Weapons and Materials of Mass Destruction. In July 2006, President Bush and Russian president Vladimir Putin announced the Global Initiative to Combat Nuclear Terrorism, which focused on improved protection, control, and accounting of deadly materials, increased cooperation for detecting and suppressing illicit trafficking, and enhanced capabilities to deal with the consequences of terrorist acts.[4]

Constructing a second floor of the global nonproliferation system was needed, and the Bush administration deserves much credit for these initiatives. The Bush administration's design, however, had a fundamental flaw: It focused almost entirely on the second floor while leaving the first floor to its structural weaknesses. The administration focused on the second floor precisely because it fundamentally disagreed with previous builders over what constituted the first floor's load-bearing walls.

The master builders of the global nonproliferation system considered these load-bearing walls to be the norms against using or threatening to use nuclear weapons, testing these devices, and producing the fissile material that made these weapons so lethal. Some—but not all—of these norms are embedded in treaties. The architects of the first floor believed that the structural integrity of their building required the rebar provided by treaties—especially the treaty banning nuclear tests.

Moreover, construction during the first nuclear age was built on the core principle that rules needed to apply to all. This principle was essential to bridge the divides created by nuclear weapons and by a bipolar world. The entire first floor could never have been built had its builders chosen to construct one set of rules for responsible states and another for bad actors because the construction crew couldn't agree on who belonged in which category: The two primary architects for the first floor were, after all, Washington and Moscow. No rules preventing proliferation could have been written by differentiating good guys from bad actors and without the commitment to abolition by all states possessing the Bomb.

The Bush administration used fundamentally different building principles for the second story. It has postulated a new guiding principle for proliferation: that the fundamental problem was not related to the Bomb but to the bomb holder. The character of the state mattered most, not whether the state was building bombs. Consequently, the administration has proposed a loose set of rules for responsible states such as India and tight rules for bad actors such as Iran. It rejected ratification and entry into force of a treaty banning all nuclear testing for all time while carving out exceptions to global rules on nuclear commerce for India, a responsible state.

The Bush administration also significantly qualified a norm-based approach to nonproliferation: Rules and norms were good, except where norms constrained U.S. freedom of action or the actions of U.S. friends and allies, especially those who might serve as counterweights to China or Iran. Informal arrangements established in codes of conduct were good, but formal rules embedded in new treaties were to be avoided. Because a treaty ending fissile material production for bombs would impose restraints on responsible, but not irresponsible, states, it was hardly a priority. The Nonproliferation Treaty obligation on nuclear weapon states to disarm need not be taken seriously, but far more serious penalties were required for new bomb seekers.

The adoption of such a structurally unsound approach to strengthening the global nonproliferation system could only have occurred in a country that enjoyed dominant power and that was prone to black-and-white formulas. America's closest allies and the lead architects of the global nonproliferation system were dismayed by these formulas—and somewhat confused by them as well. They were familiar and comfortable with bedrock conservative principles, especially the need for rules and regulations that provided order while permitting freedom of action that was not harmful to others. Indeed, the global nonproliferation system was built on these conservative principles.

No reputable construction company would build atop a shaky foundation without strengthening its load-bearing walls, but the Bush administration questioned the value of some of these walls. It argued that the cold war was over, that the United States needed to maximize its freedom of action, and that rules could be bent for responsible states. Treaties were irrelevant for bad actors, who would cheat. Verification was either impossible or ineffectual. Nor did the Bush administration think highly of diplomatic engagement, deterrence, and containment—hallmarks of success during the cold war—against bad actors. Traditional American conservatism became one of the casualties of 9/11.

The results of the Bush administration's new approach to the global nonproliferation system were not pretty to look at. The first floor of the global nonproliferation system was built along classical lines, and the second story was designed by deconstructionists. No matter how useful the rooms were on the second floor, the construction as a whole did not work properly. Worse, the architectural principles for the second story were antithetical to those used for the first. The entire construction became wobbly because the architects of the first floor and the Bush administration pursued fundamentally different principles of design.

The Bush administration was right to conclude that the Nonproliferation Treaty needed to be shored up and that a more proactive approach was needed in light of the new threats of proliferation and nuclear terrorism. On balance, however, the Bush administration has done more harm than good to the global system it inherited to prevent proliferation. Its war of choice to prevent nuclear proliferation in Iraq accelerated nuclear programs in North Korea and Iran, which, in turn, accelerated nuclear hedging strategies elsewhere. Reinforcing the building's foundations as well as constructing a second story were both required. The Bush administration's approach has left much repair work for its successor.

2 APOCALYPTIC WARNINGS

A CONSTANT DRUMBEAT of messages reminds Americans that they live in scary times. Television ratings appear to depend on discomforting viewers sitting in easy chairs. Local news broadcasts lead with stories about murder, mayhem, and random acts of violence. The national and international news is relentlessly grim, filled with suicide bombings, killer storms, combat deaths, and the murder of the innocent. Even weather forecasts prey on viewer insecurities. Commercials offer no respite, focusing on the fear of infirmities, hair loss, sexual impotency, and weight gain. More anxiety awaits in doctors' offices and transportation hubs. Washington, in particular, is awash in anxiety. Members of Congress, on both sides of the aisle, trumpet warnings and preparedness shortfalls, just as, in the wake of Sputnik, "the nation's legislators leaped forward like heavy drinkers hearing a cork pop."[1] The reverberations of attacks on the Twin Towers and the Pentagon are with us still.

In the depths of America's depression, President Franklin Delano Roosevelt told Americans that the only thing they had to fear was fear itself. After the surprise attacks on 9/11, Americans heard very different messages from their national leaders. The George W. Bush administration and members of Congress dwelled on America's vulnerabilities and anxieties in an open-ended "war on terror."

Fear became deeply embedded in the country's psyche, a critical element of competing policy and political agendas. President Bush's severest critics were no less anxiety prone, warning that the administration was compounding dangers through neglect and poor judgment.[2] Warnings from the White House and its critics reinforced each other, creating an echo chamber of public fears.

Washington no longer projected hope and optimism. Instead, the Bush administration, as former deputy secretary of state Richard Armitage observed, was exporting fear and anger.[3] After World War II ended, in earlier years of maximum danger, when the Soviet Union was beginning to consolidate its grip over Eastern Europe, Secretary of State Dean Acheson advised President Harry S. Truman to mobilize a war-weary public for a long campaign against a ruthless foe by being "clearer than truth." Exaggerating the threat in support of freedom and national security was no vice, he contended, just as modulation was no virtue. As Acheson later recounted in his memoirs:

> The task of a public officer seeking to explain and gain support for a major policy is not that of the writer of a doctoral thesis. Qualification must give way to simplicity of statement, nicety and nuance to bluntness, almost brutality, in carrying home a point. . . . If we made our points clearer than truth, we did not differ from most educators and could hardly do otherwise.[4]

Nuclear anxieties after 9/11 also prompted the Bush administration to be clearer than the truth. President Bush and his inner circle realized that it would be risky to wage a preventive war in Iraq but concluded that it would be riskier still to permit Saddam Hussein to rearm. To gain public support to wage this war of choice, senior Bush administration officials artfully conflated the threats posed by Osama bin Laden and Saddam Hussein. President Bush declared in June 2002 that "the reason I keep insisting that there was a relationship between Iraq and Saddam and al Qaeda [is] because there was a relationship between Iraq and al Qaeda."[5] In February 2003, Secretary of State Colin Powell asserted "a sinister nexus" between Hussein and al Qaeda in his United Nations speech making the case for war. "Iraqi officials deny accusations of ties with al-Qaeda," Powell said. "These denials are simply not credible."[6] Speaking to Rush Limbaugh's radio audience in April 2007, Vice President Dick Cheney focused on Abu Musab al-Zarqawi as the link between Hussein and al Qaeda. Al-Zarqawi "organized the al Qaeda operations inside Iraq before we even arrived on the scene," the vice president declared.[7] When public support for the second Iraq war reached new lows in 2007, President Bush returned to this theme: "The al Qaeda terrorists we face in Iraq are part of the same enemy that attacked us on September the 11th, 2001."[8]

The U.S. intelligence community could not validate any of these claims. There were no operational ties between Saddam Hussein and al Qaeda because Hussein viewed al Qaeda as a threat to his authority and because collusion with al Qaeda would constitute an open invitation for a U.S. invasion. Despite prodding to conclude otherwise, the Central Intelligence Agency, in the words of its former director, "found absolutely no linkage between Saddam and 9/11."[9] Nonetheless, the Bush administration's repeated assertions of linkages between Saddam Hussein and the attacks on U.S. soil gained significant traction. An anxious electorate was hard-pressed to make distinctions between Saddam Hussein and al Qaeda that its leaders were intent on erasing. A Harris poll taken in February 2005 found that 64 percent of those surveyed believed that Hussein had strong links to al Qaeda, 47 percent believed that Hussein helped plan and support the hijackers on 9/11, and 44 percent believed that the hijackers were Iraqi.[10]

The clinching argument for waging a preventive war against Saddam Hussein was that Americans would never know for sure how quickly the Iraqi leader could acquire nuclear weapons. While the mental image of the smoking ruins of the World Trade Center was still burnished in the public's consciousness, national security adviser Condoleezza Rice stated on national television that "we don't want the smoking gun to be a mushroom cloud."[11] President Bush used similar phraseology four weeks later: "America must not ignore the threat gathering against us. Facing clear evidence of peril, we cannot wait for the final proof—the smoking gun—that could come in the form of a mushroom cloud."[12]

Vice President Cheney propounded a new calculus for U.S. action after the attacks on the Twin Towers and the Pentagon. Illicit nuclear transactions could provide shortcuts to the Bomb. The immediate focus of this particular anxiety was A. Q. Khan's entrepreneurial black market in nuclear commerce. "If there's a one per cent chance that Pakistani scientists are helping al Qaeda build or develop a nuclear weapon," Vice President Cheney asserted, "we have to treat it as certainty in terms of our response. It's not about our analysis, or finding a preponderance of evidence. It's about our response."[13]

U.S. armed forces could not possibly be sent into battle everywhere there was a 1 percent chance of impending danger. But Cheney was clearly fixated on a particular target. Saddam Hussein was quite good at hiding things from inspectors and, as the vice president told a national television audience, "He has been absolutely devoted to trying to acquire nuclear weapons." Hinting that the U.S. intelligence community agreed with him, Cheney asserted that "we believe he has, in fact, reconstituted nuclear weapons."[14] Ends justified means during anxious times. The 1 percent doctrine provided 100 percent license to stretch available evidence.

Saddam Hussein was in the Bush administration's crosshairs before the 9/11 attacks, and his days were numbered afterward.[15] He had much to lose by directly confronting the United States and thus needed to keep Osama bin Laden and al Qaeda at arm's length. Tyrants and dictators enjoying the privileges of power and seeking to pass on those privileges to their offspring do not wish to be unseated. If traditional instruments of U.S. statecraft, such as containment, deterrence, and diplomacy, could work effectively against a succession of Soviet and Chinese leaders, they presumably could also work against Hussein. But traditional approaches were deemed insufficient after 9/11, in part because the standard routes to proliferation could now be shortened with the help of middlemen. The essence of the proliferation problem had mutated. It was no longer just about a few states of concern. Now it extended to shadowy networks, to back-alley deals, and to mosques. State-based proliferation was worrisome but manageable. Proliferation by extremist groups was another ball game entirely. Besides, UN sanctions in Iraq were in danger of unraveling. For the Bush administration's inner circle, the usual instruments of containment, deterrence, and diplomacy did not apply.

Threat estimates after 9/11 were feverish. Graham Allison, a sober-minded political scientist, predicted that "on the current course, nuclear terrorism is inevitable. Indeed, if the United States and other governments keep doing what they are doing today, a nuclear terrorist attack on America is more likely than not in the decade ahead."[16] In 2005, Senator Richard Lugar polled eighty-five leading nongovernmental proliferation experts to survey their probability assessments of different types of terrorist attacks. Their median estimate of the risk of the terrorist use of a nuclear weapon somewhere in the world was 10 percent over five years and 20 percent over ten years. As for a "dirty bomb" attack—a weapon of terror that dispersed radiological material without creating a mushroom cloud—the experts predicted a 25 percent chance over five years, jumping to 40 percent within ten years. The combined risk of any kind of attack involving weapons of mass destruction was estimated at 50 percent over five years and 70 percent over ten years.[17] Former secretary of defense William Perry, former senator Sam Nunn, and others estimate that the probability of a nuclear weapon detonating in an American city has grown, not declined, since the 9/11 attacks.[18]

These nuclear anxieties were warranted, but they left many Americans unhinged. If America's leaders had tried to still these anxieties, the way President Eisenhower did after the launch of Sputnik in 1957, they would likely have been ridiculed and marginalized. Eisenhower, intent on keeping a lid on military spending, referred to the first-ever man-made satellite as "a small ball" that did not change military equations. Ike's apparent nonchalance—Sputnik in no way affected his tee times on the golf course—along with the early failures of the U.S. space effort led to a 30 percent drop in presidential approval ratings.[19] The attacks against America on 9/11 were too grievous and too bold to be downplayed in any way. Restraint was unsound and cautionary notes unpatriotic. America was again living in years of maximum danger, and war needed to be declared in response to devastating attacks on U.S. soil. But war against whom? Or what?

The White House's choice to prosecute an unbounded war against terror was politically adept. There would be little room for second guessing—at least initially. The challenge of terrorism was quite real and open-ended. The years of maximum danger that lay ahead left no room for encroachment on executive authority. How could one argue against a war on terror or split hairs between terrorists and bloody dictators in the Islamic world with a penchant for weapons of mass destruction? True belief was fused with cunning against a clear and present danger. The Taliban, al Qaeda, and Saddam Hussein became the same enemy.

Saddam Hussein and his sons were removable and disposable threats who might some day, if left in power, engage in nuclear terrorism. Preparations for war, especially troop deployments, became faits accomplis. Undoing these acts would damage America's credibility in the region and embolden Hussein. Members of Congress obliged by granting permission for military action. The UN Security Council did not, but this was a mere detail. Most U.S. politicians, policy experts, and concerned citizens agreed that a preventive war was preferable to another surprise attack on U.S. soil.

Few analysts or academics, and no prominent politicians, argued that the threat of nuclear terrorism was being hyped. To diminish the threat would have left any politician open to devastating ridicule or irrelevance in policy debates if or when the next attack came. Only a few brave souls did not join the national plunge into the depths of anxiety. Political scientist John Mueller argued at book length that "our reaction to terrorism has caused more harm than the threat warrants" and that opportunistic politicians found it "politically expedient to be as hysterical as possible." He concluded that "concern over terrorism is justified, but alarm, hysteria, and panic, are not."[20] Former national security adviser Zbigniew Brzezinski agreed, arguing that "the 'war on terror' has created a culture of fear in America. The Bush administration's elevation of these three words into a national mantra since the horrific events of 9/11 has had a pernicious impact on American democracy, on America's psyche and on U.S. standing in the world."[21]

WORST CASES

It was not hard to envision worst cases after 9/11, but it was difficult to place them in historical context. In actuality, nuclear dangers after 9/11 were modest compared to the most dangerous passages of the cold war. In the formative stages of this monumental contest, America's primary competitors were two nuclear-armed, megalomaniacal mass murderers, Josef Stalin and Mao Zedong. During the first nuclear age, the United States and the Soviet Union maintained thousands of nuclear weapons on hair-trigger alert. Americans and the world lived under the threat of a nuclear arms race that produced tens of thousands of weapons. On average, the United States or the Soviet Union tested one nuclear weapon per week from the Cuban missile crisis to the fall of the Berlin wall, a constant reminder of nuclear dangers.

When the Soviet Union dissolved in 1991, power imbalances replaced the bipolar cold war competition, and the threat of asymmetric warfare replaced the threat of arms racing. Horizontal, not vertical, proliferation became the trend line to watch and worry about in the second nuclear age, especially the nuclear programs in Iran and North Korea. The primary fear was a surprise attack, not by the Kremlin but by terrorists armed with nuclear weapons.[22]

Dealing with North Korea and Iran is not easy, but managing relations with the Soviet Union and Communist China was even more challenging. As worrisome as Kim Jong Il and Mahmoud Ahmadinejad may be, they are no match for Stalin and Mao. With patience, persistence, and wise policies, previous American leaders managed to contain and reduce nuclear dangers. With better leadership, relentless effort, and sound strategies, new nuclear dangers can also be surmounted.

In the formative stages of the cold war, it was widely expected that, sooner or later, the Bomb would again be used on the battlefield and that humankind would be placed at dire risk. The expectation of disaster initially prompted an ambitious effort to ban the Bomb and place the means of its production under international control. When this effort failed, safety became the sturdy stepchild of terror, as Winston Churchill predicted. Nuclear overkill and national vulnerability became the odd guardians against another crossing of the nuclear threshold.

There could be no comfort in such means of "protection." America's earlier nuclear anxieties could have driven the country to distraction, or to wildly unsound policies. Instead, a progression of U.S. leaders of both political parties settled on deterrence, containment, military strength, and diplomatic engagement to reduce nuclear dangers. Diplomatic engagement eventually led to protracted negotiations that produced treaties limiting and then reducing the most powerful weapons in the world. Arms control produced surprisingly positive results despite widespread skepticism.

Two keys to the successful reduction of nuclear dangers during the cold war were exceptional leadership and dogged persistence. Both were exemplified by Paul Nitze. No one sounded the tocsin of nuclear dangers more powerfully or more often than Nitze when he was excluded from the corridors of power. But when given positions of responsibility, he did much to reduce nuclear dangers. Early in the cold war, Nitze offered the following counsel to those who despaired of preventing mushroom clouds: "Try to reduce the dangers of nuclear war within the relevant future time period as best you can; you just get depressed if you worry about the long-term future."[23] This advice—to work the nuclear problem day by day, month by month, and year by year—is no less relevant today, when a different set of nuclear dangers has prompted widespread public anxiety.

Taking snapshots of previous years of presumed maximum danger can help place current fears into a historical context while providing baselines to assess the Bush administration's strategic concept for reducing nuclear dangers. An administration's central strategic concept matters greatly, because the component parts of a strategy to reduce nuclear dangers need to be coherent, properly prioritized, and able to engender national and international support. If the central strategic concept of dealing with nuclear dangers is misconceived, the mix of supporting strategies will be deficient. Prioritization matters because the problems of nuclear proliferation and terrorism are so multifaceted that multiple, overlapping initiatives are required, and they will not always be in alignment.

A different set of difficulties can befall an administration that does not clarify a central strategic concept to reduce nuclear dangers. When this occurs, executive branch policies are more likely to become ad hoc, more susceptible to being taken hostage to external events, and harder to defend against domestic criticism and false interpretation. The administration of President Bill Clinton, which inherited a challenging, new nuclear environment, accomplished much in its first term, particularly in securing the nuclear holdings of the former Soviet

Union and in convincing newly independent states on Russia's periphery to give up their sudden inheritance of nuclear weapons. But President Clinton never defined and articulated a strategic concept for these efforts, and his administration progressively lost control of the nuclear agenda, unable to implement his plans for adapting the Anti-Ballistic Missile Treaty or ending nuclear tests.

YEARS OF LIVING DANGEROUSLY

There have been five particularly horrific years of living dangerously in the nuclear age. The first was 1945, when the Bomb made its spectacular appearance. To many, the Bomb's threat to civilization required radical solutions, including a well-functioning world government, the abolishment of war, and international control over atomic energy. But radical solutions were not possible, so national leaders undertook the long, hard slog to prevent a third use of nuclear weapons on the battlefield. Partial solutions and incremental effort proved to be effective counters to nuclear dangers.

The second year of living dangerously was 1949–1950, when the Soviet Union tested its first atomic bomb, President Truman endorsed a crash program to proceed with far more powerful thermonuclear, or hydrogen bombs, and the prolonged Korean War began. It was an open question whether or not atomic bombs would again be used to end another land war in Asia that was at times going badly for the United States before it ground into a bitter stalemate. The editors of the *Bulletin of the Atomic Scientists*, a newsletter (and later a journal) conceived by veterans of the Manhattan Project who felt remorse over their handiwork, created a clock to symbolize nuclear danger. During 1949, the minute hand of the clock stood at three minutes to midnight, the doomsday hour. Presidents Truman and Eisenhower considered preemptive attacks against the Soviet Union and Communist China but rejected this advice as infeasible and unwise.

The third year of living dangerously was 1962, when the Cuban missile crisis played out over thirteen days. This crisis occurred before the era of communication satellites or "hotlines"—it took half a day to code, transmit (via Western Union), and translate Nikita Khrushchev's first letter to President John F. Kennedy. In the meantime, dramas unfolded in a matter of minutes that could have changed the course of our nuclear history. Three officers on a Soviet submarine debated whether to disobey orders and fire a nuclear weapon while being depth-charged to the surface; an American U-2 spy plane was shot down over Cuba at the height of the crisis; and the U.S. Air Force, in the most ill-timed training exercise ever, tested an intercontinental ballistic missile carrying a dummy warhead over the Pacific.[24] The *Bulletin*'s clock registered seven minutes to midnight in 1962—a generous call.

The fourth year of living dangerously was 1983. This was the year that President Ronald Reagan declared the Soviet Union to be the focus of evil in the world, when he surprised nearly everyone by announcing the Strategic Defense Initiative aimed at providing an astrodome-like protection against missile attack, when Soviet air defense forces shot down a Korean Airlines jet that had strayed hopelessly off course, when the United States began to deploy new missiles based in Western Europe, and when the Kremlin walked out of nuclear negotiations. Reagan and the Kremlin's leader, the dialysis machine–tethered former KGB chief Yuri Andropov, each believed that trend lines were deeply adverse. Key advisers of both leaders worried about a bolt-from-the-blue nuclear attack.

Matters reached a boiling point in late 1983, when an intense Kremlin muscle-flexing campaign failed to block the deployment of missiles by NATO that could fly so fast or so stealthily as to be undetectable. Their likely targets were the nerve centers of the Soviet command and control system. For once, the United States had trumped the Soviet "medium machine-building" factories that pumped out missiles; NATO's rejoinder to the Kremlin's missile buildup, in the view of the Soviet defense establishment's most paranoid denizens, could leave the Kremlin deaf, dumb, and blind to attack. At the very time when some in the Reagan administration were convinced that the Soviet Union had achieved and would exploit its strategic superiority, the Kremlin's intelligence apparatus was checking on U.S. blood banks and how many lights were on late at night in the Pentagon and State Department, searching for clues of an impending surprise attack.

The fifth year of living dangerously was 2001, when Americans became acutely conscious of their vulnerability as a result of the seething rage of nineteen young men, mostly Saudi, who used jet fuel as bombs against the Twin Towers and the Pentagon. Islamic rage against the United States was nothing new; in anxious times that now seem quaint by comparison, hijacked airliners were used to seek the freedom of imprisoned comrades. Now they were used to kill innocents on a massive scale and to send tremors through an entire society. The workings of America's great cities, whose countless moving parts somehow manage to mesh, are largely taken for granted. A significant act of urban terrorism breaks down the intricate mechanisms supporting daily routines, bringing close to home the horror of mass death and awakening imaginations to even more gruesome possibilities. The reverberations from September 11, 2001, are with us still, the latest of many deeply unsettling passages from our nuclear history.

PREDICTIONS OF MAXIMUM DANGER

Americans have somehow managed to live through many projected years of maximum danger. Perhaps the most famous of all clarion calls to gird against external threats was NSC 68, a report principally drafted by Paul Nitze for President Truman.[25] Truman had been tugged by some advisers to pursue nuclear disarmament and pulled by others to authorize massive rearmament. NSC 68 was released in April 1950, eight months after the first Soviet nuclear test and four months after Chiang Kai-shek fled to Taiwan, ceding the mainland to Mao. The Korean War would begin barely less than ten weeks after NSC 68 was transmitted to President Truman.

NSC 68 could not have been written at a time of more profound national anxiety; contemporary concerns over nuclear terrorism are modest by comparison. While America was demobilizing, the Soviet Union was beginning to consolidate its grip on Eastern Europe. The authors of NSC 68 feared that the Kremlin would not stop at Poland, Czechoslovakia, and the Baltic states. The Soviet Union was "animated by a new fanatic faith" and sought "to impose its absolute authority over the rest of the world."

Not surprisingly, NSC 68 came down squarely on the side of rearmament, including the fastest possible pursuit of the H-bomb, before Stalin added thermonuclear weapons to his conventional military superiority. At the time of the release of NSC 68, Stalin's acquisition of atomic bombs was considered probable but not yet proven. It was by no means clear that the H-bomb was feasible. The authors of NSC 68 acknowledged that a successful effort by the United States and the Soviet Union to detonate and stockpile thermonuclear weapons would have profound "moral, psychological, and political" consequences, but if the USSR raced to the H-bomb ahead of the United States, the risk of "Soviet pressure against all of the free world, or an attack against the U.S., will be greatly increased."

NSC 68 reasoned that "in a very real sense, the Kremlin is a victim of its own dynamism. This dynamism can become a weakness if it is frustrated. . . . Yet the Kremlin cannot relax the condition of crisis and mobilization, for to do so would be to lose its dynamism." Under these circumstances, conflict with the

USSR had become "endemic," whether "by violent or non-violent methods in accordance with the dictates of expediency." The threat could come by means of a surprise attack, by cold war, or by "piecemeal aggression."

The authors of NSC 68 warned that "with the development of increasingly terrifying weapons of mass destruction, every individual faces the ever-present possibility of annihilation should the conflict enter the phase of total war." The sum total of all these fears was the conclusion that "this Republic and its citizens in the ascendancy of their strength stand in their deepest peril." The most powerful nation in the world was now facing its severest test: "The integrity and vitality of our system is in greater jeopardy than ever before in our history."

The United States needed to pursue a policy of containment "to block further expansion of Soviet military power." To do so required "superior overall power," whether alone or in "dependable combination with other likeminded nations." The United States would "always leave open the possibility of negotiation with the USSR," but not when America was in decline with the Kremlin growing bolder.

The authors of NSC 68 reasoned that "it would be to the long-term advantage of the United States if atomic weapons were to be effectively eliminated." But this prospect was not in the cards, and in the meantime, Soviet aggression needed to be checked. It was therefore necessary to "increase our atomic capability as rapidly as other considerations make appropriate." Years of maximum danger were forecast "within the next four or five years." All means necessary to prevent this outcome must be pursued, but "due care must be taken to avoid permanently impairing our economy and the fundamental values and institutions inherent in our way of life." A military buildup was necessary but insufficient. The United States also needed to have an "affirmative program" to "light the path to peace and order among nations in a system based on freedom and justice." Without accentuating the positive, the United States could not hope to "regain and retain the initiative."

The next significant clarion call of nuclear danger was the "Gaither Committee" report, named after H. Rowan Gaither Jr., a senior figure at the RAND Corporation and Ford Foundation, who was tasked by President Eisenhower to "study and form a broad-brush opinion" of the value of civil defenses against nuclear attack.[26] Eisenhower was under withering criticism for his seemingly relaxed view of growing Soviet nuclear capabilities. His second administration was marked by warnings from domestic critics of bomber and missile gaps and by the unsettling successes of the Soviet space program. Eisenhower steadfastly deflected these critiques, remaining wary of the "military industrial complex" he warned about in his farewell address and constant to his belief in fiscal conservatism.[27] One consequence of these policies was a heavy U.S. military reliance on nuclear weapons; another was a growing chorus of impending doom. The Gaither Committee report, *Deterrence and Survival in the Nuclear Age*, became a vehicle to highlight security concerns and address perceived laxities in the administration's nuclear and military posture. The principal drafter of the Gaither Committee report was, once again, Paul Nitze.

The report was transmitted to Eisenhower in November 1957, four days after the second Sputnik launch. Its bottom line: "The evidence clearly indicates an increasing threat which may become critical in 1959 or early 1960." Trends were ominous. "The singleness of purpose with which they have pressed their military-centered industrial development has led to spectacular progress." The Gaither report estimated that the Soviet fissile material stockpile was sufficient for an arsenal of at least 1,500 nuclear weapons. (In retrospect, the Natural Resources Defense Council estimates the size of the Soviet arsenal that year at approximately 660 weapons.)[28] America's nuclear deterrent, which then resided primarily at strategic bomber bases, was far too vulnerable, calling for "prompt remedial action." The report warned, most ominously, that by 1959 the Soviet Union "may" be able to attack U.S. bomber bases using intercontinental ballistic missiles, or ICBMs, carrying megaton warheads, against which the Strategic Air Command would be "almost completely vulnerable." Missile defenses were needed, as well as a nationwide system of fallout shelters. Early warning systems of an impending attack were inadequate. A sixfold increase in missiles based around the Soviet periphery was needed, as well as a sevenfold increase in ocean-spanning missiles. The development of new submarines and submarine-based missiles needed to be accelerated.

In one of the greatest understatements of any accentuated threat assessments, the Gaither Committee report concluded that implementing its recommendations "will probably involve expenditures in excess of the current $38 billion defense budget." The fourteen-page top secret report ended with this thought: "The next two years seem to us critical. If we fail to act at once, the risk, in our opinion, will be unacceptable." Six weeks after the Gaither Committee report was submitted to Eisenhower, its conclusions were leaked to the press.[29] The drumbeat of perilous assessments by distinguished outside experts was echoed in the intelligence community's National Intelligence Estimates in the latter years of the Eisenhower administration. The 1959 estimate, for example, concluded that "the USSR will in 1961 have its most favorable opportunity to gain a decided military, political, and psychological advantage over the U.S. by rapid deployment of operational ICBMs."[30] Why Eisenhower would invite such a damning condemnation of his administration's perceived laxity remains the subject of debate among cold war historians.

The next clarion call of nuclear danger took place in the Gerald R. Ford administration. President Ford and his secretary of state, Henry Kissinger, were pursuing policies of détente and seeking to conclude an agreement to limit strategic arms at a time of growing disquiet. The Soviet arms buildup was showing no signs of subsiding, and the Kremlin seemed to be increasingly bold about challenging the United States, especially in the Middle East. Ford was also being reprimanded in presidential primaries by Governor Ronald Reagan for letting down the nation's guard.

As the Ford administration was winding down, Central Intelligence Agency director George H. W. Bush authorized a fresh look at his agency's estimates of the Soviet threat. The reason for an "independent" review of the CIA's National Intelligence Estimate (Team A), was later recounted by the head of the group providing the competitive assessment (Team B), Harvard University historian Richard Pipes. Team B's job, according to Pipes, was to determine "whether a good case could be made that Soviet strategic objectives are, in fact, more ambitious and therefore implicitly more threatening to U.S. security" than they appeared to intelligence community professionals. Pipes was joined by fellow skeptics of détente William Van Cleave, Lt. General Daniel Graham, Paul Wolfowitz, and Paul Nitze.

A Senate committee that subsequently assessed the Team B exercise concluded that its composition predetermined its analysis.[31] Team B found that the official estimate "substantially misperceived the motivations behind Soviet strategic programs, and thereby tended consistently to underestimate their intensity, scope, and implicit threat."[32] One reason for such a systematic bias was that Team A relied too much on "hard data" while "slighting or misinterpreting the large body of 'soft' data concerning Soviet strategic concepts." Agency analysts were not being clear enough about superpower differences; instead they were guilty of "mirror imaging" America's adversary. Just because many Americans were interested in stabilizing the strategic competition did not mean that the Kremlin was playing by the same rules. Team B concluded that Soviet strategic objectives were fundamentally different from those of the United States. Because the intelligence community failed to take into account "the broader political purposes which underlie and explain" these objectives, Team B concluded that the CIA's assessments were deeply flawed.

The Ford administration, like its predecessors, believed that détente was mutually rewarding and that both superpowers acknowledged mutual assured destruction, which permitted a stabilizing process of strategic arms limitation agreements. So what would a correct interpretation of Soviet strategic concepts conclude? The Team B estimate provided what it thought was a badly needed tutorial necessitated by the intelligence community's failure to juxtapose, monitor, and synthesize Soviet nuclear force capabilities, global activities, theoretical pronouncements, and actions in the military political and economic spheres. The intelligence community missed the big picture because separate agencies were competing with each other, the skeptical view of military intelligence was being trumped by their civilian counterparts, troubling developments were being viewed in isolation, and "political pressures and consideration" were being exerted.

Given that the Team B exercise might easily be construed as a form of political pressure, Team B's suggestion that estimates were subject to politicization—a charge that did not figure in the NSC 68 and Gaither Committee reports—was quite sensitive and required explication. "On some occasions," Team B reported, the CIA's estimators displayed "an evident inclination to minimize the Soviet strategic buildup because of its implications for détente, SAL [strategic arms limitation] negotiations, congressional sentiments as well as for certain U.S. forces." The meaning of this last reference is unclear and perhaps relates to the negative ramifications that might result if the intelligence community acknowledged dramatic Soviet advances. Team B then speculated that "this is not to say that any of the judgments which seem to reflect policy support are demonstrably directed judgments: rather they appear to derive mainly from a strong and understandable awareness on the part of the NIE [National Intelligence Estimate] authors of the policy issues at stake."

Having identified the reasons for faulty assessments, Team B offered corrective judgments: The strategic arms limitation talks were a "means to further unilateral advantages"; "the pace of the Soviet armament effort in all fields is staggering"; the Warsaw Pact buildup could best be interpreted "in terms of intimidation and conquest"; and "the intensity and scope of the current Soviet military effort in peacetime is without parallel in twentieth century history, its only counterpart being Nazi remilitarization of the 1930s." The purpose of the Soviet buildup was the pursuit of "world hegemony," the means by which "the

United States can be preventively neutralized, or, if necessary, actively broken." Team B was left with "little reasonable doubt" that Soviet leaders were "determined to achieve the maximum attainable measure of strategic superiority over the U.S."

What did this mean for the timeline of maximum danger? Team B concluded that "in Soviet perceptions the gap between long-term capabilities and short-term objectives is closing. This probably means that the Soviet leaders believe that their ultimate objectives are closer to realization than they have ever been before." Over the coming decade, "the Soviets may well expect to achieve a degree of military superiority which would permit a dramatically more aggressive pursuit of their hegemonial objectives." Unless urgent measures were taken to reverse current trends, there was a distinct "possibility of a relatively short term threat cresting, say, in 1980 to 1983, as well as the more obvious long range threat."

Henry Kissinger, one of the obvious targets of the Team B assessment, considered the report an exercise to "sabotage" the strategic arms limitation treaty he and Ford were then seeking to conclude against the wishes of Secretary of Defense Donald Rumsfeld.[33] President Ford subsequently dropped the word *détente* from his political vocabulary, and although he effectively beat back Governor Ronald Reagan's challenge, his hopes for a strategic arms limitation agreement were effectively stymied before his election night defeat to Jimmy Carter in 1976. Carter, who was eager to conclude a new treaty, then replaced Ford and Kissinger in the line of fire for those most concerned about the Soviet threat. The results of the Team B exercise were first leaked to the press when Carter was selecting his cabinet.[34]

Team B members such as Paul Nitze and Eugene Rostow became the core group of the Committee on the Present Danger, which offered trenchant criticism of the Carter administration's negotiating stances and dire warnings of Soviet strategic objectives.[35] A few weeks after Carter's inauguration, the Committee issued a pamphlet endorsed by its executive committee asserting that "Soviet pressure, when supported by strategic and conventional military superiority, would be aimed at forcing our general withdrawal from a leading role in world affairs and isolating us from other democratic societies, which could not then long survive."[36]

The critiques offered by members of the Committee on the Present Danger and their congressional allies had their intended effect. President Carter dropped or scaled back one arms control initiative after another, including negotiations to ban space weapons, restrict small arms transfers, and limit nuclear testing. Carter also scaled back his ambitions in the Strategic Arms Limitation Talks (SALT) to protect U.S. nuclear modernization programs deemed essential by his critics. By the time it took to complete the text of the second Strategic Arms Limitation Treaty, this agreement was hanging by a slender thread. Leonid Brezhnev and a select group of Politburo advisers then cut this thread by deciding to invade Afghanistan in December 1979.

The Soviet invasion appeared to provide incontrovertible proof of the warnings pronounced by the Committee on the Present Danger, Team B, the Gaither Committee, and the drafters of NSC 68. But history takes its time to reveal profound ironies. The Kremlin's ill-conceived occupation of Afghanistan was not to be a stepping-stone to more ambitious conquests. Instead, it provided an opportunity for the Soviet Union's foes to lay ambushes and to grind down the Red Army on hostile terrain. The ironies of the Afghan resistance ran deep, including a U.S. partnership of convenience with Osama bin Laden and his cohorts. The Kremlin's daring venture backfired, accelerating the Soviet Union's demise and sowing the seeds for the dangers of the second nuclear age.

Before these ironies became evident, many predictors of maximum danger assumed positions of responsibility in the new administration of President Ronald Reagan. Richard Pipes became the Soviet expert on the national security council staff. Eugene Rostow, the titular head of the Committee on the Present Danger, became the director of the Arms Control and Disarmament Agency, and Paul Nitze became a key adviser at the State Department. Government-issued threat estimates now reflected the conclusions of the Committee on the Present Danger and Team B. The Pentagon's annual report for 1983, *Soviet Military Power*, warned that the Soviet Union's "main objective is to capitalize, in peacetime, on the coercive leverage inherent in powerful nuclear forces, to induce paralysis and create disarray in the free societies. In wartime, they regard employment of those forces as the key to their survival and winning."[37]

The Central Intelligence Agency's Soviet experts were now in full accord with heightened threat estimates. The U.S. intelligence community's National Intelligence Estimate, "Soviet Capabilities for Strategic Nuclear Conflict, 1982–92," issued on February 15, 1983, concluded that the Kremlin sought "superior capabilities to fight and win a nuclear war with the United States, and have been working to improve their chances of prevailing in such a conflict."[38] The following year, U.S. intelligence assessments concluded in effect that the Kremlin believed its own propaganda: Soviet leaders "view strategic arms policy in the context of a persistent long-term struggle between two world systems of socialism and capitalism, in which socialism—with Moscow in charge—is destined ultimately to triumph."[39] In the run-up to a direct confrontation with the United States, the CIA's analysts predicted that Soviet intelligence agents would "heighten their surveillance . . . to acquire detailed information on a wide range of U.S. strategic force capabilities and readiness."[40] What the intelligence community failed to notice was that Soviet operatives had begun doing precisely this in 1981, on the orders from then KGB chief Andropov.

Andropov and his fellow paranoids in the Kremlin and in the Soviet intelligence services were not preparing to initiate a direct confrontation with the United States. Instead, they feared that the Reagan administration was preparing to initiate such a confrontation. Nor did Andropov and company believe, as U.S. intelligence estimates assumed, that the correlation of forces had swung in the Kremlin's favor. Instead, they feared that the Soviet Union was in decline and that the United States could capitalize on its rearmament programs, even to the point of launching a surprise missile attack.[41] At the very time when Reagan administration officials were declaring their intent to reverse Soviet strategic superiority, Soviet intelligence officers were scanning for indicators of an impending U.S. attack.[42] The danger that U.S. and Soviet leaders would misinterpret each other so profoundly was missing among the apocalyptic forecasts of the 1980s.

These overheated predictions during the Reagan years mirrored the U.S. intelligence community's frightening assessment of Iraqi weapons of mass destruction capability during the George W. Bush administration.[43] The Iraq estimate concluded, with high confidence, that Iraq was "reconstituting its nuclear weapon program." Most worrisome of all, "If Baghdad acquires sufficient fissile material from abroad it could make a nuclear weapon within several months to a year." If not, and if left to his own devices, Saddam Hussein could acquire the Bomb by 2007–2009. The estimate found "compelling evidence" that Hussein was reconstituting his uranium enrichment effort. He had "largely rebuilt" his biological weapon programs, and he "had begun renewed production" of a number of different chemical weapons.

As for the crucial questions of whether or when Hussein would use these weapons of mass destruction against the United States, the estimate offered low-confidence judgments. The most probable scenario would be one in which a desperate Hussein had little to lose by lashing out. As for Hussein's links to al Qaeda, which might provide Osama bin Laden's shock troops with the nuclear, chemical, or biological weapons they wanted, the estimate concluded that "for now" Hussein would not engage in collusion or transfers, "fearing that exposure of Iraqi involvement would provide Washington a stronger cause for making war."

The State Department's intelligence shop dissented from these judgments. The Department of Energy dissented on one particular conclusion. The Central Intelligence Agency and the Defense Intelligence Agency concurred entirely in these judgments. This time around, the pressures for offering a worst-case assessment came not from outsiders disturbed by an administration's complacency but from those within the George W. Bush administration who were most intent on going to war.

MISESTIMATING NUCLEAR DANGER

The ominous U.S. intelligence estimates in the run-up to the second U.S. war against Saddam Hussein were therefore new—not in kind but in effect. During the cold war, when governmental critics offered overhyped estimates of the Soviet nuclear threat, they usually succeeded in accelerating the production of U.S. bombs, planes, submarines, and missiles. The Kremlin presumably adopted similarly jaundiced views of U.S. military capabilities. The resulting nuclear competition was not as much about mirror imaging, as critics contended, as it was about the imperatives of what could be considered prudent military planning. The cold war's nuclear arms race was nerve-racking, expensive, and sometimes dangerous, but it did not result in war and may have had a perversely ironic, cautionary effect. Because the superpower nuclear arsenals were so bloated and because damage expectancies in the event of war were so great, sane leaders sought to avoid a crossing of the nuclear threshold, regardless of ideological predilection. Deterrence held, despite acts of adventurism and proxy wars.

The worst-case thinkers who dwelled on such matters believed themselves to be big-picture hyperrealists. Their instinct—that it was better to be safe than sorry in a dangerous world—was well-founded, so they erred on the side of caution. Their big picture was drawn on pointillist brushstrokes of missile payloads and nuclear exchange ratios; their prescriptions called for nuclear weapon programs and war-fighting plans that resembled the Soviet threat. Team B members who warned against ascribing America's peaceful intentions to the Kremlin instead ascribed the worst possible intentions to the Kremlin. Team B's big picture was not grounded in close contact with the Soviet Union but on readings of graphs, military doctrine, and tsarist history. Team B took these graphs and doctrinal statements more seriously than did the Kremlin leadership.

It is challenging for those who interpret foreign military doctrine for a living to guard against inflated threat estimates. Threat assessments of military and nuclear doctrine are mostly for the literal minded. Doctrinal specialists, by habit as well as by instinct, are trained to filter out silver linings; military doctrine is, after all, about inflicting punishment. In the exegesis of doctrine, the warrior ethos is usually carried over from the writer to the reader. The interpreters of doctrine are not paid to factor in the concerns of political leaders, who have the final say about, for example, whether nuclear war plans are actually executed.

The U.S. intelligence community has a hard job, and getting threat estimates exactly right is an impossible task. Sometimes threat estimates are too low; more often, they are too high. The penalties for underestimating significant threats include being sidelined from public life and government service. On the other hand, those who overhype threats usually do not incur penalties, because their warnings can be credited with preventing worst cases from occurring. Threat inflation was—and is—therefore usually more likely than threat deflation.

To give the threat inflators their due, the harm that was done by issuing overheated warnings was but a mere fraction of the harm that would be done if their warnings turned out to be true. Overhyped threat estimates during the cold war resulted in excessive public expenditures, and they were politically damaging to those who could be characterized as being asleep at the switch. But these cold war estimates were not vehicles to justify waging preventive wars or launching preemptive strikes. During the cold war, being safe rather than sorry had its limits.

Inflated threat estimates of Saddam Hussein's weapons of mass destruction programs had quite different consequences. During the cold war, being safe rather than sorry meant buying more nuclear weapons and the means to deliver them. In the wake of the 9/11 attacks, the Bush administration made a sufficiently persuasive case that being safe rather than sorry meant waging a war of choice rather than waiting for another surprise attack.

The dangers of misestimating threats changed after 9/11, not only because threat levels were elevated but also because the United States possessed dominant military power and because Iraq's superpower patron had dissolved. During the cold war, taxpayers were victimized by predictions of years of maximum danger. During the war on terror, Saddam Hussein, countless Iraqis, and America's armed forces became the victims of apocalyptic threat predictions. More than ever, being safe rather than sorry required better intelligence collection and assessment.

APOCALYPSE NOW

The United States survived many years of projected maximum danger during the cold war. Public anxieties were high during these periods, but contemporary nuclear threats have a different, more pervasive feel. The Soviet nuclear threat was quantifiable and geographically contained. Moreover, the threat was most often framed and understood as a contest between two military establishments, not between the American people and the Soviet people. In contrast, terrorist threats have become far more personal. Active diplomatic engagement and nuclear negotiations between Washington and Moscow provided a sense of assurance that national leaders were reducing threats. In contrast, the Bush administration's engagement with North Korea was much delayed, its contacts with Iran were minimal, and U.S. concerns with al Qaeda and the Taliban could not be assuaged by diplomatic engagement.

After the 9/11 attacks against emblematic targets on U.S. soil, threat assessments soared. America's list of adversaries extended beyond states to shadowy groups and alienated freelancers who lived far away from home or found safe haven among coreligionists. Warfare was no longer confined to men and women in uniform; innocent bystanders were now prime targets. The visceral, optical profile of a terrorist could be met by a neighbor or by a passenger in a bus, subway, or airplane. Strategies used to deal with the Soviet nuclear threat, particularly nuclear overkill and national vulnerability, were of absolutely no use against the threats of "loose nukes" and nuclear terrorism. Strategies, especially preventive war and preemptive strikes, that were dismissed against old adversaries were revived in the wake of attacks on the U.S. homeland during a period of unparalleled American military superiority. These policy debates compounded public anxieties.

After 9/11, relaxed threat perceptions had no place in the public square. Those who minimized the threat of nuclear terrorism invited exclusion from policy debates, just like those, for example, Robert Oppenheimer, who argued that H-bombs were not needed to respond to the Soviet threat during the formative stages of the cold war. Critics of hard-line policies back then had a leavening effect. In contrast, critics of the Bush administration's policies reinforced grim threat scenarios. They argued that muscular policies were not only failing to counter new threats but also exacerbating them. The revenue-producing methodology of broadcasting local news, which featured stories of personal victimization and random violence, now extended to the 24-hour news cycle. The mugging down the block was extended to world news, which provided daily reinforcement of public anxieties. Talk show hosts gained prominence as the mouthpieces of the victimized, using their platforms as radar, pinging targets for even deeper reasons for outrage and grudges. Individual years of living dangerously were now a quaint artifact of the cold war. The United States was now living in an age of anxiety.

THE GEORGE W. BUSH ADMINISTRATION

The Bush administration's central strategic concept for reducing nuclear dangers was well suited to these anxious times. Simply put, the Bush strategic concept was to use U.S. military, political, and economic dominance to keep Americans safe. The traumatic events of 9/11 presaged new threats of nuclear terrorism, loose nukes, and poorly controlled fissile material. The Bush administration excelled at framing either/or choices. America could wait to be struck again or adopt proactive strategies. The answer to this binary choice seemed clear after the 9/11 attacks.

The foundation of a compelling strategic concept rests on a succinct definition of the problem, which the Bush administration correctly characterized as the risk of having the most deadly weapons fall into the most dangerous hands. The war on terror was born, as ambitious as the scope of the problem it sought to defeat. This label was well chosen to galvanize domestic political support and quiet dissenters but poorly chosen to succeed with the problem at hand. Waging war on a symptom is different from waging war on an enemy. If taken seriously, the war on terror would be endless, and if assessed honestly, would be as likely to produce victory as, say, a war on global poverty. Great simplifiers and outrage mongers unhelpfully translated the war on terror as a war on Islam, thereby exacerbating the problem and alienating potential allies who could offer the most assistance.

The attacks on the Twin Towers became totems of nuclear anxiety, as emblematic in their own way as the atomic devastation of Hiroshima and Nagasaki. The scale of the devastation was massively different, of course, as was the immediacy of the shock. The full horror unleashed by the atomic bombs did not begin to seep into public consciousness until *The New Yorker* devoted an entire issue to John Hersey's reporting more than a year later. In contrast, the demolition of the Twin Towers was watched by countless people across the globe in real time. Endless replays drilled public anxieties down to a cellular level. Viewers reacted in the same elemental way as those who first absorbed the Bomb's dark meaning in 1945: It can happen anywhere. And next time, the damage could be much, much worse.

The Bush administration's response to this danger was perfectly captured in its National Security Strategy, issued one year after the 9/11 attacks. This strategy fused extraordinary American power projection with a missionary zeal to prevent the most dangerous weapons from falling into the most dangerous hands. U.S. military dominance and coalitions of the willing would be used to "act against such emerging threats before they are fully formed. . . . History will judge harshly those who saw this coming danger but failed to act." A freedom agenda would be pursued in parallel to the antiproliferation and counterterrorism agendas: "We will defend the peace by fighting terrorists and tyrants. We will preserve the peace by building good relations among the great powers. We will extend the peace by encouraging free and open societies on every continent."[44] The battle with Islamic extremism was joined. If considered a screenplay of the administration's subsequent overreaching, the 2002 National Security Strategy would have been mercilessly panned for blatant foreshadowing and heavy-handed irony.

The key elements of the new national security strategy were soon evident. New global norms to prevent nuclear terrorism would be identified, but building new international institutions and bureaucracies would be avoided. Existing global norms dealing with proliferation would be treated in a new fashion. Not all states with nuclear weapons were to be treated equally. The Bomb was no longer the problem per se; instead it was the character of the bomb holder that mattered. Responsible, friendly nations, such as India, should not be penalized for past deeds and, by inference, for future actions. The essence of the problem was, after all, the most dangerous weapons in the most dangerous hands.

The post-9/11 world was not for the timid and fainthearted in the Bush administration's view. Those who dwelled in shades of gray were sidestepping difficult but critical choices. World War II was not about shades of gray, and success in the cold war came when Ronald Reagan framed important issues in black-and-white terms. America was once again at war. After the attacks on the World Trade Center and the Pentagon, U.S. national security policy was again about binary choices.

George W. Bush's strategic concept for preventing new nuclear dangers relied primarily on U.S. military dominance to check and, if need be, nullify hostile nuclear programs and transactions. Homeland security would naturally take center stage in this strategic concept after the worst attacks on American soil in U.S. history. U.S. freedom of action would be a paramount objective. A war without boundaries would be taken to the enemy; preemptive strikes and preventive wars were preferable to waiting to take another hit. Norms that constrained others would be welcomed; those that pinched U.S. military options would be opposed. Existing treaties that facilitated muscular initiatives were worthy of support. Old treaties or new ones that did not would be treated dismissively.

The track record compiled by the Bush administration to reduce nuclear dangers has been mixed at best. In the administration's defense, it has had to operate under extremely difficult circumstances. A world with one dominant military power tilts toward proliferation because the Bomb becomes an equalizer for states that feel particularly threatened by U.S. military power. It is also hard for a dominant nation to secure the support of other major powers to check proliferation when, for example, Russia and China do not view all proliferation cases with the same degree of alarm (or favor) as does the United States. In comparison, the old, bipolar structure of international relations worked reasonably well against proliferation. Both superpowers could work in tandem against this common threat while providing a reliable nuclear umbrella to friends and allies.

There are other reasons that the Bush administration has struggled. Reversing vertical proliferation during the cold war was hard; reversing post–cold war horizontal proliferation is harder, because diminishing wretched excess is easier than convincing new aspirants to forgo the Bomb. Moreover, the scope of the problem facing the Bush administration had expanded greatly to include shadowy groups not subject to the traditional dictates of deterrence, defense, and punishment. Previous predictors of years of maximum danger did not need to be concerned about Internet chat rooms used to transmit deadly orders, entrepreneurial middlemen who trafficked in centrifuge parts, and radiological material that could also be used for dirty bombs as well as for cancer treatments.

Even before the 9/11 attacks, the Bush administration's inner sanctum resolved to pursue a different approach to proliferation threats. To be safe rather than sorry meant relying more on muscle and less on diplomacy. Coercive and military elements—"counterproliferation" in the lingo of the trade—would take pride of place over tedious nonproliferation negotiations. The term "arms control" would be stripped from all but one title in the State Department's organization chart. Creative initiatives would be undertaken to form "coalitions of the willing" to intercept contraband and set norms for criminalizing proliferation. But norm building would not interfere with differentiation: The administration adopted a good guy/bad actor approach to proliferation. The good guys deserved some slack. Isolation, rather than engagement, would be the game plan for bad actors.

This sweeping agenda became more radical still after 9/11. Isolation of bad actors was now insufficient. Instead, safety against new nuclear dangers meant knocking off not just Osama bin Laden but also Saddam Hussein. In the administration's view, sanctions were wasting away, and efforts to keep Saddam Hussein in a box were wearing down U.S. forces in the field. Hussein was pocketing money for illicit oil sales, and his ambitions for weapons of mass destruction remained constant. In this view, sooner or later Hussein would succeed, which meant that neighboring Iran would redouble its efforts to acquire nuclear weapons. The first U.S. war against Iraq, in which victorious American troops did not carry the fight to Baghdad to topple Hussein, needed to be properly finished.

In retrospect, it is easy to mock this train of thought, but in the aftershocks of 9/11, the aphorism of being safe rather than sorry took on new meaning. Had Franklin Delano Roosevelt enjoyed sufficient political leeway to strike at Nazi Germany before the great and gathering danger reached full force, many lives would have been saved and Europe would have been spared wholesale devastation. But FDR was hemmed in by a severely divided country and by the isolationist wing of the Republican Party. George W. Bush also led a severely divided country after his contested election. The attacks on 9/11 had a liberating effect. After early missteps, he found the role he claimed that his Maker had intended for him: He would protect the country from evildoers through force of arms.

International relations, unlike the Old and New Testaments, are suffused with irony. The adverse political and diplomatic consequences arising from the war of choice against Saddam Hussein in 2003 might have been mitigated if combat operations had revealed hidden stocks of weapons of mass destruction and if the U.S. game plan after the initial military campaign had been brilliantly conceived and executed. Even then, the remaking of Iraq would have been a hugely difficult enterprise, as it was pure hubris to think that Iraq's fractious cast of characters, once liberated from Hussein's tyranny, would take their cues from a foreign director. Adverse proliferation consequences from the second Iraq war were unavoidable when Hussein's weapons of mass destruction proved to be illusory and when poorly conceived decisions turned American military forces from liberators into occupiers of a fractured land. When a dominant power fights a war of choice, even for compelling reasons, ties with allies and major powers will become strained. When that war of choice is fought on the basis of false assumptions and faulty intelligence, negative proliferation consequences multiply.

Cohesion among major powers, one precondition of effective international efforts to prevent proliferation, was one of the casualties of the second U.S. war against Saddam Hussein. The two countries that felt most in need of a deterrent to prevent subsequent wars of choice aimed at them—North Korea and Iran—accelerated their nuclear activities. Because U.S. intelligence was so wrong and U.S. diplomacy so unpersuasive before toppling Hussein, the Bush administration was poorly positioned to lead diplomatic efforts to stop and then reverse the North Korean and Iranian nuclear programs. Beijing engaged seriously with North Korea, whereas diplomatic engagement with Iran was contracted out, episodically, to European allies. By bogging down U.S. ground forces in Iraq, the Bush administration lost leverage to sway the Iranian and North Korean nuclear programs. Worse, by turning Iraq into a Shia-dominated fractured state, Iran became the primary beneficiary of the second U.S. war against Iraq.

3 THE FIRST NUCLEAR AGE

THE FIRST NUCLEAR AGE was defined by the cold war, nuclear overkill, and mutual assured destruction. The nuclear stockpiles of the United States and the Soviet Union peaked at approximately 69,000 combined weapons in 1986.[1] Thousands of these weapons were teed up, ready for use in a matter of minutes, at all times. Even under these grim conditions, the search for relative advantage—and the avoidance of disadvantage—was ceaseless.

The bipolar structure of the cold war competition was virtually the only neatly arranged aspect of the first nuclear age. The nuclear competition itself was sprawling, messy, and occasionally quite dangerous. With so much at stake—power, influence, and ideology, for starters—it was not clear what the boundaries of this competition would be or if there would be boundaries at all. Soviet premier Nikita Khrushchev once promised to bury America, and President Ronald Reagan predicted that the Soviet Union would end up on the ash heap of history. These declarations came at two particularly rough junctures during the cold war, of which there were many.

Severe crises became the substitute for direct warfare between the two superpowers during the first nuclear age. No one could confidently predict how these crises, which brought the armed forces and the nuclear weapons of both countries into close proximity, would be sorted out. When the worst of these crises over Berlin and Cuba were over and when Washington and Moscow were both inclined to avoid more high noon confrontations, the competition shifted to proxy wars to punish each other's overreaching and miscalculation, first in Vietnam and then in Afghanistan.

Beginning with the second Strategic Arms Limitation Treaty (SALT II), completed in 1979 but never ratified, the superpowers eventually learned to channel their rivalry by constraining the buildup of their nuclear arsenals. The Intermediate-Range Nuclear Forces Treaty, signed in 1987, began the process of mutually agreed nuclear arms reductions. This was not the first time that great powers tried to negotiate limits on their most powerful weapons of war. In the 1920s and 1930s, major powers tried to limit the size and armament on their capital ships—the strategic forces of a bygone era that could travel long distances and train big guns on important targets. These efforts foundered on irreconcilable national interests. Harsh skeptics of strategic arms control during the cold war confidently predicted a similar fate.

Nuclear negotiations naturally became one more theater of the superpower rivalry. Efforts to reduce the dark shadow cast by the Bomb were bound to be as contentious and anxiety provoking as exertions to increase nuclear firepower. Fierce debates raged over the equities of negotiated outcomes and adversarial intentions behind the deals that were struck. The binary problems of the first nuclear age were well suited to those inclined toward black-and-white solutions. The debaters were called hawks and doves, although they often called each other more vitriolic names.

Hawks and doves found mutual reinforcement in adversarial arguments. The central irony of these well-rehearsed debates was that each camp needed the other's opposition. Most Americans, on the other hand, intuitively wanted synthesis. Raw power without diplomatic engagement seemed only half-right, as did trustful idealism without reference to real differences. Nuclear dangers mandated engagement as well as vigilance. A continuous war footing was acceptable, but only if it was accompanied by arms control negotiations and agreements that were supposed to reduce nuclear danger. This synthesis never went smoothly, in part because expert debates were so fierce and in part because diplomatic engagement also fueled anxieties and greater nuclear precautions.[2]

This dialectic continued until the abrupt and surprising demise of the Soviet Union, to which hawks, with their armament, and doves, with their engagement, both contributed. The nuclear peace was cobbled together through deterrence, containment, military strength, diplomatic engagement, and arms control. The strange but inescapable cold war marriage of nuclear overkill and national vulnerability—the former anathema to doves, the latter anathema to hawks—helped keep nuclear dangers in check during the first nuclear age.[3]

The existential facts of nuclear overkill and national vulnerability did not prevent appalling risk taking during the cold war. Naval combatants armed with nuclear weapons played chicken on or under the high seas. Bombers carrying thermonuclear weapons in their bellies flew continuously in precise patterns, awaiting orders and "go codes" to head for enemy territory. Fighter aircraft made beelines for foreign coastlines to light up air defenses, the better to refine targeting plans for the real thing. Troops in the field possessed tactical nuclear weapons for handheld artillery launchers.[4] So much could have gone badly wrong during the first nuclear age but somehow did not. The prospect of mushroom clouds certainly did not prevent severe crises over Berlin and Cuba. Accidents occasionally happened, but none triggered a nuclear detonation. A small sampler: On January 24, 1961, a B-52 bomber carrying two hydrogen bombs broke up in midair over Goldsboro, North Carolina. Five of the six safety devices on one of the bombs failed, but the bomb did not detonate. Portions of the other weapon were buried in swampland and never recovered. On January 17, 1966, a B-52 carrying four hydrogen bombs collided with a tanker during aerial refueling. Two of the bombs fell on farmland near Palomares, Spain. The high explosives surrounding the bomb cores exploded, dispersing radioactivity, but the nuclear weapons did not detonate. Another bomb was recovered intact; the fourth was initially lost at sea and recovered four months later. On January 22, 1968, another B-52 carrying four H-bombs crashed near Thule Air Force Base in Greenland, scattering radioactive material. A massive cleanup effort removed contaminated ice, snow, and water. On September 15, 1980, a B-52 sitting on the runway in Grand Forks, North Dakota, caught fire, engulfing its nuclear weapons for more than three hours. The bomb cores, which were surrounded by sensitive high explosives, did not detonate.[5]

Compared to the nuclear weapons used on bombers and ocean-spanning missiles, tactical nuclear weapons used by forces in the field were far less secure. In January 1977, the radical Baader-Meinhof Gang stormed a NATO facility in Giessen, West Germany, where these compact weapons were stored. The intruders tried to create a diversion by blowing up a fuel storage tank outside the base perimeter. They used a shaped charge to explode the fuel tank, but they misread the gauge, believing the tank to be almost full. Instead, it was nearly empty. The shaped charge penetrated the tank above the fuel line. Had they aimed lower or had the tank been full, this diversion tactic might have succeeded. Gang members penetrated the base's security perimeter but were stopped, after an exchange of gunfire, from breaching another security perimeter around the nuclear weapons storage site.[6]

Each of these events—and many other close calls—could have been epochal. Instead, they are remembered vividly by very few. But nuclear accidents were not the only whispers of Armageddon during the first nuclear age. Miscalculations, intelligence failures, wrongheaded policy guidance, and overzealous military officers also could have produced disastrous results. In 1983, when the Reagan administration was asserting that the Soviet Union was achieving strategic superiority, the Kremlin was convinced that it was falling behind and that war hawks in the Pentagon and White House were preparing preemptive strikes to take advantage of growing U.S. strength. Soviet intelligence agents in the United States canvassed blood banks and checked to see how many lights were on late at night at the Defense and State Departments as indicators of a possible attack.[7] The Pentagon was indeed working overtime during this period—to issue glossy publications highlighting new Soviet military advances to advertise the need to catch up to the Kremlin's firepower.

The chart topper of all these tales occurred during the Cuban missile crisis, when President John F. Kennedy ordered a quarantine of Cuba, which the U.S. Navy zealously enforced against Soviet submarines as well as surface ships. Soviet Foxtrot submarines, unbeknownst to U.S. naval commanders, were each carrying one nuclear-tipped torpedo. The submarines were under orders not to use their nuclear weapons unless and until they received authorization from Moscow, but the three senior officers on board Foxtrot submarine B-59 made their own plans. They decided that, in extremis, they would disregard their orders: If they were under attack and could not reach Moscow, they would use their torpedo if all three agreed to do so.

On October 27, 1962, the same day that an American U-2 reconnaissance plane was shot down over Cuba, submarine B-59 was being heavily depth-charged to rise to the surface. Under great duress, the sub's captain, second captain, and deputy political officer discussed the fate of the Earth. Two of the officers were inclined to use their nuclear weapon. The vote of the second captain saved the world from a nuclear cataclysm. The hidden hero of the Cuban missile crisis was Vasili Alexandrovich Arkipov.[8] He was unknown to *Time* magazine, which selected Pope John XXIII as its man of the year.

Somehow, none of these intelligence failures, miscalculations, and accidents spiked a mushroom cloud, which then could have prompted a cataclysmic spasm of nuclear detonations. Such episodes were not featured in deterrence theory, whose architects did not dwell on what they could not control. Instead, the kingpins of nuclear deterrence focused on what they could manipulate.

Quantitative and qualitative aspects of the nuclear balance became paramount, which meant that nuclear weapon requirements during the cold war were always relative—the two superpowers never had enough of the absolute weapon.

Amazingly, the United States produced approximately 70,000 weapons and tested them more than 1,000 times during the cold war. The USSR built approximately 55,000 nuclear weapons and tested them more than 700 times.[9] This adds up to a grand total of 125,000 nuclear weapons, not one of which was used in battle or was detonated inadvertently or accidentally. Instead, to clarify deadly intent and affirm abstract deterrence theory, Washington and Moscow tested, on average, one nuclear weapon per week from the Cuban missile crisis to the fall of the Berlin Wall.

DETERRENCE AND REASSURANCE

Nuclear deterrence during the first nuclear age was based on threats of annihilation. To make deterrence more "credible," both superpowers conveyed messages of steely resolve, which required demonstrations of nuclear might that came in the form of testing nuclear weapons along with the rollout of new and better bombers, missiles, and submarines. Dozens of missiles were flight-tested and hundreds more were produced annually.

These messages were deeply jangling. Saber rattling mandated a parallel effort to assure worried publics that statesmen were hard at work to prevent nuclear nightmares from occurring. This was, to be sure, a tightrope act. Deterrence without reassurance would set nerves too much on edge, but efforts to reassure could undercut deterrence.[10] A parallel track of diplomatic engagement was required so that the threat of nuclear annihilation would not be left to chance. Beginning around 1960, a form of reassurance called arms control was conceived in academia and think tanks in the United States and the United Kingdom. One of the central purposes of arms control, as conceptualized by two of its founders, Thomas C. Schelling and Morton H. Halperin, was avoiding a war that neither side wanted and minimizing the costs and risks of arms competition.[11] Arms control, like nuclear deterrence, was a unique product of the Bomb.

The business of sending mixed messages between ideological foes, both threatening and reassuring, was politically contentious. One former head of the Strategic Air Command, General Thomas Power, whose job it was to be prepared to back up deterrent threats, once said that this was like dressing and undressing at the same time.[12] Arms controllers, who practiced the reassurance part, were ridiculed for being naïve and for giving away the store; nuclear weapon strategists, who practiced the threatening part, were ridiculed for their otherworldly plans to incinerate and irradiate civilization. These two cultures were bound to clash; successful negotiations would inevitably crimp the plans of strategists and war fighters, and strategic modernization programs would inevitably crimp the ambitions of negotiators.

After the Bomb's shocking appearance, deterrence theory began to coalesce quickly, starting with a slender volume edited by Bernard Brodie, *The Absolute Weapon.* "Thus far," wrote Brodie, "the chief purpose of our military establishment has been to win wars. From now on its chief purpose must be to avert them."[13] The appearance of arms control theory postdated the development of deterrence theory for several reasons. To begin with, the destruction of Hiroshima and Nagasaki by a single weapon provoked (in addition to the beginnings of deterrence theory) the immediate impulse to ban the Bomb, not to control its numbers. A collection of essays published in 1946, *One World or None,* summarized this impulse. The threat of sudden destruction of cities, wrote Albert Einstein, "could well bring about the result that even responsible statesmen might find themselves compelled to wage a preventive war."[14] The contributors to *One World or None* focused on the need to abolish war between major powers to prevent further use of the Bomb. And to abolish war, new supranational institutions needed to be given unprecedented powers. The problem, wrote Brodie, was finding a way for politics to catch up with physics.[15]

A heroic plan to ban the Bomb was drafted in just over two months by Robert Oppenheimer, the physicist who did as much as anyone to create atomic weapons, at the behest of Under Secretary of State Dean Acheson and David Lilienthal, chairman of the Tennessee Valley Authority. The crux of the Acheson-Lilienthal plan was to secure international control over the mining and manufacturing of bomb-making material. A variant of this plan was retooled by Bernard Baruch, a businessman whom Truman chose to present this plan to the United Nations. Baruch's changes, including veto-proof decision making by the international body to be created to implement the plan, ensured its veto by the Soviet Union. The Kremlin was not ready for the intrusive inspections required under any realistic scheme of international control. While furiously seeking his own bomb, Josef Stalin demanded that President Harry S. Truman give up his before considering any plan for disarmament. Despite his best efforts, Oppenheimer himself acknowledged that Stalin's behavior left no "shred of hope" that his blueprint could be implemented.[16]

After the Acheson-Lilienthal plan crashed and burned, Moscow and Washington traded rhetorical volleys over their mutual desire for general and complete disarmament. Then, in August 1949, the Soviet Union tested its first atomic bomb. Shortly thereafter, the next major opportunity to seek controls over the destructive power of the Bomb was missed when President Truman decided to undertake a crash program to produce fusion weapons. The hydrogen bomb would make atomic bombs look puny by comparison. Their differentiation could be identified by collecting radioactive particulate matter in "sniffers" carried by specially equipped planes. There was, in other words, a rudimentary means to monitor mutual U.S.-Soviet restraint against testing H-bombs.[17] But it was too early to consider such a radical idea, and once again, the U.S. push to maintain nuclear advantage, combined with the fact that there was no way to trust Stalin to exercise uncommon restraint, led to the exponential growth of nuclear arsenals.[18]

In the 1950s, many nuclear strategists became disaffected with President Eisenhower's fiscal restraint, which resulted in his administration's heavy reliance on nuclear weapons and plans for massive nuclear attacks, while constraining defense budgets for conventional forces. One of the most articulate critics of the Eisenhower administration's plans was Henry Kissinger, who directed a study group at the Council on Foreign Relations that became the springboard for his influential book *Nuclear Weapons and Foreign Policy*. Kissinger focused on the disconnect between nuclear doctrine, which then relied on massive retaliation, and the dictates of diplomacy and alliance management. This wide chasm led Kissinger to endorse the concept of limited nuclear war.[19]

Kissinger's proposed remedy was both controversial and questionable, because convincing the American public—let alone the Soviet Union—to accept the concept of limited nuclear war would be rather challenging. But by making the central point that a one-dimensional nuclear doctrine was insufficient to carry the burdens of deterrence and diplomacy, Kissinger facilitated the conceptual framework of arms control that would follow. He was no doubt right in arguing that the Eisenhower administration's brief embrace of massive retaliation was a dead end for military strategy as well as for foreign policy. Kissinger was, however, far too narrow in his approach: U.S. diplomacy and alliance management could not be advanced by refining nuclear war–fighting options without also offering greater reassurance against the Bomb's use.[20] Limited nuclear options were a necessary precaution against a well-armed adversary, but they were hardly reassuring.

If limited nuclear options were to be avoided and if general and complete disarmament was not in the cards, what path made the most sense? Stalin was dead and buried, which raised hopes that new Kremlin leaders might entertain new ideas. The Eisenhower administration began to break the diplomatic ice with the Kremlin, discussing without success concerns over surprise attacks. A new mechanism was needed to make surprise attacks less likely and to serve as a fallback position to general and complete disarmament. This new construct was required to provide public reassurance, to place constraints on the nuclear arms race, and to prevent the burgeoning arsenals of H-bombs and tactical nuclear weapons from being used in anger or by accident. Two groups of academics worked in parallel in London and Cambridge, Massachusetts, to consider these questions. They arrived at largely the same place, and they called that place arms control.

The study group in London convened to discuss papers written by Hedley Bull at the Institute for Strategic Studies.[21] These essays subsequently appeared in Bull's book, *The Control of the Arms Race*, in 1961. Arms control was defined as "restraint internationally exercised upon armaments policy, whether in respect of the level of armaments, their character, deployment, or use." Bull began his thesis by arguing in the negative: Arms control was not really about saving money, or morality, or preventing arms races that led inevitably to wars— propositions he rejected. Instead, arms control was about shaping policies and international arrangements "that will reduce the dangers of a world still armed and divided." In such a world, arms control could not be expected to produce wonders. "Arms control does not provide a technique of insulating a military situation from the future will of states to change it: it cannot bind, nor settle in advance, the future course of politics." Arms control would be, in effect, a steering mechanism that sensible political leaders might use to lessen nuclear dangers. "There can only be relative security" when dealing with the absolute weapon. Arms control measures might just help wise leaders "to increase their security against war."[22]

A broader and more ambitious agenda for arms control was conceptualized in the Boston area. Working under the auspices of the American Academy of Arts and Sciences, Donald Brennan and Bernard Feld coordinated a series of brainstorming sessions that produced two remarkable books in 1961: a volume edited by Brennan, *Arms Control, Disarmament, and National Security*, and the classic of the genre, *Strategy and Arms Control*, by Thomas C. Schelling and Morton H. Halperin.

The Brennan volume gathered an eclectic group, ranging from Herman Kahn, a Strangelovian character who wrote on how wars might start, to Erich Fromm, a Freudian psychologist and the author of *The Art of Loving*, who wrote on complete unilateral disarmament. This august group of contributors included Edward Teller, the "father of the H-bomb"; Jerome Wiesner, a staunch advocate of arms control who became President Kennedy's science adviser; Henry Kissinger; and Senator Hubert Humphrey, who was the strongest supporter in Congress for the creation of a new arms control and disarmament agency. It would have been pure folly for Brennan to have tried to get this collection of thinkers to agree on what constituted sound arms control. Instead, they offered, in effect, first drafts on subjects that would be fiercely contested over the next quarter-century.

Brennan hesitated to define arms control in his introductory chapter, in part because of its "experimental" nature—a characterization that could also have been applied to nuclear deterrence theory. His working hypothesis was that it would be "useful to think generally of arms control as a cooperative or multilateral approach to armament policy," which included "not only the amount and kind of weapons and forces in being, but also the development, deployment, and utilization of such forces, whether in periods of relaxation, in periods of tension, or in periods of shooting wars."[23] Another contributor, Robert R. Bowie, who later headed the State Department's policy planning shop, defined arms control as "any agreement among several powers to regulate some aspect of their military capability or potential."[24]

The slim book by Schelling and Halperin offered what Brennan's group could not possibly produce: a coherent, tightly reasoned concept of what would soon become the practice of arms control. Arms control was not, they argued, a stand-alone enterprise. Rather, it was a "natural" complement to foreign and military policy and an "enlargement of the scope of military strategy." Schelling and Halperin argued that, with the advent of the Bomb, "our military relation with potential enemies is not one of pure conflict and opposition, but involves strong elements of mutual interest in the avoidance of a war that neither side wants, in minimizing the costs and risks of the arms competition, and in curtailing the scope and violence of war in the event it occurs." It followed from these propositions that, in some circumstances, there could be "a mutual interest in inducing and reciprocating arms restraint." The art of the possible began with the recognition that "there is a feedback between our military forces and the conflicts that they simultaneously reflect and influence."[25]

Schelling and Halperin viewed the "new business" of arms control "as a rich and variegated subject whose forms and whose impact on security policy and world affairs have only been dimly perceived." In shining a spotlight on this new world of possibilities, they stressed that "arms control, if properly conceived, is not necessarily hostile to, or incompatible with, or an alternative to, a military policy properly conceived."

> The aims of arms control and the aims of national military strategy should be substantially the same. Before one considers this an excessively narrow construction of arms control, he should consider whether it cannot just as well be viewed as a very broad statement of what the aims of military strategy should be.

The co-authors of *Strategy and Arms Control* ended on a somber note: "Sophistication comes slowly. Military collaboration with potential enemies is not a concept that comes naturally. . . . It is the conservatism of military policy that has caused 'arms control' to appear as an alternative, even antithetical, field of action."[26] The conceptualization of arms control faced deep skepticism from the outset. Critics pointed out that the only prior effort that remotely approximated what Schelling and Halperin had in mind—the attempt by American, British, French, German, and Japanese diplomats to place limits on the size and firepower of their naval forces—were foiled by great power rivalries and opposing geopolitical ambitions. Failed efforts by the naval powers in the 1920s and 1930s to place agreed-on constraints on capital ships ended in a global war. Why, then, seek to emulate this failure?

The newly elected American president, John F. Kennedy, felt otherwise. The founders of arms control at Harvard and the Massachusetts Institute of Technology appeared at precisely the right time and place. Some followed Kennedy to Washington, where they attempted to put academic theory into practice. Kennedy agreed that an arms control and disarmament agency, affiliated with the State Department, was needed. Then, out of crisis came opportunity: The Cuban missile crisis forced another intense look into the nuclear abyss, prompting the first measures that were designed not for general and complete disarmament but to prevent accidental war and to reassure worried publics. A new hotline agreement was finalized in 1963 to speed up crisis communications, with terminals installed in the Pentagon and in the Kremlin, eight months after the Cuban standoff.

Later that year, Kennedy and Khrushchev agreed to stop nuclear testing in the atmosphere. The mushroom cloud had become a far too familiar reminder of nuclear dangers, and those dangers were becoming far too real. The fallout from atmospheric testing was becoming a public health hazard, with alarming indicators of strontium-90 and other by-products of the Bomb's fallout showing up in mothers' milk and dental x-rays. Deterrence strategists expressed alarm that key demonstrations of nuclear prowess would be closed off by a limited test ban treaty that would drive future testing underground. But for the first time in the first nuclear age, street demonstrations were more powerful than the dictates of deterrence theory: The public's need for reassurance trumped the desires of bomb designers and nuclear war strategists.[27] Support for the Limited Test Ban Treaty was mirrored by the four-fifths majority support it received in the Senate. A far greater achievement of arms control during the first nuclear age was soon to come—a treaty that would lay the foundation for a global system to prevent proliferation.

THE ORIGINS OF NONPROLIFERATION

The first nuclear age was primarily about vertical, not horizontal, proliferation; the size of superpower nuclear arsenals grew enormously, while surprisingly few additional states acquired the Bomb. It was also about how two ideological foes managed to begin talking to one another about how to avoid a war that could destroy them both. This engagement started simply enough, with the hotline and tacit agreements not to try to shoot down newfangled satellites launched to spy on each other. The conversation evolved with great difficulty to include negotiations over quantitative and qualitative aspects of the nuclear competition, eventually resulting in treaties hundreds of pages long, with provisions for challenge inspections and detailed procedures for dismantling missiles, bombers, and submarines. This extraordinary progression produced many achievements, but none was more important than the partnership the United States and the Soviet Union formed to try to prevent proliferation.

The origins of superpower collaboration to prevent horizontal proliferation can be traced to a secret 1965 study commissioned by President Johnson. At the beginning of the quagmire in Vietnam, Johnson's administration faced another tough decision: whether to create nuclear counterbalances to the Soviet Union and Communist China, which had just tested its first nuclear weapon, by arming India, Japan, and America's NATO allies with nuclear weapons. The alternative was to champion a global diplomatic effort against proliferation.

The Johnson administration was deeply divided about which course of action to pursue. The Pentagon and the newly created Arms Control and Disarmament Agency pushed LBJ to champion nonproliferation; the State

Department, attuned to the security concerns of friends and allies, viewed the transfer of nuclear weapons to them as a means of reassurance. LBJ decided to form a panel of "wise men" to break the deadlock. This ten-person commit-tee was headed by Roswell Gilpatric, recently retired as Robert McNamara's deputy in the Pentagon. Gilpatric was joined by hard-core veterans of the cold war—heavyweights such as former CIA director Allen Dulles, General Alfred Gruenther, the former supreme allied commander in Europe, and presidential envoys John J. McCloy and Arthur Dean.

The Gilpatric committee unanimously chose to make nonproliferation a top-tier national security priority, recommending that "if we are to have any hope of success in halting the spread of nuclear weapons," the United States would need to "greatly intensify" an engagement strategy that included talking not only with Moscow but also with Beijing.[28] Finding common cause with Mao was a bridge too far, but the cold warriors of the Gilpatric panel guessed correctly that, if the United States chose not to share nuclear weapons with West Germany, then the Soviet Union might just become a strong partner in preventing proliferation.

In hindsight, making nonproliferation a top-tier national security prior-ity was a no-brainer. It should have been obvious, as the Gilpatric committee concluded, that the spread of nuclear weapons in tense regions could nullify American might and "eventually constitute direct military threats to the United States." But the remedies proposed by the Gilpatric panel were truly radical in 1965. They included recommendations that LBJ strenuously support multilat-eral treaties, work hard to end all nuclear testing, promote nuclear-weapon-free zones and stop fissile material production for weapons.

LBJ took this advice to heart, strongly backing what soon became the Treaty on the Nonproliferation of Nuclear Weapons (or Nonproliferation Treaty), overriding the State Department's qualms about damaging U.S. ties with key friends and allies. No treaty has gained more adherents than the Nonprolifera-tion Treaty, with more than 180 faithfully participating states. States without the Bomb agreed to join because nuclear proliferation was perceived as a signif-icant threat and because of promised benefits of nuclear power and the pledges by the permanent members of the UN Security Counsel to pursue abolition. No treaty has more wide-ranging safeguards and inspections than the Non-proliferation Treaty, covering more than 150 nations. Other recommendations of the Gilpatric committee subsequently contributed to U.S. nonproliferation policies for the duration of the cold war.

The bipolar geometry of the superpower competition fueled vertical proliferation, but it worked well against horizontal proliferation. The United States and the Soviet Union shared a common interest in preventing new members from joining the nuclear club. They possessed the carrots and sticks to keep potential strays (e.g., Taiwan and South Korea) in the fold. Two states were beyond the orbit of superpower influence on nuclear matters—Israel and South Africa—and two more, India and Pakistan, placed themselves on the threshold of acquiring nuclear weapons during the first nuclear age.

Otherwise, superpower security guarantees were bankable, their alliances were stable, and few nations wished to cross both Washington and Moscow. The global system to prevent proliferation could not have been built without this odd couple. Nor could it have been constructed without linking the norm of abolition to promoting peaceful uses of the atom. The fault line in international politics created by the Bomb could be bridged only by accepting zero as the end-state for all and by promoting nonmilitary uses of atomic energy. The pledge to help nations with nuclear power, exemplified most dramatically in President Eisenhower's Atoms for Peace program, inadvertently sowed the seeds for the proliferation headaches of the second nuclear age.

This system meant, in practice and in principle, that the Bomb was the central problem—not a particular state that had the Bomb or wanted to get it. It was easier and more effective to prevent proliferation by making the Bomb the issue rather than by trying to distinguish "good guys" from "bad guys," especially since the superpowers could not possibly agree on the identification of bad actors. The foundation of the global nonproliferation system remained sturdy during the first nuclear age, partly because when the superpowers could actually agree on something, they could usually make it happen. Vertical proliferation was dangerous enough; horizontal proliferation could make matters far worse. Consequently, even—or especially—during rocky stages of the superpower competition, key stakeholders in the Nonproliferation Treaty became more protective. Eventually, they hoped, Washington and Moscow would get past their differences and succeed in negotiating arms control and reduction treaties. In these rough patches, there was little enthusiasm for holding the treaty hostage, demanding success in superpower negotiations. Playing brinkmanship with the global nonproliferation system—on top of the brinkmanship practiced by the superpowers—would only court further nuclear danger.

The leisurely pace of proliferation during the first nuclear age was crucial because it allowed major powers, neighbors, and international institutions to accommodate to unwelcome change. After the United States and the Soviet Union demonstrated "mastery" over the atom in the 1940s, Great Britain followed suit in the 1950s. Then France, China, and Israel joined in the 1960s,[29] followed by South Africa, briefly, in the late 1970s.[30] Pakistan acquired an operational nuclear capability in the late 1980s,[31] just as the first nuclear age was ending, and India followed in the early 1990s.[32] This slow progression lent itself to global and regional adaptation, in part because the countervailing growth in nonproliferation institutions, controls, and norms was also slow but steady. Export controls were strengthened, membership in the Nonproliferation Treaty grew, and treaties were negotiated that limited nuclear weapon tests.

The anticipated slowness of the Bomb's spread has always been a key condition for proliferation optimists in academia, who believe in the stabilizing consequences of nuclear proliferation. The leader of this school, Kenneth Waltz, argued that "if weapons are not well suited for conquest, neighbors have more peace of mind."[33] Those who have followed in Waltz's footsteps, who view proliferation as a stabilizing force in international relations, tend to be theorists whose constructs hinge on the rational actions of nation states. The short form of this litany is that the Bomb enforces caution and that adversaries possessing the means to make mushroom clouds would not be so dumb as to cross the nuclear threshold.

Proliferation optimists presume sound decisions, tight command and control, and proper implementation of decisions made in deep crisis. The word *jihad* is not found in the indexes of their books, and cataclysmic accidents are not seriously considered. Proliferation optimists, like deterrence theorists, focused their formidable intellects on what could be controlled, not what could go badly wrong. Bomb holders were like two scorpions in a bottle, "each capable of killing the other, but only at the risk of his own life." Robert Oppenheimer, the Manhattan Project's scientific director, offered this evocative image early in the nuclear standoff, and it stuck, despite the obvious problem of assuming that scorpions had sufficient control to exercise restraint.[34] The first books that applied Murphy's Law to nuclear weapons did not appear until the mid-1980s.[35] Proliferation optimists rested their case by pointing to the unarguable fact that no bomb was used in anger during the cold war. The rejoinder of proliferation pessimists was a series of hair-raising vignettes that clarified how fortunate the world was to have escaped Armageddon, especially during the Cuban missile crisis.

Whether by design, wise human decisions, divine intervention, or plain dumb luck, no mushroom cloud darkened the first nuclear age after Nagasaki.

Surely, deterrence played a key role in keeping the cold war from becoming hot, but deterrence required continuous displays of nuclear prowess in the form of missile flight tests, the rollout of new weapon systems, and, of course, nuclear tests. The demonstration effect of nuclear muscle flexing had the unwanted but quite reasonable consequence of making the Bomb more attractive to lesser powers. These were the good old days, when proliferation remained a manageable, state-centric enterprise.

THE NUCLEAR VERNACULAR

The first nuclear age brought with it the bikini (named after the atoll where atomic and hydrogen bombs were exploded), Dr. Strangelove, the doomsday clock advising us how close our nuclear follies were taking us toward midnight, and duck-and-cover drills at school, in case the Bomb disrupted studies. A group of Harvard professors wrote a book about learning to live with the Bomb (their answer was moderation),[36] but this sage advice was rarely followed. Everything about the Bomb was over the top: targeting plans, stockpile sizes, and the exquisite complexity of bombs designed to pack the most wallop within a confined space. (Compact warhead designs permitted many warheads to be squeezed atop a single missile.) The most complex U.S. design appears to be the B83 gravity bomb, with 6,619 parts.[37]

The Bomb acquired its own foreign language, befitting a strange, alien power. Bomb-speak was required because it was far too chilling and politically incorrect to discuss the use of the Bomb in plain language. At the outset of the first nuclear age, clinical volumes describing weapon effects were published and quietly shelved; they were too grim to read. Besides, the whole purpose of the Bomb was deterrence, not use. Of course, to deter, one had to be prepared to use the Bomb. A convoluted and yet anodyne language related to nuclear deterrence was therefore needed to explain huge public expenditures and to dissuade potential adversaries while avoiding public unrest. Discussions of weapon effects were not encouraged.

One inconvenient truth was that a single use of a Bomb on a single city would contravene the rules of war, which mandated that civilized societies do their utmost to abstain from targeting noncombatants, especially using weapons with long-lasting and indiscriminate effects. The targeting of cities was not called unlawful; it was called "countervalue" targeting. U.S. nuclear war plans did not target cities per se; instead, Washington (and Moscow) targeted military facilities and war-supporting industry located within and near cities.

(More than 150 thermonuclear weapons were targeted against the ballistic missile defense system built around Moscow.)[38]

Another key phrase of the first nuclear age was escalation control. Escalation control had to be a linchpin of deterrence theory, because if escalation were uncontrolled, genocide and perhaps even planetary suicide would result. The word *genocide* was absolutely verboten in bomb-speak. This became clear early on, at a crucial juncture in the Bomb's evolution, when this word was used sparingly but jarringly by a few remorseful scientists who worked on the Manhattan Project. They were serving as private consultants to the Truman administration, which was struggling with the decision about whether to build hydrogen bombs. The "super," as it was called then, would dwarf the destructive powers of the atomic bombs that vaporized, fireballed, and irradiated Hiroshima and Nagasaki.

The majority view of the scientific luminaries on this advisory panel, led by Robert Oppenheimer, held that "if super bombs will work at all, there is no inherent limit in the destructive power that may be attained with them. Therefore, a super bomb might become a weapon of genocide." A concurring opinion was more pointed: "Necessarily such a weapon goes far beyond any military objective and enters the range of very great natural catastrophes. By its very nature it cannot be confined to a military objective but becomes a weapon which in practical effect is almost one of genocide."[39] This line of thought was particularly dangerous because it could be extended to the entire nuclear enterprise on which deterrence was based. Not all remorseful Manhattan Project scientists were willing to extend their argument this far. (As an alternative to the super, Oppenheimer advocated more choices of less devastating atomic bombs.)

Truman's H-bomb decision crossed multiple thresholds. Henceforth, those uttering the word *genocide* were unwelcome company in any advisory or official capacity dealing with the Bomb. In a particularly brutal knife twist, Oppenheimer's security clearances were revoked exactly one day before they were to lapse, and he was then subjected to a star chamber proceeding that found him to be a security risk—an object lesson for the Bomb's skeptics if there ever was one.[40] President Truman had decided that he had no choice but to proceed with the super, given that he was dealing with Josef Stalin, who could not be trusted to exercise restraint in developing a trump card to the A-bomb. From the 1950s onward, hydrogen bombs became the staple of the U.S. and Soviet arsenals.

Extirpating the word *genocide* from policy deliberations on the Bomb was simple enough; achieving escalation control and avoiding genocide in the event of spasmodic nuclear exchanges were much harder. To deal with this co-nundrum, two new anodyne phrases were added to the vocabulary of bomb-speak: damage limitation and escalation dominance. Damage limitation was certainly most welcome when dealing with nuclear dangers of any kind. In terms of nuclear targeting, however, damage limitation meant striking an ad-versary's nuclear forces before they could strike first. And because superpower arsenals during the first nuclear age were so bloated (in their heyday, Moscow and Washington each had perhaps 6,000 weapons that could be launched in a matter of minutes to reach the other's homeland), damage limitation required the release of Armageddon-like waves of nuclear strikes.

The Eisenhower administration dealt with the contingency of a numerically superior Red Army rolling across Europe by relying heavily on tactical nuclear weapons carried by troops in Europe and by declaring that nuclear weapons were to be considered integral to war fighting. Ike's classified Basic National Security Policy put it this way: "In the event of hostilities, the United States will consider nuclear weapons to be as available for use as other munitions."[41] Dur-ing this period, massive nuclear strikes were not just an option, they were the primary nuclear targeting option.

One of the strategists who influenced these plans was Paul Nitze, who served as vice chairman of the U.S. Strategic Bombing Survey in the Pacific, where he assessed the effects of air power on World War II's outcome. Most of those who saw firsthand the Bomb's impact on Hiroshima and Nagasaki either entered the Church of Nuclear Strategy or became apostates. Nitze's choice was clear at the outset, as he applied himself to the survey with characteristic dog-gedness and precision. "Our task," he recalled forty years later, "was to measure precisely the physical effects [of the Bomb] . . . to put calipers on it, instead of describing it in emotive terms. I was trying to put quantitative numbers on something that was considered immeasurable." For the entirety of Nitze's long career in public service, he attempted to "put calipers on the rubble" in order to prevent another use of the Bomb during the first nuclear age.[42]

Writing about nuclear war-fighting strategy in 1956, Nitze asserted that "it is to the West's interest, if atomic war becomes unavoidable, that atomic weapons of the smallest sizes be used in the smallest area." Nuclear numbers and capa-bilities mattered greatly, because they could determine the relative postwar posi-tions of the adversaries—assuming that all-out war and spasm attacks could be avoided. "In this sense," Nitze argued, "it is quite possible that in a general nuclear war one side or the other could 'win' decisively. Even a small initial imbalance in relative capabilities, other things being equal, could grow rapidly into a decisive imbalance as the war progressed." This was the same hard logic that subsequently turned Nitze against the strategic arms limitation talks. It was "of the utmost importance that the West maintain a sufficient margin of superior capability," both to dissuade the Soviet Union from starting a general war and to achieve relative advantage if a war began. The greater the marginal postwar advantage, the more the victor would be in a position to dictate terms and the more the loser would need to obey these terms "or face complete chaos or extinction."[43]

This was the unvarnished Nitze, the steel-trap mind, the brutally severe logistician, and the conveyor of harsh truths. But Nitze's hard logic was built on tenuous assumptions, starting with the assumption that command and control of opposing nuclear forces would remain intact despite the stresses of nuclear exchanges. Another key assumption was that Soviet leaders would also accept his logic and avoid spasmodic attacks. Nitze acknowledged that uncontrolled nuclear exchanges were "technically conceivable" but were likely only if war were to be fought "in an entirely irrational way."[44]

Nitze's preferred strategy was reflected in the Pentagon's war-planning documents because the presumption of an illogical and irrational foe would make such plans utterly groundless. These war plans led to an abundance of short-range as well as ocean-spanning nuclear weapon "delivery vehicles." Secretary of Defense Robert McNamara subsequently used his prodigious and razor-sharp intellect to provide more discrete nuclear attack options, but for all his efforts, the resulting calculations still looked genocidal. The damage limitation targeting plans bequeathed to the Nixon administration involved no less than 4,200 nuclear weapons targeting 6,500 Soviet bloc installations.[45]

The progression of nuclear targeting plans that followed McNamara became increasingly varied. "Limited nuclear options" entered the lexicon in the 1970s. The conundrum of authorizing the use of potentially genocidal weapons was dealt with by improving the product line and making the product more sophisticated. Deployed ocean-spanning nuclear forces grew to more than 10,000 per side. Warhead lethality grew with accuracy; the most sophisticated U.S. warheads launched from ocean-spanning missiles were expected to land within a football field's distance of their targets, and cruise missiles were expected to be far more accurate than this. The growth of these war-fighting capabilities and options gave credence to theories and fears of escalation dominance.

Escalation dominance basically meant that after nuclear exchanges began, the superpower with more weapons, more telling strike options, and better defenses could dictate the course of the war by forcing the weaker side to cry uncle. Only those with the steely courage to stare unblinkingly at the exchange ratios of megadeath could enter this domain. Their underlying premise—that all wars have winners and losers and that nuclear wars would be no different— led inexorably to ghoulish preparations, because the side that was better prepared with bomb shelters and nuclear attack options would be victorious.

The first nuclear age was framed by stark choices. The Senate's most powerful voice on national security matters in the 1960s, Senator Richard Russell, clarified matters in this way: "If we have to start over again with another Adam and Eve, then I want them to be Americans and not Russians."[46] Russell did not need to be apologetic about this elemental choice; he was, after all, the chairman of the Senate Appropriations Committee. Others got into deep trouble when they became this emotional or specific about nuclear war-fighting strategy. It was therefore crucial for advocates of civil defenses and offensive preparations to remain clinical and composed at all times. The tall edifice of nuclear war planning was built on rational calculation and sold to the public in the safety blanket of deterrence theory. Relentless efforts to build up offenses and defenses were required for comparative advantage, so that the plans would never have to be executed. But the more real nuclear planning became, in the form of atmospheric tests, the stronger public resistance grew. Atmospheric testing in such places as Nevada, the Kazakh steppes, the Arctic, Australia, and Algeria generated global fallout and increased radiation levels in breast milk, teeth, and bones, which drove testing underground in 1963. Much to the consternation of deterrence theorists, local and global protests eventually prompted a treaty in 1996 that banned even underground tests.

Some defensive measures also prompted opposition to nuclear war-fighting plans. Home fallout shelters had a brief period of acceptance in the 1950s before the American public decided to redirect its collective attention to home appliances, new cars, and the pursuit of happiness. Missile defenses near major U.S. metropolitan areas such as Boston and New York were widely unwelcome in the late 1960s and early 1970s because the only reliable way to "defend" against a long-range missile attack was by using interceptors armed with nuclear weapons. The Spartan interceptors proposed by the Nixon administration carried a wallop of 5 megatons—more than 300 times more powerful than the warheads that leveled Hiroshima and Nagasaki.

The Nixon administration's test of this warhead on November 6, 1971, was the biggest U.S. underground nuclear blast. The administration's decision to test this warhead at full yield remains a testament to the urgencies of the first nuclear age. This test required significant engineering feats. The warhead weighed no less than 850,000 pounds. A weapon of this size and explosive power needed to be buried deep underground to prevent the leakage of radio-activity and to ease political concerns. The locals, in this instance, needed to be as remote and politically unsophisticated as possible. The "not in my backyard" syndrome was sidestepped by choosing for the test site an island in the Aleutian Island chain, which juts out from the coast of Alaska into the Bering Sea. The Auke Tribe's leadership, based in Juneau, tried to call President Nixon's atten-tion to the Tlingit belief that the Aleutians are imbued with spirit and ought not to be violated, but the tribe's voice was not heard in Washington. The sacri-ficial island, Amchitka, was located just 50 miles off the Soviet coast.

The particulars of this test spoke volumes about the compulsions of the first nuclear age. As recounted by Dean Kohlhoff, the author of *Amchitka and the Bomb*, the test required a borehole drilled down to 6,150 feet—a distance equivalent to four Chicago Sears Towers stacked end to end. The horizontal blast chamber for the bomb at the bottom of the borehole, which needed to be drilled by hand, had a radius of 26 feet. The test registered 7.0 on the Richter scale—the same reading as the earthquake that rocked San Francisco in 1989, interrupting the World Series. The Amchitka test uplifted a fault line in the Bering Sea by 42 inches.[47]

The Soviet Union, which was far less constrained by public opinion, tested an appalling 57-megaton device in the atmosphere on August 30, 1961. This test prompted demands by Air Force chief Curtis LeMay and Senator Henry M. Jackson for a comparable weapon to avoid being placed at a competitive dis-advantage.[48] U.S. deterrence strategists felt greatly disadvantaged by the work-ings of American democracy, which repeatedly rebuffed efforts to promote civil defenses. One civil defense enthusiast and former Pentagon official, T. K. Jones, used as supporting evidence a picture taken weeks after Hiroshima was incinerated showing a lone trolley car in service.[49] To Jones, this was evidence of the wisdom of planning for nuclear disasters and the powers of national recovery. Most listeners found his argument unconvincing. The Kremlin's cal-culations differed: To this day, Moscow remains "defended" by nuclear-tipped interceptors.

During the administration of President Reagan, when the goal of prevailing in a nuclear war was unapologetically and publicly embraced by the Pentagon, Jones opined that 98 percent of the Russian population could survive an all-out nuclear attack because of Soviet evacuation procedures and civil defense plans. To be competitive, he said, the Americans had to follow suit: "If there are enough shovels to go around, everybody's going to make it," referring to the utility of bomb shelters. "It's the dirt that does it."[50]

Such pronouncements had the opposite of their intended effect. Repeatedly frustrated from pursuing defenses, U.S. strategists could execute plans for escalation dominance only by accentuating the offense. But escalation dominance required truly heroic assumptions, starting with the ability and willingness of national leaders to fight a "rational," calibrated nuclear war. The resulting war plans raised too many unanswerable questions. If superpower differences were so profound as to prompt a deliberate nuclear war, why would one side be willing to accept defeat? How could war-fighting scenarios be choreographed like a ballet? How could either superpower be sure that it could assess the other's intentions during nuclear exchanges or, for that matter, assess its own damage? And how could thousands of nuclear weapons spring-loaded for launch be held in reserve for escalation dominance when they were extremely vulnerable to attack?

One central irony of living with the Bomb was that rationalism produced nuclear deterrence theory, but nuclear deterrence was also deeply irrational. The best and the brightest strategists of the first nuclear age tried to hold out the promise of safety with scenarios of mass destruction and by increasing the credibility of threatening weapons that were too deadly to use. No wonder these efforts lent themselves so well to parody.

No one was more susceptible to parody than Herman Kahn, who wrote books bracketing the Cuban missile crisis: *Thinking About the Unthinkable*, *On Escalation Control*, and *On Thermonuclear War*. From Kahn's fertile, febrile mind came the following illustrative passage:

> One side might wish to escalate specifically to threaten the other side with all-out war, to provoke it, to demonstrate committal or recklessness, and so forth. A nation may also escalate for prudential as well as coercive reasons: to prevent something worse from happening, to meet a problem, to prepare for likely escalations on the other side, and so on.[51]

Nobody parodied bomb culture better than Stanley Kubrick in *Dr. Strangelove or: How I Learned to Stop Worrying and Love the Bomb*. Filmed one year after the Cuban missile crisis, *Dr. Strangelove* was greeted with deep critical ambivalence. With memories of the crisis still raw, the movie-going public sought escapism, not a parody of Armageddon. *Dr. Strangelove* grossed only $8 million in 1964. The top moneymaker that year was *Goldfinger*, the Academy Award for Best Picture went to *Tom Jones*.[52]

Kubrick was even more prescient than he knew. Transcripts of the Kennedy administration's secret deliberations during the Cuban missile crisis later revealed real-world analogs to General Buck Turgidson and General Jack D. Ripper, the characters played by George C. Scott and Sterling Hayden. Both the air force chief, General LeMay, and the chief of naval operations, Admiral George W. Anderson Jr., staunchly advocated preemptive strikes against Cuba, followed by a military invasion. Although these members of the Joint Chiefs were unaware that Soviet tactical nuclear weapons were already in Cuba, they surely understood that their advice, if taken, could well have led to what was euphemistically known as "central strategic exchanges" with the Soviet Union. This prospect would, in turn, no doubt have led to recommendations for preemptive strikes against Mother Russia.[53] These private offerings were eerily similar to the classic line spoken by the George C. Scott character in *Dr. Strangelove*, who argued, after calling for massive U.S. strikes, "I'm not saying we won't get our hair mussed."

The doomsday device used by the Soviet ambassador at the end of *Dr. Strangelove* also had a real-life equivalent. The Soviet system was called Perimetr and was nicknamed the Dead Hand system by U.S. analysts who belatedly learned about it. In case of a U.S. nuclear attack and the inability of Soviet leaders to communicate the authorization to launch nuclear weapons, command and control procedures could be overridden by previously assigned designees located at hardened, underground command posts. Upon receiving a warning (true or false) of an impending attack, the Perimetr system could be activated. If detonations on Soviet soil occurred and if the Kremlin leadership could not communicate launch orders, their designated substitutes could launch missiles, broadcasting orders to fire the surviving nuclear forces. Authorization for the Perimetr system was begun in 1974. It was deployed in 1985, when some in the Kremlin were particularly concerned about a preemptive nuclear attack from the Reagan administration. The Perimetr system presumably remains in place to this day, when the United States enjoys strategic superiority, adheres to a doctrine of using nuclear weapons first, and continues to maintain many hundreds of missiles on hair-trigger alert.[54]

The Perimetr system clarified the limitations of deterrence theory. Further clarification was provided after the collapse of the Soviet Union, with the publication of reliable characterizations of Soviet nuclear war-fighting plans. U.S. deterrence strategists did not have a compliant partner. Instead, the Soviet nuclear war-fighting machine was designed around massive attacks and, in the event of a surprise U.S. attack, the Samson option.[55] Much as hawkish U.S. nuclear strategists railed against mutual assured destruction, they were powerless to negate such an outcome.

Dr. Strangelove, as played by Peter Sellers, was sex starved as well as Bomb obsessed. Loving the Bomb and playing out Bomb-related anxieties were considered particularly male traits. Indeed, in real life, all the leading Bomb strategists were male, as were the politicians and military officers who worked these precincts. Women finally entered the picture as crusading anti-Bomb activists who were roused by the confrontational policies of the Reagan administration in the 1980s. Gender politics and anti-Bomb politics were a combustible mix, with Bomb lovers tagged as deficient males suffering from missile envy.[56]

No matter how much the atomic supermarket grew in the United States, there remained only one male consumer who mattered most: the U.S. commander in chief. If command and control systems worked properly, the president remained in charge. And no matter how variegated and discriminating these plans became—whatever the weapon's yield or tailored effect, whatever the subset of targets—no amount of refinement could make this choice easier.

There was no greater safeguard during the first nuclear age than the distance between the plans of nuclear strategists and the political instincts of national leaders. The separate worlds of the weapon strategists and political leaders became the most important fail-safe mechanism to prevent a nuclear holocaust. Fail-safe mechanisms were supposed to prevent accidents or unauthorized use of a nuclear weapon. Typically several fail-safe mechanisms—mechanical, procedural, and related security measures—would be in place to prevent screwups. And eventually, the mechanical safeguards became so refined that weapons needed to be certified as being "one point safe" before entering the U.S. inventory, which meant that, if, for whatever reason, the high explosive encasing the fissile material at the Bomb's core was detonated at any single point, the probability of producing a nuclear yield exceeding 4 pounds of TNT was less than 1 in 1 million.[57]

McGeorge Bundy, who stood by President Kennedy's side during the Cuban missile crisis, wrote with particular feeling about a very different kind of safeguard.

> In light of the certain prospect of retaliation there has been literally no chance at all that any sane political authority, in either the United States or the Soviet

Union, would consciously choose to start a nuclear war. . . . There is an enormous gulf between what political leaders really think about nuclear weapons and what is assumed in complex calculations of relative "advantage" in simulated strategic warfare. . . . [Nuclear strategists] are in an unreal world. In the real world of real political leaders—whether here or in the Soviet Union—a decision that would bring even one hydrogen bomb on one city of our own country would be a disaster beyond history.[58]

Two key words in this passage are "sane" and "consciously"—words that may be less applicable in the second nuclear age, to which I turn next (in Chapter 4). Sane, rational choice was a hallmark of the first nuclear age. Nuclear weapon strategists and arms controllers disagreed vehemently about policy choices and weapon programs, but they did so based on rational premises. For arms controllers, it was rational to presume that the Soviet Union wished to avoid a nuclear war as well as a nuclear arms race and was therefore willing to accept mutual constraints in this domain. For nuclear weapon strategists, it was rational to presume that the Kremlin thought differently about benefits and risks—and that safety lay in staring frightening possibilities down—including the possibility of a nuclear war.

Rational, state-centric choice during the first nuclear age resulted in abstract and endless arguments over the requirements of deterrence and the wisdom or folly of sheathing the most powerful swords available. Nuclear abolitionists, arms controllers, and nuclear war planners all feared the same outcome—that, sooner or later, the Bomb would again be used in anger, and then all hell would break loose. That was why abolitionists wanted to eliminate the Bomb, arms controllers wanted to manage nuclear risks, and nuclear war planners planned.

Everyone tried to use their intellect to get out of this mosh pit. Rational calculation led to starkly different remedies and strange convergences. Nuclear weapon strategists were convinced that Bundy and his ilk were wrong in "mirror imaging" the Kremlin's calculations about the Bomb. These nuclear weapon strategists were guided by analogy, even though the Bomb was sui generis. Surely, in their view, a nation that took 10 million casualties in defeating Nazi Germany was made of sterner stuff than to accept a strategic stalemate. Because the Kremlin presumably believed that it was possible to fight and win a nuclear war, the United States needed to convince the Politburo otherwise by being able to deny the Kremlin's war-winning aims.[59] These hard-line strategists, led by Paul Nitze, pushed a different kind of mirror imaging, one calling for the United States to trump presumed Soviet war-winning nuclear capabilities and strategies.

NUCLEAR OFFENSES AND DEFENSES

Deterrence during the first nuclear age rested on threats of overwhelming punishment. Missile defenses were effectively ruled out by the Anti-Ballistic Missile Treaty, signed by two prototypical cold warriors, Richard Nixon and Leonid Brezhnev, in 1972. This treaty permitted only minimal defenses of limited areas. Public relief after this treaty, and a companion agreement placing bare limitations on offensive forces, was short-lived. The Anti-Ballistic Missile Treaty failed to realize its intended promise. Arms controllers, who finally succeeded in convincing the executive and legislative branches that safety lay in the counterintuitive notion of mutual vulnerability, had hoped that preventing defenses would take the wind out of the sails of the offensive nuclear competition. Nothing of the sort happened. Instead, mutual anxieties and uncertainties related to remaining defenses fueled hedging strategies that redoubled both sides' efforts to build up offenses.

The most damaging hedge of all was the decision by the Nixon administration, followed by the Kremlin, to place more than one warhead atop ocean-spanning missiles. Multiple, independently targetable reentry vehicles (MIRVs) were, unlike missile defenses, cost-effective and technically feasible. Depending on its size, a single ballistic missile could carry three, six, eight, ten, or twelve warheads to separate targets within approximately 30,000 square miles. Put another way, a Soviet targeter aiming for Washington, D.C., could also destroy Philadelphia, Baltimore, and Richmond with weapons atop a single missile.

The story of MIRVs reflects how politically "safe" decisions fueled the arms race. Safety against a powerful, untrustworthy foe meant not falling behind in the arms race against a ruthless adversary. Safety required an excess of caution and an excess of firepower. Cost-effectiveness meant increasing firepower by placing more warheads atop missile launchers rather than digging more missile silos. Not competing, on the other hand, was fraught with risk, not just for national security but for political careers. Being safe rather than sorry required precisely what President Eisenhower warned against: the "military-industrial complex," including no less than three major laboratories focusing primarily on nuclear weapon design and systems engineering. (The Soviet Union had two.)

In retrospect, it is not at all surprising how often hawks trounced doves in domestic political debates over the Bomb. They could frame domestic debates with circular arguments that were usually true: New and better nuclear weapon capabilities were needed because the Soviet Union could not be trusted. Then, when the Soviet military-industrial complex produced its own new and better nuclear capabilities, U.S. prudence was prescient. Hawks then demanded more of their preferred remedies. Doves, on the other hand, had to argue that the leopard could change its spots. Hawks were not often wrong because their preferred remedies ensured the arms race they predicted. In contrast, doves could be proven wrong because their hoped-for restraint usually did not materialize. As long as Armageddon did not happen, hawks could never be proved wrong and doves could never be proved right.

The nuclear arms race reached unanticipated heights during the first nuclear age because neither leadership was willing to buck powerful domestic political and institutional forces that were deeply skeptical of anything that smacked of restraint and naïveté, the precursors to appeasement. The entire enterprise of arms control was, as one of its strongest backers, Paul C. Warnke, used to say, an unnatural act.[60] The smart money bet on muscle, not negotiations. And yet none of the smartest nuclear strategists in the early years after the Bomb's arrival predicted that superpower arsenals would reach such dizzying heights. Back then, the best and the brightest had a deep appreciation of the Bomb's awesome destructive power. Consequently, they could not envision rational choices that would yield tens of thousands of nuclear weapons.

The first big wave of nuclear weapons was built to accompany forces in the field—either, in the Soviet case, to shock and awe NATO and facilitate a swift advance across Western Europe or, for the United States, to prevent this blitzkrieg. The apogee of huge superpower arsenals of tactical nuclear weapons occurred in the late 1960s—just as the second big wave was building. The second wave consisted of ocean-spanning warheads, driven by the concurrent technologies for ballistic missile defenses and MIRVs.

The Soviet Union initially seemed more advanced on the missile defense front, as might be expected from a nation that had suffered greatly from invasion and that had erected a huge air defense network for homeland defense. The United States was clearly ahead on MIRVs. But, as was always the case, how much comparative advantage the two sides presumably had was a matter of dispute, which the intelligence community could not or chose not to clarify sufficiently. One source of controversy was whether, or to what extent, the Kremlin was upgrading defenses designed to shoot down high-flying aircraft to also intercept incoming ballistic missiles. Another controversy was whether the Soviet Union had already begun to flight-test MIRVs or whether they were instead just beginning to put several unguided warheads atop some of their missiles.

This distinction was crucial but easily lost in political debate and technical obfuscation. Simply put, a world of unguided warheads would be far less provocative than a world of precisely targeted nuclear weapons. With continued flight testing, unguided warheads could be upgraded with precise guidance, and the multiplication of these warheads atop missiles would feed directly into concerns over surprise attacks. Compensating steps would then be inevitable, resulting in a significant ramping up of strategic nuclear weapons just as tactical nuclear weapons were being tamped down.

It would have been far better and easier to stop the flight testing of unguided warheads in their tracks—but this was not to be. Once again, it was better to be safe than sorry—and once again, rational analysis led to an irrational outcome. Arms controllers clearly understood that the advent of missile defenses and MIRVs would be mutually reinforcing, because the prospect of deploying defenses would provide the spur for more offenses, and vice versa. So they tried to stop both in their tracks. Bare Senate majorities supported this bold plan at the outset of the Nixon administration. But resolving the offense-defense mix in a way that was politically sustainable and strategically sound was too tough for too many reasons.

To begin with, the timing was awful. MIRV and missile defense technologies were forcing hard decisions before the United States and the Soviet Union had even begun to sit down to discuss strategic arms control. Deals needed to be struck quickly if flight tests of MIRVs could somehow be frozen. LBJ and his top advisers were prepared to make the effort, which worried hardened skeptics. The need to move quickly meant that little groundwork had been laid for deal making. At last, on August 19, 1968, the Soviet ambassador informed the White House of the date when the first-ever summit would be held to discuss nuclear arms control. The next day, Soviet troops invaded Czechoslovakia, and the talks were postponed until the Nixon administration took office.[61]

Differing strategic cultures also made it hard to reach agreement. It was initially unthinkable for the Kremlin to accept any constraints on defenses that might protect Mother Russia from attack. When, in 1967, Secretary of Defense McNamara explained to Premier Alexei Kosygin why it might be best not to deploy ballistic missile defenses, Kosygin thought the idea was stranger than fiction. Defenses were not, in the Soviet view, weapons of aggression.[62] Eventually, the Kremlin, fearing U.S. technological advantages, came around to the view that they could do without national missile defenses. This switch only reinforced the opposite conclusion among hawkish U.S. skeptics of strategic arms control.

Mistrust was so deep that convergence in negotiations was repeatedly foiled by surprising position shifts. Whatever seemed reasonable to the other side had to be a bad deal—even if your side originally proposed it. Those who had not lost their sense of humor during the strategic arms limitation talks quipped that there was plenty of basis for agreement; the problem was that the United States and the Soviet Union just did not agree on key issues at the same time.[63] An early example: When the Kremlin finally came around to accepting national vulnerability against ballistic missile attack, the Nixon administration switched gears, calling for a light national missile defense shield.

Mistrust, poor timing, and the pliability of the intelligence community conspired to avoid controls on MIRVs. The Pentagon began to flight-test MIRVs the year before the strategic arms limitations negotiations got under way. The Kremlin had begun to flight-test a precursor to MIRVs, which hawkish intelligence community officials, with an assist from the Pentagon, conveniently concluded were indistinguishable from MIRVs. Washington and Moscow could not trust each other to stop and reverse course. Nor did the Nixon administration want to: The Soviets were deploying 200–300 new ballistic missiles annually— big bruisers that were well suited for multiple warheads. The White House and Pentagon chafed at congressional pressures to show flexibility on MIRVs, because they were the primary near-term counter to the Soviet buildup and because hawks on Capitol Hill would have jumped ship if Nixon and Kissinger had thrown MIRVs overboard.

It took no great gift of prophesy to realize that the Kremlin would catch up to the U.S. warhead totals by deploying MIRVs, but it was hard enough for Moscow and Washington to forgo national ballistic missile defenses. Forgoing MIRVs and offensive buildups was way more than the traffic would allow. So both superpowers offered proposals in the strategic arms limitation talks to stop MIRVs that were obvious nonstarters. Nixon and Kissinger demanded on-site inspections to determine that MIRVs were not being covertly deployed and constraints on Soviet defenses against bombers as well as missiles. (It took fourteen more years of negotiating effort and the advent of Mikhail Gorbachev for the Kremlin to finally accept on-site inspections, and it would have taken forever for Moscow to accept constraints on air defenses.) The Kremlin re-turned the favor. It demanded the right to match the U.S. MIRV flight tests while promising not to deploy what it would be able to perfect and what the United States would be unable to verify. After taking a pass on attempting to constrain MIRVs, the Kremlin and the Nixon White House signed off on a deal that significantly limited missile defenses while accelerating their strategic arms competition.

SALTING WOUNDS

The Strategic Arms Limitation Talks (SALT) produced two accords in 1972, the Anti-Ballistic Missile Treaty and an interim agreement limiting offenses. These agreements were doomed to disappoint. A truly successful outcome would have required stopping both MIRVs and ballistic missile defenses. This was clearly a bridge too far. The next best outcome would have been to deploy defenses and halt the multiplication of offenses. But defenses were defective, and offenses were a sure thing. Foreclosing defenses and letting offenses multiply—the box that Richard Nixon, Henry Kissinger, and Leonid Brezhnev checked—was not a good outcome, but not as bad as leaving both offenses and defenses completely unconstrained.

When pressed, Kissinger later expressed something akin to remorse about letting MIRVs run free, acknowledging, "I wish I had thought through the implications of a MIRVed world more thoughtfully in 1969 and 1970 than I did."[64] Later still, when the Reagan administration shifted gears from strategic arms control to strategic arms reductions, Kissinger wrote that "the age of MIRVs has doomed the SALT approach."[65] Foresight was supposed to be Kissinger's and Nixon's forte. But they were trapped in circumstances that not even they could manipulate. Codifying national vulnerability was hard—or, as critics contended, foolhardy—enough. Stopping the most promising new offensive moves at the same time was beyond the pale.

The early 1970s was a bad time to crimp the most powerful weapons ever invented. As a Soviet defector who closely observed the negotiating process later wrote:

> SALT was as painful as childbirth to the Soviets, particularly the military services. After decades of complete secrecy regarding military developments, it seemed inconceivable to disclose to the enemy even the names of Soviet weapon systems. Ridiculous as it appeared, the Soviets simply could not bring

themselves to use their own terminology and decided to adopt NATO designations for their weaponry. Defense Minister Grechko remained permanently apoplectic during SALT. . . . Grechko would repeatedly and irrelevantly launch into admonitory lectures on the aggressive nature of imperialism, which, he assured us, had not changed. There was no guarantee against a new world war except a continued buildup of Soviet armed might.[66]

The Grechko equivalent in the U.S. Senate was Senator Henry "Scoop" Jackson, a defense-minded Democrat and a force to be reckoned with on the Armed Services Committee.[67] Jackson was aided by a young staffer named Richard Perle, whose extraordinary skills at setting the terms of debate were honed during this period. When the 1972 SALT accords were signed, the United States had almost four times as many warheads on its missiles and bombers—mostly carried by bombers, an area of great U.S. advantage during the first nuclear age.[68] But the first agreement on offensive limits covered only missiles—an area of Soviet advantage—the Kremlin's offset to the U.S. four-to-one advantage in warheads and other qualitative leads.

Because of the Soviet advantage in missile launchers permitted under SALT, Jackson and Perle succeeded in characterizing this agreement as a terrible deal for the United States, bordering on nuclear appeasement. Not only were the Soviets permitted far more missiles, but also their missiles were bigger than those of the United States, twin advantages that the Kremlin would surely exploit by equipping missiles with MIRVs. (On this score, and given the Grechko effect, they were entirely correct, which made U.S. MIRVs even more essential.) Jackson's rhetorical question, "What is wrong with parity?" hit the bull's-eye, because the rejoinder required a mountain of words, numbers, and technical detail.

Jackson offered an amendment that could not be refused, mandating that any future treaty not limit the United States to "levels of intercontinental strategic forces inferior to the limits provided for the Soviet Union." What could be more like motherhood or apple pie? And yet this amendment did not pass overwhelmingly (the vote was 56–35), reflecting the reluctance of many senators to endorse the new panoply of nuclear programs that the Pentagon and White House were teeing up to offset the Kremlin's hedges.[69] The Jackson amendment was also brilliantly designed to secure the support of President Nixon and national security adviser Henry Kissinger, whose negotiating skills were being rebuked. It also foreshadowed a purge of arms controllers associated with SALT in the executive branch.

The 1972 SALT accords codified national vulnerability and nuclear over-kill—the two defining features of the first nuclear age—but did so in particularly damaging ways. As fully expected, Washington and Moscow raced forward to build new submarines, ballistic missiles, bombers, and MIRVs, confirming the misgivings of both hawks and doves. Secretary of Defense Melvin Laird was candid on this score, testifying that "peace cannot be bought cheaply."[70] Acknowledging the concerns of skeptics, the Nixon administration chose not to call the first SALT agreement limiting offenses a treaty of indefinite duration like its companion governing defenses; instead, it was to be a five-year interim agreement that would be superseded by a more comprehensive and presumably better treaty.

The big push on offense belied many of the justifications for the deals struck, which were badly oversold by Nixon, Kissinger, Laird, and Secretary of State William Rogers. Speaking before a joint session of Congress, upon returning from the Moscow summit, President Nixon hailed SALT as "the first step toward a new era of mutually agreed restraint and arms limitation. . . . We have begun to check the wasteful and dangerous spiral of nuclear arms."[71] Kissinger subsequently testified before the Senate Armed Services Committee that the Anti-Ballistic Missile Treaty "reduces the incentives for continuing deployment of offensive systems."[72] Rogers, who was cut out of the negotiations by Kissinger, went even further out on a limb, testifying that "a brake has been applied to the build-up of Soviet strategic forces."[73] Laird, a man with few illusions, nonetheless volunteered that SALT "stops the momentum of the Soviet Union in the strategic offensive weapon area."[74]

The backlash to SALT was fierce and was led by those, like Senator Jackson, who accurately predicted the arms buildup to follow and who relentlessly opposed measures to prevent its occurrence. The twin outcomes of a surge in offenses and national defenselessness offended just about everyone. Hawks argued that national vulnerability was contrary to Soviet doctrine and was morally objectionable. Doves found the arms buildup senseless, especially once effective defenses were prohibited. Consequently, the deals struck in 1972 invited repeated efforts to overturn them. While in academia, before negotiating the SALT agreement, Henry Kissinger authoritatively argued the case for a far different negotiating outcome.

A control system will add to stability if it complicates the calculations of the attacker and facilitates those of the defender. Or put another way, the objective should be to increase the uncertainty about the possibility of success in the mind of the aggressor and to diminish the vulnerability of the defender.[75]

Hawks agreed. They pounded Kissinger and proposed remedies in the form of better offenses and more defense. Doves advocated more restraint, which made them look naïve and feel politically vulnerable during the entirety of the first nuclear age. Errors in judgment by hawks could be fixed with more of the same old remedies. Errors in judgment by doves—such as predicting that the Soviet Union would slow down on offense once reaching rough parity with the United States—undercut their favored remedy of further restraint. The machinery of the nuclear arms competition was self-perpetuating. The missile design bureaus in the Soviet Union, the defense contractors in the United States, the weapons labs, the powerful politicians, the cautious bureaucrats, the depths of anxiety, and the radiating power of the Bomb were stronger than countervailing forces. Hawks usually got their way, except when their proposed remedies were too worrisome, such as atmospheric nuclear testing, or when they wished to locate the Bomb near U.S. metropolitan areas. Doves therefore succeeded in driving nuclear testing underground and in stopping nationwide missile defenses and space weapons.

The deck for an arms race was stacked during the first nuclear age. The "arms control process" made modest inroads, but the insurance policies taken out to cover mistrust and to guard against failure were overriding. The margin of safety required to engage in nuclear negotiations would not permit transformative results until game-changing national leaders who were unwilling to settle for marginal gains appeared. In retrospect, the extent of the nuclear arms competition during the SALT years was not as surprising as the modest inroads made to slow it down, despite such long odds.

Pro–arms control negotiators and bureaucrats were repeatedly scapegoated for their efforts. The first purge was carried out by the Nixon White House to mollify critics of SALT and to signal that the next treaty would be pursued more vigilantly. The manner in which SALT was negotiated compounded grievances. Nixon and Kissinger gave the American negotiators one set of instructions and then secretly negotiated different terms, often without U.S. interpreters present. Government experts assisting the negotiations were often directed to sift through various negotiating options that the Nixon White House viewed as nonstarters. The first SALT agreements were hurriedly concluded at a Moscow summit while U.S. negotiators were left cooling their heels in Helsinki. Earlier, as an academic, Kissinger warned against high-wire nuclear diplomacy.

> It is trivial to pretend that problems of the complexity of those which have rent the world for a decade and a half can be solved in a few days by harassed men meeting in the full light of publicity. It cannot be in the interest of the democracies to adopt a style of diplomacy which places such a premium on the authority of a few leaders.[76]

This was, of course, precisely what national security adviser Kissinger and President Nixon did when they flew off to Moscow, determined to clinch a deal.

Those who felt most burned by the process became the staunchest critics of SALT. No one seethed more than Paul Nitze, who was the secretary of defense's representative on the negotiating team. Nitze's proposed major overhaul of the negotiations did not elicit a response from the Nixon White House, which was enmeshed in the Watergate scandal. After tendering his resignation, Nitze joined forces with Jackson and other defense-minded Democrats to derail a negotiating process that, in their view, blessed the growth of Soviet strategic forces and prevented the defense of the nation. The bottom line of Nitze's critique was that the Kremlin managed to achieve through negotiation "a theoretical war-winning capability" that it would surely exploit.[77]

It is dimly remembered now that only two senators and two members of the House of Representatives voted against the agreements that became the object of such harsh critiques. But in 1972, Congress and the American public were longing for a thaw in the cold war and relief from nuclear anxiety. Disenchantment with SALT grew quickly, however. Nixon's replacement, President Gerald Ford, found it necessary to delete the word "détente" from his vocabulary. In 1974, two short years after Capitol Hill overwhelmingly voted to support SALT, Kissinger sought to strike a deal with the Kremlin at the equal levels mandated by the Jackson amendment. This proposed deal, which would have capped the number of missile launchers and bombers at 2,400 each—every one of which would be able to carry a large complement of warheads—met stiff opposition, led by Secretary of Defense Donald Rumsfeld, Governor Ronald Reagan, who was challenging Ford for the Republican presidential nomination, and Senator Jackson, who had naturally become the arbiter of compliance with his own amendment.

THE DEMISE OF SALT

Strategic arms limitation talks were resumed under a new Democratic president, Jimmy Carter, a down-home moralist with traits that seemed at the time to be welcome antidotes to Watergate. Anxieties about SALT grew perceptibly with the changing of the guard. If Nixon and Kissinger were taken to the cleaners by the Kremlin, how would a neophyte in the White House advised by fervent arms controllers fare? These concerns were immediately confirmed during Carter's inaugural address, in which he decried "a massive armaments race" and promised a step within one year "toward our ultimate goal—the elimination of all nuclear weapons from this Earth."[78] (President Carter's interest in abolition actually paled in comparison to the next neophyte governor-turned-president, Ronald Reagan, a spectacular White House act discussed later.)

Carter named as his chief negotiator Paul Warnke, a caustic critic of nuclear worrywarts. Hawks obsessed about missile size and throw-weight differentials. Warnke asserted that "when both sides have assembled thousands of warheads, the numbers game is not worth playing."[79] Garden mulch, he intimated, would have more utility than new bargaining chips in the form of bombers, missiles, and submarines. Before taking the job, Warnke wrote, "It is futile to buy things we don't need in the hope that this will make the Soviet Union more amenable. The Soviets are far more apt to emulate than capitulate." Instead, Warnke suggested trying "to evoke a process of matching restraint." This sentiment was based not just in opposition to the arms buildup that accompanied SALT but also in Warnke's previous service in the Pentagon, where he worked with the incoming secretary of state, Cyrus Vance, during the Vietnam War. This searing experience left them both with a healthy skepticism toward hawkish maneuvers and upping the ante. "We are spending too much on military arms and manpower," Warnke wrote, and "to continue to do so worsens our economic position and jeopardizes our true national security." If this were not incendiary enough, Warnke took a few roundhouse swings at the military-industrial complex: "We need not and cannot be the world's policeman," and "we face a single military threat, not a hostile world."[80]

The stage was clearly set for a battle over national security and military preparedness that favored hawks, because the Soviets could usually be counted on to run up their nuclear numbers and to be worthy of mistrust. Warnke was roughed up during his confirmation hearings, the highlight or lowlight of which was Paul Nitze impugning his Americanism.[81] Forty senators voted against Warnke's nomination to be the SALT negotiator—a shot across the bow clarifying that Carter would be hard-pressed to secure the two-thirds vote needed to ratify a SALT treaty.

Prospects for SALT dimmed further when President Carter instructed Vance to propose deeper cuts than Kissinger negotiated in 1974 and then, when the Kremlin balked, quickly fell back to the basic outlines of Kissinger's deal. In the first three months of his presidency, Carter managed to confirm hawkish fears and dovish anguish. To make matters worse, the Kremlin played hard to get. The longer the negotiations strung out, the more dyspeptic critics felt. The Kremlin was making mischief in faraway places while Americans were reeling from high fuel prices and interest rates. President Carter continued to make ambitious arms control initiatives—on conventional arms transfers, preventing an arms race in outer space, and abolishing nuclear testing—that were eviscerated. His high intentions were ground down by the combined intransigence of Soviet and domestic hard-liners. This unsuccessful track record reinforced jaundiced views about Carter's naïveté, negotiating skills, and stewardship of the Bomb.

It had taken two years for President Ford and General Secretary Brezhnev to reach the outlines of a second SALT agreement, which Ford backed away from when the deal was challenged by Secretary of Defense Rumsfeld and a rising conservative tide within the Republican Party. It took three more long years for President Carter and Brezhnev to reach an agreement that was more comprehensive but only marginally better. The fine print of the SALT II treaty—which was three times longer than the 1972 interim agreement—provided much grist for hawkish mills. These details, however, mattered less than the atmospherics at a time when public anxieties over the state of the union were free ranging. Critics of détente pointed to a Soviet "combat brigade" belatedly discovered in Cuba and to the Kremlin's adventurism in the Horn of Africa—which was viewed in some quarters as a launching point for more ambitious Kremlin schemes. Washington's ability to leverage Moscow's behavior dwindled, as Carter was unable to deliver on increasing trade with the Soviet Union, which was blocked by Senator Jackson's insistence that trade be linked to freedom of emigration from the USSR.

Treaty advocates asked for patience. They argued that the second SALT treaty finally got a handle on nuclear competition, closed the barn doors left open by Nixon and Kissinger, and provided a framework for progressive reductions over time. True, the treaty's constraints remained modest, but as Paul Warnke wryly testified, "In any negotiation, what you can get from the other side depends in very large part on what you are willing to give up yourself. . . . We have given up very little in SALT II."[82] Besides, killing this treaty would have invited more of an arms race and weakened America's standing in the world. These arguments made little headway. Hawks, led by defense-minded Democrats that felt displaced by the Carter administration, joined forces with Republicans to form the Committee on the Present Danger. They sounded the tocsin against what they perceived to be a successful Soviet drive to achieve strategic superiority that the United States "appeared willing to relinquish."[83]

Hopes for détente were waning. The SALT II treaty was characterized as "modest but useful" by the Joint Chiefs of Staff, hardly a ringing endorsement and no match for over-the-top critiques by treaty foes. On the eve of the treaty's signing, Senator Jackson delivered a speech at the Friends of Freedom award dinner, hosted by the Coalition for a Democratic Majority, in which he characterized the 1970s as a decade of appeasement and retreat.[84] Eugene Rostow, the chairman of the Committee on the Present Danger, declared that ratifying SALT II would be "an act of submission."[85]

During the first nuclear age, the passage of time invariably worked against strategic arms control; the longer the talks dragged on, the more reasons hardliners in the United States and Soviet Union found to be disaffected with the results. Negotiators were continually playing catch-up to technological advancements. In the run-up to the first SALT agreement, the biggest technological foe of the negotiators was MIRVs; in the run-up to the second agreement, it was cruise missiles.

Unlike ballistic missiles, which traveled in great arcs to distant targets, cruise missiles never left the earth's atmosphere. They could travel slowly or speedily; either way, they would be hard to detect and thus provided little warning of attack. Cruise missiles could take direct or meandering routes to further complicate defensive preparations. These weapons were first introduced as crude buzz bombs used by the Nazis to terrorize Great Britain. They reappeared as technological marvels, as bargaining chips, and as U.S. counters to the huge blunderbusses that were being turned out like sausages by the Soviet missile design bureaus. Cruise missiles were flexible and agile; they played to America's comparative advantages in the cold war arms race. They negated the huge Soviet investment in air defenses with radar-evading capabilities and could be delivered from the ground, sea, and air. Needless to say, the Soviet Union also got into the cruise missile business. Typically, the second SALT treaty kept options open for cruise missiles.

Cruise missiles offered far too much versatility and accuracy to be confined to nuclear war-fighting plans. Of all the bargaining chips gestated during SALT, they had the most military value, once their nuclear warheads were replaced with conventional explosives. Ironically, with the passage of time, cruise missiles eventually helped redirect the Pentagon away from the nuclear business, because conventionally armed cruise missiles had enormous military utility, whereas their nuclear-armed cousins could be used only for Armageddon. In the 1970s, however, the focus on cruise missiles was primarily on nuclear war fighting.

In the SALT decade, not one additional land-based missile silo was constructed, but existing missiles were much improved. Warheads on U.S. and Soviet ocean-spanning missiles rose 200 percent; their estimated explosive power grew 30 percent; and their lethality against hardened targets—the combination of explosive power plus accuracy—grew 200 percent.[86] SALT II added cruise missiles to this mix, yet another example of a strategic arms control "process" that seemed better at producing new strategic arms than new arms control agreements.

By the time SALT II eventually emerged from protracted negotiations in 1979, Jimmy Carter's approval rating was 29 percent—lower than George W. Bush's in 2007 when he called for a troop increase in Iraq after Democrats regained majorities in both houses of Congress. One formidable challenger to Carter, Governor Ronald Reagan, was strongly against the deal, which set the template for other Republican candidates. No major treaty has ever secured passage over the opposition of the Senate's minority leader—in this instance, Howard Baker, someone who was also angling for Carter's job and who opposed the deal. Henry Kissinger could have modulated opposition to SALT II—the second treaty, after all, offered modest improvements to his handiwork—but he weighed in with reservations as well. Kissinger's opposition was mild compared to hard-line treaty opponents like Scoop Jackson and Paul Nitze.

Hearings droned on for four months in the House and Senate, breaking for the political conventions, yet another indicator of inauspicious timing. Warnke found it prudent to remove himself as a lightning rod and resigned as chief negotiator eight months before the treaty-signing ceremony. Secretary of State Vance, the administration's lead witness in support of the treaty, argued that it preserved a stable military balance, increased predictability and U.S. understanding of Soviet military capabilities, and strengthened U.S. alliances and global leadership. On balance, Vance concluded, the United States would be better off with SALT II than without it. This tepid endorsement did not fare well against hyperbolic critiques. Secretary of Defense Harold Brown hardly helped the administration's case by arguing that without SALT II the Kremlin could exploit its advantages even more.[87] No supportive argument for a treaty is less compelling than "things could be worse."

After ten volumes and 4,399 pages of testimony by the Senate Foreign Relations Committee and the Senate Armed Services Committee, the SALT II treaty was hanging by a slender thread. The treaty limped out of the Senate Foreign Relations Committee by a nine to six vote, with a majority of Republicans and one Democrat voting against. The chairman and ranking minority member of the committee, Frank Church and Jacob Javits, both SALT supporters, were subsequently defeated for reelection. The Senate Armed Services Committee, where Senator Jackson held sway, delivered a stinging indictment, declaring the treaty "not in the national security interests" of the United States and its limits on Soviet forces "not militarily significant." Jackson and his committee demanded "major changes."[88] The Kremlin's invasion of Afghanistan in December 1979 was the final straw. Carter expressed deep regret and some surprise over the invasion and asked the Senate's Democratic leadership to delay further consideration of the treaty.

This was in many ways a merciful result compared to a vote in the Senate. When, twenty years later, President Bill Clinton similarly asked the Senate leadership—then in Republican hands—to suspend consideration of the treaty banning all nuclear testing for all time, he was handed a stinging rebuke. Seeking to embarrass Clinton and keep the testing option very much alive, Senate majority leader Trent Lott called the roll and Republicans voted down the treaty.

Had SALT II somehow entered into force, it would have been plagued by endless domestic and Soviet challenges. Beleaguered senators, seeking to demonstrate support as well as deference to the concerns of treaty foes, attached dozens of extraneous and niggling conditions to their resolution of ratification. No less a figure than Andrei Sakharov, living in internal exile in Gorky, argued that "the problem of lessening the danger of annihilating humanity in a nuclear war carries an absolute priority over all other considerations."[89] But this did not stop senators from attaching provisions to SALT II relating to Soviet military advisers in Cuba, the range and payload of a medium-range Soviet bomber, reentry vehicle weights on new types of ballistic missiles, and reentry vehicle maneuvers associated with a particular Soviet missile. These were the relatively kind offerings of SALT supporters; foes wished to kill the treaty outright.

Strategic arms limitations were the centerpiece of détente, which made their demise so essential to anti-Soviet crusaders and so inevitable when superpower ties deteriorated.[90] These negotiations became a magnet for cold war anxieties ranging from Fidel Castro's extended tenure in Havana, to Soviet military advisers in Cuba, to a warlord imbalance in the Horn of Africa. Geostrategic concerns were reinforced by anxieties associated with the shifting nuclear balance. The Soviet Union was playing catch-up when SALT started; at the end of the SALT decade, it had certainly caught up and, in the view of hard-liners, was on the cusp of strategic superiority. When the SALT process was launched, President Nixon declared that nuclear sufficiency would be America's standard, not nuclear superiority, which would only fuel an unlimited arms race and doom the negotiations to failure. This shift was necessary, because neither superpower could accept a codification of inferiority, but it was also unsettling to domestic audiences in the United States.

One great irony about nuclear negotiations during the cold war was that the American public wanted reassurance but could be persuaded not to trust treaties meant to reassure. The first treaty constraining nuclear options—the 1963 Limited Test Ban Treaty—was an exception to this rule, for instructive reasons. This treaty banned nuclear testing in the atmosphere, which posed a health hazard and greatly worried most Americans. This treaty was also negotiated during a period of clear U.S. strategic superiority and was defended in terms of reinforcing that superiority. SALT was different. SALT was about numbers, and the numbers were mind-numbingly hard to measure because the U.S. and Soviet nuclear arsenals were configured differently. U.S. and Soviet SALT negotiators were relearning the lessons that British prime minister Ramsey Mac-Donald and President Herbert Hoover discovered during the London Naval Treaty negotiations in 1930 to regulate the tonnage and armament on capital ships. "This parity business is of Satan himself," MacDonald wrote. "I am sure it has struck the President as it has me as being an attempt to clothe unreality in the garb of mathematical reality."[91]

There were many more variables in measuring U.S. and Soviet nuclear capabilities than in calibrating rough equality for capital ships. Those inclined toward worst-case thinking—and all those who took nuclear war-fighting scenarios seriously were, by nature, worst-case thinkers—believed that the categories in which the Soviet Union enjoyed advantages were decisive. And not surprisingly, those who thought that seeking relative advantage in nuclear warfighting scenarios between the superpowers was a fool's errand did not bother themselves with comparisons of missile throw weight.

Nuclear numerology provided experts with endless debating points. Most Americans took their cues from the overall state of U.S.-Soviet ties. During the stolid Brezhnev years, numbers mattered because the loss of America's nuclear superiority was deeply unsettling and because the numbers seemed to reinforce a more generalized sense of U.S. decline and Soviet adventurousness. Under Mikhail Gorbachev's leadership, the particulars of the nuclear balance mattered far less because most Americans accepted Gorbachev's transformative potential. And if a conservative American president, Ronald Reagan, blessed the deals struck, why worry?

Strategic arms reductions were negotiated two decades after the SALT process was first conceived. In the meantime, every detail under negotiation seemed crucial to the contending camps of experts. Issues that in other contexts would constitute fine print became front-page news. One example: The Soviets "cheated" in SALT by refusing to abide by U.S. unilateral statements laying down markers about permissible volumetric growth when upgrading older missiles for newer ones. The previous sentence reads like Aramaic—a strange, forgotten tongue with little relevance to world affairs. But in SALT debates over Soviet perfidy and the Nixon and Carter administrations' laxity, this became a core issue in building public anxieties over the Kremlin's nuclear war-fighting capabilities. In this strained calculus, every nuclear advantage counted: "The side better able to cope with the operational consequences of raising the stakes has the advantage," warned Nitze. "The other side is the one under greater pressure to scramble for a peaceful way out."[92] Worse yet, hawks argued that U.S. officials looked the other way while the Soviets cheated to secure nuclear war-fighting advantages. The United States was trapped in a process of self-deception and denial; extrication and national revival depended on killing SALT.

SALT supporters were at a great disadvantage in these debates, in part because public anxieties could not be assuaged with detailed explanations. In anxious political discourse, details work far better as assertions than as rebuttals. Anxiety, once attached to detail, can be dislodged only by major positive shifts in the political climate, overriding troubling details. During the SALT decade, anxiety could be readily attached to details and could not be dislodged because major trend lines were, in fact, negative. Nuclear capabilities and numbers governed by SALT were rising alongside tensions on various regional fronts.

The Kremlin's inner circle effectively pulled the plug on SALT when it decided to invade Afghanistan. But, in truth, there wasn't much of SALT left at this stage. Paul Warnke, the bête noire of hawks during the first nuclear age, was often prophetic, but his powers of prognostication could also be wrong. Warnke predicted during the SALT II hearings that "a better treaty can be negotiated, but only after this treaty comes into effect."[93] Warnke, as well as the hawks who bitterly opposed him, did not foresee what eventually followed the demise of SALT. From 1987 to 1993, Washington and Moscow managed to negotiate not one but three extraordinary treaties that seriously undermined nuclear theology and broke the back of the nuclear arms race.

Before reaching this destination, those sitting on the edge of their seats needed to survive another severe passage of nuclear danger, outlast the death of three decrepit Soviet leaders, become introduced to a radical reformer in the Kremlin named Mikhail Gorbachev, await the outcome of an extended battle between pragmatists and hard-liners advising President Reagan, and discover that Reagan's antinuclear instincts were even stronger than his anticommunist tendencies.

After the demise of SALT, a new start was needed, one with more ambitious objectives. A reversal of fortunes and perceptions were required as well. America needed to feel better about itself, and a new Kremlin leadership needed to internalize the need for shifting priorities away from the arms race. Put another way, American anxieties needed to be assuaged, and Soviet concerns needed to grow sufficiently to take new kinds of risks.

ENTER STAGE RIGHT: RONALD REAGAN

The Kremlin was not prepared for the Reagan administration, expecting another Nixon-like experience—a conservative Republican who bad-mouthed the Soviet Union before coming into office but who would sit down to bargain pragmatically over nuclear arms. Reagan clarified during his first press conference that he was not another Nixon by volunteering that the Soviets "reserve unto themselves the right to commit any crime, to lie, [and] to cheat."[94] The demise of SALT, the Soviet invasion of Afghanistan, and the evolution of the Republican Party's conservative wing had changed superpower relations in ways that the sclerotic Kremlin leadership was unprepared for.

Ronald Reagan was a gifted, blue-sky politician; his opposite number in 1983, Yuri Andropov, was a paranoid intelligence apparatchik. Andropov was supposed to be skilled in keeping America's leaders off balance, but it was Reagan whose avuncular anticommunism was deeply unnerving to the old men in the Kremlin. Reagan's in-house Soviet expert was Richard Pipes, a historian specializing in the Russian Revolution and the origins of Soviet Communism, who had lately turned his attention to Soviet nuclear doctrine, concluding that the Kremlin was entirely serious about fighting and winning a nuclear war with the United States.[95]

Reagan chose as his secretary of defense Caspar Weinberger, a dogged advocate of building up U.S. defenses that, in a widely shared Republican view, were shamefully degraded during the Carter years. Weinberger agreed with his most influential policy adviser, Richard Perle, that arms control was a "soporific."[96] For Weinberger and Perle, the problem was not just Soviet ruthlessness but also American mushy-headedness. U.S. officials negotiated among themselves what a "fair" deal might be and then split the difference with the Kremlin for an even weaker deal. Under these circumstances, gaining half a loaf was worse than going hungry. "Democracies will not sacrifice to protect their security in the absence of a sense of danger," Perle said. "And every time we create the impression that we and the Soviets are cooperating and moderating the competition, we diminish that sense of apprehension."[97]

Weinberger set about recasting what he viewed as politically correct language surrounding U.S. nuclear policy. The Pentagon's new Defense Guidance Document, issued in April 1982, did not mince words: "The United States must prevail and be able to force the Soviet Union to seek earliest termination of hostilities on terms favorable to the United States." U.S. defense guidance, according to published leaks of the classified document, included both decapitation strikes and capabilities to engage in protracted nuclear exchanges.[98] This was an almost perfect match for Pipes's interpretation of Soviet nuclear doctrine. Even though U.S. nuclear capabilities were not about to change appreciably any time soon—improvements endorsed by the Carter administration were coming online, but it would take the better part of a decade or more for new nuclear programs initiated by the Reagan administration to be fielded—the Kremlin was unnerved by the candor of the new secretary of defense.

Weinberger was from the "don't give an inch" school of public affairs. His new defense guidance was leaked to the press within one month, causing much consternation and eliciting from the pugnacious Pentagon chief this rejoinder to the weakhearted: "You show me a Secretary of Defense who's planning not to prevail and I'll show you a Secretary of Defense who ought to be impeached."[99] As head of his Arms Control and Disarmament Agency (ACDA), Reagan chose Eugene Rostow, the chairman of the executive committee of the Committee on the Present Danger, which viewed SALT as a trap to ensnare the United States in strategic inferiority. Rostow was joined by sleuths who sought to find

Soviet treaty violations that more pliant administrations preferred to cover up. The fallback plan of hard-liners, in the event that domestic and allied pressures forced the administration to retreat from preferred outcomes, was to go public with a charge sheet of violations that made new deals harder to strike.

The first order of nuclear business in the Reagan administration was to accelerate weapon programs, not as bargaining chips but as essential instruments of deterrence and, if need be, war fighting. Arms control talks were put on hold until the United States rebuilt a position of sufficient strength. The centerpieces of this rebuilding program were the B-1 bomber that Carter canceled to pursue more technically advanced and cost-effective cruise missiles and a big blunderbuss missile carrying ten warheads that Carter endorsed, subsequently named the Peacekeeper by Reagan. The Reagan administration kept the Kremlin cooling its heels as long as domestic opinion and allied sensitivities would allow; when it did offer negotiating proposals, they were so lopsided as to signal disinterest in negotiations.

Preliminary talks on "Euro-missiles"—new intermediate-range ballistic and cruise missiles that would be deployed in the United Kingdom, Italy, Belgium, the Netherlands, and, most telling to the Kremlin, West Germany—began in the Carter administration. Reagan's initial proposal, which called for the Kremlin to remove and dismantle its Euro-missiles, in return for which the United States would not proceed with counters, was offered ten months after taking office. The administration's opening gambit on ocean-spanning missiles was cut from the same bolt of cloth: deep across-the-board cuts in Soviet forces and modest U.S. reductions in some categories but not in others. This offer emerged sixteen months after Reagan's inauguration.

A YEAR OF LIVING DANGEROUSLY

In January 1983, President Reagan signed off on National Security Decision Directive 75, which called for placing "internal pressure on the USSR to weaken the sources of Soviet imperialism" and for exploiting "a number of important weaknesses and vulnerabilities within the Soviet empire."[100] In March, Reagan spoke before the National Association of Evangelicals in Orlando, denouncing Soviet Communism as the "focus of evil in the modern world." (The previous summer, speaking before the British Parliament, Reagan famously predicted that the Soviet Union would end up on the "ash heap of history.") The evangelicals gave Reagan a standing ovation as the orchestra played "Onward Christian Soldiers."[101] Later that month, Reagan sent tremors through the Kremlin, the

U.S. nuclear and military establishment, and allied capitals by announcing his vision of a missile defense shield that would make nuclear weapons "impotent and obsolete."

Reagan's heartfelt Strategic Defense Initiative (SDI), he declared, "could pave the way for arms control measures to eliminate the weapons themselves. We seek neither military superiority nor political advantage. Our only purpose—one all people share—is to search for ways to reduce the danger of nuclear war."[102] There were more heresies to the established nuclear order and deterrence theology in Reagan's surprise unveiling of SDI than had ever been vocalized by any previous U.S. president. Because few believed that Reagan could seriously hold these views, the search for—and subsequent pursuit of—hidden agendas completely preoccupied Washington and Moscow. After four days of internal deliberations, the Kremlin's evaluation of Reagan's speech was vocalized by Soviet leader Andropov, who declared SDI to be "a bid to disarm the Soviet Union in the face of the American nuclear threat."[103] On September 1, 1983, in the dead of night over the Kamchatka peninsula, Soviet Air Defense Forces shot down a badly off-course Korean Airlines plane carrying 269 passengers, including the Congress's only card-carrying member of the John Birch Society. Secretary of State George Shultz quickly characterized this event as an inexcusable, cold-blooded, and barbaric act,[104] not as a tragic screwup, as U.S. intelligence sources and methods were beginning to suggest. Reagan administration officials released highly classified voice recordings at the United Nations to reinforce their case. The true story of this tragic event was entirely different: The Soviet Air Defense Command and their interlocutors on the General Staff had been pinged repeatedly by U.S. reconnaissance flights along their Asian periphery. These flights were designed to light up Soviet air defenses, the better to locate them and monitor their frequencies in the event of a third world war. One of the planes was operating at the time of the Korean airliner's ill-fated flight.[105] This was also a period of aggressive U.S. attack submarine operations trailing Soviet submarines.

With the clock ticking and unable to distinguish between the Korean airliner and another presumed U.S. "provocation," Soviet military officials concluded that it would be better to be safe than sorry. They followed standard operating procedures and shot down "the intruder." The circumstances surrounding these tragic events made it virtually impossible for the Reagan administration to react charitably. But by going public with the worst interpretation of Soviet motives, President Reagan fueled paranoid Kremlin interpretations of his own motives. Notes of Politburo meetings released nine years later revealed that the entire Soviet leadership believed this episode to be a "deliberate provocation" and that, under the circumstances, the shoot down was entirely justified.[106] When Anatoly Dobrynin, Moscow's long-time ambassador to the United States, published his memoirs, he characterized Andropov's reaction to the shoot down as "a gross blunder" by "those blockheads of generals." He also reported that

> the whole grievous event left a lasting and bitter memory in our relations with the United States and with President Reagan personally. Our leaders were convinced that he deliberately and disproportionately used the incident against them, and that American secret services were involved one way or another.[107]

In early November, the United States conducted a high-level command and control exercise, Able Archer 83, to test communication procedures for the release and use of nuclear weapons in the event of a war with the Soviet Union. This exercise was monitored by Soviet intelligence agencies and their closest comrades in the Politburo with grave concern. Soviet minister of defense Marshal Dimitri Ustinov remarked shortly afterward that it was becoming "more and more difficult" to distinguish exercises "from the real deployment of armed forces for aggression."[108] Soviet intelligence agencies sent out additional messages to operatives in the United States to be on the alert for signs that the Reagan administration was planning a nuclear first strike.

In mid-November, the first U.S. cruise and ballistic missiles began to arrive in Europe, along with parliamentary votes to proceed with deployments. Marshal Nikolai Ogarkov, chief of the Soviet General Staff, concluded in print that "the United States is intensively building up its strategic nuclear forces with a view of giving them the capability to inflict a disarming nuclear strike." He likened the Reagan administration's tactics to fascist governments in the 1930s that resorted to "rude lies and slander."[109] On November 20, 1983, ABC television broadcast in prime time *The Day After*, a gruesome drama about the aftermath of a nuclear war. Three days later, Soviet negotiators picked up their papers in Geneva and walked out of the negotiations.

In 1983, the United States and the Soviet Union were like two ships passing in the night, with key crew members holding themselves hostage to worst-case assessments. The *Bulletin of the Atomic Scientists* doomsday clock stood at four minutes to midnight. The clock ticked one minute closer to midnight in 1984.[110]

FROM CONFRONTATION BACK TO DÉTENTE

At the midpoint of the Reagan administration, in 1984, the president became far more open to shifting gears in his dealings with the Kremlin. Some reasons for this shift are fairly straightforward. Conservative Republican presidents usually preside over internal fights between pragmatists and hard-liners. In the Reagan administration, Secretary of State Shultz referred to intramural disputes over nuclear negotiations as the "ship of feuds."[111] Hard-liners are usually strongest in the first term and subsequently lose standing the longer they remain in office, when domestic, congressional, and allied opinion grow weary of confrontationist policies that usually bring out the worst in America's foes. Hard-line arguments fit all facts into the same conclusions, and rote repetition loses credibility the more the facts change.

The facts began to change greatly when Mikhail Gorbachev was elevated by his peers to replace Konstantin Chernenko as general secretary of the Communist Party of the Soviet Union on March 11, 1985. After three frail, old-school Communist leaders, the Politburo opted for a change of pace. Soviet experts in the U.S. intelligence community predicted old wine in new bottles, but Margaret Thatcher held a different and more prescient view. She met with Gorbachev at Chequers, the prime minister's country estate, before his elevation and then shared with the BBC her assessment that "I am cautiously optimistic. I like Mr. Gorbachev. We can do business together."[112] Thatcher's interventions with Reagan, then and subsequently, helped steer the administration toward a safe harbor in its dealings with the Kremlin, countering Washington's insiders who continued to express skepticism that a Kremlin leader could seek radical revisions to Soviet dogma. Skepticism ran so deep that even Reagan's successor, President George H. W. Bush, initially sought to review the bidding before proceeding with Gorbachev. Bush senior's press secretary famously declared four months after taking office that Gorbachev was a "drugstore cowboy"—all sizzle and no steak.[113]

A third reason for Reagan's shift from confrontation to deal making in his second term was no doubt the president's commitment, shared by his closest adviser and marriage partner, Nancy Reagan, to accomplish major feats in reducing nuclear danger in his remaining years in the White House. Shultz discovered, when he was able to meet Reagan without his hard-line bodyguards, that the president was genuinely interested in reaching historic achievements with the Kremlin and confident in his persuasive abilities. This was music to the secretary of state's ears. The CIA director, William Casey, "wanted no dealings with the Soviets." His "ideological bent on foreign policy issues was so strong" that Shultz "worried about the objectivity of his and his agency's intelligence assessments." Shultz wrote in his memoirs that "our knowledge of the Kremlin was thin, and the CIA, I found, was usually wrong about it." He was determined that "American foreign policy should not be the prisoner of an exercise in Kremlinology."[114] The president's personal interest provided a lifeline to reinvigorated negotiations.[115] Reagan's public remarks began to reflect his wishes to engage, even during the horrific events of 1983.

A fourth reason for the turnaround was Reagan's secular religion, which called on him to take heroic measures to prevent a nuclear holocaust. Reagan's premier biographer, Lou Cannon, found his subject "hooked on Armageddon," the biblical concept of a world-ending battle between Good and Evil that would usher in the second coming of Christ. Reagan's profound commitment to SDI was rooted in his belief that the scourge of nuclear annihilation must be countered. Robert Macfarlane, the national security adviser when SDI was unveiled, recalls the president speaking of Armageddon in the following terms: "'I'm telling you, it's coming,' he would say. 'Go read your Scripture.'"[116] Macfarlane's reading of the president was "as a romantic, heroic figure who believes in the power of a hero to overcome even Armageddon."[117] Reagan could not achieve heroic results by relying only on SDI; he also needed to engage his antagonists face to face.

A fifth factor that may have helped Reagan to shift gears must remain somewhat conjectural, at least until the complete story of the U.S. intelligence community's misreading of the Kremlin in the early 1980s is fully told. Reagan had swallowed hook, line, and sinker his advisers' threatening assessments of Soviet military power and intentions. This was a key part of his "evil empire" critique and why he felt so strongly that a major U.S. military buildup was essential, not just to deter but also to dissuade the Kremlin from exploiting its military advantages in warfare. Sometime around the halfway point of his presidency, Ronald Reagan learned that his rhetoric and his policies were making the prospect of Armageddon far too real.

The conveyor of this surprising news appears to have been a double agent named Oleg Gordievsky, who was the deputy chief of the KGB's London station.[118] Gordievsky's message, conveyed by his British handlers, was that, far from believing that the Soviet Union was enjoying strategic nuclear superiority, key leaders in the Kremlin feared that the United States was pulling ahead and might seek to exploit its advantages through preemptive strikes.

The full story of Gordievsky's role in creating an opening for nuclear diplomacy after Reagan's first term remains shrouded in secrecy. His name does not appear in any of the memoirs of the key participants, although he met privately with both Reagan and Thatcher after defecting in 1985. When British intelligence began passing along his information to Washington has not been publicly established, but available evidence suggests that Gordievsky's disturbing information was conveyed to Washington shortly after the Able Archer military exercise in November 1983.[119] Published material from Ronald Reagan's diaries includes this passage, dated November 18, 1983: "I feel the Soviets are so defense minded, so paranoid about being attacked that without being in any way soft on them we ought to tell them no one here has any intention of doing anything like that."[120]

Far from confidently marching toward world domination, Gordievsky reported that there were strong currents of anxiety jolting the aging Kremlin leadership, especially those with intelligence backgrounds, including the ailing party leader, Andropov. When Reagan learned about these reports, he reportedly remarked to Macfarlane, "I don't see how they could believe that." This revelation again turned Reagan's thoughts to the biblical prophecy of Armageddon. He worried that this scenario could generate a sequence of events "that could lead to the end of civilization as we know it."[121] In November 1983, Reagan authorized the creation of a small planning group to open new channels of communication to the Kremlin.[122]

Reagan was a believer in Armageddon, but he was powerfully moved to prevent its occurrence on his watch. Without mentioning Gordievsky, Reagan wrote in his memoirs that he was stunned to learn that Soviet leaders "feared us not only as adversaries but as potential aggressors who might hurl nuclear weapons at them in a first strike." Reagan began this year of living dangerously asserting that "in virtually every measure of military power, the Soviet Union enjoys a decided advantage."[123] He ended the year realizing that key Kremlin leaders were feeling profoundly vulnerable. This reinforced his instinct "to get a top Soviet leader in a room alone and try to convince him that we had no designs on the Soviet Union and [that the] Russians had nothing to fear from us."[124]

THE NEGOTIATING ROLLER COASTER RIDE

After an initial shakedown, when Reagan's first choices as secretary of state and national security adviser, Alexander Haig and Richard Allen, and Arms Control and Disarmament Agency director Eugene Rostow departed, the fundamental cleavage within the Reagan administration for and against doing deals with the

Soviets became fixed. Hard-liners were led by Secretary of Defense Weinberger, ably assisted by Richard Perle, and CIA Director Casey, with well-placed allies on the National Security Council staff, the intelligence community, and the Arms Control and Disarmament Agency. The locus of deal making was, naturally enough, in the State Department, led by Secretary of State Shultz, ably assisted by the "Silver Fox," Paul Nitze. Nitze was a force to be reckoned with, whether sidelined or included in the inner circle of an administration's nuclear gambits. No outsider could be fiercer in opposition, and no insider could be more dogged in the trenches, advancing a cause. Perle, whose gifts lay in framing issues rhetorically and in erecting roadblocks, correctly labeled Nitze "an inveterate problem solver" and "result-oriented to a fault."[125] Key wild cards in this competition were the procession of political and national security advisers to the president. But the biggest wild card of all was Ronald Reagan.

What Weinberger and Shultz and their advisers learned early on, and what became clear to the outside world only belatedly, was that Reagan was a unique hybrid: the most anticommunist and antinuclear president ever to sit in the Oval Office. The president was, as Rostow's replacement at the Arms Control and Disarmament Agency, Kenneth Adelman, observed, "a man singularly endowed with an ability to hold contradictory views without discomfit."[126] The separate compartments in Reagan's mind prompted a buildup in U.S. nuclear forces, harsh anti-Soviet rhetoric, and an offer to share with the Kremlin missile defenses that would make nuclear weapons "impotent and obsolete." The surprise unveiling of Reagan's Strategic Defense Initiative at the end of a speech devoted to defense spending was privately opposed by both Shultz and Weinberger, who clearly recognized the difficulties SDI would pose to alliance management, the nuclear umbrella the United States had extended to its allies, defense budgeting, and congressional relations.

Reagan's anti-Soviet and antinuclear stance gave his advisers as well as the Kremlin fits. Shultz's immediate reaction to SDI's sudden unveiling was that "the Joint Chiefs of Staff should have their necks wrung" for failing to impose a reality check.[127] Weinberger worried that SDI would make it harder for America's NATO partners to follow through with countermeasures to the Soviet buildup. His memoirs are deeply protective of Reagan and of his own subsequent position supporting SDI. The only misgiving Weinberger acknowledges was related to the secrecy preceding the president's initiative and his last-minute efforts (as if this wasn't even more of a concern at the State Department) to inform key partners so that they were not "totally surprised by their major ally."[128] But Weinberger quickly signed up. No negotiating gambit could be a stronger blocking move than Reagan's fervent commitment to futuristic missile defenses, which was sure to produce apoplexy in the Kremlin.

After a first term marked by fierce infighting (but not in front of the president) and negotiating deadlocks, Shultz and Nitze recommitted themselves to use SDI to leverage deep cuts in the Soviet Union's nuclear forces. SDI, as Shultz recounted in his memoirs, "proved to be the ultimate bargaining chip. And we played it for all it was worth."[129] Weinberger and Perle recommitted themselves to shoring up the president's commitment to SDI and to reductions that would cut deeply into Soviet nuclear war-fighting capabilities while pushing ahead with U.S. strategic modernization programs.

The opening U.S. negotiating positions had the patina of equality and symmetry, but their uneven effects were designed to elicit a rejection by the Kremlin. In the view of deep skeptics of superpower negotiations, the more improbable the arms control initiative, the better.[130] The Reagan team smartly trumped Democrats who supported arms control and grassroots activists who pushed for a freeze in new nuclear arms with negotiating proposals calling for deep cuts. SALT was replaced with a new acronym—START—signaling the administration's interest in strategic arms reduction talks, not mere arms control. The opening U.S. position on Euro-missiles called for the abolition of these weapons, which presumably would be a nonstarter for the Kremlin because its missiles were already deployed, whereas U.S. missiles were still being built. For the most worrisome ocean-spanning missiles, the Reagan team proposed equal limits of 2,500 deployed warheads each—which would result in a 60 percent cut in Soviet weapons and a 16 percent increase in U.S. warheads.

Once Gorbachev decided to play this same game—fighting fantasy with fantasy and trumping Reagan's proposals for deep cuts with offers to completely eliminate nuclear weapons—the negotiations swerved deeply into the realm of the surreal.[131] Adelman was reminded of a verse from Sir Walter Scott, "Oh what a tangled web we weave when first we practice to deceive." Strange bedfellows were now appealing to Reagan's deeply conflicted instincts. Perle, who viewed the president's vision of a world without nuclear weapons "a total delusion,"[132] "absurd," and "hopelessly unrealistic,"[133] joined with Gorbachev in back-of-the-envelope negotiations to eliminate all nuclear weapons. ("Ours was," as Adelman later wrote, "an accountability-free administration.")[134] For his part, Weinberger continued to reinforce Reagan's belief in SDI to foil the designs of Shultz, Nitze, and Prime Minister Margaret Thatcher to leverage SDI to reap the benefits of deep cuts. Weinberger and Shultz, who worked together at Bechtel before joining the Reagan administration, battled over which of Reagan's instincts—anti-Soviet or antinuclear—would prevail. Shultz recounted in his memoirs that "once a certain arrangement of facts was in [President Reagan's] head, I could hardly ever get them out."[135]

Shultz won the battle. He, Nitze, and Thatcher moved methodically to constrain SDI in ways that fit within Reagan's mental constructs and in ways that Weinberger and Perle could not effectively rebut. Thatcher visited Washington after Reagan's reelection in December 1984 and hammered out a joint communiqué on SDI affirming that the aim of the program was not to achieve superiority but to maintain balance; that SDI deployments would be a matter of negotiation and not dictation; that the aim of SDI was to enhance, not undermine, deterrence; and that forthcoming negotiations should seek arms reductions (with no mention made of making nuclear weapons impotent and obsolete).[136]

Two months later, Nitze received the White House's clearance to publicize criteria for the development of SDI that tied fervent supporters of missile defenses into knots. In a speech delivered to the World Affairs Council in Philadelphia, Nitze offered the following guidelines:

> The technologies must produce defensive systems that are survivable; if not, the defenses would themselves be tempting targets for a first strike. This would decrease rather than enhance stability.
>
> New defensive systems must also be cost effective at the margin—that is, it must be cheap enough to add additional defensive capability so that the other side has no incentive to add additional offensive capability to overcome the defense. If this criterion is not met, the defensive systems could encourage a proliferation of countermeasures and additional weapons to overcome deployed defenses, instead of a redirection of effort from offense to defense.[137]

These simple, commonsense, and unobjectionable criteria—survivability, stability, and cost-effectiveness—effectively grounded SDI. A simple explosive device positioned in space alongside a far more expensive SDI battle station would flunk the "Nitze criteria." Nor could SDI proceed to deployments if the end result would mean more offenses, which would go directly against President Reagan's vision of a nuclear-free world.

Nitze, as Shultz's surrogate, also needed to connect his criteria for SDI to President Reagan's vision of eliminating nuclear weapons. In his Philadelphia speech, he offered the bare outlines of a strategic concept in which the United States and the Soviet Union would shift from an offense-dominated world of many thousands of nuclear weapons to a defense-dominated world in which all nuclear weapons would eventually be abolished. Nitze offered in a few spare paragraphs the most ambitious government-issued blueprint to prevent nuclear danger since the 1946 Acheson-Lilienthal plan to internationalize the means of producing nuclear weapons.

The first ten years of Nitze's strategic transition proposal would be marked by radical reductions in nuclear arms and by the stabilization of the offense-defense equation. This transition would be a "cooperative endeavor" between the superpowers. Defenses would be deployed "at a measured pace." The process of further nuclear arms reductions could last for decades. The end of the transition would be marked by the complete elimination of nuclear weapons and widespread deployments of effective nonnuclear defenses.[138]

Had Nitze been in exile from government, he probably would have been an unmerciful, caustic critic of this simplistic plan. For starters, political conditions were nowhere near ripe for such a radical transformation of the nuclear order. Trust was absent. Verification arrangements would be daunting. Hedging strategies against cheating went unmentioned. A world without nuclear weapons would be a world of Soviet conventional military superiority as well as a world without America's protective nuclear umbrella for friends and allies in rough neighborhoods. The nuclear weapons of third countries needed to be taken into account, and so on. But Nitze was now an insider whose job it was to make a silk purse out of the sow's ear of SDI.[139]

Nitze emerged relatively unscathed from delivering these remarkable nostrums. Boosters of SDI could not really take issue with Nitze's criteria. Nor did those who supported deal making with the Kremlin, because Nitze's strategic concept was widely viewed as part of a hidden agenda to put the president's irreconcilable twin passions of SDI and nuclear abolition into time phases that prioritized deep cuts. By lending his considerable intellectual gravitas to Reagan's twin passions, the Silver Fox gave the president's paper-thin notions some intellectual standing. (Only later did it become apparent that Nitze himself was beginning to think more seriously about nuclear abolition.)

At the midpoint of the Reagan administration, it was extremely hard to find anyone other than the president who truly believed in both SDI and nuclear abolition. Reagan's conflicting desires provided fertile ground for hidden agendas to flourish, seeking to move the president toward one pole or the other. But with the public interventions of Thatcher, Shultz, and Nitze—as well as with the president's belated understanding of Soviet anxieties and his long-standing desire to become the leading man in a drama of biblical proportions to save humankind from the scourge of nuclear weapons—the scales within the administration had clearly shifted away from hard-liners and toward deal makers.

The president's tone changed markedly. At the end of 1983, Reagan sent the ailing Andropov a letter indicating that the United States "had some fresh ideas on trying to break the stalemate over nuclear arms control."[140] A series of speeches in 1984 indicated a renewed interest in soothing ruffled feathers. In January, speaking from the East Room of the White House, Reagan declared, "We are determined to deal with our differences peacefully, through negotiations." Later that month, Reagan declared 1984 to be "a year of opportunities for peace," proposing a "major effort" to make progress. Well on his way to a landslide reelection victory, the president gave a speech at the United Nations in September that included not one word of chastisement or negativity about the Soviet Union. In the speech, Reagan talked about "our oneness as inhabitants of this planet" and said that "we recognize there is no sane alternative to negotiations on arms control."[141] With Gorbachev's elevation right around the corner, the stage was now set for negotiations unlike any other in the first nuclear age.

ENTER STAGE LEFT: MIKHAIL GORBACHEV

U.S. and Soviet leaders were always odd couples: the haberdasher and city machine politician Harry S. Truman and the paranoid, ruthless Josef Stalin; the urbane John F. Kennedy and the proletariat's Nikita Khrushchev, who pounded his shoe at the United Nations; the born-again Jimmy Carter and the weary, cynical Leonid Brezhnev. But never has there been a more compelling pairing than Ronald Reagan and Mikhail Gorbachev, and never did U.S. and Soviet leaders ever negotiate for higher stakes. Reagan and Gorbachev could not have had more different life experiences and temperaments. But this odd couple shared common traits that made their interactions mesmerizing to outsiders and deeply unsettling to their advisers. Both men were supremely confident in their abilities, comfortable with risk taking, impatient with received wisdom, and completely beyond the thrall of nuclear weapons.

As deal makers in the Reagan administration hoped and as hard-liners feared, the initial one-sided U.S. negotiating positions were whittled back in the course of the Euro-missile and strategic arms reduction talks. Before the Soviet walkout in late 1983, Nitze and his opposite number, Yuli Kvitsinski, engaged

in off-line conversations that would have downsized existing Soviet deployments and new U.S. deployments. This back-of-the-envelope deal received an
unenthusiastic reception in the Kremlin and was nixed by Defense Department
hard-liners who appealed to Reagan's abolitionist instincts.

With Reagan's overwhelming reelection victory, the Kremlin was ready to
resume negotiations. The campaign to prevent NATO missile deployments had
fizzled, and by walking out of the talks, Moscow had lost all leverage to influence outcomes. Harsh denunciations and threats did not work; new leadership and new tactics were clearly needed. Both arrived in the person of Mikhail
Gorbachev.

Gorbachev offered a flurry of dramatic new initiatives. On Easter Sunday,
1985, he announced a freeze on Soviet deployments of Euro-missiles and asked
the United States to reciprocate. He also proposed a freeze on strategic offensive
arms and a moratorium on the development of space weapons. In September,
he proposed a 50 percent reduction in offensive nuclear arsenals.[142]

In November 1985, Gorbachev and Reagan met for the first time in Geneva,
agreeing in principle on 50 percent cuts in strategic arms and an interim agreement on Euro-missiles. The most important outcome of this summit may well
have been atmospheric, with Reagan agreeing to Gorbachev's formulation that
"a nuclear war cannot be won and must never be fought."[143] In one rhetorical
stroke, both leaders undercut hard-liners in Washington and paranoids in the
Kremlin. Gorbachev remained adamantly opposed to SDI but was beginning to
understand that his best counter was proposals for nuclear abolition and deep
cuts, which would weaken support for Reagan's dream of a defensive shield.

Soviet proposals for nuclear abolition, a staple of the early cold war confrontation, reappeared in January 1986, when Gorbachev proposed the complete elimination of nuclear weapons in three stages, to be accomplished by
the year 2000. If nuclear weapons were abolished, what need would there be
for SDI? Gorbachev's grand scheme for nuclear abolition had another consequence: It put the Reagan administration's initial zero option for Euro-missiles
back in play. Reagan encouraged Gorbachev's outside-the-box thinking by re-
plying that if both superpowers could agree to radical reductions, he would
consider time-limited constraints on testing and deploying futuristic defenses.

The stage was set for an impromptu summit, which was quickly arranged
for Reykjavik, Iceland, in October 1986. The Reagan administration was expecting informal conversations; Gorbachev arrived with sweeping proposals. What
followed was, in George Shultz's memorable and accurate characterization,

· "the highest stakes poker game ever played."[144] In START, Gorbachev reaffirmed the objective of 50 percent cuts, and he endorsed Reagan's call for zeroing out Euro-missiles. These cuts would be contingent on a ten-year moratorium on the right to withdraw from the Anti-Ballistic Missile Treaty.

Reagan and his team proposed a modification of Gorbachev's framework: The 50 percent cuts in strategic offensive arms would take place within five years, and in the next five years, all ocean-spanning ballistic missiles would be eliminated. During this ten-year period, the Anti-Ballistic Missile Treaty would remain in effect, but afterward the United States would be free to deploy whatever defenses it desired. Gorbachev rejected this plan on two major counts. First, after eliminating missiles, the United States would retain major advantages in bombers, and second, the prospect of SDI deployments remained unacceptable. Gorbachev's rejoinder was to propose the elimination of all nuclear weapons, not just ballistic missiles—a goal that Reagan readily agreed to in Reykjavik. But there was a catch: Gorbachev continued to insist that space-based testing and deployment of SDI remain prohibited. This Reagan could not accept, and the summit ended with drawn faces and a somber mood.

This wild ride was widely viewed at the time as an object lesson of how not to engage in summitry. The U.S. side suffered from poor intelligence about what Gorbachev was up to, and the most consequential U.S. proposals ever offered in nuclear negotiations were completely ad hoc; America's allies were appalled by negotiations that would remove their nuclear umbrella. Verification issues went unaddressed, and Reagan and his beloved SDI were set up to take the fall when the summit collapsed.

In less than a year, however, it became clear that the Reykjavik summit paved the way for the most ambitious treaties ever negotiated during the first nuclear age—the Intermediate-Range Nuclear Forces Treaty, signed in 1987, which zeroed out Euro-missiles, and radical reductions in two strategic arms reduction treaties that were completed after Reagan left office. These treaties set new standards for intrusive, on-site inspections, a demand of every American president since Truman. Intrusive inspections were required because deep cuts raised the stakes for Soviet compliance and because the Kremlin could not be trusted. Gorbachev convinced his military leadership and Politburo colleagues to break with the past to accommodate future arms reductions. His embrace of openness, glasnost, even extended to Soviet nuclear forces.

Reagan and Gorbachev accomplished what all their predecessors wished for but were unable to do: They succeeded in breaking the back of the nuclear

arms race. They did so by rejecting decades of heavily encrusted nuclear theology. Both leaders scoffed at nuclear numerology and nuclear war plans. Reagan
believed deeply that getting rid of nuclear weapons was more important than
abstract notions of providing a nuclear umbrella—the sacrosanct concept of
extended deterrence—over worried allies. Unlike his predecessors, Gorbachev
understood that there was no need to confront SDI frontally, because skeptics
on Capitol Hill, who were in the majority, could ground SDI if the political
dynamics between the superpowers changed for the better. And if, somehow,
futuristic defenses could surmount technical challenges and political opposition on Capitol Hill, the Soviet Union would deal with this threat with relatively inexpensive countermeasures (such as cheap "space mines" that would
loiter near U.S. battle stations) rather than with noisy political campaigns.
"There will be a reply to SDI," Gorbachev said in the postmortem to Reykjavik.
"An asymmetrical reply, but there will be a reply. And we shall not sacrifice
much at that."[145] This sober appraisal allowed deep cuts to take center stage,
with momentous results.

Reagan's successful embrace of the zero option left many U.S. nuclear strategists and commentators unsettled, including Richard Nixon, Henry Kissinger,
and Reagan's former ambassador to the United Nations, Jeane Kirkpatrick.
Caspar Weinberger and Richard Perle, who left the Pentagon before their presumably nonnegotiable offer on Euro-missiles was accepted by the Kremlin, sup-
pressed their misgivings. Reagan's enthusiasm for deep cuts in ocean-spanning
nuclear forces was no less a cause for concern in these quarters. Nixon's critique
was that deep cuts would increase, not decrease, U.S. strategic vulnerability.
Kissinger's qualms about deep cuts were that they would "mark another major
step away from the deterrent strategy pursued for the entire postwar period"
and would "be another step toward stripping away the legitimacy of nuclear
weapons" without also reducing conventional imbalances that favored the Soviet Union.[146] Reagan was blissfully unconcerned about these critiques. In his
view, nuclear weapons were the problem, not the solution; SDI and deep cuts,
even elimination, were the solution.

A SURPRISINGLY HAPPY ENDING TO THE FIRST NUCLEAR AGE

The Intermediate-Range Nuclear Forces Treaty and deep cuts in strategic nuclear forces were an astounding and widely unexpected result. Doves, who were
appalled by the Reagan administration's early policies and pronouncements,
could not conceive of these outcomes. Nor did hawks ever expect that Reagan

would become the champion practitioner of arms control. Reagan's implacability and Gorbachev's inventiveness proved to be a perfect match. Neither leader could have accomplished these achievements without the other. Theirs were the lead roles in an inconceivable script with an absurdly happy ending. This oddest of all pairings of U.S. and Soviet leaders reversed decades of vertical proliferation. Their heresies released the stranglehold that deterrence theory held on nuclear negotiations.

The deals that Reagan and Gorbachev cut to delegitimize nuclear weapons received decidedly mixed reviews. Gorbachev was lionized in the United States and widely criticized at home. (Dobrynin, for example, found Gorbachev "helpless in the face of practical problems," which he tried to solve "by taking spontaneous, feverish, rash steps," becoming "the helpless witness to the consequences of his own policy.")[147] Reagan, on the other hand, was lionized at home for hastening the demise of the Soviet Union, but his role in nuclear negotiations was widely discounted, partly because his supporters also championed nuclear deterrence and partly because his detractors dismissed the president's abilities to engineer successful outcomes.

Reagan's simplistic views provided much fodder for caricature, especially his adherence to SDI. Four heavyweight practitioners of diplomacy and arms control—McGeorge Bundy, George Kennan, Robert McNamara, and Gerard Smith—dismissed the notion of a protective defense umbrella by declaring, "The end is unattainable, the means hare-brained, and the cost staggering."[148] The critique from protectors of nuclear deterrence was no less severe. SDI was, in the view of former secretary of defense and energy James Schlesinger, an uncalculated venture in personal diplomacy.

> We were all to learn rather suddenly that deterrence was "immoral" and "flawed." Such phrases seemed to have been borrowed from the Catholic bishops. While there may be considerable satisfaction in dishing the left by stealing its clothes, it hardly seems necessary to undermine the foundation on which Western security must rest for the foreseeable future.[149]

Reagan's lack of interest in the particulars of nuclear deterrence and his rejection of its central tenets provided his detractors with much ammunition. Reagan's embrace of nuclear abolition and SDI and his profound antinuclear and anticommunist instincts were deeply embedded in his DNA. They defied analytical cohesion. Even Reagan, the Great Communicator, could not articulate how his views meshed. Nonetheless, these simple nostrums coexisted peacefully in Reagan's mind, providing many opportunities for his fractious advisers to pursue diametrically opposed agendas. SDI, in the words of one detractor, was Reagan's "greatest triumph as an actor-storyteller."[150] But SDI also became the means to extraordinary ends. Reagan was often deprecated as "a detached, sometimes befuddled character"[151] and as "a President who confused nostrums with policies and dreams with strategy."[152] Gorbachev, Shultz, and Nitze rise in stature in these accounts because they succeeded in confining the ambit of hard-liners and in paving the way for Reagan's antinuclear sentiments to triumph.

There is certainly much truth in these accounts, but they also belittle Ronald Reagan's role. Anatoly Dobrynin, on the other hand, gives Reagan his due.

> His overriding strength lay in his ability, whether deliberate or instinctive I was never quite sure, to combine the incompatible in the outward simplicity of his approach and in his conviction that his views were correct, even if they were sometimes erroneous or untenable. The point is, he knew they were nevertheless supported by the population and by his own evident stubborn and even dogged determination to put his ideas into effect.[153]

Reagan did not achieve the zero outcome he wanted by dint of analysis, standard negotiating behavior, or deterrence theory. He got there, as Dobrynin writes, by sticking to his guns. Similarly, Reagan's instinctual and nonanalytical embrace of SDI forced Soviet strategists "to reconsider their position . . . and this brought us closer to arms control."[154]

This more charitable view toward Reagan's role in the positive events that closed the first nuclear age deserves wider appreciation. Reagan was central, not incidental, to the zeroing out of some missile deployments and deep cuts in others. It is quite true that Reagan could not have broken the back of the nuclear arms race without significant assists from Gorbachev, Thatcher, Shultz, and Nitze. But neither could this extraordinary cast have succeeded without Reagan in one of the two lead roles. The first nuclear age ended not with a bang—as so many had feared during the cold war—but with verifiable treaties that slashed missile deployments and trashed the deterrence rationales behind them.

ANOTHER SURPRISING OUTCOME: THE NUCLEAR TABOO HOLDS

In days of old, the transfer of power and authority was symbolized by the handover of the crown and scepter. With the advent of the Bomb, the transfer of authority is marked by who has the nuclear "football" as a constant companion.

The football is the carrying case containing the codes and communication links that national leaders can use to authorize the use of nuclear weapons. The most important legacy of the first nuclear age was that the football was never used.

Despite years of living dangerously, close calls and accidents, and grotesque stockpiles of nuclear weapons and despite the unforgiving nature of Murphy's Law, no nuclear weapons were used in anger during the cold war. To be sure, the Bomb was used repeatedly as a leveraging device and as a sharp reminder of national power—more than 2,000 nuclear weapon tests served these purposes—but a legacy of nonuse grew year by year and war after war. Credit for this extraordinary accomplishment goes to a diverse procession of national leaders who were, on occasion, sorely tempted and heavily lobbied to fire a nuclear weapon but who chose to keep their most powerful and shocking war-fighting instruments under wraps.

Every forgone opportunity to use the Bomb made every subsequent decision to cross this threshold more difficult. The legacy of nonuse owes much to Presidents Truman and Eisenhower, who were enmeshed in a stalemated ground war in Korea early in the Bomb's maturation. Eisenhower, in particular, threatened to use the Bomb to break this stalemate against Communist China, which had no such means to fight back. Ironically, Eisenhower, the president who placed more emphasis on the Bomb than any of his successors, was crucial in strengthening the nuclear taboo. Had he, or Truman before him, actually detonated the Bomb, the first nuclear age would have unfolded quite differently. Thomas C. Schelling has homed in on this point: "If the tradition of nonuse is shattered, it is important to consider what new traditions will be launched. The way in which the weapons are used will set precedents for wars in which nuclear weapons will no longer be excluded."[155] Had the use of nuclear weapons against a foe without the Bomb been established in the Korean War—or shortly thereafter, when the French faced defeat in Indochina and asked President Eisenhower to provide the deus ex machina in the form of a mushroom cloud—proliferation would have run rampant during the first nuclear age.

The slow accretion of a record of not detonating nuclear weapons in warfare, like the astounding growth of superpower arsenals, was largely unanticipated. When the Bomb made its sudden, shocking appearance, most onlookers were so shaken because they assumed subsequent use. This fear animated the creation of nuclear deterrence and arms control theory. The early shock of the Bomb also animated ambitious plans for abolishing war, creating the United Nations, and promoting international control over the means of producing material needed for the Bomb.

After the limits of idealism were established early in the first nuclear age, after the iron curtain dropped down to divide Europe, and after Josef Stalin acquired atomic and hydrogen bombs, the prospects of establishing a record of not using these weapons on the battlefield seemed highly improbable, if not impossible. Paul Nitze yielded to no one in his willingness to face hard facts and to prepare for the use of these dreadful weapons. But Nitze was a visionary as well as a realist. His advice for dealing with the Bomb's possible use in warfare was remarkably wise: "Try to reduce the dangers of nuclear war within the relevant future time period as best you can; you just get depressed if you worry about the long-term future."[156] Many wars were fought during the first nuclear age, including wars between states that possessed the Bomb and those that did not. Day by day, month by month, year by year during the first nuclear age, the legacy of nonuse in warfare was established.[157] Nitze, the man who raised alarms, advocated nuclear buildups, and took nuclear war fighting seriously, played a crucial role in engineering a soft landing to the nuclear arms race. Later, he became an advocate of nuclear disarmament.

There were many significant achievements during the first nuclear age. Superpower cooperation in preventing proliferation, as embodied in the negotiation of the Treaty on the Nonproliferation of Nuclear Weapons was surely a major accomplishment. So, too, were the treaties that stopped nuclear testing in the atmosphere and prevented a wasteful and futile superpower competition in building national missile defenses. Treaties that zeroed out entire categories of ballistic missiles and mandated deep cuts in ocean-spanning missiles were extraordinary accomplishments. But no achievement during the first nuclear age was more central to reducing nuclear dangers than the record of not using nuclear weapons in warfare, even when doing so might have conferred short-term gains. The most important accomplishment of arms control, according to Schelling, was establishing the belief "that nuclear weapons are in a class apart from conventional weapons. They are under a curse, a taboo, despite the awe in which they are held and the prestige that may go with having them."[158]

The first nuclear age ended with the demise of the Soviet Union in 1991. What began with widespread expectations of a nuclear holocaust ended with genuine surprise over extraordinary treaties to slash frontline nuclear forces. Profound ironies attended this outcome. Hard-liners inadvertently created the conditions for deep cuts. The slayers of the nuclear dragon previously served as its guardians. Hawks used the instruments championed by doves to realize results that doves could not achieve on their own. Nuclear overkill and Reagan's cherished SDI made deep cuts possible. Vulnerability to the Bomb offered protection throughout the first nuclear age.

The first nuclear age began with ambitious plans to create world bodies for global governance and central control over the means of making nuclear weapons. These plans went unrealized, as did the worst fears of their proponents. New theories of nuclear deterrence and arms control were devised to prevent nuclear exchanges and, clashing every step of the way, both contributed to the tradition of nonuse. Technological advances in support of deterrence outpaced arms control, until the end of the first nuclear age, when two extraordinary risk takers and shibboleth breakers, Ronald Reagan and Mikhail Gorbachev, reversed the nuclear arms race.

The first nuclear age ended abruptly, with memorable flourishes. The second nuclear age was just around the corner. It, too, would begin with momentous events.

4 THE SECOND NUCLEAR AGE

THE SECOND NUCLEAR AGE[1] began in 1991, when the Soviet Union dissolved and when victorious U.S. troops in Iraq discovered an advanced nuclear weapon program that inspectors from the International Atomic Energy Agency had previously failed to notice. The Agency was supposed to be the watchdog of the nuclear nonproliferation treaty; the first Iraq war proved that the watchdog had little bark and no bite. During the first nuclear age, the dominant thrust of proliferation was vertical, with Washington and Moscow building tens of thousands of nuclear weapons. During the second nuclear age, these stockpiles would contract, as would those of Great Britain and France. Vertical proliferation is continuing, as India, Pakistan, and China continue to modernize and expand their nuclear forces, but this triangular competition is proceeding at a measured pace, primarily because economic growth is far more of a priority for Beijing and New Delhi than the growth in their nuclear arsenals. Horizontal, not vertical, proliferation is the primary concern of the second nuclear age.

The Bomb's newest and most worrisome aspirants are Iran and North Korea. In Iran, medievalist mullahs vie for control with a younger generation of revolutionary guards led by a Holocaust denier. In North Korea, the globe's last Stalinist regime is led by a puerile aficionado of luxury goods who rules by paranoia and starvation and who pays for his cognac, nuclear programs, and army through illicit exports.

The third aspirant for nuclear weapons was Saddam Hussein, who survived one war with the United States and continued to rule by delusion, paranoia, and repression. The weapons of mass destruction he sought to deter a second war with the United States did not exist, but to publicly acknowledge this would, he feared, embolden his enemies.[2] Nor did Hussein's scientists dare to tell him how little progress they were making. President George W. Bush, Vice President Dick Cheney, and almost everyone else—besides the United Nations inspectors who were actually on the ground in Iraq—assumed otherwise. Hussein's presumed weapons of mass destruction were the Bush administration's rationale for a preventive war, which could only have been initiated in the anxiety-laced aftermath of surprise attacks on U.S. soil.

The first-ever preventive war against proliferation by the Bush administration accelerated nuclear programs in North Korea and Iran to deter against another potential U.S. military strike. Using nuclear-related maneuvers against dominant American power thus became another defining feature of the second nuclear age. Because the Iraq war of choice was based on faulty assumptions and bad intelligence, yet another defining feature of the second nuclear age is that the dominant power's coercive options against such nuclear hedging are greatly constrained.

The second nuclear age's power imbalances also mean that asymmetric warfare has replaced arms racing as another of its distinctive features. Asymmetric warfare is about using unconventional means to counter an adversary's strengths, such as improvised explosive devices against armored patrol vehicles. Arms racing, in contrast, is symptomatic of a contest between equals, as between the United States and the Soviet Union. The cold war competition was internal as well as external: Nuclear laboratories, defense contractors, and design bureaus in both countries competed against each other to produce marginally more effective warheads and missiles, which were then tested and deployed. Every test and new missile fueled the superpower competition.

After the cold war ended, power imbalances made arms racing pointless, because far more efficient ways were available to deter or tie down a much stronger adversary, ranging from a rudimentary nuclear weapons program to unconventional warfare. The second nuclear age is still punctuated with alarms over potential arms races by arms controllers and by weaker parties in power equations who seek to gain traction against stronger foes by using this argument.

Another defining worry of the second nuclear age is the possible acquisition of the Bomb or of its key elements by religious extremists or nihilists. This problem extends beyond the Islamic world, where border regions and the occasional failed state provide safe havens, into Europe and Asia, where Muslim wanderers feel doubly alienated from their home countries and from their adopted homes. Cellular, highly motivated local franchises of extremists network using Internet cafes. The academic literature on proliferation from the first nuclear age makes no mention of madrassa-schooled freelancers. Nor does classical deterrence theory provide much help for these additions to the threat column.

Supply-side proliferation also became more complicated during the second nuclear age with the discovery that Pakistan's state-run nuclear procurement operations had spawned A. Q. Khan's parallel network of entrepreneurial profit centers. Khan, the self-monikered father of Pakistan's nuclear program, also became the mother of all nuclear nightmares, selling weapon designs, centrifuges, and who knows what else to interested buyers. Proliferation during the first nuclear age was state centric. Now the list of potential buyers extends to transnational groups and religious extremists, assisted by entrepreneurial middlemen.

Nonproliferation successes during the second nuclear age are harder to achieve because horizontal proliferation is more difficult to stop than the vertical kind. Put another way, wretched excess is easier to reverse than proliferation prompted by regional security concerns and religious zeal. Statecraft and intelligence tradecraft need to play catch-up in the second nuclear age; they were designed and better equipped to deal with familiar, country-specific proliferation challenges. Nuclear terrorism and decentralized cells are a whole different ball game. The contours of proliferation challenges during the first nuclear age were linear; in the second nuclear age, these contours are potentially viral as well as linear. Reality, to paraphrase Herman Melville in *Moby Dick*, is in danger of outrunning apprehension.

The classic drivers for proliferation in the first nuclear age were deterrence, improved security, added leverage on neighbors and foes, status, and domestic factors, including the influence of powerful internal lobbies. Another motive for proliferation was added to this list in the second nuclear age: the impulse to shake up the established nuclear order. New entrants are driven by feelings of weakness, humiliation, righteousness, and vulnerability.

The 1971 war between India and Pakistan, which vivisected Pakistan and created the new nation of Bangladesh, generated not one but two nuclear programs. India, the overwhelming victor, deeply resented the Nixon administration's attempt to curtail the war by sending an aircraft carrier into the Bay of Bengal. Subsequently, Prime Minister Indira Gandhi gave the go-ahead for India's "peaceful" nuclear test. And after its drubbing by India, Pakistan's leader,

Zulfiqar Ali Bhutto, famously vowed to acquire the Bomb "even if we have to eat grass."[3] A former Chinese foreign minister, Chen Yi, offered an equally colorful variation on this theme, recalling that China needed the Bomb "even if we had to pawn our trousers."[4] (During the cold war, Beijing was on the receiving end of nuclear threats from both superpowers.) Future chroniclers of the Bomb are likely to add to this list of memorable quotations.

After the Soviet Union's demise, religious fault lines sharpened as ideological divisions faded. As a consequence, proliferation during the second nuclear age took on religious overtones—another ominous development. The "Islamic Bomb" was a figment of anti-Muslim imaginations during the first nuclear age, because Pakistan's military leaders were not inclined to sell the nation's crown jewels to coreligionists across national borders—with the possible exception of Saudi Arabia. Pakistan's military establishment, which may have been complicit in some of A. Q. Khan's dealings, took great offense at the designation of an Islamic bomb—did anyone talk of a "Hindu bomb" or a "Jewish bomb"?—until even they were embarrassed by the extent of Kahn's side deals.

It is doubtful that an authoritative, comprehensive account of A. Q. Khan's freelance operations will emerge. At the outset of Pakistan's nuclear program, many corners were cut, oversight was shoddy, and highly personalized ad hoc procedures were followed. Competing centers of authority and changes in authority resulted in shifting alliances and opportunities for illicit commerce. Khan did not make deals simply for the sake of venality; he also talked about the dictates of faith and the need to support the Muslim community, or *umma*, against external threats. The many compartments and intrigues of Pakistan's nuclear program warrant skepticism about sweeping assessments regarding the extent to which Khan's transactions were blessed by higher authorities.[5]

The most troubling fault line for proliferation during the second nuclear age is not the clash of civilizations but the clash within Islam. If Iran succeeds in obtaining what will likely be viewed as a "Shia bomb," Pakistan's "Sunni bomb" is unlikely to be viewed as a sufficient counter by other Sunni states, such as Saudi Arabia, Egypt, and Turkey. Islamabad will go to great lengths to maintain cordial relations with Iran, not wishing to add a Sunni-Shia feud to its list of regional security concerns. But Pakistan's nuclear requirements will grow if Iran succeeds in obtaining the Bomb. Pakistan, with a long-standing, symbolic military contingent stationed in Saudi Arabia, might someday be called on to help Riyadh in more substantial ways.[6] Extended deterrence—whereby a nuclear power provides a security umbrella to weaker friends—was an established fact of the first nuclear age in Europe and the Far East. During the second nuclear age, extended deterrence might be stretched to the Islamic world as well.

The more horizontal proliferation extends beyond the major powers—the five permanent members of the United Nations Security Council—the more perturbations will result from the progression of Bomb holders. International relations theorists and proliferation optimists in the first nuclear age worked within limited geographic parameters. Until China forced its way into the club in 1964, proliferation was a distinctly Western phenomenon. Once China's revolutionary zeal gave way to the more traditional aspirations of accumulating power and wealth, the five permanent members of the Security Council endorsed the Nonproliferation Treaty's injunction that they should eventually achieve nuclear disarmament while enjoying the privileges that nuclear weapons provide.

During the first nuclear age, the two superpowers were tenacious competitors in many ways, but they were partners in supporting the global system to prevent proliferation. China's extraordinary restraint in forswearing a large nuclear arsenal and in pledging never to use nuclear weapons first also kept the system in decent working order.[7] Great Britain and France became peripheral to nuclear dynamics because status, rather than security concerns, played such a large part in their calculus to retain the Bomb. So long as both countries whittled down their nuclear arsenals, they too contributed to the health and well-being of the global nonproliferation system during the first nuclear age.

During the second nuclear age, club membership opened for a more diverse clientele. The newest members lived in the tough neighborhoods, such as South Asia. India and Pakistan had fought wars over inheritance, religion, sovereignty, and territory—a witches' brew that became more poisonous by adding nuclear weapons to the pot. Newcomers that barged into the nuclear club were, by definition, outliers who could not rely on others for protection. (Leave aside, as all deterrence theorists must, that the means of existential protection were indistinguishable from the means of societal destruction.)

Domestic politics and powerful interest groups continue to be important drivers for horizontal proliferation during the second nuclear age. Democracies have been no less susceptible to the Bomb's siren song than the most brutal dictatorship. Indeed, democracies have found it more difficult to give up the Bomb than leaders in one-party states because they are more constrained by domestic politics.[8] Not surprisingly, the most successful cases of nuclear disarmament have occurred during peaceful regime changes in nondemocratic countries—South Africa and the newly independent states of the former Soviet Union. Libya's Muamar Qadafi's U-turn against acquiring the Bomb fits into this mold as well. Democratization, however, does have an upside in retarding or halting the early stages of proliferation, before Bomb programs gain sufficient political and interest group traction. For example, newly elected civilian leaders in Brazil and Argentina were able to pull the plug on nascent nuclear weapon programs favored by disgraced military leaders in 1991.

The entry of Pakistan and India into the nuclear club as the Soviet empire was crumbling foreshadowed a far more uncertain nuclear future. "Islamic" and "Hindu" Bombs now joined the fold—although leaders in both countries would vehemently reject these characterizations. More accurately put, pride in the status derived from this technological achievement spread for the first time to the Muslim world and the Hindu heartland. Both countries had obvious security imperatives in seeking the Bomb—India to offset a rising China and Pakistan to offset a rising India.

NUCLEAR TRIANGLES

During the first nuclear age, only the triangular relationship among Washington, Moscow, and Beijing mattered. China, the weakest leg of the triangle, at first linked up with the Soviet Union and then normalized ties with the United States. During the second nuclear age, a second nuclear triangle emerged. The original alignment of the Washington—Moscow-Beijing triangle returned, as China and Russia had no need to compete over leading the Communist movement and much reason to counterbalance predominant U.S. power. The second triangular nuclear relationship involved China, India, and Pakistan. The newer triangular competition was fueled by keen status consciousness, contested borders, and grievances from previous warfare. Both triangles bear watching.

All sides of the China-India-Pakistan triangle are unequal, which makes for awkward geometry, instability, and the potential for increased competition. But all three parties have publicly resolved not to repeat the wretched excesses of the cold war competition between the Soviet Union and the United States, including the mistake of arms racing. At the same time, the existing nuclear hierarchy in southern Asia—China followed by India followed by Pakistan—grates on New Delhi and Islamabad. Beijing has not yet deigned to accept India's interest in dialogue on the Bomb, including discussions on nuclear stabilization and confidence-building measures. Perhaps China's leaders will think differently after New Delhi captures Beijing's attention by testing thermonuclear weapons that can be placed atop new missiles able to reach Beijing and Shanghai. Pakistan cannot compete with India in conventional arms, but Pakistan's generals have demonstrated every intention to compete with India with respect to nuclear weapons.

The triangular nuclear jockeying among China, India, and Pakistan is far less freewheeling than the triangular competition during the first nuclear age. The geometry of the earlier competition took the shape of an isosceles triangle, with two equally powerful sides—the United States and the Soviet Union—and the third connecting side, Communist China. Beijing, holding the short straw, became the object of superpower threats and diplomatic maneuvering. China was also the most unconventional participant in this triangular competition, at first mocking the Bomb as a "paper tiger" and then acquiring and remaining surprisingly satisfied with a modest nuclear arsenal.

The Chinese leadership had not yet obtained the Bomb during the Korean War, when it was subject to repeated nuclear threats by the United States. General Curtis LeMay, then head of the Strategic Air Command, argued within the councils of government that "there are no suitable strategic targets in Korea. However, I would drop a few bombs in proper places in China [and] Manchuria." For good measure, LeMay proposed bombing Russia with nuclear weapons. "We have never raised the ante—we have always just called the bet. We ought to try raising sometime."[9] President Eisenhower, like Truman before him, chose not to use nuclear detonations to break a stalemated land war, thereby giving the nuclear taboo a chance to take hold.

U.S. threats clarified the Chinese need to acquire the Bomb. The Kremlin pledged to help its fraternal Communist neighbor but then had second thoughts as jockeying between the two Communist giants increased. The withdrawal of Soviet support for China's nuclear program was ostensibly tied to the nuclear test ban talks that the Kremlin was beginning to have with the Eisenhower administration, but this was a flimsy excuse. Beijing and Moscow were clearly going their separate ways. In 1959, Moscow conveyed the news that its promises of a prototype bomb, blueprints, and other technical data would not be forthcoming and that there would be a two-year suspension of assistance. A few months later, Soviet specialists took their leave, never to return. During the test ban negotiations in Moscow, President John F. Kennedy directed his chief negotiator, Averell Harriman, to broach the subject of carrying out preemptive strikes against the emerging Chinese nuclear program with Nikita Khrushchev.[10] Khrushchev was nonresponsive. Later, it was Leonid Brezhnev's turn to ask Richard Nixon about strangling China's nascent nuclear program. Again, no sale.[11] Nixon and his national security adviser, Henry Kissinger, were beginning to contemplate a bold opening toward China.

The lonely passage of being the object of hostility from not one but both nuclear superpowers reinforced Mao Zedong's resolve to join the nuclear club. A government pamphlet issued in 1963 declared, "It is absolutely impermissible for two or three countries to brandish their nuclear weapons at will, issue orders and commands, and lord it over the world as self-ordained nuclear overlords, while the overwhelming majority of countries are expected to kneel and obey orders meekly, as if they were nuclear slaves."[12] Nie Rongzhen, the head of China's strategic weapons program, succeeded in testing his first bomb in 1964, four years after the Kremlin pulled the plug on nuclear cooperation. He turned next to a thermonuclear weapon design, which was tested three years later, at the beginning of the Cultural Revolution.

China's bomb makers rejected the manic nuclear targeting requirements of their American and Soviet counterparts. Beijing's minimal nuclear deterrent did not require obsessive care and constant improvements. Zhang Aiping, who worked on nuclear testing and eventually rose to become deputy chief of the General Staff, once said, "It is unnecessary for us to achieve tremendous accuracy. If a nuclear war breaks out between China and the Soviet Union, I don't think there is too much difference [if] . . . China's missile misses its predetermined target, the Kremlin, and instead hits the Bolshoi Theater."[13]

This degree of relaxation for the requirements of nuclear deterrence was both puzzling and welcome to the two nuclear superpowers. When Deng Xiaoping visited Washington in January 1979 and confided to President Carter and his key advisers that China was about to teach Vietnam a lesson by way of a border war, he was asked whether Beijing might be concerned about how Moscow, Vietnam's nuclear patron, might react. No, replied Deng; a few nuclear weapons would suffice to prevent the worst that Moscow could offer.[14] Comparable U.S. targeting plans would have involved many hundreds, if not thousands, of warheads.

The Chinese model of nuclear deterrence has subsequently rubbed off on India. Both countries have given priority to economic development and have so far refused to get sucked into a nuclear numbers game. Whereas the United States and the Soviet Union developed and deployed a robust triad of bombers, missile-carrying submarines, and intercontinental ballistic missiles, Beijing has been largely content to rely on land-based missiles. Despite being in the crosshairs of both nuclear superpowers and being on the receiving end of multiple nuclear threats during the first nuclear age, Beijing announced a doctrine of no first use of nuclear weapons. Its meager strategic arsenal consisted of perhaps two dozen lumbering liquid-fueled missiles, hidden in caves, that took hours to prepare for launch. No major power embraced the concept of minimal deterrence more wholeheartedly.

China's pace of nuclear modernization is picking up because the U.S. Air Force during the George W. Bush administration has endorsed a muscular military doctrine of "space control," which predicates American freedom of action in space on denying it to others. In addition, missile defense advocates within the Bush administration sought to deploy more long-range ballistic missile interceptors than China's number of ocean-spanning missiles—ostensibly to foil threats from rogue states. At the same time, the Bush White House adopted a proactive national security strategy after the 9/11 attacks that explicitly endorsed preemptive military action.

In response, China has become less relaxed about its nuclear requirements. Beijing is picking up the pace in improving and enlarging its force of ocean-spanning missiles, and eventually it will field new ballistic missile-carrying submarines. Even so, China's strategic modernization programs will remain extremely relaxed by cold war standards.[15] Beijing's primary focus will continue to be on its periphery and the contingency that matters most: a clash with the United States over Taiwan. China is mass producing and deploying approximately 100 short-range missiles annually that can be launched in fusillades against Taiwan and that can also reach nearby U.S. bases.[16] By making this deterrent message clear, the modernization of China's longest-range nuclear forces can continue to proceed at a slower pace.

Beijing has conveyed another deterrent message by blowing up one of its aging satellites in January 2007 with a medium-range missile. The antisatellite test, only the second of its kind—the first was carried out by the Reagan administration in 1985—most probably was meant to clarify that the Pentagon would not own the high ground of space in the event of a clash over Taiwan. During the first nuclear age, the mutual vulnerability of cities to missile attacks provided the basic underpinning of superpower deterrence. During the second nuclear age, major powers will seek to deter each other in space as well as on the ground.

Even if the Bush administration had not issued its proactive national security strategy and deployed missile defenses, U.S. military dominance mandated closer ties between Russia and China, the two major powers that feel most uncomfortable with American might. By reflexively homing in on two objectives that are sensitive to Moscow and Beijing—controlling the high ground of space and deploying missile defenses around their peripheries—the Bush administration accentuated anxieties that it would seek to exploit American military dominance to negate their nuclear deterrents.

The cold war's old isosceles triangle was gone, but the old partnership between Beijing and Moscow was back. The Bush administration's projected nuclear needs were sized to stay ahead of the combined nuclear capabilities of Russia and China. Moscow was prepared to help Beijing to become more of a counterweight to Washington's dominance, even at the risk of encountering difficulties with a muscular China later on. In the meantime, the two weak legs of this triangle shared a common interest in securing minimal nuclear deterrence against U.S. power projection capabilities, missile defenses, and space warfare options.

Beijing's partner in the second nuclear triangle is its old friend Pakistan. Before tightening its export controls, Beijing helped Pakistan to offset India's nuclear ambitions by transferring missiles and, according to some reports, by providing the design of a nuclear warhead, even welcoming Pakistani officials to its nuclear test site.[17] Pakistan may well have returned these favors. After the attacks by al Qaeda on the U.S. embassies in Kenya and Tanzania in August 1998, the Clinton administration sent volleys of cruise missiles over Pakistani territory into Afghanistan to strike camps where Osama bin Laden was presumably present. The attacks killed Pakistani nationals who were helping the Taliban and al Qaeda, but bin Laden was elsewhere. The most important consequence of the failed strikes was that a few of the cruise missiles fell on Pakistani soil, where they were presumably exploited by Pakistan and China to upgrade their deterrents.

New Delhi, like Beijing, claims adherence to minimal nuclear deterrence and a no-first-use doctrine. India has been in no hurry to build up its arsenal, partly because of its ambivalence toward nuclear weapons, befitting a nation that reveres Mahatma Gandhi while seeking a seat at the high table of international affairs with other possessors of the Bomb. Gandhi once said, "An eye for an eye only ends up making the whole world blind." But if China and the rest of the permanent members of the Security Council had blinding mechanisms, India was going to have them as well, in its own peculiar way. Perhaps the clearest indicator of India's ambivalence can be measured by the twenty-four years that elapsed between India's first and next nuclear weapon tests.[18]

Decision making in New Delhi is highly consensual—another reason for India's deliberate approach to all things nuclear. Defense procurement decisions have produced scandals in the past, breeding caution that further slows down the pace of decision making. Powerful bureaucrats and civilian leaders in the defense research and nuclear establishments jealously guard their prerogatives, even from senior military officers. The subsequent lack of civil-military coordination has hampered India's nuclear progress. An integrated defense staff that would be led by an equivalent to the U.S. chairman of the Joint Chiefs of Staff remains in limbo because of infighting between the services over which branch should be in charge. Consensus building is an important trait for vigorous democracies, but rarely has it been taken to such lengths as in India.

Pakistani leaders also claim allegiance to a minimal credible deterrent, but their actions suggest otherwise. Pakistan has less money to spend for conventional forces and fewer opportunities to buy. (Moscow, which is not known for restraint in arms sales, has not sold to Pakistan, apparently in deference to its significant dealings with India.) Nor can Pakistan's leaders resume support for a jihad against India without risking more domestic unrest and increased pressure from its two primary supporters, the United States and China. With constrained conventional and unconventional military options, Pakistan's military leaders have spared no expense in competing with India on nuclear weapons and their means of delivery. They have so far afforded the luxury of both highly enriched uranium and plutonium production programs along with competing nuclear weapon design teams and ballistic missile programs.

The prerequisites of minimal credible deterrence for Pakistan are substantial because Pakistan's generals do not believe India's pledge not to use nuclear weapons first and because New Delhi has espoused a doctrine of massive retaliation if struck first.[19] Consequently, Pakistan's nuclear requirements will be relative, depending on what India has and on what India seems to want. Because India intends to have the ability to deliver nuclear weapons from the sea and from land-based missiles and aircraft, Pakistan wants a triad as well. Because India is developing and fielding cruise missiles to complement its ballistic missiles, Pakistan is too. If India resumes nuclear testing to certify a more powerful weapon design, Pakistan is likely to follow suit.

The requirements of minimal credible nuclear deterrence for China will also be relative, not absolute. All three corners of the India-Pakistan-China nuclear triangle will seek to avoid arms racing, but they will still compete with one another. That competition is heating up. Beijing has noted that the Bush administration has taken steps to retain nuclear offenses and deploy missile defenses that could negate its deterrent and also that India seeks to move up in class, so China is taking compensatory steps. As China increases its nuclear holdings and capabilities, India will as well. And as India goes, so goes Pakistan. In the Beijing–Islamabad–New Delhi triangle, India is the odd man out. These dynamics make for unstable geometry because a triangular competition is more complicated that a bipolar one. This particular competition relies on the primacy of economic growth and bureaucratic sluggishness as moderating factors.

NUCLEAR CONVULSIONS

Another defining apprehension of the second nuclear age is the collapse of states that possess nuclear weapons or other disruptions that could result in the loss of control over the Bomb or its key ingredients. A precedent for the possible implosion of a nuclear-armed state occurred during the first nuclear age, when China experienced the convulsive decade of the Cultural Revolution. Those responsible for the development of China's Bomb had no interest in exchanging catechisms with the Red Guards. Nie Rongzhen had an H-bomb to test, and he had sufficient clout to order the Xinjiang regional military command to secure his facilities from unauthorized personnel and overzealous youth.[20] Although China's bomb program suffered delays during the Cultural Revolution, its bomb makers were mostly insulated from the craziness around them.[21]

During the second nuclear age, many fear that Pakistan could also break apart or be taken over by Islamic extremists who would then gain control over the country's nuclear weapons and fissile material. Although this scenario cannot be completely discounted, it seems overdrawn. Given the extent of Pakistan's ills and its governmental failings, it is striking how little popular ferment and upheaval there has been against military and civilian rulers who have overpromised and underperformed. Street demonstrations are usually well-scripted affairs in Pakistan financed by political parties and designed for signaling purposes, not for a revolution from below or for the radical overthrow of a sitting government. The specter of spontaneous, combustible, uncontrollable street rebellion is regularly advanced by military and political leaders in Islamabad as a compelling reason for continued support from Washington. In all such scenarios, the beneficiaries of domestic upheavals are religious zealots wearing long beards.

Perhaps one day this dire prediction might come to pass, but even after decades of misrule, there remains little evidence of a stampede in Pakistan toward the religious parties. The Pakistani government's writ is weak along the border with Afghanistan and in other peripheral locations, where the Pakistani military's nuclear weapons and fissile material are unlikely to be found. And if Pakistan were to dissolve into chaos, the military guardians of the nation's nuclear crown jewels would likely protect these assets with the same grim resolve as the Chinese military units that fended off the Red Guards during the Cultural Revolution. The biggest threat to nuclear stability and a breakdown of command and control in Pakistan is a split within the army, not a takeover by radical Islamic elements.

The specter of Pakistan's possible collapse figures prominently in nuclear nightmares because the implosion of a nuclear-armed state has already occurred. The collapse of the Soviet Union kicked off the second nuclear age, creating unprecedented opportunities for nuclear fission. At the time of its dissolution, the Soviet Union was estimated to have 27,000 nuclear weapons and enough plutonium and highly enriched uranium to make 90,000 more.[22] These estimates were necessarily rounded off, because no one needed to keep accurate counts during Soviet rule. Bombs and bomb-making material were well guarded, and there were no signs of breakdowns in command and control in the military and internal security organs of the Soviet state. The brutal efficiency with which a totalitarian state could suppress dissent provided an object lesson to anyone foolish enough to contemplate the theft of a nuclear weapon or fissile material from the closed cities in which they were produced.

When the Soviet Union began to fall apart, all of this changed. Nuclear guardians, bomb makers, and the military chain of command were first presented with the question of whether their allegiance was to Boris Yeltsin or Mikhail Gorbachev. When Yeltsin and the Russian Duma dissolved the Union of Soviet Socialist Republics, most of those watching were transfixed by the historic geopolitical changes that were about to unfold. A few discerning eyes were focused instead on the whereabouts of the military aide who accompanied the Soviet leader carrying the briefcase with the nuclear launch codes. After the issue of political allegiance was resolved quickly and without a struggle, another set of problems immediately arose over the sudden nuclear inheritance of the newly independent states of Ukraine, Kazakhstan, and Belarus.

When the Soviet Union dissolved, nuclear weapons were stored at more than fifty locations, including four in Ukraine and three in Kazakhstan.[23] Ukraine instantaneously inherited the better part of the Soviet Black Sea Fleet, key missile-building factories, 176 intercontinental ballistic missiles, and approximately 5,000 nuclear weapons—making Ukraine the third largest nuclear weapon state in the world, with more weapons than Great Britain, France, and China combined. Newly independent Kazakhstan inherited a major space launch complex, advanced space tracking and laser facilities, a nuclear test site, 104 intercontinental ballistic missiles, and 1,410 nuclear weapons, instantaneously becoming the world's fourth largest nuclear power. Belarus's nuclear inheritance was less problematic, because its leaders in Minsk were inclined to maintain close ties with Moscow and were thus unlikely to want to keep their newly acquired nuclear weapons.

If the Bomb were nothing more than a great equalizer to a more powerful neighbor, Ukraine and Kazakhstan would have held on to at least some of their sudden nuclear inheritance. Russia's authoritarian tendencies were deeply rooted, and Moscow would surely seek to reaffirm its primacy in neighboring countries. Nuclear weapons were ideally suited to promote cautious behavior by a stronger neighbor and conferred special status on their owners. Why look a gift horse in the mouth?

Ukraine and Kazakhstan were, however, deeply scarred by the atom. The explosion at the Chernobyl nuclear power plant in Ukraine in 1986 required the creation of a 4,300-kilometer exclusion zone and the resettlement of more than 200,000 residents.[24] The Soviet nuclear test site in Kazakhstan also had left a bitter legacy. The Soviets conducted 116 atmospheric tests at Semipalatinsk and another 340 tests underground, using shoddy test practices that resulted in the venting of radiation into the surrounding countryside, which was used for farming. Soviet testing has produced a trail of genetic havoc and sorrow across the Kazakh steppes.[25]

The United States and other key stakeholders in the Nonproliferation Treaty had many good reasons to seek to persuade Ukraine, Kazakhstan, and Belarus to give up their nuclear inheritance. The Nonproliferation Treaty could withstand slow, singular proliferation, but it had never been tested by multiple, instantaneous members in the nuclear club. If nuclear wannabes from Central Asia joined those in South Asia, the Middle East, and the Far East, the treaty's protective blanket against proliferation would feel more like a badly tattered quilt.

Another reason to convince Ukraine and Kazakhstan to give back their nuclear inheritance was that Moscow insisted on retrieving its nuclear weapons before the strategic arms reduction treaties negotiated at the end of the cold war could be implemented. The importance of these treaties now lay not in Russia's ability to maintain and build up its nuclear capacity but in its inability to do so.

A structured and verifiable drawdown of Russian nuclear forces provided some insurance against a chaotic nuclear future while providing a framework for broader nuclear cooperation with the United States. Training, maintenance, safety, and security practices on Russian soil were now deeply problematic, but the chances of something going badly wrong were even greater in newly independent states that would be starting from scratch in terms of nuclear stewardship. Although there would be no guarantees of cordial relations with Russia by giving back their sudden nuclear inheritance, Ukraine and Kazakhstan would ensure troubled relations with their aggrieved neighbor—and with the West—by refusing to do so.

All these factors combined to give the administrations of George H. W. Bush and Bill Clinton running room to convince the newly independent states around Russia's periphery to return their nuclear inheritance to Russia. Whatever their value, nuclear weapons could not heat homes and factories in the bitter cold, so Russian energy supplies might therefore be a suitable trading commodity. Moreover, without help from the United States and the West, Ukraine and Kazakhstan would be greatly disadvantaged in a confrontation with Russia. Washington and NATO capitals conveyed telling messages that better ties required a commitment to nonproliferation. In addition, the nuclear weapons inherited by Ukraine and Kazakhstan had limited shelf lives. They would need to be replaced over time with skills and money that these newly independent states did not have. Nor was Moscow about to help them figure out the protective measures and launch codes designed to prevent the unauthorized use of these nuclear weapons.

The Clinton administration's success in convincing leaders in Ukraine, Kazakhstan, and Belarus to voluntarily give back their nuclear inheritance to Russia was an enormous achievement. Had these efforts failed, the global nonproliferation system would have been badly shaken, and subsequent cases of nuclear ambition would have been even harder to stop. The strategic arms reduction process would have remained in limbo, and friction between Moscow and Washington would have greatly impaired the start-up of cooperative threat reduction programs to safeguard dangerous weapons and materials in the former Soviet Union. The Clinton administration sealed the denuclearization deals without offering security guarantees to Ukraine and Kazakhstan. Instead, the provision of energy from Moscow and the likelihood of improved relations with the United States and NATO were the key ingredients in persuading the leadership in Ukraine and Kazakhstan to give up the Bomb.[26]

Other nuclear convulsions followed. The Russian economy suffered several meltdowns under Boris Yeltsin, whose "free market overhaul" had disastrous effects. When basic necessities were available, they could be purchased after waiting in line for hours. The cost of butter rose sixfold, to one-thirtieth of the average Russian's monthly salary. By 1997, the Russian government owed almost $9 billion in back wages and benefits to workers. In 1998, the ruble crashed and the Russian stock market lost half its value. During the 1990s, Russia's gross domestic product fell by 40 percent. By contrast, U.S. gross domestic product fell by 30 percent during the Great Depression.[27]

The old Soviet system to protect nuclear weapons and fissile material was in shambles, with reports of guards leaving their posts to forage for food for their families. There was initially no accurate accounting of Russian nuclear weapons and bomb-making material. Research facilities housing portable highly enriched uranium were poorly secured. "Orphaned" sources of radioactive material suitable for dirty bombs were all over the map.

One of the second nuclear age's most puzzling questions is why opportunity and motive have not already produced a nuclear catastrophe. For example, on November 24, 1995, Shamil Basayev, a Chechen rebel leader, alerted journalists to search for a parcel in Ismailovsky Park, a popular recreation site in Moscow. There security forces found a box containing 1 gram of cesium-137, a substance well suited for a dirty bomb. The radiological material appears to have come from nuclear waste located in Grozny, the battered capital of the Chechen Republic.[28] Basayev told his interviewers, "People these days say we are always bluffing. They think we can no longer hurt the Russians. So we will give them a little sign of what we have. Consider it a small disarmament. But remember that we are completely prepared to commit acts of terrorism that will be tangible for Russia." Basayev was killed in 2006 by Russian forces in their extended, brutal campaign in Chechnya. The response Basayev promised has yet to occur.[29]

Other scare stories and close calls are plentiful, but so far, they have not led to tragedies. Some examples:

- A worker at a laboratory in Podolsk skimmed off small samples of highly enriched uranium while his co-workers were taking smoke breaks, accumulating 1.5 kilograms of the bomb-making material. He was arrested in 1992 for an unrelated crime while he happened to be carrying lead containers of highly enriched uranium.[30]
- In December 1994, Prague police, acting on an anonymous tip, searched a Saab and found almost 3 kilograms of highly enriched uranium. The

ringleader, a former worker in the Russian nuclear complex who sub-sequently tried and failed to run a bakery, teamed up with two smug-glers working at an import-export trucking firm operating in Eastern Europe. The origin of the highly enriched uranium was believed to be a fuel fabrication plant serving the Russian navy in Obninsk. The bomb-making material was identical to that seized in Landshut, Germany, six months earlier.[31]

- In Moscow, a worker at a plant producing fuel for nuclear reactors stole 2 kilograms of uranium-235. The worker and three associates were looking for a foreign buyer when they were arrested by Russian au-thorities in March 1994.[32]

- In February 2006, a Russian smuggler from North Ossetia was arrested in a sting operation by Georgian authorities; the smuggler was trying to sell 100 grams of highly enriched uranium to a man he thought was a representative of an Islamic organization. The Russian government re-fused to work with Georgian authorities on the case because of frayed relations, describing the entire affair as a provocation.[33]

- In June 2007, Georgian authorities stopped a car at a border check-point carrying plutonium and beryllium (a substance used to trigger nuclear explosions). The car was sent back to Azerbaijan rather than confiscated because, according to one Georgian official, "It would have been very expensive to keep it in Georgia and special conditions" were needed to secure the material.[34]

The International Atomic Energy Agency created a database to monitor illicit trafficking; the database covers reported incidents since January 1993. By the end of 2005, the database had logged 827 confirmed incidents reported by 91 countries. A parallel database initiated by Stanford University and now maintained by the University of Salzburg, draws on open-source material. It lists 1,440 cases of nuclear smuggling, theft, and orphaned radiation sources. Most of these incidents did not pose public hazards, but at least twenty-five of these cases were serious, involving the diversion of highly enriched uranium or plutonium.[35]

To prevent nightmare scenarios from occurring, Senators Sam Nunn and Richard Lugar—then the Democratic chairman of the Armed Services Com-mittee and the second-ranking Republican on the Foreign Relations Commit-tee, respectively—conceived of a cooperative threat reduction program to secure dangerous weapons and materials in the former Soviet Union. With only one exception, major nonproliferation initiatives have been conceived by the executive branch. The exception was the Nunn-Lugar program. Nunn-Lugar funding was used to help transport nuclear weapons back to Russia from Ukraine, Kazakhstan, and Belarus and to dismantle the missiles and bombers designed to carry them. The first authorization of $400 million was passed in November 1991, with eight senators opposed. Funding for the panoply of cooperative threat reduction programs grew annually during the Clinton and George W. Bush administrations, topping the $1 billion mark in 2006, when Congress overrode the Bush administration's proposed budget cuts.[36]

Although the Nunn-Lugar programs enjoyed considerable bipartisan support, both the executive and legislative branches had lingering qualms over whether these funds would be properly expended and whether Russian authorities would use the money saved by having others pay for security upgrades to rebuild their nuclear forces. Counterarguments were far more persuasive because many upgrades would not be a high priority for Moscow. Russian authorities would also proceed far more slowly without outside assistance—unless propelled by the very act of nuclear terrorism that cooperative threat reduction initiatives were designed to prevent. And although it was certainly true that Moscow would be able to spend rubles on its nuclear forces that it would not spend on improved nuclear security, Russian force levels would continue to plummet as cold war–era missiles faced block obsolescence.

The Nunn-Lugar program produced significant results. With U.S. assistance, the Russian Federation deactivated more than 6,900 nuclear warheads, dismantled more than 600 intercontinental ballistic missiles, destroyed more than 150 strategic bombers, eliminated more than 900 nuclear-armed air-to-surface missiles, and cut up more than 30 missile-carrying nuclear-powered submarines. Slightly more than 80 percent of Russian facilities storing weapons-usable fissile material have received security upgrades. Two hundred eighty-five tons of highly enriched uranium from dismantled weapons have been blended down for use in civilian power reactors. Forty-nine facilities that were once involved in biological weapons work have now engaged in joint partnerships with U.S. institutions.[37] In November 1994, approximately 600 kilograms of weapons-grade uranium was removed from the Ulba Metallurgy Plant in Kazakhstan. An even larger stash of enriched uranium was removed from a research reactor on the outskirts of Tbilisi, Georgia, in August 1998. Nunn-Lugar funds have also been used to construct a storage facility in Mayak, designed for the safekeeping of fissile material from approximately 25,000 nuclear weapons.

These impressive results occurred despite significant obstacles. Many Russian authorities had less of a sense of urgency than their U.S. counterparts, notwithstanding confirmed incidents of nuclear smuggling from Russian facilities. Russian mistrust of U.S. motives curtailed the scope of facility upgrades. For example, the consolidation of nuclear weapons at fewer storage sites made excellent sense from a security standpoint, but it also could facilitate U.S. nuclear targeting plans. In addition to weapon storage sites, Russian officials were reluctant to provide intrusive access to waste storage facilities, warhead manufacturing sites, and former biological weapons sites.[38]

Russian authorities were also reluctant to provide waivers or liability limits in the event of accidents resulting from or associated with Nunn-Lugar–type initiatives. Authorities in the newly independent states of the former Soviet Union also wished to impose taxes on foreign imports related to Nunn-Lugar programs. Limiting liability and imposing taxes were unacceptable to Congress and the executive branch, so programs were slowed while government lawyers haggled. Although unwilling to cede ground on these issues on a permanent basis, Moscow consented in 2006 to a seven-year umbrella agreement providing blanket protection for U.S. workers engaged in cooperative threat reduction projects.

Not all the reasons for the limited scope of Nunn-Lugar programming had to do with foot-dragging in Moscow. Many U.S. agencies were involved in cooperative threat reduction programs, resulting in less than optimal prioritization and coordination. Skeptics on Capitol Hill set legislative conditions to Nunn-Lugar funding, including that Russia needed to forgo any military modernization program that exceeded "legitimate defense requirements" and a prohibition on reusing fissionable material and other components of destroyed nuclear weapons in new ones. Congress also attached conditions relating to Russia's human rights practices. But Capitol Hill permitted presidential waivers, implicitly recognizing that, for such matters, principle could be trumped by necessity or, to cite Voltaire and the old Soviet Ministry of Defense, the best could also be the enemy of the good. The level of U.S. and allied funding for cooperative threat reduction initiatives could also have been more appropriate to the scope of the problem. One billion dollars was by no means a trivial sum of money to appropriate annually for preventing the most dangerous weapons and materials from getting into the most dangerous hands. But it is a pittance compared to, say, the transportation bill passed by Congress in 2005 that included the infamous "bridge to nowhere" in Alaska. This legislation included 6,373 earmarks of special interest to members of Congress. The tab for these add-ons was in excess of $24 billion.[39]

TWO PERSONIFICATIONS OF THE SECOND NUCLEAR AGE

Two individuals personified the new dangers of the second nuclear age, where nuclear terrorism, "loose nukes," and viral, horizontal proliferation have become paramount anxieties. Both individuals are intimately connected with Pakistan: the self-promoting father of Pakistan's bomb, A. Q. Khan, and Osama bin Laden, the incendiary behind the 9/11 attacks who, with an unwitting assist from the George W. Bush administration, has inspired a new generation of Islamic extremists. Since the revelations of his nuclear transactions, Khan has spent his declining years confined to one of his properties in Islamabad; bin Laden's whereabouts have been hard to pin down, but he is widely presumed to be on Pakistani soil.[40]

Both men benefited greatly from Pakistan's state sponsorship. Khan ran not one but two nuclear supply networks. He imported critical material and equipment to support his nation's bomb-building program. For this essential service, Khan received the accolades of a grateful nation, whose leaders looked the other way when he skimmed off the top. This practice was, after all, hardly uncommon for state-related transactions, and besides, Khan's surcharges came with priceless national security benefits. He was encouraged to cut corners to obtain the Bomb, and he was not someone to be trimmed by mere security procedures.

Since about 1987, Khan's entrepreneurial talents have extended beyond government-sanctioned imports to a parallel, shady, lucrative export program. During this fifteen-year period, Khan became the world's worst proliferator, helping neighboring Iran jump-start its uranium enrichment program and offering North Korea a second route to the Bomb, undermining the deal struck by the Clinton administration in 1994 to suspend Pyongyang's plutonium reprocessing programs. Under close scrutiny by foreign intelligence services,[41] Khan provided deadly shortcuts to the two most worrisome proliferation cases of the second nuclear age.

The Khan network's first substantial export deal, in 1987, offered centrifuge technology to Iran in return for $3 million.[42] The delivery of first-generation Pakistani centrifuges to Iran began in 1991; drawings for second-generation centrifuges were offered in 1993 and conveyed the next year. Complete second-generation centrifuges were delivered to Iran in 1997, the same year that Libyan authorities approached Khan for nuclear assistance. Centrifuge and bomb-making kits were delivered to North Korea in the late 1990s. Libya's first centrifuges were shipped in 2000 along with feedstock. By 2001, the evidence of illicit activities and U.S. démarches were sufficient for President Musharraf to remove

Khan from the directorship of his laboratory. The network's hub then shifted to Dubai, where orders were filled without constraint until the impoundment of the *BBC China*, a ship bound for Libya, in October 2003. This vessel, flagged in Antigua and owned by a German firm, was carrying precision machine tools, aluminum tubes, molecular pumps, and components for building thousands of gas centrifuges.[43]

Seven months before the *BBC China*'s seizure, in March 2003, Libya's leader for life, Colonel Muamar Qadafi, sent out feelers to British intelligence about ceasing his efforts to acquire weapons of mass destruction in return for an end to sanctions.[44] Libyan bomb makers had acquired the tag in some circles as "the gang that couldn't proliferate straight," and it was surely becoming evident to some members of the Qadafi family that the value of nuclear deterrence against the United States—assuming that the equipment from Khan's network, which remained mostly in crates, could ever be operationalized—was less than the value of his oil fields, which desperately needed foreign investment. The impoundment of the *BBC China* clarified matters further: Qadafi effectively swapped his crates for foreign help in the oil drilling business. The other recipients of Khan's illicit commerce placed a far greater value on nuclear deterrence.

Punitive action against Khan required evidence that his overseers could not deflect or rebut, which the impoundment of the *BBC China* provided. President Musharraf showcased Khan on television to deliver a contrite apology (in English for a foreign audience, not in Urdu), after which he was confined to quarters.[45] Khan attempted to justify his bomb-selling kits as an excess of Islamic solidarity, an argument that would have been more persuasive had he not accumulated $8 million in various banks and even more in real estate assets.[46] Nor was Islamic solidarity a convincing argument in explaining sales to North Korea.

The sleuthing that led to the impoundment of the *BBC China*'s cargo was heralded by the George W. Bush administration as a major intelligence coup, which it most certainly was. Left unspoken was that Khan was on intelligence service watch lists even before absconding to Pakistan in 1975 from his place of employment in Holland with centrifuge specifications and drawings. From this point onward, he became a central figure in Pakistan's efforts to produce enriched uranium for bombs, where his presumed indispensability—along with his ability to tell inconvenient truths and to create domestic political firestorms—made him impervious to mounting evidence of gross venality and odd travel itineraries.

Why did it take so long for Khan's odyssey from nuclear procurer to exporter to be publicly exposed and rolled up? Several answers are plausible, but none are satisfactory. It took time for intelligence services to gather enough information to make a persuasive private case and, once they did, the information was still not compelling enough to force Pakistani authorities to face the negative consequences that would result from exposing a man who worked very hard to make himself untouchable. Western intelligence services also held off on orchestrating a sting to discover more about the scope of Khan's operations. As former CIA director George Tenet later recounted, "The natural instinct when you find some shred of intelligence about nuclear proliferation is to act immediately. But you must control that urge and be patient, to follow the links where they take you, so that when action is launched, you can hope to remove the network both root and branch."[47]

Pakistani authorities cannot put A. Q. Khan's misdeeds in the rearview mirror because their network for critical nuclear imports is still operational.[48] Nor can Pakistani authorities allow foreign sleuths to interrogate Khan about his illicit exports without jeopardizing state secrets regarding nuclear imports. Pakistan's nuclear stewardship has improved greatly since Khan was confined to his quarters in Islamabad. Security oversight of nuclear facilities is now handled by the Strategic Plans Division at Joint Staff Headquarters, which has assigned approximately 10,000 personnel, mostly undercover, to keep watch over key personnel and the country's nuclear and missile complexes.[49] The Strategic Plans Division has also belatedly put in place serious personnel reliability programs, borrowing from best practices learned from outsiders. Agreements with India have been reached to upgrade hotlines, provide prenotification of ballistic missile flight tests, and establish procedures in the event of nuclear accidents. Further security upgrades and nuclear risk-reduction measures can be expected, but the stain of having a national hero also become the world's most damaging proliferator will continue to haunt Pakistan.

A. Q. Khan sold bomb-making material to make a profit. Osama bin Laden, the other key personification of the second nuclear age, sought bomb-making material to make mayhem. Khan was a son of the middle class who sought upward mobility; bin Laden spurned his royal lineage to become a revolutionary. For him, wealth was a means to the end of toppling the Royal House of Saud and generating pain for its protector, the United States.[50] Khan was an enabler for states that wanted the Bomb and posed a threat to the United States. There is no public evidence, as yet, that Khan's network sold to freelancers. Bin Laden was the ultimate freelancer. No one made more trouble for Washington merely by using conventional explosives and jet fuel. But bin Laden's ambitions were greater: He wanted nuclear weapons and fissile material.

The earliest reports of bin Laden's interest in nuclear weapons date back to 1993, when he was in Sudan.[51] Other assessments, including the *9/11 Commission Report*, date al Qaeda's interest in nuclear material to 1997.[52] Former CIA director George Tenet testified that bin Laden considered the acquisition of weapons of mass destruction to be a "religious obligation."[53] Three veterans of the Pakistani nuclear establishment, Sultan Bashuruddin Mahmood, Mizra Yusuf Baig, and Abdul Majeed, were detained in late October 2001 by Pakistani authorities, after U.S. officials provided damning evidence of their travels and meetings in Afghanistan, where they reportedly met with bin Laden, his closest associate, Ayman Zawahiri, and Mullah Mohammed Omar, the Taliban head. Mahmood was the former director of the Pakistan Atomic Energy Commission; Baig and Majeed worked under Mahmood, whose trips to Afghanistan ostensibly reflected their deep commitment to refugee relief operations there. Before retiring from the Pakistani Atomic Energy Commission in 1999, Mahmood held senior positions at the Khushab heavy water reactor used for plutonium production. Earlier in his career, he worked on uranium enrichment before A. Q. Khan took over this program. Majeed, who retired in 2000, was a nuclear fuels expert at the Pakistan Institute of Nuclear Science and Technology.

At least fifteen scientists from Pakistan's atomic energy complexes were detained for questioning by Pakistani authorities for their involvement in the Khan export network or for visiting Afghanistan to meet with al Qaeda leaders, including one trip after the 9/11 attacks. Most were released quickly; Mahmood and Majeed were detained for three months and were subsequently confined to their residences.[54] The government of Pakistan has declared that none of its scientists had the specific expertise or access required to help the Taliban or al Qaeda and that they were guilty of poor judgment, not the transfer of state secrets or bomb-making material. Authorities in Pakistan will not allow access to these scientists to prove otherwise.

It is hard to conclude from the sketchy evidence publicly available that the Pakistani scientists who traveled to Afghanistan took part in Khan's schemes. His laboratory was in competition with Mahmood's lab to build bombs and missiles, and Khan's relations to the Pakistan Atomic Energy Commission leadership were badly strained. This does not necessarily mean, however, that Khan was incapable of working surreptitiously with individual Pakistan Atomic

Energy Commission employees to assist bin Laden and al Qaeda operatives. Assistance to al Qaeda would serve all of Khan's motives—profit taking, Islamic solidarity, and challenging the United States. But al Qaeda could not make good use of centrifuge equipment, uranium feedstock, and bomb designs, the stock-in-trade of Khan's network. Al Qaeda's nomadic circumstances required finished products, not infrastructure. For its cells to pose a nuclear threat to the United States, U.S. forces, or allies, al Qaeda needed to acquire someone else's nuclear weapons, highly enriched uranium, or the radiological material ideally suited for dirty bombs.

Pakistan is not the only potential source of fissile or radiological material to al Qaeda. Uzbekistan is another possibility.[55] Uzbekistan has a nuclear power reactor and irradiated fuel elements containing highly enriched uranium. Another batch of highly enriched uranium and reactor fuel from Uzbekistan was removed to Russia for down-blending, courtesy of Nunn-Lugar funding. Uzbekistan also inherited Soviet biological and chemical weapon facilities.[56] When detained for questioning, Mahmood and Majeed reportedly told their Pakistani inquisitors that bin Laden had acquired radiological material from the Islamic Movement of Uzbekistan but not highly enriched uranium or plutonium usable in nuclear weapons. Searches of the house used by Mahmood when he was in Kabul did not uncover nuclear-weapons-related material, but they did produce pamphlets and reports dealing with biological warfare, especially anthrax.[57] In 2002, one of bin Laden's biographers concluded that there was "absolutely no evidence" that al Qaeda had succeeded in weaponizing "any of the chemical and nuclear materials it has flirted with."[58]

Insider and outlier, seller and buyer, entrepreneur and revolutionary: A. Q. Khan and Osama bin Laden reflect a wide spectrum of challenges in the second nuclear age. Objects of intense scrutiny by many intelligence services, they were still free to go about their business until 2001, providing object lessons of how the most dangerous weapons and materials might fall into the most dangerous hands. Khan and bin Laden both believed that this scenario had already come to pass, because the United States had nuclear weapons in abundance. The same was true for Israel. Bin Laden added Musharraf to his list of enemies of Islam after 9/11, when the government of Pakistan turned against the Taliban and al Qaeda leadership.

Khan and bin Laden did not need to connect to produce momentous shifts in American national security policy. The mere prospect of their liaison—or of other illicit and deadly transactions—was sufficient to motivate the Bush administration to wage its war on terror. America's ground forces were thrown into this fight with woefully insufficient help or understanding of the countries they were fighting to liberate. The war in Iraq granted bin Laden's wish to produce countless recruits consumed by grievances who were willing to give meaning to their truncated lives, as well as honor (and remittances) to their families. The second nuclear age was all about asymmetric warfare, and no form of asymmetric warfare was more chilling and harder to defend against than the sacrificial act of suicide bombing. And no act of immolation would be more consequential than if accompanied by a mushroom cloud, the Bush administration's ultimate argument for deposing Saddam Hussein. Threat and response were mutually reinforcing.

CONCILIATORS AND DOMINATORS

During the first nuclear age, the United States competed effectively against the Soviet Union. During the second nuclear age, the United States had great difficulty adjusting to a new adversarial matchup. The gift of the Soviet Union's collapse produced smugness, petty diversions, and then expectations that America's sudden and pronounced dominance would generate compliant behavior. For a short while after the Soviet Union dissolved, the old camps of hawks and doves that argued about nuclear weapons, arms control, and America's proper place in the world morphed into dominators and conciliators. Conciliators hoped that dominant U.S. power might promote cooperative threat reduction programs that progressively reduced nuclear dangers. They also sought new treaties to reduce the salience of nuclear weapons. Dominators viewed the demise of the Soviet Union as confirming the utility of a muscular national security strategy and as enabling the unapologetic use of American power. In their view, U.S. dominance ought not to be constrained by treaties that either presumed equality or limited U.S. military options.[59] These divergent plans were tried out in the administrations of William J. Clinton and George W. Bush.

The second nuclear age started out promising enough. During the first term of the Clinton administration, the Nunn-Lugar initiatives proceeded surprisingly well, dismantling aging bombers, missiles, and submarines in the former Soviet Union. Thousands of nuclear weapons were relocated from the furthest reaches of the Soviet Union into safer and more central storage sites. At the same time, the Clinton administration successfully convinced Ukraine, Kazakhstan, and Belarus to join the Nonproliferation Treaty as non-nuclear-weapon states, breathing new life into nonproliferation efforts.

These were historic achievements, but Nunn-Lugar programs lost rather than gained momentum in the latter half of the Clinton administration. Part of the problem was that Russia was a major work in progress and a disappointing partner. Moscow felt the same way about Washington, especially after President George W. Bush replaced Clinton and began to shed treaty constraints of interest to Moscow and began to strengthen ties with countries around Russia's periphery. Not surprisingly, the more Russia reverted to authoritarian tendencies under Vladimir Putin, who came to office in December 1999, the harder it became to develop a strong, functioning partnership to reduce nuclear dangers.

Russia's regression is but one thread in this disheartening story. The decade between the collapse of the Soviet Union and the 9/11 attacks was a time of wasted opportunities, unwise priorities, and foolish digressions in the United States. The second term of the Clinton administration constituted an extended diversion from growing nuclear dangers. Republican majorities in Congress elevated an appalling sexual indiscretion by President Clinton into impeachment proceedings constructed around high principles of the rule of law and the sanctity of judicial proceedings. Impeachment became a vehicle of political castration and infotainment. The Senate ultimately declined to oust Clinton but not before placing a scarlet letter on his chest. From Clinton's public admission of sexual indiscretions on August 17, 1998, to the Senate's vote on February 12, 1999, a Lexis Nexis data search netted 82,329 references to Monica Lewinsky, the pizza-delivering intern who caught the president's eye, compared to 10,253 references to Osama bin Laden and 4 to A. Q. Khan.

During this poisonous period, Republican senators summarily rejected a treaty banning nuclear testing for all time, which for decades had been a key element of U.S. nonproliferation policy and a load-bearing wall for the Nonproliferation Treaty. Congress's focus was elsewhere. The House Government Reform Panel was a particular nemesis of the Clinton White House, issuing no less than 1,052 subpoenas from 1997 to 2002 to investigate presumed Democratic misdeeds. Republican-led committees took 140 hours of testimony alone on the Clinton administration's Christmas mailing list and whether it was improperly used as a vehicle for political fund-raising. By way of comparison, the Republican-led Congress spent twelve hours holding hearings on the Abu Ghraib prison practices that did so much to inflame the Islamic world.[60]

While seeking to broker peace between Israel and the Palestinian leadership and fending off his tormentors, President Clinton had difficulty focusing on the loss of momentum of Nunn-Lugar programs. Nor did he pursue sustained measures to disrupt bin Laden's operational base in Afghanistan, as Pakistan was not providing the help required and covert U.S. intelligence assets in the region were meager. When Clinton finally authorized military action against al Qaeda in Afghanistan in the form of ineffectual cruise missile strikes in August 1998, he was widely accused of seeking a diversion from the Monica Lewinsky scandal.

9/11 AND PRESIDENT GEORGE W. BUSH

The traumatic events of 9/11 provided a national wake-up call to the dangers of Islamic extremism and the bitter realities of the second nuclear age. The prospect of nuclear terrorism, when added to loose nukes and poorly controlled fissile material, truly focused the mind. The problem, correctly defined by President George W. Bush as the most deadly weapons in the most dangerous hands, required grand strategy. The war on terror was born, as ambitious as the scope of the problem it sought to defeat. This label was well chosen to galvanize domestic political support and quiet dissenters but poorly chosen to succeed with the problem at hand.

The attacks on 9/11 ended the debate between dominators and conciliators. The World Trade Center became the new ground zero of the second nuclear age. After the Bomb's gruesome unveiling to end World War II, idealists reacted by calling for radical new institutions and a redefinition of national sovereignty to deal with unprecedented nuclear danger. A group of wise men, bomb makers, and giants from the world of science, led by Dean Acheson, David Lilienthal, and Robert Oppenheimer, sketched out a blueprint for a nuclear-weapon-free world in which the means of producing the Bomb were in the hands of an international organization policed by global civil servants. This plan was discussed in a brand new forum created to keep the peace, the United Nations. These ambitious blueprints were worthy of the unprecedented problems of the day but incapable of surmounting them. The Bomb's power and superpower distrust were too great for the Acheson-Lilienthal plan to succeed.

After the Twin Towers fell, global sympathies for America were at an all-time high. The most powerful country in world history had been victimized, and the Bush administration had wide latitude and great capacity to react. This was America's unipolar moment—the apt title of an essay written by the gifted polemicist Charles Krauthammer as the Soviet Union was coming apart. After the Bomb's shocking appearance, diplomats gathered to discuss remedial action. Krauthammer and other tribunes of the transformative powers of American might did not advocate a conclave of diplomats. They framed the unipolar moment as an elemental choice between power or parchment.

In Krauthammer's view, the time had come to quit being apologetic about the use of power in pursuit of national interests—to stop paying false obeisance to "pseudo-multilateralism," where "a dominant great power acts essentially alone, but, embarrassed at the idea and still worshiping at the shrine of collective security, recruits a ship here, a brigade there, and blessings all around to give its unilateral actions a multilateral sheen."[61] Good guys followed the rules embedded in international agreements; bad actors disregarded them. Why, then, should the United States limit its military options in the defense of its global responsibilities and its way of life? And why should America feel restrained by the timidity and fecklessness of allies?[62]

There was a haunting echo in Krauthammer's powerful prose of Barry Goldwater's famous peroration from his 1964 presidential campaign—that extremism in defense of liberty was no vice and that moderation in pursuit of freedom was no virtue. Goldwater's charge was downright scary in the context of a superpower competition and a nuclear arms race. Krauthammer's call to action was far more positively received at a time of unparalleled U.S. military superiority.

Missing in Krauthammer's ringing declaration for the unapologetic exercise of U.S. power was any reference to the classic injunction in the Declaration of Independence about paying decent respect to the opinions of mankind. Instead, America's power was now so unsurpassed that the successful application of force would confer its own legitimacy. Henceforth, norm building would need to take into account American exceptionalism. Canvassing the views of other nations may have made sense for the Founding Fathers governing a fledgling America but not for the cold war's victor and the globe's sole superpower.

After 9/11, a new America would be on display—part throwback to an earlier era and part future-tense change agent. The old television show from the 1950s, *Father Knows Best*, was given a makeover, with the all-powerful father figure played not by a benevolent Robert Young but by an amalgam of Vice President Dick Cheney and Secretary of Defense Donald Rumsfeld. The object of their tutoring was "the Decider,"[63] George W. Bush, a man elevated to the presidency from the governor's mansion in Austin, Texas, an office rich in symbolism but much of whose executive powers had been ceded to the state legislature.

George W. Bush epitomized the "fortunate son" that Credence Clearwater Revival sang about during the Vietnam war, born "silver spoon in hand," gliding through life while others marched off to war. Carefree and incurious, he collected degrees from America's most prestigious institutions of learning, performed indifferently at the offerings lined up by family friends, and then moved up to try something else, as if by birthright. The swagger came naturally; the aimlessness disappeared when he found a good wife and his Savior, Jesus Christ. The man who emerged reborn by religious belief gained confidence, ambition, and prepared for the challenge of a lifetime.

Beyond neighboring Mexico, Bush made three foreign trips before becoming president. He visited his father when he was the ambassador to China during graduate school; he led a U.S. delegation to celebrate Gambia's independence day during his father's administration; and when contemplating a run for the presidency, he visited his daughters in Italy before joining other governors on a tour of the Middle East.[64] A few sound bites woven around the national interest and the need to rebuild a military worn down from service in peacekeeping and nation-building assignments served as the basic national security text of his presidential campaign. His most memorable campaign quote was delivered at a speech before the Veterans of Foreign Wars in Milwaukee. Candidate Bush promised to fix "a military in decline."

> The reasons are clear. Lack of equipment and material. Undermanning of units. Overdeployment. Not enough time for family. Soldiers who are on food stamps and soldiers who are poorly housed. Dick Cheney and I have a simple message today for our men and women in uniform, their parents, their loved ones, their supporters. Help is on the way![65]

During the presidential campaign, national security matters were staffed by the "vulcans," capable, confident, and ambitious high-risers led by Condoleezza Rice, Paul Wolfowitz, and Robert Blackwill, who worked in responsible positions for President George H. W. Bush and who sought even more challenging assignments in another Bush administration.[66] In their view, Bill Clinton had far too many naïve enthusiasms, including trying to make peace between Israel and the Palestinians and sending U.S. soldiers off to wars in the Balkans to stop men with ancient feuds from behaving badly. A new Bush administration would follow a different playbook.

This game plan was previewed in a *Foreign Affairs* article written by Rice, soon to be appointed as national security adviser. Rice's criticisms of the outgoing Clinton administration included a failure to set priorities by trying to "be all things to all people." A new Republican administration, she promised, would refocus the United States on the national interest rather than engaging in

Wilsonian pipe dreams, such as Clinton's "pursuit of, at best, illusory 'norms' of international behavior," which had reached "epidemic" proportions.

Rice promised that a new Republican administration would end the neglect of America's armed forces. The Clinton administration's misuse of the military produced "devastating" effects—"military readiness declined, training suffered . . . morale plummeted, and the services cannibalized existing equipment. . . . Moreover, the administration began deploying American forces abroad at a furious pace. . . . Means and missions were not matched and (predictably) the already thinly stretched armed forces came close to the breaking point." The result was "an extraordinary neglect of the fiduciary responsibilities of the commander in chief." Clinton's handling of the Kosovo war received withering scorn, as it was "conducted incompetently, in part because the administration's political goals kept shifting and in part because it was not, at the start, committed to the decisive use of military force." The key lessons to be learned from Clinton's misuse of the armed forces were that "if it is worth fighting for, you had better be prepared to win. Also, there must be a political game plan that will permit the withdrawal of our forces." Clinton's mistakes were not to be repeated: "The president must remember that the military . . . is not a civilian peace force. It is not a political referee. And it is most certainly not designed to build a civilian society."[67]

This playbook was thrown away after 9/11. George W. Bush was again reborn, this time as part Wilsonian idealist and part Terminator. New initiatives were required to protect against the viral threat of Islamic extremism. The new enemy could be within, requiring eternal vigilance and secret prying. External enemies were already in plain view, having secured safe havens in Afghanistan and Pakistan. They were in hiding elsewhere, making plans for spectacular funeral pyres.

President Bush emerged from the fire and anguish of 9/11 with a new mission: as a defender of the nation against Islamic extremists. Senator Henry Cabot Lodge once said of his nemesis, President Woodrow Wilson, "If he had been a soldier and a man of fighting temperament, the Government of the United States would have been in grave danger."[68] President George W. Bush did not serve on the battlefields of Vietnam, but he was most definitely a man of fighting temperament. With no tempering experience or feel for the world he was about to shake up, the nation girded for war. Preventive war is a deeply un-American military tradition. The public mood, as Bernard Brodie wrote during an earlier U.S. debate on this subject, "inclines to support really bold action only in response to great anger and great fright." Both were present in full measure after 9/11. "A decision for 'timely action,'" Brodie wrote, "would require an extraordinary, indeed almost boundless, degree of conviction and resolution on the part of the President."[69] President George W. Bush had such conviction and resolution. A new crusade was at hand.

The ethos of the moment was perfectly captured in the Bush administration's National Security Strategy, issued one year after the 9/11 attacks. The "America First," realism-based approach was tossed overboard, replaced by an ambitious agenda fired by missionary zeal. The battle against Islamic extremism was joined. The 2002 National Security Strategy was the foundation document for this crusade. A modest sampler:

- "These values of freedom are right and true for every person, in every society."
- The objective of U.S. national security strategy is "to create a balance of power that favors human freedom."
- "We will defend the peace by fighting terrorists and tyrants. We will preserve the peace by building good relations among the great powers. We will extend the peace by encouraging free and open societies on every continent."
- "America will act against such emerging threats before they are fully formed. . . . History will judge harshly those who saw this coming danger but failed to act."
- In the new world we have entered, "the only path to peace and security is the path of action."
- We will defend America "by identifying and destroying the threat before it reaches our borders."
- "This strategy will turn adversity into opportunity."[70]

These passages fused George W. Bush's true belief and unfamiliarity with far-off places with Cheney's and Rumsfeld's comfort with the raw exercise of American power. The resulting high-octane mix of transformational zeal and hyperrealism was unique in the annals of U.S. national security policy. The immediate fixation was Afghanistan, where al Qaeda and the Taliban needed to be routed. The next fixation was Iraq—a war that would have been inconceivable had there not been surprise attacks against emblematic targets on American soil.

The administration's hyperrealism was expressed in deep skepticism about the ability of multilateral institutions and traditional diplomacy to turn back threats posed by the most deadly weapons in the most dangerous hands. Its transformational zeal was applied to hugely ambitious projects, most notably the remaking of Iraq, which was subsequently defended in more grandiose terms as a remaking and democratization of the greater Middle East. Niccolo Machiavelli wrote in *The Prince* that "nothing is more difficult to plan, more doubtful of success, nor more dangerous to manage than the creating of a new order of things."[71] Bush, Cheney, and Rumsfeld were more ambitious than Machiavelli.

President Bush and his closest advisers believed deeply that bold maneuvers must not be compromised by the fainthearted or by cautious bureaucrats, naysayers, and second-guessers. This leadership team did not occupy their posts during a time of crisis to fiddle at the margins of momentous events. To shape the future, they were prepared to seize the initiative, accept the slings and arrows of critics, and await history's verdict. They acted on an unshakable determination that they, and not their sworn enemies, would dictate the terms of engagement in a war worthy of America's blood and treasure. In their view, the essence of leadership in trying times was the fait accompli.

This mix of hyperrealism and transformational zeal may seem mutually exclusive, or at least contradictory. Can it be possible for U.S. leaders to be hyperrealistic and extraordinarily idealistic at the same time? Actually, American national security policy has long reflected both impulses, although rarely to such an extent and never concurrently. The Bush administration managed this merger by refusing to allow its deep skepticism about traditional diplomacy and multilateral institutions to result in a sense of defeatism, which was a totally unacceptable response to the challenges America faced. Instead, the administration's inner circle resolved to choose heroic initiatives to defeat evil, promote freedom, and remake the world from a position of unparalleled strength. The radical concept of a preventive war against Iraq could be executed only in the context of the post-9/11 belief that half-measures against presumed existential threats were insufficient and that profoundly difficult choices were required to avoid calamity. It was better to be safe than sorry. This confluence of men and moment resulted, quite paradoxically, in the most powerful nation in the world rejecting, rather than seeking to affirm, the status quo.[72]

After routing the Taliban and al Qaeda leadership, the Bush administration's inner circle turned its full attention to a military campaign against Saddam Hussein. This fateful choice was rooted in the unfinished business of the past, and it was about to mortgage the future. During the first American war against Saddam Hussein, President George H. W. Bush and his closest advisers decided not to follow up the rout of Iraqi troops by overrunning Baghdad and bringing the dictator to justice. When asked about this decision, then secretary of defense Dick Cheney responded that toppling Hussein was not worth the cost.

> Because if we'd gone to Baghdad we would have been all alone. There wouldn't have been anybody else with us. There would have been a U.S. occupation of Iraq. None of the Arab forces that were willing to fight with us in Kuwait were willing to invade Iraq. Once you got to Iraq and took it over, took down Saddam Hussein's government, then what are you going to put in its place? That's a very volatile part of the world, and if you take down the central government of Iraq, you could very easily end up seeing pieces of Iraq fly off: part of it, the Syrians would like to have to the west, part of it—eastern Iraq—the Iranians would like to claim, they fought over it for eight years. In the north you've got the Kurds, and if the Kurds spin loose and join with the Kurds in Turkey, then you threaten the territorial integrity of Turkey. It's a quagmire if you go that far and try to take over Iraq. The other thing was casualties. Everyone was impressed with the fact we were able to do our job with as few casualties as we had. But for the 146 Americans killed in action, and for their families—it wasn't a cheap war. And the question for the president, in terms of whether or not we went on to Baghdad, took additional casualties in an effort to get Saddam Hussein, was how many additional dead Americans is Saddam worth? Our judgment was, not very many, and I think we got it right.[73]

The attacks on 9/11 clearly altered Cheney's balance sheet. Saddam Hussein remained quite capable of reconstituting his weapons of mass destruction and creating havoc for U.S. interests in the Middle East. Although he had no record of doing so in the past, he could also provide these instruments of mass death to Islamic extremists. Sanctions were eroding. The younger President Bush resolved to finish the job that his father started but failed to complete.

Bush chose Colin Powell as secretary of state to handle the disquiet of allies. Powell was peripheral to decisions of war and peace, which revolved around Cheney and Rumsfeld, the musclemen Bush chose to help him exercise raw power. Rumsfeld—famously known for asking countless questions of underlings—appears to have not asked the right ones, or at least he accepted faulty answers, in the run-up to the second U.S. war against Saddam Hussein. How much persuasion Bush needed, or whether the president needed any persuasion at all, has yet to be clarified by first-person accounts and early chroniclers of the Bush presidency. What does seem evident from the first drafts of history that have thus far appeared is that there were no searching National Security Council deliberations on whether to fight America's first preventive war against proliferation. It also appears that Secretary of State Powell, believing that the die was already cast, never made a sustained case against a preventive war in the Middle East or laid out in brutal detail the downside risks of going to war.[74]

The White House did not ask the U.S. intelligence community too many difficult questions about the upcoming Iraq campaign, and the CIA did not volunteer very many unpleasant answers. The director of central intelligence, George Tenet, records no effort in his memoirs about trying to speak directly to the president or the National Security Council about his agency's findings of the most likely postinvasion consequences in Iraq.[75] These findings, which were mostly prescient, were prepared late in the run-up to war, just two months before the onset of hostilities. The request for this critical evaluation came not from the White House or from the CIA director but from the director of policy planning at the State Department.[76] This telling estimate was buried in other war-planning material sent to the White House.[77] The intelligence community's prewar assessments of Iraqi weapons of mass destruction capabilities that proved to be so faulty were also generated by outside requests—this time from Capitol Hill.[78]

Never has a more consequential White House decision been made with less vetting. No senior officials placed their bodies before this moving train, and no serious political capital was expended to try to stop a decision that was implicitly made without debate by the National Security Council. No one of consequence forced an unpleasant weighing of downside risks against the rosy scenarios in Bush's truncated war cabinet.

The absence of a systematic weighing of pros and cons by Bush's National Security Council was crucial because Congress, still reeling from the 9/11 attacks, would have consented by large majorities to virtually any plan of action the president proposed to punish those labeled as a grave and gathering danger to the country. Few media outlets raised red flags about the course of action the president appeared set on or about the supporting evidence that was offered to justify a preventive war.[79] A sufficiently persuasive case could be made for Hussein's removal, given the anxieties and hubris of the moment and the abdication of responsibility within the executive branch, Congress, media outlets, and senior military officers.[80]

The Bush administration's transformational zeal ran roughshod over careful planning. Force requirements necessary for an invasion and occupation were whittled down by the Pentagon's supremely confident leadership team of Rumsfeld and his deputy, Paul Wolfowitz, and whittled down further by a balky ally, Turkey. Few members of Congress read the intelligence documents on which the war was prosecuted, and fewer still questioned them before authorizing the use of force in Iraq. The handful of senators and representatives who absorbed these intelligence reports were constrained to speak about them publicly because of their classification.

On October 10, 2002, 296 members of the House of Representatives consented to President Bush's impending war against Iraq. In the wee hours of the following day, seventy-seven senators provided similar consent. Public anxieties gave license to action. Analogies to Munich and warnings of waiting too long to deal with gathering dangers, including the prospect of a mushroom cloud on U.S. soil, sealed the outcome. Many Democrats voted against authorizing the first war against Saddam Hussein, warning of a quagmire, only to be proven decisively wrong by America's armed forces. Few wished to be on the wrong side of history the second time around, especially those in Congress with national political ambitions. Capitol Hill was painfully late in recognizing the dangers posed by Nazi Germany: The Selective Service Act imposing a draft proposed by President Franklin Delano Roosevelt in the summer of 1941 passed Congress by a single vote. Capitol Hill would not be caught napping this time around—not after surprise attacks on U.S. soil.

Cold, hard logic, based on Saddam Hussein's previous use of chemical weapons, his prior quest for nuclear weapons, and his need for weapons of mass destruction to deter another U.S. invasion, led most to assume that he was flouting United Nations inspections for good reason. Cold, hard logic, alas, did not take into account the dysfunction, intrigue, and deception of Hussein's regime. The Bush administration was also extraordinarily adept at framing policy choices. International sanctions against Hussein did not appear to be sustainable. The buildup of U.S. forces around Iraq's borders was well under way when Congress was asked to vote on authorizing war. To insist on climbing back down from the Bush administration's choreography for war could have emboldened Hussein, weakened the confidence of U.S. friends and allies in the region, and invited more trouble down the road. The administration succeeded in placing members of Congress and concerned citizens between a rock and a hard place.

Buyers' remorse has subsequently fallen hard on Capitol Hill and in more than two out of three homes across the United States. Being safe rather than sorry in Iraq has generated lasting sorrows. A succession of poor decisions has yielded only bad choices with painful outcomes. America's ground forces have been badly worn down. They were sent initially into battle on false premises and faulty intelligence. They were deployed understrength, with woefully insufficient diplomatic and military backup. They were resent into battle for two, three, and four tours of duty to keep a fractious foreign land from dissolving into chaos. The mission of victory evolved into the mission of staying long enough to avoid a far worse bloodbath and to prevent Iraq from becoming a safe haven for those planning massive attacks on American soil.

U.S. forces were quite capable of ending Hussein's brutal regime and completely unsuited for the mission that would inevitably follow. It is usually appropriate for visitors in much of the Islamic world to take off their shoes before entering someone's home. Soldiers on patrol in sullen neighborhoods, however, needed their combat boots to kick down doors. They were the same troops that the Bush administration was asking to win over hearts and minds, an elusive goal attempted earlier in the Vietnam War.

The Bush administration's fusion of missionary zeal and power projection could only be transitory. Domestic politics in the United States and alliance politics among free nations cannot sustain faits accomplis of this magnitude, especially ones that are executed badly. By 2006, America's armed forces were nearly broken (to use Colin Powell's characterization) by the Iraq project.[81] Too few soldiers had been asked to do far too much. The sobering historical truth, since relearned by the Bush administration, is that foreign military forces labeled as occupiers have not compiled good track records of transforming the Arab world.

The pursuit of heroic measures by politically divisive and preemptory means does not work very well for very long in American politics, especially on matters of war and peace. A Republican administration that goes places where traditional conservatives fear to tread established the conditions of its own demise. Traditional conservatism abhors transformational zeal and would not attempt to construct grand new architectures of this sort—at least not until something better than the existing order was clearly within reach. But the George W. Bush administration was anything but traditional or conservative— at least as measured by the yardsticks of deficits, limited government, separation of church and state, protecting personal privacy, or the remaking of the international system. Domestic support for the Iraq project began to unravel when its burdens on U.S. servicemen and women became clear. The toppling of Saddam Hussein did not justify their losses, grievous injuries, and the hidden scars—as well as the public expenditure of $800 billion to $1.2 trillion.[82] An ill-conceived and ill-executed war was unworthy of such great sacrifice.

THE SPECTER OF NUCLEAR TERRORISM

The U.S. military campaigns in Afghanistan and Iraq—one essential, the other unwise—provided Osama bin Laden with his recruits, the sacrificial bodies for his guerrilla war against the United States and its allies in the Islamic world. Some of these angry young men might become nuclear terrorists. Databases of theft and diversion from nuclear facilities reflect successful detective work; failures will not become apparent until dreaded acts occur. And yet, almost two decades after the dissolution of the Soviet Union, there has not been an act of nuclear terrorism.

There are several reasons that nuclear nightmares have not yet occurred. Nuclear weapons are the crown jewels of national nuclear programs, and crown jewels are usually not for sale. Because of cooperative threat reduction initiatives, dangerous weapons and materials are better protected. Acquiring them, even with insider help, is extremely difficult. Even if nuclear weapons can be purchased, they might well have disabling devices to prevent unauthorized use. Acquiring highly enriched uranium is easier than buying a nuclear weapon. The elementary designs needed to turn highly enriched uranium into a mushroom cloud are accessible, but recruiting a team with the requisite skills to execute this assembly is far from simple and could provide telltale signs for intelligence agencies.[83]

Acquiring the radiological material needed for crude dirty bombs is well within the capability of terrorist networks. These devices will not kill as many innocents as massive conventional explosions, but they could still have profound psychological effects. Perhaps the reason that dirty bombs have not yet been used is that extremist groups have demonstrated all too often that they can create havoc and destruction by means of conventional explosives, car bombs, and hijacked airliners without having to resort to radiological warfare.

Other reasons for the absence of nuclear nightmares since the Soviet Union collapsed include heroic counterintelligence efforts by national authorities. With the A. Q. Khan network broken up, there may also be a dearth of middlemen with the means to provide terrorist groups with nuclear assistance. Plain dumb luck and divine intervention may also be explanatory factors. For whatever combination of reasons, the absence of significant acts of nuclear terrorism thus far in the second nuclear age gives reason to hope that, with sound policies and relentless effort, this successful track record can be extended.

Only fools would be complacent about existing nuclear dangers. Despite impressive gains in cooperative threat reduction efforts in the former Soviet Union, there is still much work to do. A mid-2006 survey of cooperative threat reduction efforts in the former Soviet Union concluded that comprehensive upgrades had been completed for slightly more than half the buildings housing weapons-usable nuclear material.[84] Of the $20 billion pledged by the eight industrialized nations at their June 2002 summit to assist with cooperative threat reduction programs, less than 20 percent of this amount had actually been spent four years later.[85]

Enough fissile material remains in Russia to produce approximately 40,000 nuclear weapons. At current rates, U.S. efforts to secure bomb-making materials there and elsewhere could take between fifteen and twenty-five years.[86] In the decade before 9/11, cooperative threat reduction programs that locked down dangerous weapons and materials received modest increases in funding, but their funding remained a pittance compared to the Pentagon's budget: By 2007, the Bush administration was spending the equivalent of one year's worth of funding on cooperative threat reduction programs in three days of military operations in Iraq.[87] A distinguished bipartisan panel led by former senator Howard Baker and presidential adviser Lloyd Cutler recommended that a sum of $30 billion over a period of eight to ten years would be an appropriate amount to prevent the misuse of deadly weapons and materials—"the most urgent unmet security threat to the United States."[88] This amounts to a four- or fivefold increase in annual funding for cooperative threat reduction programs.

THE END OF THE SECOND NUCLEAR AGE?

How long will the second nuclear age last? Given that the first two nuclear ages began with severe shocks, it might be best to avoid a third nuclear age. Of course, the next severe discontinuity could be positive rather than negative. The demise of the Soviet Union, which initiated the second nuclear age, had extremely positive ramifications for those suffocating under the heavy red cloak of Communism. But a new set of nuclear dangers accompanied this welcome event, dangers that have not gone away and that could erupt at any time. Even positive epochal events have crosscutting negative ramifications.

The next epochal event is more likely to be negative than positive. The most worrisome game-changing nuclear developments that could usher in a third nuclear age are considered in the next chapter. These include the third use of a nuclear weapon by a state at war, the use of a nuclear weapon by an extremist group, the first use of radiological weapons or dirty bombs that prompts copycat attacks, the resumption of nuclear testing by many states, and the demise of the global system of proliferation controls, to which these acts would be major contributors. Measured against these developments, a continuation of the second nuclear age is to be welcomed—but not if it continues to be marked by sparring among major powers, the progressive hollowing out of the Nonproliferation Treaty, widespread hedging strategies by states that fear the nuclear ambitions of their neighbors, and surreptitious nuclear transfers to extremist groups.

The second nuclear age need not be marked by these trends. Brighter scenarios are also possible, ones in which relations among major powers are repaired and the nuclear weapon program of Iran can be checked, as may now be the case in North Korea. Cooperative threat reduction programs can be more generously funded and accelerated. No new mushroom clouds need appear in the nuclear future, and acts of nuclear terrorism can be foiled or averted. The future is not foreordained at this troubling juncture.

5 ALTERNATIVE NUCLEAR FUTURES

TREND LINES have shaped the nuclear past and will shape the nuclear future as well. But trend lines are usually set by major events, and major events usually have crosscutting effects. The use of atomic weapons to end World War II, the appearance of the H-bomb, close calls such as the Cuban missile crisis, and other game-changing events such as the dissolution of the Soviet Union generated countervailing impulses to control the atom and to build bombs. Just as the shift from the first to the second nuclear age entailed the shedding of old worries and the accumulation of new ones, whatever the future holds, it is reasonable to expect more addition and subtraction.

Alternative nuclear futures do not occur in a vacuum or by happenstance. Nor can the future be masterfully engineered by deliberate choice. Game-changing events can waylay the best made plans. Serendipity—as well as misfortune—happens. Whether the net effect of game-changing events is negative or positive depends on the nature of the event and on how national leaders and their publics react to it. These reactions, in turn, will be shaped not just by the shock of the new but also by the political context that precedes major headline events. This is especially true when both positive and negative trends occur concurrently. If the preceding political context to a headline event is generally positive, the probability increases that negative consequences will be contained and that the net effect of the event will be positive. If the preceding context is negative, the headline event will likely accelerate negative trends.

For example, dreadful acts of terrorism occur in Pakistan and India. Escalation is most likely to result in periods of deteriorating bilateral relations, in

the context of high infiltration rates across the Kashmir divide and prior in-
cidences of terrorism. If a headline act of terrorism occurs in the context of a
deep crisis or border skirmishing, it can generate military mobilizations. Triggering events could include an act of nuclear terrorism involving a dirty bomb,
attacks with conventional explosives in city centers that produce mass casualties, or explosions at highly symbolic national monuments or religious shrines.
The more egregious the triggering event, the greater the likelihood of escalation. The most escalatory event of all would be an act of terror that produces a
mushroom cloud. If, however, a headline act of terrorism occurs when national
leaders are working hard to improve bilateral relations and are making progress
in pursuit of a Kashmir settlement, there is a reasonable chance that leaders will
seek to redouble their efforts, or at least insulate the process of reconciliation
from those who seek to reverse it.[1]

Trends can build imperceptibly at first and unmistakably over time. Headline
events can accentuate these trends, slow them down, or reverse them. Change
entails positive as well as negative elements. Opportunity can flow from misfortune, or opportunity can encourage hubris. Choice matters, especially when
nations are confronted with game-changing events. It is easier to predict major
events—at least in generic form—than it is to forecast their net consequences.
In this chapter I briefly summarize countervailing trends and then move on to
major events that could well arise, the fulcrums on which the nuclear future
may turn. Constructive actions now and in the years ahead—or sins of omis-
sion and commission—will shape the trend lines that follow, for good or ill.

This is, of course, a speculative exercise. The great difficulty in following
George Santayana's famous dictum about being condemned to repeat history is
determining which lessons among the large menu of choices bear remember-
ing. Our shared nuclear history will assuredly shape future choices, but as Bernard Brodie once observed, "The phrase 'history proves' usually signals poor
logic and worse history."[2] Brodie, a military historian who became one of the
first, and perhaps the best, thinker about the Bomb, warned that "history is at
best an imperfect guide to the future, but when imperfectly understood and
interpreted it is a menace to sound judgment."[3] International relations theorist
Kenneth N. Waltz also suggests caution in this regard: "History," he wrote, "tells
us only what we want to know."[4]

Unpleasant as well as pleasant surprises happen in life, and it would be quite
extraordinary if they did not apply to the Bomb as well. Some big events make
sense in retrospect but still come as surprises. Continuities can accumulate to

the tipping point where they produce significant discontinuities. Sound analysis and common sense suggest that every act of proliferation has unique aspects, but every new aspect of proliferation also connects in some fashion to some preceding step. One proliferation problem can lead to the next, and as the problem becomes more complex, it also becomes less predictable and less manageable.

The flip side of this process could also apply: One wise decision or fortunate development can lead to the next, and the scope of the proliferation dangers can progressively contract. Wise decisions that produce fortunate consequences may also produce only temporary relief from proliferation problems, but buying time in the nuclear business can often be considered a victory. For example, by belatedly working with North Korea to suspend and dismantle its nuclear programs, the George W. Bush administration has improved prospects for nonproliferation in East Asia.

TREND LINES

The most positive trends of the second nuclear age are that the nuclear taboo continues to hold and that nuclear weapons are decreasingly useful for major powers. Several indicators point to the growing military disutility of nuclear weapons for major powers, beginning with continued reductions in the nuclear inventories of the United States and Russia. This measure of declining utility is not definitive because superpower arsenals were so overstocked during the cold war. A more compelling measurement that nuclear weapons provide less bang for the buck relates to nuclear testing. Russia last tested nuclear weapons in 1990, Great Britain in 1991, the United States in 1992, and France and China in 1996.[5] This prolonged hiatus does not mean that nuclear testing has ended forever, but it does suggest that national calculations regarding testing have shifted. The political fallout from resuming testing has remained high enough to override the lingering interests to do so within national nuclear enclaves. With the 1996 Comprehensive Test Ban Treaty in limbo, nuclear detonations have subsequently been confined to three states: India, Pakistan, and North Korea. The eight-year global testing moratorium between the Indian and Pakistani detonations in 1998 and the North Korean test in 2006 was the longest in the history of the Bomb. Whether this trend holds or folds will be a critical fulcrum for the nuclear future.

Another positive trend is that conventional military options are growing for major powers, which means that potential roles for nuclear weapons can continue to shrink. This trend is most advanced in the United States, which has added long-range conventional strike capabilities to nuclear war plans. As other major powers improve the accuracy and lethality of conventional strike options, they are likely to reinforce this trend.[6] With the passage of time since 1945, all major powers have shared the same fundamental calculations when considering the first use of the Bomb against an adversary: If used as a conscious choice against another nuclear-armed foe, this would invite horrific retaliation in kind. And if used against a far weaker foe, especially one that practices a different religion or wears a different skin color, the adverse political, diplomatic, and international consequences are likely to far outweigh presumed military benefits.

These considerations do not apply to the possible use of a nuclear weapon by a weak country against a major power or its use by freelancers and extremists. Nonetheless, the Bomb's declining utility for major powers—when the reverse was perceived as true during the first nuclear age—remains a significant positive trend.

The resilience of the global system to prevent proliferation, despite the occasional disregard by key stakeholders, attests to its fundamental importance. The multiple weaknesses of global arrangements to prevent nuclear proliferation are evident, but remedies remain within reach. No international regime to control dangerous weapons and materials has broader membership and more intrusive inspections. Major powers recognize how harmful the demise of this system would be, which has led to cooperation in difficult proliferation cases, especially with regard to North Korea and, to a lesser extent, Iran. The common recognition of the importance of the global nonproliferation system has also served to limit the extent to which major powers have sought exceptions to these rules. Most states that can export nuclear technology and fuel have formed a unique cartel whose purpose is to prevent profit taking when it would result in proliferation. States belonging to this nuclear suppliers group have agreed to make such decisions by consensus. A united front among suppliers has been crucial to preventing proliferation, because the most important cartel members stand to make the most profit if the rules of nuclear commerce are relaxed.

Positive developments in chemical nonproliferation have paralleled those in the nuclear field. The last use of chemical weapons in interstate conflict was in the 1980s, during the Iran-Iraq war.[7] Many countries have the ability to produce chemical weapons, and U.S. officials have testified that covert stockpiles are presumed to exist in Iran, North Korea, Syria, and China.[8] Russia, like the United States, is destroying cold war stocks of chemical weapons under international inspections. As with nuclear weapons, there are no guarantees against the next use of chemical weapons. This constraint is clearly weaker than the nuclear taboo, but revulsion against chemical warfare appears to be growing alongside the recognition that these weapons are not militarily useful for countries except to stop human wave assaults and to break localized stalemates on the battlefield.[9] In contrast, concerns over the prospective use of biological weapons are growing, and with good reason. Biological weapons can be harder to trace back to their source and can create large-scale loss of life.[10] Biological weapons are, however, hard to control on the battlefield, and their confirmed use by states would generate widespread revulsion. These constraints provide a basis to prevent a bleak future associated with the use of biological weapons.

Encouraging signs coexist with negative trends during the second nuclear age. The opportunities for the most dangerous weapons and materials falling into new hands remain great, and yet there have been no mushroom clouds or acts of nuclear terrorism—yet. Although good fortune could end quickly and repeatedly, it remains difficult for states and extremist groups to succeed in the multiple steps required to obtain the Bomb. The many skills and steps required to obtain nuclear weapons provide the basis for sound preventive strategies.

NEGATIVE DRIVERS

This decidedly mixed but far from pessimistic picture provides context for the headline events that can shape the nuclear future. Perhaps the easiest way to assess these drivers—and to prioritize preventive measures—is to identify the events that would produce the most harm if they were to occur. Conversely, identifying the most damaging drivers clarifies the most important positive steps that national leaders might take to reduce nuclear dangers. Because the context in which drivers occur is so mixed, crosscutting effects can be expected. Troubling events could generate positive reactions that contain damage and make worse events less likely. Alternatively, negative events could trigger more backsliding. A short list of negative, game-changing developments must therefore factor in the potential for even worse downstream consequences. In order of their potential damage to nonproliferation norms, rules, and treaties, my list of the nine worst drivers for a negative nuclear future is as follows:

1. The next use of a nuclear weapon in warfare between states
2. Failure to stop and reverse the Iranian and North Korean nuclear weapon programs
3. The breakdown and radical change of governance in Pakistan

4. The further spread of enrichment and reprocessing plants to nations that are hedging their bets and might want to be a "screwdriver's turn" away from the Bomb

5. Failure to lock down and properly safeguard dangerous weapons and nuclear materials that could be used for acts of terrorism

6. Acts of nuclear terrorism directed against states by extremist groups

7. The demise of international inspections and other nuclear monitoring arrangements

8. A resumption and cascade of nuclear weapon testing

9. Continued production of highly enriched uranium and plutonium for nuclear weapons

This list does not presume to be definitive, and good cases can no doubt be made for additions and reordering. The reasons for this particular list and its rank ordering follows.

The Next Mushroom Cloud

The biggest shock to global nonproliferation norms, rules, and treaties and the most likely prod to new proliferation would surely be the next use of a nuclear weapon on a battlefield. The next mushroom cloud could occur as a deliberate act of a desperate leader facing a crushing defeat or as a war-winning weapon against a foe without the means to respond in kind. A mushroom cloud could also result from a breakdown in command and control, where someone in a position of responsibility disregards orders and has the means or the connections to launch a nuclear weapon without authorization. Or a mushroom cloud could result from a terrible accident during a crisis or in wartime, when nuclear weapons are readied for possible use. When moved from vulnerable locations to positions where they are harder to find and presumably less subject to attack, nuclear weapons are more subject to Murphy's Law than in repose, where they are usually heavily protected. If a weapon were to detonate by accident during a period of intense crisis or during the outbreak of war, the causes of the detonation might be hard to determine. The nuclear forensics required to determine cause and ownership might be a difficult and lengthy undertaking. Political leaders possessing insufficient and unreliable information would be under severe pressure to take action, especially if the mushroom cloud were believed to be an act of sabotage or a deliberate strike by a nuclear-armed foe.[11]

Horrific wars, including wars that have not gone well for states possessing nuclear weapons against foes without the Bomb, continue to occur. And yet the taboo against the battlefield use of nuclear weapons has held since 1945. The importance of this taboo can best be appreciated by imagining what might happen if it were broken.[12] The immediate focus of world leaders would be the loss of life and damage resulting from the Bomb—as well as efforts to keep this detonation an isolated event. If the use of a nuclear weapon occurs between two nuclear-armed states, stopping detonations could be a tall order. Even a singular nuclear detonation could prod further proliferation if the user appears to benefit and if other states feel increasingly threatened as a result, thereby accelerating national strategies to obtain the Bomb.

If a nation uses the Bomb against a non-nuclear-weapon state, the load-bearing walls of the Nonproliferation Treaty could crumble. If a state benefited from a mushroom cloud, with the victim suing for peace, or could deflect severe consequences by threatening subsequent use, the global nonproliferation system's protections and incentives would be effectively nullified. Whether states withdraw from or remain affiliated with the Nonproliferation Treaty, they would likely place little reliance on its provisions. Many countries might then seek to become a screwdriver's turn away from possessing the Bomb.

Negative consequences might be contained if the user of nuclear weapons gains no benefit and suffers significant economic, political, and diplomatic penalties, but this outcome is far from assured. Under these circumstances, the next battlefield use of a nuclear weapon could also lead to renewed efforts to shore up the Nonproliferation Treaty. The surprise discovery of Saddam Hussein's advanced nuclear weapon program in 1991 had the effect of strengthening the International Atomic Energy Agency's inspection rights, but subsequent implementation has been spotty. Perhaps an actual detonation would lead to far more strenuous and long-lasting efforts by the international community at damage control and prevention, but there are ample grounds for skepticism about the ability of the Nonproliferation Treaty system to recover from such a blow.

The negative proliferation consequences of a small number of nuclear detonations between two warring states could be more containable, depending, in the first instance, on the ability of leaders to halt a nuclear war quickly. However, the chain of command would be under terrible pressures to use more nuclear weapons on the assumption that additional volleys from an adversary's nuclear arsenal would be arriving soon. Stopping a nuclear exchange after a few "demonstration shots" has long been part of the literature of nuclear deterrence and has always seemed more likely on the printed page than in the crucible and chaos of a nuclear battlefield.

It is possible that, if both victimized states possess and use the Bomb, the net effect of a small-scale nuclear exchange could conceivably be positive. States possessing the Bomb might then recommit to abolition and make more concerted efforts to draw down their arsenals. Treaties banning nuclear tests and the production of fissile material might receive a boost, and new steps might be taken to rethread the Nonproliferation Treaty's interlocking obligations for states with and without the Bomb. These positive steps depend, however, on what lessons are learned by key states about the horrific and nullifying consequences of the first nuclear exchange in world history.

States possessing the bomb could also learn contrary lessons from the first limited nuclear exchange in history. If mutual use led to the nullification of the Bomb's utility, other states possessing the Bomb might conclude that war-winning capabilities were needed; otherwise, the great expense and risks associated with nuclear weapons could not be justified. This response would result in an intensified nuclear arms competition. Larger stockpiles, new types of weapons, and more complex nuclear targeting plans could all result from the first nuclear exchange in history—all of which would damage the global structure of nonproliferation that depends, in part, on reducing the salience of the Bomb by shrinking existing arsenals and prohibiting new nuclear weapon tests.

The only time that nuclear weapons were used on the battlefield was to end a global war decisively and quickly. Their use in 1945 was against a nation on the brink of defeat that was not able to respond in kind. This historical experience generated both of the divergent scenarios suggested here—a strong impulse to ban the Bomb and a strong impulse to build bombs. Which of these two contrary scenarios would apply in the event of the first limited nuclear exchange in history? The first nuclear exchange, like the first use of nuclear weapons, would be likely to generate contrary impulses. The stronger impulse would depend on which set of anxieties associated with the Bomb—possession and possible use versus victimization and possible defeat—becomes paramount.

As dreadful as these scenarios are, they could be worse yet if the first nuclear exchange in history is uncontrolled. Many tens or perhaps far larger numbers of nuclear weapons could be used in war, the result of spasm attacks, the breakdown of command and control, or the stubborn execution of war plans. The proliferation consequences of worst-case scenarios become lost in a grim accounting of megadeath and planetary disaster. It would be difficult to identify the "winner" from such exchanges. Instead, the focus would be on the extent of loss. The two warring nations would be left to their own radioactive ruins, the breakdown of social order, and economic collapse. Other nations would try to fend as best they could against the global lethal hazards created by nuclear exchanges of this magnitude.[13] The cautionary lessons learned would, of course, be profound. But it would be rather late to learn them.

Iran and North Korea

Soon after the George W. Bush administration decided to topple Saddam Hussein, the outlook looked bleak that the North Korean and Iranian nuclear programs could be stopped or reversed. Both regimes were on the administration's "axis of evil" list, and both were widely expected to accelerate their nuclear programs as a deterrent to another U.S. attempt at regime change. Production of enriched uraniun did, indeed, follow in both countries, but worst-case predictions have yet to be realized. The Bush administration's delayed diplomatic engagement with North Korea, strongly supported by China, Russia, South Korea, and Japan, has resulted in the cessation of bomb-making material and the beginnings of dismantlement of the North Korean nuclear program. The situation in Iran appears to be far more problematic. According to a 2007 National Intelligence Estimate, Tehran's production of enriched uranium continues, but its work on producing nuclear warheads was suspended in 2003, "primarily in response to increasing international scrutiny and pressure resulting from exposure of Iran's previously undeclared nuclear work."[14]

The resumption of the Iranian nuclear weapon program could have profoundly negative proliferation consequences. The clash within Islam, and not the clash of civilizations, is the most troubling hinge for new proliferation. It is no coincidence that several neighbors of Iran, including Egypt, Jordan, Turkey, and the Gulf Cooperation Council, have developed a newfound interest in nuclear power plants and related infrastructure after the Iranian nuclear program became well developed.[15] These states are concerned about Iran's rising ambitions, its ability to foster discord within their Shia minorities, and America's reliability as an ally and protector in the aftermath of a searing occupation in Iraq. Iran remains in a stage of active rebellion against the status quo, providing financial and material support to well-armed extremist groups in Iraq, Lebanon, Syria, Afghanistan, and the Palestinian territories. Another complicating factor is that the Iranian nuclear program increases Israeli nuclear requirements, which in turn, raises the salience of the nuclear issue in the Arab world. Iran's nuclear ambitions also have to be a concern to neighboring Pakistan. The Pakistan-Iran border is one of the fault lines of the Sunni-Shia divide.

In contrast, the proliferation consequences of a breakdown in the dismantlement process for North Korea's bomb program are not nearly as consequential. U.S. ties with countries along North Korea's periphery are more solid than in the Middle East. North Korea does not have potential third columns in place in neighboring countries, and Pyongyang's ideological appeal to outsiders is nonexistent. Moreover, a well-developed multilateral contact group is working to engage the North Korean leadership to trade nuclear weapons for normal ties, financial support, and economic investment. If the terms of the deal struck in 2007 can be properly implemented, they will probably not become a source of domestic friction between groups contending for power in North Korea, as would likely be the case in Iran. The easiest (but far from easy) cases for reversing proliferation are in countries ruled by a maximal leader.

Why rank the Iranian proliferation case so high in this listing of negative structural impacts? Because, unless suspended or reversed, the Iranian case in particular is likely to generate pernicious second-order effects. Many countries will hedge their nuclear bets against Iran's ascendancy and the decline in America's standing in the Middle East. Another reason for such a high ranking comes from George H. Quester.

> Every additional country that comes into possession of nuclear weapons, whether a seemingly unstable and aggressive state or one that would act only in response, would pose the same concerns about whether they could settle into an enduring pattern of deterrence and non-use. Our concerns about this increased danger of nuclear weapons use thus forms a powerful argument for greater efforts to prevent nuclear weapons proliferation.[16]

Proliferation optimists might contest this assessment, on the assumption that, with the passage of time, nuclear weapons would invariably induce caution and restraint in Iran, as elsewhere.[17] This assumes a great deal, particularly that the proliferation consequences of the Iranian nuclear program would be limited. If, however, countries most concerned about Iran's nuclear ambitions lose confidence in America's security guarantees and its nuclear umbrella, proliferation might not be limited. Proliferation optimists also assume stabilizing results if other countries, such as Saudi Arabia and Turkey, take refuge in the Bomb as a result of Iran's nuclear program and a loss in confidence in the United States. The chain of proliferation within the Islamic world, however, is unlikely to end with Turkey and Saudi Arabia, which might seek protection from Pakistan's nuclear umbrella, thereby further complicating ties between Tehran and Islamabad.

The rosy scenarios of proliferation optimists also assume that limited wars, severe crises, and nuclear detonations can be avoided in the troubling passage between acquiring the Bomb and attaining its presumed stabilizing benefits. The last such passage, between India and Pakistan, included one limited war along a contested border, one ten-month standoff involving the mobilization of more than 1 million troops, and two other severe crises.[18] Similar passages associated with the Iranian nuclear program would provide severe tests for the global nonproliferation system. This structure has borne the weight of slow accretion of new nuclear weapon states in the past, partly because this weight has been offset by nonproliferation success stories. Successful proliferation by Iran, however, is unlikely to be accompanied by offsetting success stories and could well accelerate proliferation at a faster rate than the structure can withstand. Successful proliferation by key states in the Middle East and the Far East could well put proliferation optimists out of business.

Pakistan

Pakistan has been poorly governed for so long—both by military rulers and by civilians—that its demise has been repeatedly predicted. The nation's cadres of civil servants, its public education system, and its social services have progressively degraded. Political leadership in Pakistan has become a lifetime appointment; few business opportunities offer as much prospect of success as being an elected official. Growing areas in the country have become autonomous from central rule, not only the tribal belt adjacent to Afghanistan but also parts of Baluchistan and the North-West Frontier Province. Islamic extremism, once a favored tool of the Pakistan military to dislodge the Soviet Union from Afghanistan and to punish India across the Kashmir divide, has turned against the organs of the state. Acts of violence are on the rise in Pakistan and have been directed against former paymasters in the Pakistan military. National elections are rarely fair and usually do not produce representative governments.

Pakistan's strains have grown appreciably after the 9/11 attacks, when the ruling chief of army staff, Pervez Musharraf, abruptly turned against al Qaeda and repositioned his country as a U.S. ally in the war on terror. The Pakistan army's links to the Taliban are harder to sever. To do so would create rifts within the country's ethnic Pashtun population, which lives astride the border with Afghanistan, but to avoid doing so would create a wider rift with the United States. Musharraf did, however, engineer a quieting of the Kashmir divide. Pakistan's military leaders follow the precept that one inflamed border is manageable, but two borders in turmoil constitutes a severe threat to the state. Consequently, the army seeks to avoid severe crises with India, prompted by high rates of infiltration and acts of terror, while the Afghanistan border remains inflamed. Pakistan's military leadership also faces growing domestic discontent over Musharraf's extended stay in power. The army has not ruled the country well, and it is poorly trained, equipped, and led to counter extremist groups that engage in domestic violence.

Despite Pakistan's many weaknesses, the country has managed to hold together and its populace has been long-forbearing of misrule. Religious parties have historically received little more than 10 percent of the vote in relatively fair elections. Pakistan remains a rare example of an Islamic state in which the two largest political parties do not define themselves primarily in religious terms. Both parties, however, have suffered from the weaknesses of their leaders, Benazir Bhutto and Nawaz Sharif, who spent most of Musharraf's rule in foreign exile.[19]

Pakistan's multiple weaknesses have long raised concerns that it could suffer a massive upheaval from below, akin to the Iranian political revolution. Iran under the shah was also a secular, progressive Islamic state until its populace and religious leaders rebelled and engineered a toxic shift in national reorientation. The United States was poorly able to monitor and predict a revolution from below because its ties to Iranian society were from the top down. The same holds true for Pakistan: Washington is poorly situated to track bottom-up changes in Pakistani society that could result in a breakdown and radical change of governance in the country. U.S. concerns over the country's future stability has reinforced Washington's support for military rule, which, in turn, has accentuated the very trends that Washington fears most.

A breakdown and revolutionary change in Pakistan would be worse than in neighboring Iran in the sense that Pakistan already possesses nuclear weapons, a large standing army and security services with ties to Islamic extremists. If religious authorities assume positions of power, command and control arrangements within the army could fissure, and Pakistan's new Sunni leaders could clash with both Iran and India. For all these reasons, the demise of Pakistan might well warrant a higher ranking on my list of drivers leading toward a far bleaker nuclear future.

The ranking offered here is based on two calculations. First, the proliferation impacts of a nuclear-armed Iran would likely have greater cascade effects than the continued existence of a nuclear-armed Pakistan. Pakistan's two key neighbors, India and Iran, already possess or seek nuclear capabilities; a radicalized Pakistan would increase its neighbors' nuclear requirements, whereas an Iran that succeeded in obtaining the Bomb would likely generate more states seeking the Bomb as well as greater nuclear requirements by its neighbors. A second reason for listing Pakistan below Iran in my list of proliferation drivers is that the country's leaders have so far demonstrated a surprising ability to muddle through periodic crises. The most hard-core Islamic extremists have turned against their former handlers in Pakistan's military and security services, but they are in no position to take over the state. Acts of Muslim-on-Muslim violence, especially those that claim the lives of innocent bystanders, do not win hearts and minds. If the takeover threat by extremists is overblown, what developments in Pakistan would most threaten the safety and security of Pakistan's "crown jewels"? One possibility is a serious crisis or a military clash with neighboring India. Another is the breakdown of the unity of command within the Pakistan army.

When tensions rise precipitously with India, the readiness level of Pakistan's nuclear deterrent also rises. The dictates of deterrence mandate some movement of launchers and weapons from fixed locations during crises. Nuclear weapons on the move are inherently less secure than nuclear weapons at heavily guarded storage sites and are also more susceptible to insider security threats. If a crisis spills over into combat, the possibility of a mushroom cloud, whether by accident, a breakdown of command and control, or a deliberate top-down decision, cannot be discounted.

Pakistan's army reflects popular sentiment. It follows that, if national governments do not address popular grievances, those grievances will grow, including within the army. If national divisions widen, they will also widen within the military. The Pakistan army is a hierarchical institution; orders are given from the top down, and senior officers follow them. This unity of command is essential for nuclear security. It will be threatened by a prolonged period of turbulence and infighting among the country's president, prime minister, and army chief. The triangular jockeying for power in Pakistan isn't new. So far, it has led to poor governance, but not to breakdowns in the Pakistan army's unity of command.

The Spread of Enrichment and Reprocessing Capabilities

The further spread of fissile material enrichment and reprocessing facilities ranks fourth on my list of most consequential steps that could result in the demise of the global nonproliferation system. The Navajos who mined uranium in the Southwest and who suffered from its effects, called this substance the "yellow monster."[20] Its monstrous potential consequences are greatest when highly enriched. Enriched uranium is easily transportable. It is also extremely lethal, having produced the Bomb that destroyed Hiroshima. Plutonium is a darker and denser agent of mass destruction; once produced, it has a half-life of more than 24,000 years. Plutonium, the fissile material that fueled the Nagasaki bomb, has modest upsides; it is hard to handle, except in metallic form, an important safeguard against its diversion for acts of nuclear terrorism. And one isotope of plutonium is used to power long-distance space probes.

Producing these key ingredients, rather than stealing or buying them in quantities necessary for the Bomb, requires learning, blueprints, imports, many workers, and complex machines—telltale signs of nascent Bomb programs. Production also requires construction projects, some on a large scale, that are of great interest to countries with picture-taking satellites. There are enough clues associated with the industrial processes associated with the Bomb that gaining early warning of such intent is usually possible. One exception was Saddam Hussein's advanced nuclear program in the early 1990s, which escaped the notice of the U.S. intelligence community.

Uranium enrichment and plutonium reprocessing capabilities can also be used for nuclear power generation by states that seek complete independence from outside suppliers or hope that, one day, the technologies associated with a complete nuclear fuel cycle will prove to be cost-effective. These arguments have been suspect, because the costs of complete energy independence from foreign nuclear suppliers are exorbitant and because cost-efficient nuclear power has so far proved to be elusive. It has been less costly—and far better to ameliorate concerns over proliferation—to import nuclear fuel from outside suppliers than to build domestic enrichment or reprocessing capabilities, as the Russian Federation has proposed to Iran. When new states with few nuclear power plants insist on their own fuel cycles—especially states blessed with significant reserves of oil and natural gas—it is reasonable to assume that they have more than electricity generation in mind.

Heading off the Iranian enrichment program has been greatly complicated by tepid and pliable statements from the head of the International Atomic Energy Agency,[21] Iran's ability to create havoc in global energy markets, and the Bush administration's decisions to engage in a war of choice against Iraq and to offer India, a nonparty to the Nonproliferation Treaty, the benefits of nuclear commerce commensurate with being a "responsible state." The proposed U.S.-India civil nuclear cooperation agreement, which was characterized by India's External Affairs minister as the dismantlement of "technology denial regimes that have targeted India,"[22] came at a particularly awkward time, when Pakistan was entering a period of profound political crisis and when the administration was attempting to tighten the rules of nuclear commerce against Iran.

The Bush administration proposed an exemption to the rules of nuclear commerce to assist India's domestic power-generation needs. New Delhi has also sought access to foreign enrichment and reprocessing technologies as well as a "fuel bank" from foreign suppliers of sufficient quantity to guard against disruption in reactor operations. (The principal reason for disruption would be an Indian resumption of nuclear testing.) Because the Bush administration's primary interests in the agreement were to help forge a strategic partnership with India and to assist India in becoming a counterweight to China, few compensatory steps were asked of New Delhi in the civil nuclear cooperation agreement and fewer still were accepted. New Delhi has resisted any constraints on its strategic autonomy and nuclear options, including the cessation of fissile material production for weapons, and has declined to sign the treaty banning nuclear testing for all time. New Delhi also kept its distance from "coalitions of the willing" favored by the Bush administration, including the Proliferation Security Initiative and The Hague Code of Conduct designed to retard ballistic missile proliferation.

The Bush administration presumed that India's coalition government would welcome the civil nuclear cooperation agreement, but this deal was met with opposition from parties on both the left and the right of the political spectrum. The precedent that the administration sought to establish—that friendly states deserve a relaxation of the rules of nuclear commerce—invites further exceptions and the erosion of norms. As enrichment and reprocessing technologies spread, more nations will be a screwdriver's turn away from the Bomb or more able to enlarge their nuclear arsenals.

Safeguarding Nuclear Materials That Can Be Used in Acts of Nuclear Terrorism

Acts of nuclear terrorism were unlikely during the first nuclear age when concerns over the use of nuclear weapons were state focused. During the second nuclear age, nonstate actors have become agents and seekers of proliferation.

Entrepreneurs such as A. Q. Khan and his cohort have highlighted the harm that can result from covert nuclear supply networks. The preferred customers of Khan's network were states, not freelancers, but some Pakistani nuclear officials also had conversations with key members of al Qaeda and the Taliban.[23]

The first act of nuclear terrorism would be a headline event. The perpetrators are likely to have connections to government officials working within nuclear complexes in states that have loose security arrangements or insider threats. States, not freelancers or extremist groups, have the industrial capacity and skills required to produce enriched uranium and to reprocess plutonium. Those who seek shortcuts to the Bomb or to nuclear terrorism will direct their attention to existing stockpiles. Prevention strategies must therefore focus on locking down highly enriched uranium and plutonium and stopping further production.

Officially sanctioned transfers of bomb-making material and nuclear weapons cannot be ruled out but seem unlikely. The inflated 2002 U.S. intelligence community threat estimate of Saddam Hussein's Iraq did not consider him likely to transfer weapons of mass destruction, unless he was under attack and about to be deposed: Despots do not typically hand off deadly weapons to those they cannot control.[24] Bomb-making materials and the weapons into which they are inserted are considered the crown jewels of the state. Unlike blueprints and spare parts, they are likely to be well guarded and nontransferable—at least under normal circumstances. Nuclear weapons in storage are typically protected by multiple gates, regular patrols, and by various sensors that provide warning of unusual activity. However, facilities that are buttoned down against external threats might still be susceptible to insiders—plant workers, guards, and officials in positions of trust at nuclear agencies who can collude with outsiders.

Guardians at nuclear facilities need to be worthy of their security clearances and sufficiently independent of bomb makers to provide proper oversight. Before the government of Pakistan revamped its security practices at nuclear facilities beginning in 2000, A. Q. Khan had a great deal to say about who was responsible for plant security at his own laboratories.[25] U.S. ties with Pakistan were deeply frayed from 1989 to 2001, when Washington imposed sanctions because of Pakistan's nuclear program. During this period, providing U.S. nuclear security assistance to Pakistan was inconceivable.

The Nonproliferation Treaty contains strictures against transferring technologies for improved nuclear safety to states that are not parties to the treaty.

Prevention strategies against nuclear terrorism require that these strictures are not interpreted so tightly that they preclude the sharing of best practices and lessons learned for improved security at sensitive sites. In the immediate aftermath of 9/11, even after Musharraf cut ties with the Taliban leadership in Afghanistan and viewed al Qaeda as a domestic threat, U.S. offers of assistance to help improve security for Pakistan's nuclear weapons and bomb-making material were still viewed with deep mistrust. Over time, U.S. offers of assistance for personnel reliability programs were accepted, but offers of "permissive action links" that would guard against unauthorized use or a breakdown in command and control were not.[26]

Locking down bomb-making material and down-blending highly enriched uranium for research reactors and naval nuclear programs are key priorities for cooperative threat reduction programs. Lesser acts of nuclear terrorism involving radiological materials such as cobalt-60, which is used in cancer treatments, and cesium-137, which is used in industrial and drilling gauges, can also be used to terrorize city dwellers. Preventing the theft and misuse of radiological materials that could produce dirty bombs but not mushroom clouds is a huge undertaking. Cooperative threat reduction programs have expanded to address these threats, but considerable work still needs to be done.

One scenario that has not received much attention is an act of nuclear terrorism during a period of intense crisis, especially a crisis between two nuclear-armed states. If an extremist group is estranged from one or both governments, it might well see opportunity in sparking a war between them. Under these circumstances a radiological weapon need not cause great damage to have profoundly destabilizing effects, especially if the target of the attack has great symbolic, cultural, religious, or economic value. This scenario seems most applicable to India and Pakistan but could extend to other countries in the future.[27]

The structural damage to the global nonproliferation system resulting from acts of nuclear terrorism could vary greatly. The most crucial distinction is between nuclear bombs that produce mushroom clouds and dirty bombs that spread radioactive material. One is a weapon of mass destruction, the other a weapon of mass disruption. Both events would break taboos. The appearance of either one could spark unintended escalation and, in the case of dirty bombs, copycat attacks by freelancers. The first act of nuclear terrorism might well generate more concerted international efforts to lock down dangerous weapons and materials. Bureaucratic, legal, economic, and political constraints that have interfered with progress on cooperative threat reduction initiatives would then seem petty and unreasonable. Positive—or negative—repercussions could be reinforced if one act of nuclear terrorism leads to the next.

The Demise of Inspections

Decades of patient effort to open up sensitive sites to foreign inspectors have resulted in widespread international inspections that have not yet become global norms. During the first nuclear age, states with smaller nuclear arsenals resisted intrusive inspections. The George W. Bush administration raised the danger that the pioneers of intrusive inspections—Washington and Moscow—may join them.

During the formative years of the cold war, the notion of inspections was a pipe dream. Lack of trust killed early efforts to create international disarmament mechanisms in the 1940s. The first serious efforts to negotiate restraints on nuclear testing in the 1950s were also foiled by disagreements over inspections. President Kennedy thought he might be able to convince the Senate to consent to a comprehensive nuclear test ban treaty in 1963 if Premier Khrushchev could accept five inspections annually. Khrushchev's limit was three. A partial test ban treaty—absent inspections—followed that drove testing underground.[28] The first strategic arms limitation accords in 1972 were troubled by accusations that their limits could not be verified. On-site inspections were still beyond the pale, so both superpowers agreed to check each other's behavior remotely by using "national technical means," a euphemism for spy satellites.

It took four full decades for the Soviet Union's hypersensitivity to foreign inspections to ease up. The first breakthrough occurred in Stockholm in 1986 at a European forum to ease tensions and build confidence. Western negotiators sought to implement the practice of providing annual calendars of military exercises, with foreign observers at exercises that involved sizable numbers of troops. Prospects for a breakthrough were not promising at the outset, when the long-standing foreign minister Andrei A. Gromyko repeated his decades-old complaint against inspections. They were, he announced in January 1984, merely an "an excuse to peek through the neighbor's fence."[29]

The Kremlin changed this tune under new management, when Mikhail Gorbachev was elevated to become general secretary of the Communist Party in March 1985. Gorbachev believed that the way to improve national security was to reduce superpower tensions. Four months after taking the reins, he met with the military high command to convey this message. One way to clarify that changes were in store and to break down enemy images was to accept on-site inspections.

The generals were reluctant to accept transparency not only out of habit but also because of concerns that inspections would reveal weaknesses. Aleksander Yakovlev, one of Gorbachev's key advisers, later recounted a conversation with one general who explained the military's reluctance in the following way: "We don't want to let them in not because they might see something there. We don't want to let them in because they would see that there's nothing there."[30]

Gorbachev overruled the generals. For the first time during the cold war, the Soviet Union provided prior notification in writing of its military exercises and was obliged to allow foreign observers—usually trained military attachés and others with intelligence backgrounds—to observe up to three exercises annually.[31] NATO countries accepted reciprocal obligations.

The 1986 Stockholm Accord opened the floodgates for intrusive inspections. President Reagan borrowed the Russian phrase "trust but verify" and made it his own, demanding openness as a condition for new arms reduction treaties. Gorbachev agreed. In 1987, the Intermediate-Range Nuclear Forces Treaty was signed. This accord mandated the complete dismantlement of 2,700 nuclear-tipped missiles and more than 5,000 other missile-related items. Over 850 inspections were carried out to monitor compliance: baseline visits to affirm data exchanges; monitoring at missile production facilities; visits to confirm the elimination of items mandated by the treaty and the "close out" of bases, missile support, and production facilities; and short-notice inspections.[32] These inspection provisions expired in 2001.

A treaty reducing conventional forces in Europe negotiated in 1990 contained extensive inspection rights.[33] More than 4,000 on-site inspections have been carried out at military units, storage sites, and repair and training facilities, and much equipment has been destroyed, as mandated by treaty provisions.[34] In 1991, the first Strategic Arms Reduction Treaty (START) was negotiated, which applied the Intermediate-Range Nuclear Forces Treaty's intrusive inspections to longer-range missiles and bombers. START mandated fourteen types of inspections, including visits to gather and update data and to eyeball production facilities, suspect sites, and deployment areas.[35] Mandatory intrusive inspections became an integral part of superpower and NATO–Warsaw Pact relations and part of the security architecture extending from the Atlantic to the Urals, including neutral and nonaligned European states.[36]

The International Atomic Energy Agency began to implement quite polite and not very intrusive inspections at nuclear facilities while the two superpowers sparred over tougher inspections. By the late 1980s, the superpowers took the lead, setting standards of intrusive inspections for other states to follow. The International Atomic Energy Agency had some catching up to do. The deficiencies of its relaxed procedures—where inspectors were permitted to visit only those rooms in particular facilities deemed acceptable by host countries—became evident after the first U.S.-Iraq war, with the belated discovery of Saddam Hussein's advanced bomb program.

The International Atomic Energy Agency then tightened its monitoring procedures, permitting its inspectors far greater leeway to open doors and take samples in countries pledging abstinence. It carried out 2,142 safeguards inspections in 2005.[37] Inspections have become a global phenomenon, but most remain rudimentary. Norm setting for intrusive challenge inspections continues to be a slow process. Only half of the Agency's 156 member states have ratified the protocol requiring stricter inspections that was devised after discovering Saddam Hussein's hidden nuclear weapon program.[38] And five states with nuclear weapons—China, Great Britain, France, India, and Pakistan—continue to resist inspections at military-related nuclear facilities.

The Nonproliferation Treaty is no longer the only significant multilateral treaty monitored by inspections. In 1997, a treaty banning chemical weapons entered into force. The Organization for the Prohibition of Chemical Weapons, headquartered in The Hague, has conducted nearly 3,000 inspections—more than half at military facilities—in seventy-nine countries since its inception, including Pakistan and India.[39] These inspections suffer from serious limitations. The procedures for challenge inspections at suspect sites are cumbersome and have yet to be initiated, primarily because of concerns that the treaty's procedures would be weakened if tested.

What begins as a breakthrough can eventually become a habit and then a norm. Alternatively, good habits can be broken. During the second nuclear age, inspections have fallen out of favor in Washington and Moscow. Skeptics in the United States argue that bad actors will circumvent inspections and that responsible states do not need them. The U.S. Senate attached conditions to ratifying the Chemical Weapons Convention, stipulating that the president could reject challenge inspections on national security grounds and that key chemical by-products and waste streams would be exempt from inspections. Sampling these streams could provide telltale signs of violations, but they could also reveal trade secrets.[40] The U.S. Congress has also shortchanged the Comprehensive Test Ban Treaty Organization in Vienna, which is establishing an effective global network to monitor low-yield nuclear tests. This monitoring system proved its worth by identifying the North Korean nuclear test in 2006, which registered less than 1 kiloton.[41]

For different reasons, the administrations of George W. Bush and Vladimir Putin have sloughed off or threatened to pull out of cold war era treaties governing missile defenses and nuclear and conventional arms reductions. A day after President Bush announced the U.S. withdrawal from the Anti-Ballistic Missile Treaty in December 2001, Putin announced that Russia would no longer abide by the provisions of the second strategic arms reduction treaty signed in 1993. Intrusive inspections mandated by a treaty eliminating intermediate-range nuclear forces expired in 2001. Putin has threatened to pull out entirely from this treaty, and in July 2007, the Kremlin announced its intention to suspend its obligations under the 1990 treaty reducing conventional armaments in Europe.[42]

The sole remaining bilateral treaty governing strategic arms reduction that contains intrusive monitoring obligations is the 1991 Strategic Arms Reduction Treaty, whose provisions expire in December 2009. The most senior Bush administration official dealing with verification has opined that the treaty's intrusive monitoring provisions were "cumbersome" and "complicated," had outlived their usefulness, and were "no longer necessary."[43] Protections of monitoring satellites and provisions for inspections are also included in the 1990 treaty reducing conventional armaments in Europe and the 1987 Intermediate-Range Nuclear Forces Treaty, from which the Kremlin has threatened withdrawal.

The value of hard-won inspection rights might best be appreciated by contemplating their disappearance. Decades of work peeling off layers of secrecy would be reversed. Intrusive inspections were crucial in transforming relations between former adversaries and in building domestic support for treaties and cooperative threat reduction initiatives. They paved the way for limits on nuclear testing and deep cuts in nuclear forces and provided rare protections of satellites. Inspections help to hold up the load-bearing walls of the global nonproliferation system. As nations lose early warning and lose the trust that intrusive inspections provide, hedging strategies will gain traction.

Routine inspections have many virtues. Transparency provides baseline indicators of how seriously states take their treaty obligations as well as early warning signs of when they do not. Challenge inspections can be even more valuable. Information gleaned from challenge inspections, as well as information withheld, can yield indicators of troubling or unusual developments that require further investigation. Inspections can serve as a deterrent and as mechanisms to gain international support for penalties, as warranted.

The off-loading of inspections cannot be attributed to misplaced trust. Although it is true that George W. Bush initially declared that he had looked Vladimir Putin in the eye and into his soul and "found him to be very straight-forward and trustworthy,"[44] this judgment was surely revised over time. Nor can the denigration of intrusive inspections be rationalized by the need to move beyond the cold war and "the balance-of-terror policy framework."[45] Other rationales for sloughing off inspections relating to cost and complexity cannot be taken seriously. Inspections cost pennies compared to other defense requirements, and burdensome procedures can be simplified if needed. Nor is it convincing to belittle inspections when they are insufficient in the hardest cases. Tax collection systems do not always catch cheaters and drivers still break traffic rules, but this does not constitute grounds for tossing monitoring overboard. Norms are still needed to bring rule breakers into account, and developing a global norm of transparency is crucial to prevent proliferation and nuclear terrorism. Only in the field of arms control do critics find the inability to succeed in the hardest cases to be disabling.

There is no substantive basis for backtracking from intrusive monitoring, because trying to confine such activities to problem states does much damage to the development of a global norm. Perhaps the Bush administration's aversion to inspections reflects a broader rejection on ideological grounds of all things related to the arms control canon. Perhaps this is part of a larger plan to free up space warfare options by stripping monitoring satellites of treaty-based protections. Or perhaps the off-loading of bilateral inspections is part of the Bush administration's philosophy of maximizing freedom of action. For whatever reason, the continued denigration of intrusive inspections will result in a far more dangerous nuclear future.

Nuclear Testing and Fissile Material Production

Every test of a nuclear weapon is a declaration of the Bomb's power and an indirect attempt to gain leverage or influence. States on the receiving end of these messages are unlikely to remain passive. Therefore every nuclear test constitutes a link in the chain of either vertical or horizontal proliferation. During the first nuclear age, testing as a form of message sending was a common occurrence. Testing actually increased threefold after it was driven underground by the 1963 Limited Test Ban Treaty. On average, thirty-nine nuclear tests were carried out every year until 1996, when a comprehensive test ban treaty was completed over the resistance of nuclear weapon establishments in testing states.[46] A nineteen-month pause in testing followed, until it was broken by India and Pakistan. The longest testing moratorium in nuclear history then ensued, until North Korea carried out a test in 2006.

Public sentiment around the globe strongly opposes nuclear testing. This has led to a standoff with nuclear enclaves in states that oppose the entry into force of the Comprehensive Test Ban Treaty. Nuclear weapon establishments in the United States, Russia, China, India, Pakistan, and perhaps elsewhere would welcome the opportunity to test, but no country is eager to shoulder the burdens of breaking a global moratorium, and none wished to follow in North Korea's footsteps. If India were to break another moratorium, as in 1998, Pakistan would almost surely follow suit. If China were to break a moratorium, both India and Pakistan could well test again. And if the United States were to break a global moratorium, many countries would resume testing.

Unlike nuclear testing, no treaty prohibits the production of fissile material for bombs. Efforts to start negotiations, after decades of lip service, for a "cutoff" treaty run counter to the interests of the few remaining countries that perceive the need to produce more bomb-making material—Pakistan, India, Israel, and perhaps China. Israel's continued fissile material production likely reflects concerns over potential requirements in the event of a successful Iranian nuclear program that could presage greater interest in nuclear weapons elsewhere in the Middle East. China has never publicly declared a moratorium on fissile material production, which might suggest an interest in resuming production in the future.[47] India's requirements appear to be uncertain and open-ended, whereas Pakistan is undertaking an ambitious military-related nuclear agenda.

Continued production of bomb-making material by a few states would not appreciably change existing facts. In this sense, the net impact on the global nonproliferation system of continued fissile material production would arguably be marginal. At the same time, continued fissile material production by Israel, India, Pakistan, and perhaps China would result in larger arsenals and continued resistance to a cutoff treaty, which undermines the status quo in southern Asia and the Middle East. The combination of resumed nuclear testing alongside continued production of bomb-making material would compound damage to the global nonproliferation system.

PROLIFERATION DRIVERS

Negative drivers are not necessarily additive—otherwise, global proliferation would be far more advanced than is the case. Negative drivers can be sufficiently dreaded that national leaders and key states will seek countervailing preventive steps. Consequently, the list of negative drivers discussed here can remain on hold, can accelerate, or can be reversed, depending on the crosscutting consequences of significant events. Only the ninth item on this list of negative drivers—the production of bomb-making material—is presently an accomplished fact. Others items on this list could also become accomplished facts, but these outcomes have yet to be determined. Their negative consequences are sufficiently grave that countervailing preventive efforts have a chance of succeeding.

There is a long list of books and articles pointing to specific steps that might be taken to prevent negative drivers from occurring.[48] Obvious places to start include helping to ameliorate regional tensions that could lead to the next use of nuclear weapons, particularly between India and Pakistan, which have experienced a succession of hair-raising crises and one limited border war since acquiring the Bomb.[49] Lessening the prospects of a possible clash over Taiwan between the United States and the People's Republic of China would also help stabilize the nuclear future,[50] as would the extension of treaty arrangements governing nuclear arms reduction and on-site inspections between the United States and Russia.[51] There is no shortage of detailed prescriptions on preventing the most dangerous weapons and materials from falling into new hands[52] or for dealing with the Iranian and North Korean nuclear programs.[53]

In this chapter and the next I do not seek to replow this ground. Instead, in the pages that follow I investigate five alternative pathways to the nuclear future, and the keys to achieving or foreclosing these outcomes. The time frame for consideration here is one decade—a mere blip on the screen of the future events and choices. One reason for such a short excursion into the future is the degree of difficulty in looking further ahead. Another reason is based on the conviction that wise choices and fortunate happenstances over this time frame will extend favorable trends beyond predictive powers. The reverse is true for poor choices and unwelcome circumstances. Constructive movement, informed by vision, is the need of this hour, this day, this year, and this decade. In the last chapter I apply this philosophy to the key elements for a safe passage into the nuclear future.

ALTERNATIVE NUCLEAR FUTURE I: ABOLITION

The idea of abolishing nuclear weapons comes and goes in cycles, usually when external events evoke uncommon fear or present great opportunities.[54] There have been three prior waves of public interest in seeking nuclear disarmament; each wave has been successively less powerful. A fourth wave is now building. The first wave was strongest because it was generated by the biggest tremor—

the atomic bombing of Hiroshima and Nagasaki. The A-bomb constituted the most powerful threat then known to humankind, and an attack could come suddenly, for which there was no defense. Tellingly, the advent of hydrogen bombs of far greater destructive effect did not generate a powerful new wave of support for abolition, in part because the U.S.-Soviet divide seemed so intractable by the early 1950s.

In contrast, the A-bomb appeared at an optimistic time, when Nazi Germany and Imperial Japan were defeated, when there was hope for a peaceful world and the success of new international institutions. During this brief spring, the Acheson-Lilienthal plan to internationalize control of the atom was conceived. Winter came quickly, in the person of Josef Stalin and in the form of the iron curtain. The Acheson-Lilienthal plan was explicit about the risks involved in seeking to internationalize control of the atom, one of which was "the probable acceleration of the rate at which our present monopoly will disappear."[55] For those who assumed that the United States could compete effectively against the Soviet Union and that Stalin could not be trusted, this risk seemed more acceptable than the risks associated with abolishing nuclear weapons.

The second wave of nuclear abolition washed up on the Reagan administration, whose tough talk about prevailing in a nuclear war, building up nuclear arms, and early disinterest in negotiations stoked public anxieties. Scientific studies about the disastrous global effects resulting from extensive nuclear exchanges—the blockage of the sun from smoke and nitrous oxides spread by prevailing winds, causing a nuclear winter effect—lent momentum to the second abolitionist wave.[56] The most influential wave runner and voice of the second abolitionist movement was Jonathan Schell, who wrote two powerful books, *Fate of the Earth* and *The Abolition*, during this period.[57]

The second abolitionist wave was less powerful than the first for several reasons. To begin with, superpower nuclear arsenals were so large and animosities so great that abolition seemed far too daunting a task. Besides, the Kremlin walked out of nuclear negotiations in 1983, leaving no negotiating vehicle for deep cuts, let alone abolition. Public opposition to the Reagan administration's initiatives in the United States and Western Europe focused on freezing new nuclear force deployments in general and blocking new NATO missile deployments in particular. The Reagan administration then trumped the freeze movement by championing deep cuts in nuclear forces. Much to the surprise of his critics, President Reagan turned out to be the true leader of the second abolitionist movement.

In the 1980s, there were too many roadblocks for abolition to gain traction. Instead, the abolition paradox held firm: When abolition seems most imperative, it is also most difficult to achieve, and when progress seems most achievable, public interest wanes. The most dangerous stages of any arms competition are accompanied by intense political fears and dysfunctions that make abolition appear impractical. Conversely, when political conditions appear favorable, hugely ambitious undertakings seem less warranted and near-term concerns crowd out visionary pursuits. Once Ronald Reagan and Mikhail Gorbachev agreed to the 1987 Intermediate-Range Nuclear Forces Treaty, which abolished entire categories of nuclear-tipped missiles, the second abolitionist wave crested.

The third wave of interest in abolition—the weakest of all three—occurred after the Soviet Union dissolved. As in 1945, the world was reborn. During this hopeful time, radical possibilities could be entertained. With America's conventional power paramount, some veterans of the cold war argued that it made good sense for the United States to champion abolition. The Bomb was, after all, the only weapon that could do serious harm to the world's most powerful nation. Paramount nuclear security concerns now related to Russian weakness, not Soviet strength—all the more reason to press for abolition. The Henry L. Stimson Center enlisted General Andrew Goodpaster and a distinguished panel of national security experts, including Paul Nitze, to take a fresh look at the role of nuclear weapons in the post–cold war world.

These reports argued for a phased approach to abolition as a matter of national interest, identifying the security conditions required to move from one stage to the next. The Goodpaster-Nitze panel concluded, "Without a more radical approach to non-proliferation, the challenges posed to the non-proliferation regime can only mount over time, and the United States, eventually, is sure to face new nuclear threats."[58] The case for abolition was also made by international panels of experts convened by the Australian and Japanese governments. These reports stressed global security and moral considerations.[59]

Once again, the abolition paradox held firm. After the cold war ended, free nations raised their own flags around Russia's periphery, the security environment was much improved, important nations had other priorities, and abolition was not a priority.

A fourth abolitionist wave is now gaining strength. This wave is unusual because it is moving from the center outward. The leading advocates of abolition this time around—statesmen such as George Shultz, Sam Nunn, Henry Kissinger, William Perry, and Max Kampelman—have not swum in previous waves. The fourth wave is also different because it is powered by subtle slow-motion events rather than sharp external shocks. All abolitionist waves are driven by anticipatory dread. The sense of dread this time around derives from the erosion of global structures built to prevent proliferation and the possibility of a horrific act of nuclear terrorism. This wave is also different because it comes at a time when all major powers face common enemies of nuclear terrorism and the demise of the global nonproliferation system.

How might progress toward abolition occur? One scenario, by far the most welcome, would be the absence of significant negative drivers and the steady accumulation of positive trends, including nuclear arms reductions, the continued cessation of nuclear testing, and steady gains to improve the security of dangerous weapons and materials. Alternatively, a more positive nuclear future could, ironically, be generated by a terrible event, such as a nuclear accident or an act of nuclear terrorism. If a negative nuclear event were so chastening and if it could somehow be isolated, traction might be generated in the direction of nuclear abolition. The global revulsion from some negative acts might prompt states with nuclear weapons and states that have abstained from acquiring the Bomb to join in common cause to enact a work plan that makes significant progress toward abolition. Less drastic but still negative nuclear drivers might also prompt the remedial steps needed to shore up the foundations of the Nonproliferation Treaty and to redesign the structure's second-floor additions constructed by the George W. Bush administration. For example, a limited resumption, but not a cascade, of nuclear testing might have a chastening effect.

The ironies of living with the Bomb could work negatively as well as positively. Positive developments could lead to negative unintended consequences, and negative developments could generate even greater backsliding. Finding traction on slippery slopes is far from easy. The chance of a negative trigger producing positive developments is probably less likely than a negative development producing even more bad news. Success in moving steadily toward abolition is difficult because it requires not only the absence of negative drivers but also the presence of positive reinforcing developments along the way to zero. The absence of disabling negatives and the profusion of positives required to reach zero may seem fanciful. And yet a succession of hardheaded practitioners with long years of public service have concluded that zero is the right destination to aim for.

Henry L. Stimson arrived at this conclusion before leaving the War Department in 1945. He came to this conclusion not out of remorse about authorizing the use of the atomic bomb but from a sense of realism about the consequences of failure. Stimson argued that

> the riven atom, uncontrolled, can be only a growing menace to us all, and there can be no final safety short of full control throughout the world. Nor can we hope to realize the vast potential wealth of atomic energy until it is disarmed and rendered harmless. Upon us, as the people who first harnessed and made use of this force, there rests a grave and continuing responsibility for leadership in turning it toward life, not death.[60]

Paul Nitze came to embrace abolition toward the end of his many decades of wrestling with the Bomb. Nitze, like Stimson, did not hold romantic notions about abolition. He arrived at this conclusion because of revolutionary advances in U.S. conventional warfare.

> The technology of our conventional weapons is such that we can achieve accuracies of less than three feet from the expected point of impact. The modern equivalent of a stick of dynamite exploded within three feet of an object on or near the earth's surface is more than enough to destroy the target. In view of the fact that we can achieve our objectives with conventional weapons, there is no purpose to be gained through the use of our nuclear arsenal. To use it would merely guarantee the annihilation of hundreds of thousands of people, none of whom would have been responsible for the decision invoked in bringing about the weapons' use, not to mention incalculable damage to our natural environment.[61]

Sam Nunn, George Shultz, Henry Kissinger, and William Perry have added a values-based rationale to the arguments offered by Nitze and Stimson. They wrote, "Reassertion of the vision of a world free of nuclear weapons and practical measures toward achieving that goal would be, and would be perceived as, a bold initiative consistent with America's moral heritage."[62] These writers could hardly be considered naïve waifs. Many other serious thinkers, religious leaders, and former practitioners of the art of the possible have reached a similar conclusion. The Reverend Billy Graham came to this conviction as a "teaching of the Bible."[63]

Sensible, hard-nosed realists have joined religious leaders in endorsing abolition because they have concluded that complete nuclear disarmament would be in the national security interests of the United States. Moreover, the serious pursuit of abolition is the glue that holds the global nonproliferation system together. If nuclear disarmament could be achieved, the worst threats to U.S. national security would be eliminated, and U.S. conventional superiority would become even more pronounced.

For these and other reasons, the complete elimination of nuclear weapons from the face of the earth would be a desirable end state. It would also be a dangerous end state without reciprocal, verifiable, and permanent elimination by all other states. Abolition is therefore both the most desirable alternative nuclear future and the most difficult to achieve. Success would require, among other factors, cooperative, or at least nonthreatening, relations among major powers; regional harmony marked by the absence of serious threats to nations that have the means to acquire nuclear weapons; strong, functional alliances that help to stop and reverse proliferation; mandatory, effective, intrusive, and global monitoring arrangements that serve as a deterrent against cheating and an early warning system against worrisome activities; and mandatory, effective global export controls.

Other items might be added to this list, but it is already long enough to clarify that, even if significant progress is made on some of these agenda items over the next decade, severe challenges to achieving a nuclear-weapon-free world would remain. The end state of abolition may remain beyond reach, but steps along this path can nonetheless reduce nuclear dangers. Most important, no other alternative nuclear future offers a greater likelihood of achieving these steps. Nor do the alternative nuclear futures discussed in the next sections have greater logic, coherence, or sustaining power than nuclear abolition. Washington may not be able to reach this destination, but it has more steering capacity than any other capital. When trying to steer, it helps to know what destination is most desirable. Even knowing the preferred destination, it is possible to get lost. Not focusing on the ultimate destination makes it easier to get lost.

Abolition as a preferred end state seems as implausible as, say, hoping in 1945 that the United States and the Soviet Union could somehow manage to avoid incinerating each other during the unfurling decades of the cold war. Paul Nitze's wise counsel, cited more than once in these pages, applies to the pursuit of nuclear disarmament as well as to finding safe passage during the cold war. Nitze counseled against despair in reaching a distant goal. Instead, he advocated relentless effort and methodical attention to detail in "working the problem" of cold war nuclear dangers. Working the problem of nuclear disarmament requires the same focus, day by day, month by month, and year by year. The destination of nuclear abolition may not be achievable, but if pursued wisely, it can systematically reduce nuclear dangers.

ALTERNATIVE NUCLEAR FUTURE II: ANARCHY

International relations theorists write about a self-help system whereby nations do what they must to protect their interests. This system produces modest forms of anarchy, because anarchy does not serve the interests of most states. If the world were truly anarchic, dozens of states would have nuclear weapons and trafficking in bomb-making material would be widespread, as would acts of nuclear terrorism. There would be no global network to prevent proliferation, no treaties, no inspection rules, and no export control regulations. An anarchic system of this order of magnitude does not exist because it is too dangerous. National leaders are usually not chosen from among the ranks of anarchists.

To help prevent nuclear anarchy, nations have agreed to a global system to prevent proliferation, with the Nonproliferation Treaty as its centerpiece. Export controls, nuclear facility inspections, and constraints on nuclear testing directly reinforce the global nonproliferation system. Strong conventional military capabilities, alliances, and "nuclear umbrellas" that powerful states extend to protect friends and allies indirectly support the global system erected to prevent nuclear anarchy.

This system offers less protection than before. Norms and export controls have been weakened, treaties have been denigrated, and new nuclear aspirants have appeared. These troubling developments are still not harbingers of nuclear anarchy. As noted, eight of the nine worst proliferation drivers are not yet faits accomplis. Some analysts link nuclear anarchy to nuclear abolition. In this view, abolition would provide an invitation to aggression and nuclear rearmament, as any state that acquired the Bomb would gain significant advantages over other states that faithfully adhered to their abolitionist pledges. With the nuclear umbrella removed from tense regions, adversaries would presumably be more prone to fight, and fights would likely lead to more proliferation.[64] A mad scramble to acquire or reacquire the Bomb would then follow.

This scenario seems misplaced for several reasons. To begin with, the prospects of abolition as well as anarchy are distant, in part because the five permanent members of the UN Security Council, all possessors of nuclear weapons, will resist both end states. Second, abolition requires a progression of small steps that lead, over time, to the transformation of international relations. If nuclear anarchy is unlikely under current, highly imperfect circumstances, it will be far more unlikely if international relations are transformed in ways that make abolition more likely. Third, if enough steps toward abolition are achieved, the end state may be reinforced if a number of nations maintain the capability to rebuild the Bomb, thereby providing an insurance policy against cheating.[65]

Because the downside risks of nuclear anarchy are so great and because so many important states will seek to prevent this outcome, this nuclear future seems unlikely. Relying on this expectation, however, would be most unwise. Identification of the key contributors of nuclear anarchy clarifies the steps required to foreclose it—and the most useful steps toward safer destinations.

ALTERNATIVE NUCLEAR FUTURE III: PROLIFERATION

Every five years, member states in the Nonproliferation Treaty gather to consider the treaty's implementation, providing a barometer of global efforts to prevent further proliferation and to achieve nuclear disarmament. As measured by the outcome of review conferences since 1995, the Nonproliferation Treaty is in uncertain health. The bilateral strategic arms reduction process between the United States and Russia has moved in the direction of fewer constraints and less monitoring. Although aging U.S. and Russian warheads continue to be dismantled, China, India, and Pakistan are adding to their nuclear stockpiles. The Nonproliferation Treaty obligation for states possessing nuclear weapons to seek nuclear disarmament has not been taken seriously. A companion treaty ending nuclear weapon tests for all time, the Comprehensive Test Ban Treaty, remains in limbo. Prospects for a successful, near-term negotiation of a treaty ending fissile material production for bombs do not look promising. The United States has also proposed changes in export controls for India's benefit that could result in a weakening of the global system of constraints on nuclear commerce.

These negative developments have been accompanied by progress in some areas related to proliferation. North Korea's nuclear programs are being dismantled. Libya's nuclear ambitions have been checked. The Proliferation Security Initiative has already demonstrated its value in intercepting proliferation-related contraband. Agreement has been reached on The Hague Code of Conduct, which sets norms against ballistic missile proliferation. The passage of UN Security Council Resolution 1540 mandates improved national controls against proliferation. Cooperative threat reduction programs are expanding. These positive developments help to compensate for the multiple weaknesses of the Nonproliferation Treaty, but in the absence of construction to reinforce the treaty's load-bearing walls, its structure will remain weak.

The 2005 Nonproliferation Treaty review was dispiriting, with participating states unable even to agree on documents reporting on their ineffectual deliberations. All the states acknowledged to possess nuclear weapons under the treaty have backed away from the pledges they accepted in return for the treaty's indefinite extension in 1995, none more so than the Bush administration.[66] The sixty-five nation Conference on Disarmament in Geneva, where some of these pledges were to be honored, remains moribund, a prisoner of the consensus rule that is required for negotiations to proceed. Iran, Egypt, and Pakistan have joined the United States and China in blocking long-standing agenda items in Geneva.

Prospects for proliferation lie between the alternative nuclear futures of abolition and anarchy. Is there a safe stopping point or a stable equilibrium between these polar opposites? Proliferation optimists in academia answer in the affirmative. This camp, which views proliferation as a stabilizing factor in international relations, is led by Kenneth N. Waltz.[67] Waltz's key assumptions are that proliferation will proceed slowly and manageably; that the future of proliferation will be much like the past; that nuclear weapons will induce caution, especially in weak states; that cautionary behavior related to the Bomb is so great that catastrophic consequences will not result; that reliable deterrence can be obtained quickly with minimal effort; that nuclear arms races are pointless; and that rational decisions will prevail over dangerous ones.[68] Even if every assumption in this long list holds true, no responsible public official can afford to rely on them all. Indeed, at least some—and perhaps many—of these assumptions have become questionable during the second nuclear age.

Proliferation may or may not proceed slowly in the future, because it is hard to predict when national hedging strategies will multiply and become mutually reinforcing.[69] The assumption that future cases of proliferation will reflect previous ones is also questionable because new factors have come into play, including the diffusion of technology and the advent of entrepreneurial middlemen, both of which can provide shortcuts to the Bomb. In addition, the spread of the Bomb to the Islamic world could well change the dynamics of proliferation. The presumption that Murphy's Law does not apply to new proliferation cases (or prior ones) seems heroic; and the presumptions of stabilization and rationality associated with the Bomb have been sorely tested in serious crises between states possessing the Bomb.

Waltz's assumptions—and those of his disciples—have been most recently tested by India and Pakistan.[70] This nuclear passage has been marked by severe crises and one limited border war. Two of the crises occurred in 1987 and 1990, when each country presumed that the other had covertly acquired the Bomb.

After exploding their bombs in 1998, they fought a border war along the Kashmir divide in 1999, which was followed in 2001–2002 by a ten-month standoff in which approximately 1 million soldiers were prepared for battle. This crisis was prompted by an attack on the Indian Parliament by Islamic extremists, a triggering event that did not figure in the literature of proliferation optimists.

Waltz and his disciples do have a point, however: Although two sets of neighboring nuclear states have clashed along contested borders shortly after testing nuclear weapons (the Soviet Union and China in 1969 and India and Pakistan in 1999), both pairings avoided a major war. Subsequently, bilateral relations improved. In both cases, it is possible to argue that border wars remained limited and full-scale escalation was avoided because of the Bomb. This record does not suggest, however, that the Bomb's acquisition has produced a fulsome record of stabilizing, rational behavior.

Instead, the Bomb's appearance has generated rough passages that have greatly challenged national leaders. This stands to reason, because when nuclear weapons are added to troubled relationships, tensions usually grow. The Bomb has also encouraged risk-taking behavior by leaders who believed that nuclear weapons would keep an adversary in check, thereby seeming to provide an insurance policy against escalation. This dynamic, known as the stability-instability paradox in academia, rests on the profound irony that nuclear weapons can be destabilizing at low levels of interstate violence while helping national leaders prevent total war.[71]

Political scientist Glenn Snyder identified the stability-instability paradox in 1961, noting that, notwithstanding the U.S. nuclear deterrent, the Kremlin could engage in "a range of minor ventures which they can undertake with impunity, despite the objective existence of some probability of retaliation."[72] Robert Jervis summarized the resulting dilemma as follows: "To the extent that the military balance is stable at the level of all-out nuclear war, it will become less stable at lower levels of violence."[73] The available evidence suggests that, before bilateral relations improve, adversaries that acquire the Bomb can expect a transition period checkered with crises and close calls.

Waltz is also correct in arguing that, at least so far, the nuclear club has expanded slowly from one decade to the next. Each new member—along with the doorkeepers to the Nonproliferation Treaty—seeks to close the door after entry, but the very act of entry leaves that door further ajar. Perhaps slow and steady growth of proliferation will remain the rule, but with each new member, more states are likely to adopt hedging strategies, especially if Iran gains entry.

U.S. national security policies have further complicated these dynamics, as Waltz himself has acknowledged. Waltz cites the George W. Bush administration's commitment to deploying missile defenses and to "rending the fabric of agreements that brought nuclear weapons under a modicum of control" as new drivers for proliferation.[74] U.S. military superiority is not, however, one of the nine key drivers for proliferation. Instead, the net effects of U.S. military power are mixed, reinforcing the impulses of some bomb seekers while reassuring friends and allies in troubled regions. However, when the use of force to prevent proliferation is accompanied by a highly selective interest in treaties, verification, and nuclear disarmament, countervailing trends tilt toward more proliferation and less reassurance.

The alternative nuclear future of stabilizing proliferation is a concept for academics to consider and for policy makers to avoid. Every new aspirant to the Bomb adds further complexity and risk to proliferation. For national leaders, the management of new proliferation cases is rightly considered a fallback position, to be undertaken with resignation and regret. Prevention strategies can mean safe passage into the nuclear future, whereas managed proliferation strategies offer the prospect of still more proliferation.

ALTERNATIVE NUCLEAR FUTURE IV: ARMS CONTROL

Among the great ironies of the first nuclear age was that the severest critics of arms control treaties produced the greatest triumphs in this field. Arms control's biggest boosters were sidelined during the Reagan administration, when hard-liners and conservative deal makers fought bitterly over treaties. The deal makers won out, with the inadvertent assist from hard-liners, who took stands that made deal making look good by comparison. The resulting treaties needed to be struck by conservative administrations, because hawks could block the most ambitious efforts of doves. Arms controllers were hamstrung by poor timing, technically "sweet" opportunities for making the Bomb more powerful, and hidebound Kremlin leaders. Only severe critics of past agreements working for a staunchly anti-Communist president named Ronald Reagan could tame naysayers. But Reagan needed a partner. He found one in Mikhail Gorbachev, who surprised everyone, especially the Kremlin establishment that elevated him.

Before the advent of the Reagan administration, one major achievement of arms controllers was to establish a global system designed to prevent nuclear proliferation. Their second major achievement was to codify national defenselessness to the Bomb in the 1972 Anti-Ballistic Missile Treaty. This agreement was both counterintuitive and realistic, because there were no prospects for effective defenses against the Bomb's awesome destructiveness. By codifying national vulnerability, arms controllers sought to provide a measure of stability into the offensive nuclear competition. This objective proved to be elusive because there were many reasons for building new offensive capabilities, only one of which had to do with overwhelming defenses. Indeed, the absence of defenses became yet another anxiety that resulted in more potent offenses.

It took fifteen more years for political conditions to become ripe for stabilizing nuclear arms reductions. Before then, national defenselessness painted an indelible bull's-eye on the backs of arms controllers, leaving them open to the charge of endorsing the immoral and unacceptable condition of mutual assured destruction. The rejoinder—that mutual vulnerability helped to keep the cold war from becoming hot—was true, but did not carry much political weight. Vulnerability was not a bankable political commodity.

The great conceptualizers of nuclear deterrence, epitomized by Henry Kissinger, did not care much for the signature accomplishments of arms control because these treaties swept too many pieces off the nuclear chessboard. They undercut nuclear targeting options and greatly complicated America's alliance relationships. Nuclear weapons and deterrence strategists such as Kissinger and his boss, President Richard M. Nixon, held their applause for the treaties that broke the back of the nuclear arms race.

The founders of arms control—Thomas Schelling, Morton Halperin, and Hedley Bull, among others—came from academia and think tanks, like their counterpart deterrence theorists. For them, mutual vulnerability was an essential ticket for safe passage during the cold war. Ironically, the clearest benefits of mutual vulnerability became apparent whenever an American president insisted on deploying defenses. The fundamentals of nuclear overkill and ineffective defenses never changed during the first nuclear age, but the Kremlin was always worried about U.S. technical virtuosity and was most willing to make concessions when the prospects of U.S. missile defense deployment were strongest.

The theory and practice of arms control, like the theory and practice of nuclear deterrence, were unique products of the first nuclear age. One required the other, because reassurance was just as crucial as deterrence in keeping the cold peace. Without arms control to reassure domestic and allied audiences, deterrence would become too unnerving. The founders of arms control hoped that their brainchild would complement, not compete with, national defense policy. This proved to be too grand an ambition because the preferences of arms controllers and deterrence strategists were rarely in alignment. Deterrence and arms control proceeded in an awkward parallelism. The preferences of arms controllers and deterrence strategists were almost always mutually objectionable, but they were sufficient to prevent dreaded outcomes.

Preventing nuclear cataclysm during the first nuclear age required the leverage that hard-liners provided and the techniques that arms controllers offered. The essence of deterrence was calculated threat and long-distance signaling. Arms control, on the other hand, required a formal partnership and patterns of cooperation. Deterrence alone was unable to engineer a peaceful accommodation to nuclear overkill; arms controllers invented the mechanisms with which the superpowers could institutionalize their joint interest in avoiding war.[75]

The irony that deterrence theorists and arms controllers needed each other was mostly lost on the domestic combatants.[76] Winston Churchill's hopeful prediction in 1955—that "safety will become the sturdy child of terror, and survival the twin brother of annihilation"[77]—required diplomatic engagement as well as deterrence and containment. Deterrence strategies became too scary and unsettling when Washington and Moscow were not trying to negotiate agreements to reduce nuclear danger. Americans accepted deterrence, but they also fervently wished to make these plans unnecessary. Because nuclear preparations were so worrisome, grand theories of nuclear deterrence needed to be accompanied by grand theories of strategic arms control. The most important arms control theorist (and Nobel laureate), Thomas C. Schelling, concluded retrospectively that "holding off disaster was what most of us aimed for in 1960" and that "the purpose of arms control was to help make certain that deterrence worked."[78] In truth, the conceptual foundations of arms control that Schelling and others built had far more ambitious objectives.

The founders of arms control correctly foresaw that, amid an intense ideological, geopolitical, and military competition, the two superpowers could still carve out a zone of cooperation over their common interest in not blowing each other up. This required new lines of communication, negotiations, the pursuit of predictability, and eventually, extraordinary transparency. These were radical notions in the early 1960s. That they have become common sense attests to how much arms control theory has been woven into military practice.

Negotiated reductions in nuclear arms came at the close of the first nuclear age. Arms control was rooted in the cold war and in a bipolar international system. The end of the cold war and the demise of the Soviet Union have made classical arms control approaches tangential. After six decades of nonuse of nuclear weapons, the oft-repeated contention by arms controllers—that a new or refurbished weapon design would somehow make it easier for national leaders to cross the nuclear threshold—makes little sense. Another key tenet of arms control that took a beating after the cold war ended was the assumption that nuclear and conventional capabilities needed to be strictly segregated. In the old days, this strengthened superpower controls against the unauthorized use of nuclear weapons while decreasing the probability, however marginal, that the nuclear threshold would be crossed in the event of hostilities. When the George W. Bush administration provided the U.S. Strategic Command with long-range conventional strike capabilities, it greatly reduced that Command's interest in nuclear strike options.

Arms controllers lost many of the arguments and much of their audience after the cold war ended. This was inevitable, partly because any conceptualization that was designed to deal with 1960s-era nuclear dangers could not be compelling a half-century later. Two of the key tenets of arms control—nuclear overkill and national vulnerability—made sense when the primary nuclear dangers were arms racing and the fear of surprise attack by the Soviet Union. These core principles make no sense in dealing with the paramount dangers of nuclear terrorism and proliferation. The second nuclear age is about power imbalances and asymmetric warfare, not arms racing.

Other key tenets of arms control, such as clarifying nonhostile intent and finding zones of collaboration with major powers, still make a good deal of sense. Arms control arrangements devised to prevent proliferation that proved their worth during the first nuclear age also remain crucial. In the first nuclear age, proliferation control required cooperation among major powers. Only after the Lyndon B. Johnson administration decided against providing nuclear weapons to U.S. allies, especially West Germany, did it become possible to work with the Soviet Union to negotiate the Nonproliferation Treaty. Cooperation among major powers remains essential to control proliferation, as the North Korean case demonstrates. Preventing horizontal proliferation to new states was, from the start, linked to superpower efforts to control and reverse their own vertical proliferation. Proliferation prevention was also linked to the ultimate goal of abolition. These linkages remain crucial because the pursuit of nuclear disarmament continues to be one of the adhesives that hold the Nonproliferation Treaty together.

Although mechanisms developed for arms control can help to provide safe passage into the nuclear future, the central organizing concepts of arms control are hopelessly dated. Moreover, the practice of arms control was, until the second Reagan administration, mostly reactive rather than preventive. Treaty negotiations were long running and not very adaptive enterprises. Preventive and adaptive nuclear threat reduction measures are now required. Arms control is too much a hallmark of our nuclear past to help shape the nuclear future.

ALTERNATIVE NUCLEAR FUTURE V: DOMINANCE

The dissolution of the Soviet Union allowed the George W. Bush administration to retrieve the strategic concept of safety through dominance from the shelf where it had been gathering dust for four decades. The strategic concept of safety though dominance was openly championed by Truman and Eisenhower but was shelved in favor of "sufficiency" by Nixon, who required a different yardstick by which to negotiate strategic arms limitation with the Soviet Union.[79] With the exception of President Reagan, every president from Nixon onward accepted sufficiency (or variations on this theme) during nuclear negotiations for the remainder of the cold war.

The George W. Bush administration's belief in the utility of nuclear war-winning capabilities transposes cold war–era thinking onto the dilemmas of the second nuclear age. One school of thought during the cold war firmly believed that the nation less damaged in nuclear exchanges and more able to impose its will if warfare continued would be able to dictate terms of surrender—even after major metropolitan areas in both countries had been destroyed.[80] Paul Nitze was a key member of this school. He advocated "high quality deterrence" on the grounds that one could still distinguish between the victor and the vanquished in the aftermath of a nuclear war.[81] In this view, the Kremlin was pursuing nuclear war-winning capabilities, and the United States could only checkmate Soviet designs by emulating Soviet nuclear doctrine.[82] This school of thought held that Russian strategic culture could accept tens of millions of fatalities in a nuclear war and thus could not be dissuaded from engaging in brinkmanship except through positions of strength.

An opposing view during the cold war held that political leaders of the United States and Soviet Union thought very differently about nuclear weapons than the developers of nuclear war-fighting plans. McGeorge Bundy reaffirmed this belief during the Cuban missile crisis. Seven years later, he wrote:

> In light of the certain prospect of retaliation there has been literally no chance at all that any sane political authority . . . would consciously choose to start a

nuclear war. This proposition is true for the past, the present, and the foreseeable future. . . . There is an enormous gulf between what political leaders really think about nuclear weapons and what is assumed in complex calculations of relative "advantage" in simulated strategic warfare. . . . In sane politics, therefore, there is no level of superiority which will make a strategic first strike between the two great states anything but an act of utter folly.[83]

Other veterans of the Cuban missile crisis, including Secretary of State Dean Rusk and Secretary of Defense Robert McNamara, came to a similar conclusion: "American nuclear superiority was not in our view a critical factor," they wrote, "for the fundamental and controlling reason that nuclear war, already in 1962, would have been an unexampled catastrophe. . . . No one of us ever reviewed the nuclear balance for comfort in those hard weeks."[84] This analysis was, of course, strongly contested, nowhere more forcefully than in the writings of Nitze and Henry Kissinger, who were then convinced that comparative nuclear advantage mattered greatly in deep crisis or in the event of warfare.[85]

Much has changed from the first nuclear age to the second. During the cold war, securing relative advantage in nuclear-tinged crises and warfare was hard to accomplish after the Cuban missile crisis, when the Kremlin resolved to counter U.S. strategic supremacy. Subsequently, the Kremlin's commitment to nuclear orthodoxy was at least as strong as the Pentagon's. With both superpowers firmly resolved to avoid disadvantage, nuclear war-winning capabilities remained beyond reach, despite warnings to the contrary. The Soviet collapse ended this hyperactive competition—and reopened the possibility that the United States could prevail in the event of a nuclear war or a severe crisis between major powers. Ironically, as Nitze ended his long career of thinking about the Bomb as a heretic calling for nuclear abolition, his cold war prescriptions for high-quality nuclear deterrence gained a new lease on life.

The George W. Bush administration had little use for nuclear negotiations predicated on equality. Russia and China could not match U.S. conventional military forces, and they lagged far behind U.S. offensive nuclear capabilities. Nor could they compete with the United States in missile defenses of various kinds, if Congress could be persuaded to pay for them and if the Pentagon could make them work. U.S. deterrence strategists, long beset by domestic constraints and their opposite numbers in the Soviet Union, could at long last hope to achieve the presumed benefits of dominant nuclear capabilities.[86] After the demise of the Soviet Union, the United States had the ability, at least on paper, to target and destroy Russia's far weaker nuclear forces and to defend against ragged retaliatory strikes.[87]

The George W. Bush administration, unlike the Reagan administration, steered clear of loose talk about prevailing in nuclear warfare, but it was unrealistic to expect key officials who believed deeply in the value of full-spectrum dominance not to extend that belief to nuclear weapons. Because U.S. nuclear war plans remain classified documents, this conclusion must rest on the size and readiness of the nuclear forces that the administration deemed essential. This conclusion can also be inferred from the portions of the administration's nuclear posture review that have been leaked to the media.[88] The closest to plain speaking that President Bush has come in these matters was a passage in his administration's 2002 National Security Strategy promising that "our forces will be strong enough to dissuade potential adversaries from pursuing a military build-up in hopes of surpassing, or equaling, the power of the United States."[89] The administration's nuclear posture is predicated on achieving U.S. strategic objectives in worst cases. The worst case of all requires being able to prevail in a nuclear war against a major power.

The actions taken and those resisted by the Bush administration are consistent with the pursuit of whatever rewards might come from nuclear dominance. In the second nuclear age, no less than in the first, these rewards remained hypothetical and deeply suspect. In the worst possible case—the use of nuclear weapons in a conflict between major powers—war-winning nuclear capabilities still could not prevent the most grievous and long-lasting damage on U.S. soil. Beijing and Moscow are intent on making clear this consequence by maintaining the capability to keep American cities vulnerable to attack. U.S. strategic superiority also reinforces the Kremlin's intent to maintain as large a nuclear capability as it can reasonably afford while accelerating the pace of China's nuclear modernization programs. High numbers of U.S. nuclear weapons on alert ensure that the Kremlin will keep its land-based missiles on alert.[90] Readiness for the worst possible case therefore increased the probability of accidents and the application of Murphy's Law to nuclear weapons.[91]

Trying to be safe against worst cases often has the perverse result of increasing negative consequences for lesser cases. U.S. war-winning nuclear capabilities do not help secure dangerous weapons and nuclear materials in Russia. Instead, they have reinforced the impulse in Moscow to maintain excessive nuclear stockpiles and to keep some beyond the reach of U.S. cooperative threat reduction programs. A war-winning U.S. nuclear posture also makes it harder to encourage Beijing to accept transparency in its nuclear holdings. U.S. nuclear war-winning capabilities did not prevent and may well have contributed to North Korea's nuclear test in 2006. Nor does U.S. nuclear superiority help with Iran because, ironically, the utility of nuclear dominance declines with the weakness of one's opponent. Would nuclear superiority help more against major powers? The primary function of nuclear weapons during a deep crisis in the second nuclear age, as in the first, is to prevent a crossing of the nuclear threshold. Whatever the imbalance of nuclear forces may be in a crisis between major powers, other equities and nonnuclear factors—diplomatic, economic, and military—are far more likely to influence outcomes. McGeorge Bundy emerged from the Cuban missile crisis convinced that the use of a single nuclear weapon would be a "catastrophic blunder" and that the use of ten would be "a disaster beyond history."[92] Bundy's arguments, subsequently endorsed by Nitze, have become stronger with every year and every crisis in which the nuclear taboo has held.

Of all the gifts resulting from the demise of the Soviet Union, America's nuclear dominance has the least utility. This gift has the most disutility when it is tightly held. The Bush administration's embrace of nuclear dominance serves to mortgage the nuclear future. The maintenance of war-winning nuclear capabilities does not help to ameliorate a single nuclear nightmare of the second nuclear age and increases prospects that some of these nightmares might become real.

· · ·

The alternative nuclear futures considered in this chapter are all unsatisfactory in one way or another. Stabilizing proliferation is an unreliable and dangerous construct that no responsible government official can endorse. Nuclear dominance offers no evident rewards and many penalties. Nuclear anarchy is an option to be avoided. Arms control speaks too much of the past to serve as a beacon for the future. The alternative nuclear future of abolition is the most suitable end state for U.S. nuclear policy, but it remains a long-term vision, many steps away. What then, is the best way for the United States to proceed? This question frames the chapter that follows.

6 FINDING SAFE PASSAGE IN THE SECOND NUCLEAR AGE

CHARLES WILSON, a car company executive tapped by President Dwight D. Eisenhower to run the Pentagon, reportedly said, "What's good for General Motors is good for the country."[1] This aphorism, which used to suggest leaving well enough alone, has taken on an entirely different meaning. Revitalization is required for the U.S. automobile industry as well as for American policies to prevent and reverse new nuclear dangers. The business community's use of best practices and lessons learned is entirely applicable to the process of reconsidering how best to improve security in the second nuclear age.

During the cold war, American presidents used five key elements to deal with the Bomb: deterrence, military strength, containment, diplomatic engagement, and arms control. These mainstays were not always pursued harmoniously or wisely. The Eisenhower administration, for example, gave nuclear weapons an oversized role in deterrence and containment, balancing the federal budget by means of massive nuclear strike options and reduced conventional forces. Advocates of containment often clashed with those who wished to pursue diplomatic engagement. Détente was sometimes politically popular and at other times a political albatross, as when President Gerald R. Ford needed to drop this word from his vocabulary in 1976 because of political heat from the conservative wing of the Republican Party.

Arms control was especially contentious. Powerful voices argued that any deals considered good enough by the Kremlin had to be suspect. In this view, the Soviet Union would cheat and gain decisive advantage if a deal were struck. Moreover, the process of engagement itself would naturally result in America letting down its guard. It was not easy to devise a comprehensive approach to check the worst dangers of the first nuclear age. Most of the creative tension came from trying to balance new nuclear programs with arms control negotiations. The founders of the novel practice of arms control argued that both sets of initiatives could be harmonized, but this rarely happened.

Nuclear overkill, one of the key defining features of the first nuclear age, did not happen absentmindedly. Deterrence strategists believed that nuclear exchange ratios mattered greatly, because victory and loss were defined in relative, not absolute, terms. Powerful domestic constituencies in the United States and the Soviet Union considered it essential to move on to the next warhead, missile, submarine, and bomber. Arms control initiatives premised on the notion that fewer was better or that some nuclear additions could actually decrease security produced bitter fights. Arms controllers lost most of these battles, as the consequences of falling behind in the nuclear arms race were not politically acceptable. Even so, the conceptual framework of arms control took hold, resulting in a negotiating process and treaties that helped to keep the cold war from becoming hot.

The five key elements for dealing with the Bomb did not always mesh, but none could be jettisoned because its exclusion increased nuclear dangers. Deterrence and containment required not only military strength but also the reassurance provided by diplomatic engagement and arms control. When national leaders appeared to be relying too heavily on any one of these key elements, public anxieties dictated reorientation. When deterrence strategies seemed to veer too much toward nuclear war fighting, arms control initiatives needed to be highlighted, and when arms control seemed to become too much of a panacea, military and nuclear initiatives gained traction. Likewise, when containment strategies seemed to crowd out diplomacy, public calls for a course correction grew; when diplomacy seemed to yield insufficient or poor returns, the defense budget received a boost. Diplomatic engagement with friends and allies made containment credible and achievable. Nuclear diplomacy with the Soviet Union raised domestic anxieties, but it also helped to assuage public fears. The mix of containment, military strength, and diplomatic engagement eventually contributed to the dissolution of the Soviet empire.

Success during the first nuclear age required creative friction as well as complementarities among the five key elements of nuclear risk reduction. Deterrence and arms control were both unnerving in different ways; they needed each other to slow, stop, and reverse the nuclear arms race. One could not succeed without the other. Arms control was based on the juxtaposition of nuclear overkill and national vulnerability, twin conditions that eventually facilitated deep cuts and the acceptance of intrusive inspections for the most powerful weapons ever created. Reducing bloated arsenals and limiting the extent of proliferation were major arms control achievements. The most important achievement of all—one in which both arms control and deterrence played major roles—was helping to prevent a nuclear war between sworn ideological and geopolitical foes.

In retrospect, it is remarkable how much was accomplished despite the friction created by trying to harness the five key elements used by presidents to reduce nuclear dangers. The combined, sustained use of deterrence, military strength, containment, diplomatic engagement, and arms control helped maintain the taboo against using nuclear weapons on battlefields. The Bomb was omnipresent, but it remained under control. The worst nuclear nightmares never became realities. Surprise nuclear attacks did not happen, and widespread nuclear proliferation did not occur. With patient and persistent diplomacy, nonproliferation became a global norm, with only a few exceptions. The nuclear arms race was always dangerous, but it was never out of control.

This record of accomplishment was accompanied by many unwise decisions. Containment required, in the judgment of Presidents John F. Kennedy, Lyndon B. Johnson, and Richard M. Nixon, that U.S. forces hold back the tide of Communism in South Vietnam. Diplomatic engagement led to dangerously unscripted summit meetings between Kennedy and Nikita Khrushchev in Vienna in 1961 and between Ronald Reagan and Mikhail Gorbachev in Reykjavik in 1986. Heavy reliance on military strength produced the oversized, budget-busting, government-directed, military-industrial-technological complex that President Eisenhower warned against in 1960. Tens of thousands of nuclear weapons were built, with thousands deployed on the front lines of the cold war and thousands more kept at further remove, ready for launch.

The cold war was all about excess, paranoia, and true danger. The impulse to add margins of safety through refinements in nuclear deterrence resulted in flirting with catastrophe. And yet, somehow, there was a happy ending: The Soviet Union dissolved, and Americans remained safe. Containment and diplomatic engagement, military strength, deterrence, and arms control all played their parts in realizing George Kennan's vision of "either the break-up or the gradual mellowing of Soviet power."[2] The same could be said for U.S. policies toward the People's Republic of China. China entered the nuclear age as a rogue state but eventually discovered the joys of making money.

Few of those who worked to reduce nuclear dangers during the first nuclear age believed that the United States would be so successful in these undertakings. Certainly not Kennan, whose visions of the demise of the Soviet Union and the wholesale devaluation of nuclear weapons coexisted with a quarrelsome view of prevailing policies and a deep streak of Spenglerian pessimism. And yet the combined application of deterrence, military strength, containment, diplomatic engagement, and arms control worked to prevent new mushroom clouds, stem proliferation, break the back of the nuclear arms race, and defeat the Soviet Union. Given this extraordinary track record, it was entirely reasonable to expect that these five key elements—suitably adapted for changed circumstances—would be applied to the challenges of the second nuclear age.

Instead, America's first MBA-holding president, George W. Bush, along with his inner circle, were widely dismissive of best practices and lessons learned. As Vice President Dick Cheney announced before the Veterans of Foreign Wars in 2002, "Old doctrines of security do not apply" when dealing with "enemies who have no country to defend."[3] The Bush administration also dismissed "old doctrines of security" when dealing with problem states. In the hardest cases of Iraq, Iran, and North Korea, it initially denigrated the value of deterrence, containment, and diplomacy and tossed overboard much of the arms control canon, including hard-won intrusive inspections.

Without question, the challenges of nuclear terrorism were new, and they mandated proactive measures. The proliferation challenges from Iraq, Iran, and North Korea were, on the other hand, familiar. Some of the particulars were novel, of course, but Saddam Hussein, Mahmoud Ahmadinejad, and Kim Jong Il were not the first mercurial leaders to seek the Bomb. The greatest novelty of all was the Bush administration's response to these challenges, which discounted old remedies in favor of muscular approaches. Saddam Hussein, unlike Josef Stalin and Mao Zedong, was deemed by the administration to be impervious to the patient and persistent application of containment, deterrence, and diplomatic engagement.

President George W. Bush's call to arms against Saddam Hussein was perfectly pitched after the trauma of 9/11. "We are now acting," he declared, "because the risks of inaction would be far greater." Containment and deterrence were bound to fail: "In one year, or five years, the power of Iraq to inflict harm on all free nations would be multiplied many times over. With these capabilities, Saddam Hussein and his terrorist allies could choose the moment of deadly conflict when they are strongest." The most reliable instrument of all in this case was deemed to be preventive war: "We choose to meet that threat now, where it arises, before it can appear suddenly in our skies and cities."[4]

No other American president had suggested, let alone endorsed, a similar course of action. Because a preventive war was so contrary to American ideals and diplomatic history, the Bush administration laid the predicate for military action with its National Security Strategy, issued one year after the 9/11 attacks and six months before the invasion of Iraq.

> We must adapt the concept of imminent threat to the capabilities and objec-
> tives of today's adversaries. . . . The greater the threat, the greater is the risk
> of inaction—and the more the case for taking anticipatory action to defend
> ourselves, even if uncertainty remains as to the time and place of the enemy's
> attack. . . . The U.S. will not use force in all cases to preempt emerging threats,
> nor should nations use preemption as a pretext for aggression. Yet in an age
> when the enemies of civilization openly and actively seek the world's most
> dangerous technologies, the U.S. cannot remain idle while dangers gather.[5]

These passages reflected an extraordinary expansion of presidential authority and ambition, conditions that result when American presidents fight wars
of global scope. These passages also reflect a radical shift in U.S. thinking about
the use of force. President Truman rejected preemptive strikes and preventive
war against the Soviet Union, not just because it would be hard to find critical
targets and because this course of action would place Western Europe at risk
but also because such attacks were what the Japanese did to the United States at
Pearl Harbor. Truman wrote in his memoirs that he did "not believe in aggression or in preventive war" and that "there is nothing more foolish than to think
that war can be stopped with war. You don't prevent 'anything' but peace."[6]
President Kennedy was also quite clear on this point: "Our arms will never be
used to strike the first blow in any attack."[7]

The attacks on 9/11 fostered a different view. Writing in "The Unipolar
Moment," Charles Krauthammer argued that there was "no alternative to confronting, deterring and, if necessary, disarming states that brandish and use
weapons of mass destruction."[8] President Bush, Vice President Cheney, and
Secretary of Defense Rumsfeld agreed. They viewed the threat of a surprise
nuclear attack, either by a "rogue" state or by a terrorist group, to require exceptional, proactive means of national protection. An analogous "forward strategy"
to roll back Communism was proposed during the cold war but was rejected
as too dangerous and impractical.[9] The primary reason for impracticality

then—Soviet military and nuclear might—was no longer a constraining factor. Roll-back strategies in the form of preventive war could now be considered not only when an adversarial strike was imminent or when there was no other recourse to avert war but also against emerging threats that were presumed not to be amenable to patient diplomacy and containment.[10] Bush's new approach constituted, in Krauthammer's approving view, "an unprecedented assertion of American freedom of action and a definitive statement of a new American unilateralism."[11] A shift of this magnitude was conceivable only in the context of the 9/11 attacks and America's military dominance.

After denigrating the value of deterrence, containment, diplomatic engagement, and arms control, George W. Bush and his inner circle had to rely heavily on the Pentagon to counter the grave and gathering dangers they faced. This process of subtraction added heavy burdens to U.S. expeditionary forces. No irony of the second nuclear age is more biting than presidential candidate George W. Bush's campaign promise to the troops and their families in 2000 that "help is on the way."[12]

Three years after the initiation of a preventive war in Iraq, pragmatists in the Bush administration's State Department finally gained presidential authorization to try diplomatic engagement with North Korea. One reason was that efforts to isolate Pyongyang produced neither regime change nor the cessation of the North Korean nuclear program. Another was that U.S. troops were heavily committed elsewhere and poorly situated to address another military contingency on the Korean peninsula. A third reason was that China, Russia, Japan, and South Korea—the "contact group" assembled by the Bush administration to help with the North Korean nuclear program—strongly urged a more proactive U.S. diplomatic strategy. The mix of carrots and sticks that the Bush White House deemed useless against Saddam Hussein was found appealing by Kim Jong Il. Soon after Washington offered incentives in return for the shutdown of Pyongyang's nuclear facilities, this deal was struck in 2007.[13] Many parallel steps will be required to implement this agreement.

REGAINING BALANCE

The belated but productive engagement of North Korea by the Bush administration strongly suggests that the time is ripe to return to first principles to reduce nuclear dangers. A comprehensive approach to threat reduction is needed, one that draws on successful formulas of the past. The five key elements of deterrence, military strength, containment, diplomatic engagement, and arms control produced many successes during the first nuclear age. Devaluing so much of this inheritance meant the loss of creative friction and complementarities in dealing with new nuclear dangers. The denigration of all but one of these key elements—military strength—produced some successes, but overall, it has not worked well. One key error in judgment was that the Bush administration devalued diplomacy, deterrence, and containment not only against extremist groups but also against countries. Another error was the extent to which the administration denigrated the techniques of arms control, including its inspection procedures.

New states that seek the Bomb and extremist groups that seek to engage in nuclear terrorism want the same materials and end products. The quickest way for both categories of seekers to succeed is through existing means of production in states that already have the Bomb. Arms control monitoring arrangements developed to impede state-based proliferation during the first nuclear age therefore have become twice as relevant during the second nuclear age. Success in stopping proliferation and nuclear terrorism now requires strengthening arms control mechanisms that have enduring value and supplementing them with less formal adaptive tools especially well suited to prevent freelancers and extremist groups from acquiring the Bomb.

The time has come to reaffirm the utility of deterrence, containment, and diplomacy as essential elements of a comprehensive national strategy to reduce nuclear dangers and as complements to military strength. All four of these key elements require adaptation to address new dangers of proliferation and nuclear terrorism. The fifth key element, arms control, requires the most adaptation. What was once known as arms control has already morphed into a far broader practice of cooperative threat reduction. The terminology of arms control takes us backwards and dredges up old arguments that are best left interred. The terminology of cooperative threat reduction is forward looking, more encompassing, and less politically divisive.

Cooperative threat reduction programs owe much to cold war–era arms control treaties, from which transparency, confidence building, and nuclear risk-reduction measures originated. Just as one new instance of proliferation usually leads to another, one new advance in cooperative threat reduction can lead to another. These practices have become more varied, informal, and geographically dispersed over time.[14] With U.S. assistance, security perimeters around sensitive sites have been upgraded in many countries. Radiation detectors and other monitoring devices have been placed at border crossings and ports. Some shipping containers are monitored before leaving these ports; others are checked when they arrive in the United States. Highly enriched uranium in some locations has been removed and blended down so that it cannot be used to make mushroom clouds. Personnel reliability screening procedures for guards at facilities where dangerous weapons and materials are housed have been improved in many countries, including Pakistan. Nuclear weapons and their means of delivery continue to be dismantled under agreed procedures.

There are no secrets to success or magic bullets to reduce the most danger- ous weapons and materials and to prevent them from falling into new hands. Success requires relentless effort to apply more broadly and speedily coopera- tive threat reduction practices that have already demonstrated their worth. Success becomes easier when relations among major powers improve; it be- comes harder when Washington, as under the Bush administration, and the Kremlin, as under Vladimir Putin, shed treaty commitments that constrain freedom of action. When treaties are weakened or dispensed with, the foun- dations on which cooperative threat reduction initiatives have been built are also weakened. It is hard to convince newcomers to accept greater transparency when those who have long accepted intrusive monitoring arrangements now find them to be inconvenient.

FROM DOMINANCE TO COMPREHENSIVE THREAT REDUCTION

During the first nuclear age, there was no widely accepted shorthand term for the combined use of deterrence, military strength, containment, diplomatic engagement, and arms control. An appealing catchphrase for the key elements required to reduce dangers in the second nuclear age may be similarly elusive. What matters most in this regard is not finding the right memorable phrase to characterize these efforts but engaging in the right practices.

For lack of a better term, the strategic concept suggested here is comprehen- sive threat reduction.[15] This terminology serves several purposes. First, it clari- fies that the five key elements of deterrence, military strength, containment, diplomatic engagement, and cooperative threat reduction will be fused to re- duce nuclear dangers. Linking all five acknowledges the scope and complexity of current challenges and the breadth of responses required for prevention. A comprehensive approach also emphasizes the value of collaborative efforts with other nations to improve national security and homeland defense. A renewed emphasis on diplomatic engagement is warranted because trying to isolate problem states fails more often than it succeeds. Diplomatic engagement, in turn, is strengthened when the United States champions rules rather than exceptions to the rules governing proliferation. Nonproliferation norms matter because rules help to identify, isolate, and impose penalties on rule breakers.

The embrace of a new strategic concept of comprehensive threat reduction will not eliminate inconsistency, because nuclear dangers are too disorderly and diverse for one-size policies to fit all problems. But without trying to articulate a strategic concept, different initiatives can be perceived as, and can become, incoherent. The more coherent and appealing the strategic concept, the more it can be passed on from one administration to the next and the more it will be able to sustain domestic and international support.

Some of the George W. Bush administration's troubles in dealing with the new challenges of the second nuclear age are not of its own making. The structural shift from a bipolar world during the first nuclear age to the "unipolar moment"[16] has accelerated preexisting proliferation dangers, as those who feel most threatened by U.S. power have sought deterrence through unconventional means. The Bush administration can, however, be faulted for policies that have compounded preexisting dangers. The Bush administration's strategic concept of leadership through dominance needs to be replaced because it has produced more negative than positive results, especially in the Islamic world, and because it has placed heavy burdens on U.S. military forces.

The best encapsulation of this strategic concept can again be found in the Bush administration's seminal 2002 National Security Strategy, issued one year after the 9/11 attacks. The strategy called for "forces sufficient to support our obligations, and to defend freedom. Our forces will be strong enough to dissuade potential adversaries from pursuing a military build-up in hopes of surpassing, or equaling, the power of the United States."[17] The term "dissuasion" was borrowed from nuclear deterrence theory to apply to far broader purposes. Like all good terms related to the gruesome subject of nuclear war, dissuasion is a perfectly anodyne word, now freighted with a larger meaning. As President Bush announced to the graduating cadets at West Point in July 2002, "America has, and intends to keep, military strength beyond challenge—thereby making the destabilizing arms races of other eras pointless, and limiting rivalries to trade and other pursuits of peace."[18] Dissuasion has become a code word for maintaining superior military capabilities against any combination of potential foes. In the view of the Bush administration, dissuasion has required, at a minimum, off-loading treaties that were based on equal numbers or that constrained freedom of action. It also required making an object lesson of Saddam Hussein's defiance against the United States and the United Nations.

Dissuading Muslim rage against the United States is far from easy. President Bush, Vice President Cheney, and Secretary of Defense Rumsfeld repeatedly argued that acts of terror were carried out by individuals who hated freedom and other values that America represented. The harshest critics of America in the Islamic world, however, did not direct their wrath against enduring and appealing American values. Instead, acts of violence were prompted by specific U.S. policies that appeared unjust to many in the Islamic world.[19] Justice, as George Perkovich has written, is the missing link in the Bush administration's campaign to spread freedom and liberty.[20] The perpetrators of 9/11 did not hate freedom, at least as they conceived it; they hated, among other things, the lack of freedom in their countries of origin and the presence of U.S. troops in the Islamic world.

Acts of terrorism directed against the United States and the West have grown precipitously during the Bush administration, many directed against U.S. expeditionary forces and against soft targets in the West. In a memo subsequently leaked to the media, Secretary of Defense Rumsfeld identified one important metric for measuring success or failure in "winning or losing the global war on terror." Rumsfeld correctly asked, "Are we capturing, killing or deterring and dissuading more terrorists every day than the madrassas and the radical clerics are recruiting, training and deploying against us?"[21] By this metric, the Bush administration has poured new kerosene on smoldering resentments.[22]

It was inevitable that acts of terrorism would increase after 9/11, especially those directed at U.S. expeditionary forces in Afghanistan and Iraq. But the Afghan and Iraq campaigns account for just half of the thirty-five-fold jump in major acts of terrorism from 2000 to 2006. The fiftyfold increase in casualties recorded by the U.S. government during this seven-year period reflects global trends that have been accentuated by the Bush administration's policies.[23] The Bush administration finds solace in a third metric: the absence of another 9/11-like act of terror on U.S. soil. A corollary argument—that it is far better to fight terrorists in Iraq than to fight them on U.S. soil—has obvious political appeal, which is why it is repeated so often. But it is safe to assume that Islamic extremists seek to carry out terrible acts of violence on U.S. soil whether or not U.S. troops are present in Iraq and Afghanistan.

The British colonial presence in India provided the stimulus for a national campaign of passive resistance led by a transcendent leader, Mahatma Gandhi.

Gandhi's movement succeeded brilliantly because it figuratively disarmed those with a moral conscience. In stark contrast, the presence of U.S. military forces in the Middle East provided stimulus for a "jihad of the sword" led by a firebrand, Osama bin Laden, who learned his tactics as a willing recruit in the U.S.-backed effort to expel Soviet troops from Afghanistan. Bin Laden's tactics sought to kill, not morally disarm, foreign occupiers, tactics that were easily extended to the Sunni-Shia division within Islam. Muslims, not Americans, were the primary victims of a jihad of the sword.

THE LIMITS OF DOMINANCE

Iraq and Afghanistan became magnets for a new generation of Islamic warriors who were not amenable to dissuasion by superior firepower. Violence was franchised out, one improvised explosive device and suicide bombing at a time. The costs of U.S. occupation were high for U.S. ground forces, America's global standing, the internal cohesion of states in the region, and the U.S. treasury. Walter A. McDougall wrote, "Strategy is a form of economy, a function of scarcity; unlimited resources render strategy unnecessary."[24] The Bush administration's strategic concept of safety through dominance was extravagant even for America's abundant resources.

The goal of warfare, according to Karl von Clausewitz, is to "harmonize entirely" policy objectives with the use of force.[25] The Bush administration's use of force—inevitably in Afghanistan and optionally in Iraq—led to prolonged military occupations. Its war on terror fundamentally violated Clausewitz's core principle of war being the extension of policy by other means. Instead, war became the prelude to destabilizing developments across a wide arc of states ranging from Turkey and Pakistan to the Levant and the Persian Gulf. The characterization of an open-ended war on terror was politically adept at home but lent itself to mischaracterization elsewhere as a war on Islam. Unlike the ideological struggle during the cold war, which was fought victoriously by nonmilitary means, the war on terror was dominated by the use of force that, in turn, made nonmilitary instruments less credible.

The Bush administration's strategic concept of leadership by dominance was doomed to be short-lived because it sought too expansive a goal through too limited means on too narrow a political base. The cold war was won through the creative friction generated by the combined application of all five of the key elements of success. The war on terror went badly because the Bush administration relied on military might and denigrated all its complements.

Dominance gave license to the old adage that when you have a hammer, every problem looks like a nail. But hammering Islamic extremism is like hammering globules of mercury, which multiply and spurt in all directions from the impact of the blow. Convinced that dissuasion would not work with Saddam Hussein, that UN inspectors were feckless, and that sanctions were failing, the Bush administration reached for its hammer. Toppling Hussein, who entertained freelance extremists with as much hospitality as the Chinese government's approach to advocates of Tibetan freedom, was a terrible misjudgment. After disposing of Hussein and his repressive control mechanisms, Iraq descended into civil war, with U.S. forces serving as policemen, domestic arbiters, and punishers. These tasks were performed with distinction but at great cost.

Another fundamental reason for the short half-life of the Bush administration's strategic concept of leadership through dominance was that it could not be publicly defended. Maintaining America's dominance was not a compelling argument for the administration's policy preferences, so other arguments were used. These rationales became widely suspect, even when they were defensible. Leadership by dominance could succeed only with a large number of willing followers. Instead, the Bush administration's strategic concept was off-putting to friends and allies who highly valued containment, deterrence, diplomatic engagement, and arms control. At the same time, China and Russia, the major powers most uncomfortable with U.S. dominance, moved to counterbalance Washington by increasing arms sales and technology transfers from Moscow to Beijing.

Leadership by dominance provided a comfortable fit for President Bush's Manichean view of good guys and bad actors, but because the administration demanded exceptions to the rules it wanted others to follow, its complaints and threats often sounded hypocritical or disingenuous. The Bush administration did not want North Korea to test nuclear weapons, but it refused to support the entry into force of a treaty banning nuclear tests. It demanded intrusive inspections for designated bad actors while rejecting intrusive inspections at home by saying it needed to protect national security and commercial secrets.[26]

DOMINANCE OVER CHINA

The most important tests of a strategic concept are its hardest cases. Besides the wars in Iraq and Afghanistan, no cases were more important for the Bush administration than its dealings with China and Russia. One zone of possible contention with China relates to space, because any clash over Taiwan would accentuate the importance of satellites providing military support for the contesting armed forces. The U.S. Air Force Space Command issued a strategic master plan in 2003 declaring that "our charter is to rapidly obtain and maintain space superiority and the space, nuclear, and conventional strike capabilities that produce desired warfighting effects. . . . We must also pursue the ability to apply conventional combat in, from, and through space."[27] After this military guidance was published, the Bush administration denied that it reflected national policy, eventually issuing an unclassified national space policy in August 2006 in which references to "space dominance," "space superiority," "warfighting," and "combat in, from, and through space" were conspicuously absent. Instead, Bush's National Space Policy borrowed heavily from the language of the more ambiguous formulations of the Clinton administration's policy.[28] At the same time, the administration continued to oppose any agreement that would limit U.S. freedom of action in outer space, including the first use of space weapons.

The awkwardness of this position was evident when the People's Liberation Army blew up an aging Chinese satellite in January 2007. The primary purpose of this test—only the second of its kind (the first was by the United States during the Reagan administration in 1985)—was most likely to send a deterrence message to Washington, clarifying Beijing's intention to deny the Pentagon space dominance in the event of a crisis or a clash over Taiwan.

The Bush administration's public rejoinder was handcuffed by its staunch resistance to negotiations that would prevent the United States from developing, testing, and using space weapons. The People's Liberation Army test was not barred by any agreement, but it was nonetheless an egregiously irresponsible act, because it produced an estimated 40,000 pieces of debris 1 centimeter or larger in size. Each of these pieces of debris is now orbiting the earth with the approximate energy of a 1-ton safe falling from a five-story building, presenting a lethal threat to any space object in its path.[29]

The White House's critique therefore focused on the particular means of space warfare that Beijing tested, which produced the worst-ever man-made debris field in the history of the space age, one that will last for perhaps a century before burning out of low earth orbit. Because an end to all forms of harmful interference against satellites would conflict with the dictates of U.S. freedom of action in space, the administration's public rejoinder was confined to the admonition that Beijing's antisatellite test made civil space cooperation with the United States more remote.[30]

The zone of cooperative threat reduction between Washington and Beijing is still being defined. Stopping North Korea's nuclear program has fallen within this zone; cooperating on space security has not, at least not yet. One constraint is that both Washington and Beijing seek to maximize their freedom of action in the event of friction over Taiwan. Another is that China, like Russia, has found hidden agendas in the stated rationales of the Bush administration's national security policies. The year before the Bush administration took office, a Defense Intelligence Agency assessment concluded, "China feels [its] deterrent is at risk over the next decade because of U.S. targeting capabilities, missile accuracy, and potential ballistic missile defenses. Beijing is, therefore, modernizing and expanding its missile force to restore its deterrent value."[31]

The Bush administration subsequently proceeded to withdraw from the Anti-Ballistic Missile Treaty, issued a revised, classified nuclear posture calling for capabilities "to defeat opponents decisively,"[32] and negotiated an agreement on civil nuclear cooperation with New Delhi that would facilitate the growth of India's nuclear arsenal. The People's Liberation Army took seriously the U.S. Air Force's military space guidance as well as the administration's plans to deploy forty-four long-range missile defense interceptors—at a time when the U.S. intelligence community estimated that China possessed perhaps twenty aging ocean-spanning missiles that required hours to prepare for launch.

By 2015, the CIA estimates that China will increase four- or fivefold the number of warheads carried by ocean-spanning missiles that would be targeted against the United States.[33] This estimate, like its predecessors, is probably overstated,[34] but the Bush administration has pushed enough of Beijing's buttons to speed up China's leisurely approach to fielding new and better nuclear forces. Beijing probably presumes that the U.S. missile defense interceptors will become more capable over time and that their number will grow, along with U.S. long-range conventional strike capabilities.

The principal author of the Pentagon's 2001 Nuclear Posture Review and a long-standing advocate of missile defenses, Keith Payne, argued that, in any crisis or military engagement over Taiwan, Chinese leaders would need to

> believe that Washington would persevere despite their nuclear threats and possible regional nuclear use. Washington would have to deny Chinese leaders confidence that such threats could deter U.S. intervention, a hope to which they would likely cling. Consequently, U.S. deterrence policy in this case could require that the United States be able to limit its own prospective losses to a level compatible with the stakes involved.[35]

In classical deterrence theory, this is known as damage limitation: the ability to destroy an adversary's deadliest weapons before they can do great harm. U.S. conventional and, if necessary, nuclear strike forces would be assigned this mission, and missile defenses would have the task of intercepting warheads that have otherwise escaped destruction. In other words, the dictates of damage limitation call for superior American offensive forces and missile defenses to serve as a deterrent and, if deterrence fails, to provide the decisive margin of victory mandated in the Bush administration's nuclear posture statement. Payne and many others offered precisely this set of prescriptions during the first nuclear age.[36] They found no reason to change these requirements against far weaker competition in the second nuclear age.

The nuclear forces required to carry out these objectives have been downsized with the dissolution of the Soviet Union, but the essential imperatives of nuclear war-fighting plans remain the same. Moscow and Beijing understand these targeting calculations, which is why they are so sensitive to small increments of U.S. missile defense deployments.[37] They have gotten some relief from poor U.S. missile defense test results, competing Pentagon priorities, and growing congressional resistance to deploying costly, unproven missile defenses in Alaska and California. These comforts will decrease over time as U.S. missile defenses improve. Perhaps as a result, Beijing's interest in a treaty ending fissile material production for nuclear weapons appears to have waned, just as its interests have grown in techniques to disrupt and destroy U.S. satellites and to deploy mobile long-range ballistic missiles that will be harder for the Pentagon to target.

In one of his more disingenuous speeches, Secretary of Defense Rumsfeld noted these and other military developments by China and asked rhetorically, "Since no nation threatens China, one must wonder: Why this growing investment? Why these continuing large and expanding arms purchases? Why these continuing robust deployments?"[38] Rumsfeld surely knew that these developments were not unrelated to the nuclear, conventional, and space postures that he championed. He also knew that domestic criticism that the Bush administration's policies brought out the worst in others had a simple, politically cunning rejoinder: Carpers were forever "blaming America first."

The practical effects of the Bush administration's strategic concept of leadership by dominance do not rise to the level of an arms race between the United States and China. Asymmetric warfare, not arms racing, is a defining feature of the second nuclear age. U.S. policies that seek to maintain dominance do, however, add up to more wariness and an accelerated pace of nuclear and space warfare programs by the two states—China and Russia—whose cooperation the United States needs most on proliferation-related issues. The U.S. strategic concept of leadership by dominance has been particularly corrosive for U.S.-Russian relations. Bilateral ties, which were excellent after the 9/11 attacks, became so strained that, by 2007, Russian president Vladimir Putin was making indirect and invidious comparisons between the Bush administration's behavior and that of Nazi Germany.[39]

STRATEGIC RECOVERY

The bad news is that the George W. Bush administration has made serious missteps by denigrating four of the five key elements to success during the first nuclear age. The good news is that all five key elements of a successful strategy to reduce nuclear dangers remain applicable and that each of these key elements can be pursued with more effective means than ever before. The United States has greater economic and military capacity to engage in deterrence, containment, and diplomacy than during the first nuclear age. U.S. economic and military capabilities require significant repair, but the U.S. economy remains fundamentally sound and responsive to wise national policies. Moreover, no institution is more adaptive and takes lessons learned more seriously than the U.S. Army. Although U.S. military forces have been badly misused in Iraq, Washington is not doomed to repeat these mistakes, at least not anytime soon. Painful lessons that are relearned lengthen the time frame in which they are again forgotten.

The most positive irony associated with contemporary dangers of nuclear proliferation and terrorism is that there have never been more preventive measures available. Transparency, confidence building, and nuclear risk-reduction measures implemented during the first nuclear age remain eminently adaptable to new challenges. A wide range of new cooperative threat reduction techniques have been added to this toolkit. Proven techniques to secure dangerous weapons and materials have expanded well beyond the former Soviet Union. There is much work left to do, but the primary challenges of implementation are not technical in nature.

The key elements to tackle new dangers of nuclear proliferation and terrorism can be revived with wise foreign and national security policies that project, rather than undercut, U.S. political ideals. Revitalization will also come with economic solvency, farsighted investment decisions, domestic cohesion, and the attraction of U.S. culture. Joseph S. Nye called the least measurable of these instruments "soft power," or the means "to get what you want through attraction rather than coercion or payments. It arises from the attractiveness of a country's culture, political ideals, and policies. When our policies are seen as legitimate in the eyes of others, our soft power is enhanced."[40] Soft power is more effective when backed up by hard military power and greatly diminished when hard power is used unwisely.

If diplomacy, deterrence, containment, military strength, and cooperative threat reduction are used creatively, Americans can become safer and sorry consequences can be avoided in the second nuclear age. Working with a much smaller toolbox, previous U.S. leaders rebounded from rough stretches during the first nuclear age. The proliferation challenges posed by Iran and North Korea are serious, but more serious nuclear threats have been overcome in the past. The United States can rebound once more by adopting the five key elements of a comprehensive strategy, by using best practices, by learning from past mistakes, and by adapting proven methods to meet new challenges.

BACK TO BASICS: CONTAINMENT

During the cold war, the United States practiced containment against two major powers, the Soviet Union and the People's Republic of China. Both countries sprawled across many time zones and possessed significant military and economic potential. Russia was blessed with oil and gas. China was a sleeping giant. Containment was more challenging during the first nuclear age because both of these major powers were initially led by fanatical and ruthless leaders who used ideology to mobilize their countries and to stifle dissent. Communism, ostensibly predicated on equality and social justice, offered an alternative to the excesses of capitalism—until its own, different excesses became widely apparent.

The U.S. policy of containment during the first nuclear age was backed up by values and by military strength. The writers of NSC 68 were crystal clear about both pillars of containment: "The principles of freedom, tolerance, the importance of the individual, and the supremacy of reason over will—are valid and more vital than the ideology which is the fuel of Soviet dynamism." These core values, together with "the essential tolerance of our world outlook, our generous and constructive impulses, and the absence of covetousness in our international relations, are assets of potentially enormous influence."[41] The United States often fell short of these core values, but containment could not have succeeded against the Soviet Union solely by military power; competing concepts of freedom and economic security, based on the promotion of individual liberty and justice, were also essential.

Military containment could not be purchased on the cheap. The Eisenhower administration tried to do so, but this resulted in an unhealthy dependency on nuclear weapons. For containment to prevent nuclear war and Soviet expansionism, large, well-equipped, and well-trained conventional forces were required, some deployed in forward areas to provide reassurance to allies and to serve as trip wires in the event of Soviet adventurism. Because these forces were outnumbered, the nuclear shadow was never far behind them on the front lines of the cold war.

In one sense, containing hostile countries is simpler in the second nuclear age than it was in the first nuclear age because America's conventional military capabilities have become far more agile, whereas those of Russia have shrunk considerably. Smaller increments of U.S. forces can mete out more punishment with far more discrimination than during the first nuclear age. U.S. expeditionary forces are not so large and well equipped, however, as to be asked to seize and hold hostile territory for extended periods. This requirement—especially in lands that were once colonial possessions and especially in the Middle East, where foreign powers can readily be viewed as crusaders and occupiers—can produce painful results. Containment in the second nuclear age rests on a different formula: the threat and, if necessary, the use of power projection capabilities without extended military occupation of hostile territory.

In another sense, containment has become more difficult because new proliferation networks can arise to provide dangerous weapons and materials to states, freelancers, and extremist groups. Stopping new proliferation networks in their tracks requires timely warning, cooperation among intelligence communities and financial institutions, assistance to states that wish to counter shadowy proliferation networks, and military capabilities to disrupt proliferation-related transactions. The prototypical proliferation network for the second nuclear age was created by A. Q. Khan; the prototypical counterproliferation operation was the collaborative effort by the United States, Great Britain, and Italy in 2003 to prevent the illicit shipment of seaborne cargos sent by the Khan network to Libya.

Fusion is the key. The State Department's nonproliferation diplomacy must work in tandem with what the Pentagon calls counterproliferation programs.[42] When muscular counterproliferation initiatives are used while treaties and diplomatic engagement are being denigrated, they are likely to result in more proliferation and less prevention. Conversely, when the United States champions diplomatic initiatives to prevent proliferation, it is more likely to succeed in collaborative counterproliferation programs. Proliferation and counterproliferation have, in essence, become network warfare. Both are in their formative stages. Strengthening networks to contain proliferation has become one of the benchmarks of successful cooperative threat reduction and containment.

Containing two huge Communist states with followers in far-off lands was challenging and costly. American military might was used on the periphery of the struggle between the United States and the Soviet Union but never in direct battlefield engagement. Costly mistakes, both strategic and tactical, were made in these proxy wars, which resulted in a frustrating standoff on the Korean peninsula and a searing experience in Vietnam that extracted heavy losses in blood and treasure. Throughout these trials and tribulations, America held its ground and kept its powder dry in Central Europe, the front line of the contest between the superpowers. Containment was frustrating during the first nuclear age because it was a long-term strategy and because it seemed to be about creating conditions for stalemate. Only later did the nonmilitary aspects of containment—the attractiveness of America's values, the vitality of its economic model, and the internal rot of the Soviet system—result in victory.

By comparison, containing Iran and North Korea is far simpler. American military strength is unparalleled, and its power projection capabilities are more than sufficient to repel cross-border aggression, as was amply demonstrated when Saddam Hussein invaded Kuwait in 1990. North Korea has produced some measure of nuclear capability, a large standing army, and a great deal of poverty. Its ideology appeals to no one beyond its immediate, suffocating thrall. North Korea has two powerful neighbors, Japan and South Korea, that are close allies of the United States and that provide forward basing for U.S. troops. The U.S. Navy remains offshore and can greatly expand its presence if need be. The U.S. Air Force can arrive in strength more quickly. The pathways leading out of North Korea that could be used to export dangerous weapons and materials are few in number and heavily monitored. Under these circumstances, patient and persistent U.S. diplomatic engagement has the potential to accomplish far more than "penalizing" North Korea by refusing diplomatic engagement—especially when diplomatic engagement is supplemented with economic inducements. When the George W. Bush administration belatedly tried this approach, it achieved positive results.

Containing Iran is harder but not nearly as hard as containing the Soviet Union was. Iran's ideological fervent seems to be following a familiar downward trajectory, as it fails to deliver on promises at home. A country that sits on huge reserves of oil and natural gas but that suffers from gasoline shortages offers negotiating opportunities as well as challenges. Iran's transnational appeal is confined to a single region and is based on the cleavage between the Shia and Sunni branches of Islam, which further limits its reach. The sectarian basis for Iran's regional ambitions offers ample opportunity for local counterbalancing, even after replacing Iran's primary regional counterweight, Saddam Hussein, with a fractured, Shia-led government.

Iran and North Korea have pursued the means to do grievous harm to the United States, its forward-deployed forces, and America's friends and allies. Nuclear proliferation in both regions is likely to have cascade effects. The threat of nuclear proliferation on the Korean peninsula is now receding, as international observers monitor the dismantling of Kim Jong Il's capacity to make nuclear weapons. Kim has also promised to relinquish his bomb-making material.[43] Whether he will faithfully implement this agreement depends on whether he values nuclear weapons more than foreign help and whether the United States and North Korea's neighbors will be willing to provide it. The Iranian nuclear program is of greater concern, despite its less-developed state, because of Tehran's ambitions and links to extremist groups elsewhere in the region. Prevention requires early warning from intelligence agencies, vigorous diplomacy, strong military ties in troubled regions, forward-deployed forces, and contingency planning.

If these means prove insufficient to prevent Tehran from acquiring bomb-making material, they can also become the fundamental pillars of a containment strategy. If containment proves insufficient, military options remain on the table. Before using military means, it is worth recalling that containment strategies worked successfully during the first nuclear age against far more formidable foes espousing transnational ideologies. This suggests that pessimism or fatalism concerning the utility of containment against a far smaller and weaker state is unwarranted.[44] Containment may indeed fail against Iran, but it should not fail for want of trying.

If containment is in danger of failing, presidents have always had the military option of preventive war to engineer regime change and to foil proliferation. Previous occupants of the White House declined to choose this option—until George W. Bush. By deposing Saddam Hussein on the basis of false assumptions and faulty intelligence and by paying such a high price for the decision to occupy Iraq, the Bush administration has raised the bar for a subsequent administration to undertake another preventive war.

Preemptive strikes against proliferation-related activities are a different matter, as they have been tried on a number of occasions. Israel carried out air strikes against the Osirak nuclear power reactor in Iraq in 1981, prompting condemnation by the Reagan administration and by many other governments. This act of preemption delayed Iraq's nuclear ambitions for perhaps a decade. Israel also struck a nuclear facility under construction in Syria in 2007, eliciting a far more muted international response.[45] President Clinton ordered the bombing of what he assumed was a chemical weapons facility in Sudan in 1998. This plant was presumed to be connected to Osama bin Laden, although this case still has not been definitively made.[46] The plant's owner, who sued unsuccessfully for damages, claimed to be making aspirin. His assets were frozen and subsequently released. And in 1994, the Clinton administration gave serious consideration to carrying out preemptive strikes against North Korea to prevent its leadership from utilizing reprocessed plutonium to make bombs.[47]

All these preemptive strikes were carried out using conventional weapons. It would be hard to identify a more hypocritical act or one that would be more likely to backfire than the world's most powerful state using a nuclear weapon to prevent nuclear proliferation by a weak state in the third world that practices a different religion. An initiative early in the George W. Bush administration to promote new bunker-busting nuclear warheads was partly predicated on these grounds.[48] The short duration of this boomlet—the bunker buster idea went up as a trial balloon in 2002 and died in 2004—attests to the weakness of the arguments presented.

The United States still reserves the right to use nuclear weapons first in defense of friends and allies that do not possess the Bomb and that have threatening nuclear-armed neighbors. By refusing to pledge never to use nuclear weapons first, the United States seeks continued abstention by friends and allies, which, in turn, supports the global system to prevent proliferation. The validity of this argument vanishes if the United States becomes the first country to break a sixty-year-old nuclear taboo. Breaking this taboo against a far weaker nuclear-armed state now seems improbable; breaking it against a non-nuclear-weapon state seems inconceivable. In either case, U.S. forces have the most to lose if the nuclear taboo is broken. Another irony of the second nuclear age is that the country enjoying superior nuclear capabilities is most hamstrung in using them.

The case for preemption against Iranian nuclear facilities has already been made, and this chorus is likely to become louder over time.[49] Serious evaluation of the pros and cons of striking Iranian nuclear facilities has been undertaken within and outside the Bush administration.[50] The negative implications if Iran succeeds in acquiring the Bomb are evident, including the probability that nuclear hedges in several Middle Eastern countries will become realities and the possibility that Mahmoud Ahmadinejad and his admirers mean what they say when they talk about destroying Israel.[51] The negative implications of carrying out preemptive strikes against Iranian nuclear facilities are also evident, including greater challenges for U.S. military forces in Iraq and further destabilization in Iraq, Afghanistan, and the Middle East. U.S. strikes against Iran could also have far-reaching effects on U.S. ties to Pakistan.

The Iranian government has sought to build a large number of centrifuge cascades and has reluctantly acknowledged obtaining this technology covertly from the A. Q. Khan network. Tehran's poor track record of compliance with the International Atomic Energy Agency and its insistence on a complete nuclear fuel cycle suggest an interest in acquiring bomb-making material rather than a desire to fuel a large number of nuclear power reactors beyond the two that are currently under construction. Iran's intentions can be clarified with credible international offers to fuel Iran's nuclear power plants in return for the padlocking or dismantling of Iran's centrifuges or placing them under international control and ensuring inspection rights to visit suspect sites.

BACK TO BASICS: DETERRENCE

Nuclear deterrence against troubling states, like containment, has become easier in the second nuclear age than in the first. During the first nuclear age, deterrence strategists claimed that qualitative and quantitative aspects of the nuclear balance mattered, even at extraordinarily high numbers. If this highly debatable proposition is true, the United States has more deterrence leverage against major powers than at any time since the Soviet nuclear buildup in the 1960s. The Russian Federation's nuclear arsenal is still large enough to do massive damage, but it pales in comparison to the former Soviet Union's nuclear arsenal, whereas China's force levels remain extremely modest. Moscow seeks to affect the decisions of its neighbors, but not by means of nuclear threats. Instead, the Kremlin's primary forms of leverage are its ability to block energy supplies and consensus at the UN Security Council. Russia is no longer a global or ideological threat and cannot regain its lost status as a peer competitor to Washington.

Because the central measure of national power and influence in the second nuclear age is based on economics and not on warhead numbers, Russia will continue to rebound, whereas China will continue to derive leverage from economic dynamism, trade surpluses, and holdings of U.S. currency. Beijing's emphasis on economic growth provides ample resources for military modernization, especially from new arms sales and military coproduction agreements with Moscow. Beijing will most likely deploy in due time a nuclear deterrent on land and at sea that is sufficiently large to foil U.S. attempts at dissuasion. Beijing will also remain ahead of India in nuclear forces while seeking to avoid generating the intense anxieties that accompanied the Soviet strategic buildup. China's primary deterrents at present are its ability to harm U.S. warships and satellites in the event of a clash over Taiwan and its ability to cause economic turbulence in the United States because of its dollar holdings. Nuclear weapons constitute a secondary, evolving deterrent.

U.S. conventional military superiority in the second nuclear age has many implications for nuclear deterrence. One consequence has been that weak countries threatened by U.S. military superiority have sought their own nuclear programs for purposes of dissuasion. Another is that long-range conventional military capabilities can substitute for some U.S. nuclear strike options. The Bush administration's nuclear posture has embraced this shift by endorsing a "new triad" composed of offensive strike capabilities (both nuclear and conventional), defenses (passive and active), and "a revitalized defense infrastructure."[52] The innovation of adding conventional strike capabilities to U.S. nuclear war plans has meant, for all practical purposes, that the U.S. Strategic Command now has at its disposal weapons with great military utility as well as weapons with extremely limited utility. With conventional and nuclear strike options available under the same command, U.S. military preferences will facilitate further contractions in the U.S. nuclear arsenal.

Nevertheless, nuclear orthodoxy remains well entrenched. The U.S. nuclear arsenal has been downsized but not fundamentally altered in structure or targeting requirements from the first nuclear age. Adding up the requirements of nuclear deterrence, the George W. Bush administration's Nuclear Posture Review concluded that approximately 2,200 deployed nuclear weapons would be required through 2012, of which 1,500 could be launched in a matter of minutes. No less than 2,500 additional weapons would be kept as reserves and spares that could be reconstituted and deployed in a matter of days to many months, as deemed necessary.[53] These projected requirements suggest no diminished value to nuclear weapons since the latter years of the Clinton administration, which reached similar numerical conclusions.[54]

A radical alternative to the Bush administration's concepts of nuclear deterrence was offered by Paul Nitze. No one defended the dictates of remorseless nuclear targeting more strongly than Nitze during the first nuclear age, but this hardened cold warrior viewed nuclear weapons in an entirely different light after the United States achieved conventional military superiority. Nitze would no doubt have been pleased by the George W. Bush administration's incorporation of conventional strike options into nuclear war-fighting plans. But he no longer endorsed nuclear weapons as war-fighting instruments, even in retaliation.

> I can think of no circumstances under which it would be wise for the United States to use nuclear weapons, even in retaliation for their prior use against us. What, for example, would our targets be? It is impossible to conceive of a target that could be hit without large-scale destruction of many innocent people. The technology of our conventional weapons is such that we can achieve accuracies of less than three feet from the expected point of impact. The modern equivalent of a stick of dynamite exploded within three feet of an object on or near the earth's surface is more than enough to destroy the target. In view of the fact that we can achieve our objectives with conventional weapons, there is no purpose to be gained through the use of our nuclear arsenal. To use it would merely guarantee the annihilation of hundreds of thousands of people, none of whom would have been responsible for the decision invoked in bringing about the weapons' use, not to mention incalculable damage to our natural environment.[55]

At the end of a long life well lived, Nitze thus joined an illustrious group of pragmatic realists, beginning with Henry L. Stimson, in advocating the idealistic goal of total abolition. (After Nitze's death, George Shultz, Sam Nunn, Henry Kissinger, William Perry, Max Kampelman, and others would share his perspective.)[56] Typically, Nitze's conversion reflected logical deduction and rigorous analysis. In his view, the world had changed drastically after the dissolution of the Soviet Union, which required a fundamental shift in thinking about nuclear weapons. Because of U.S. conventional superiority, major powers such as Russia and China would not seek confrontation with Washington. If, however, in the unlikely event that confrontation occurred, the remote possibility of crossing the nuclear threshold would work against U.S. conventional military superiority. In any event, war-winning nuclear capabilities were not needed for this contingency; small nuclear arsenals would sufficiently clarify mutual dangers of escalation.

Following this logic, the use of U.S. nuclear weapons makes even less sense for other contingencies against weak states. Nitze's view, that devastating conventional firepower could be used to punish maverick states that were foolish enough to use a nuclear weapon, is hard to contest: The best outcome in the event of another crossing of the nuclear threshold would not be retaliation in kind but a punishing defeat by conventional means, regime change, and global revulsion against the state using a nuclear weapon. Under these circumstances, the nuclear taboo might be reconstituted and U.S. conventional military superiority would be reaffirmed. Nitze's view, however, flies in the face of decades of nuclear deterrence orthodoxy. The aphorism "never say never" when it comes to war-fighting contingencies and the possible use of nuclear weapons still has a long shelf life.

Orthodoxy aside, America's conventional military dominance clearly diminishes the requirements of nuclear deterrence and the range of circumstances under which the United States would resort to the battlefield use of nuclear weapons. These requirements are modest against major powers, minimal against weak states, and of no use against freelancers and extremist groups that are, by definition, not amenable to nuclear deterrence—or deterrence of any kind.[57] U.S. nuclear strikes against extremist groups operating under the protection of a state or in ungovernable areas would do immeasurable harm to America's standing and interests abroad and would prompt severe backlashes against U.S. forces and interests overseas. It would be hard to conceive of military benefits that would be so great as to override the negative consequences of the United States initiating battlefield use of a nuclear weapon in the third world or anywhere else.

Conventional strikes against extremist groups operating in safe havens are a different matter. The threat of U.S. conventional retaliation might stiffen the resolve of host countries to take their own preventive measures. If, however, the host state lacks the resolve or the capabilities to prevent its territory from being used as a sanctuary to carry out violent acts against the United States and U.S. deployed forces, Washington must reserve the right to carry out acts of self-defense. Punishment meted out by conventional strikes would generate a significant backlash against the United States in the country where sanctuary has been given. This might, however, be the least abhorrent choice of an American president, and a far better one than the least abhorrent choice facing President Truman and Secretary of War Stimson when they were contemplating the use of nuclear weapons to end the war in the Pacific as quickly as possible.[58]

NUCLEAR WEAPONS: HOW MANY? WHAT FOR?

Because nuclear weapons can do the most harm to the United States, its armed forces, and its friends and allies and because they can negate U.S. conventional military superiority, the elimination of nuclear weapons is the best end state for U.S. national security policy. This ultimate goal has the considerable added benefits of providing the most support for global efforts to prevent proliferation and nuclear terrorism. No other nuclear end state makes more sense than abolition. "Managed" proliferation and arms control do not offer suitable destinations or compelling rationales; nuclear anarchy is to be avoided at all costs, and attempts to assert U.S. nuclear dominance would accelerate the demise of global nonproliferation and disarmament norms. Abolition is the end state best suited to assist U.S. leaders in reducing nuclear dangers and in strengthening the global nonproliferation system.

Nuclear disarmament is, however, a process, not an on-off switch. It is a journey as well as a destination. The destination will not be reached unless public safety and national security are enhanced every step along the way. If security and political conditions cannot support this journey, it will grind to a halt. How, then, to proceed? Pragmatic steps can lead to ideal objectives, and ideal objectives can open the aperture for pragmatic steps. As the panel led by General Andrew Goodpaster and convened by the Stimson Center noted, "By contemplating the unthinkable, the boundaries of the feasible might well be stretched."[59] Abolition as an end state needs to be reaffirmed and taken seriously, but emphasis is better placed on pragmatic steps than on ideal objectives. Sweeping ambition can serve to highlight shortfalls more than it provides impetus to progress. When American presidents attempt to remake the world with rhetorical flourishes, they can be deeply humbled, as when Woodrow Wilson and George W. Bush announced their intention to make the world safe for democracy. Agenda setting is best distinguished from hyperbole, because hyperbole serves only to magnify inconsistencies and hypocrisy.

The ultimate goal of eliminating nuclear weapons provides a clear direction in which to proceed, because the right trajectory for America's nuclear forces in the second nuclear age is downward. How many steps are taken in the direction of nuclear disarmament also depends on the absence of the most worrisome developments discussed in Chapter 5. Even if every one of these negatives can be avoided, significant positive developments are required to gain traction in the direction of nuclear disarmament, beginning with cooperation among major powers. The safe harbor of nuclear disarmament remains a long way off, but an impressive list of people have signed up for this journey.

Getting to zero is not about arithmetic or fixed timelines. Ironically, trying to establish a time-bound framework is likely to increase resistance against abolition rather than facilitate progress toward it. Timelines reinforce a natural tendency of the mind to telescope contemporary constraints against a distant goal. This mental juxtaposition makes visionary goals appear otherworldly. Abolition, like other visionary goals, can be achieved only if contemporary constraints are systematically removed. Visionary deadlines may appeal to some who will not have responsibilities for implementing them. Deadlines may even be helpful in some instances when much heavy lifting has already occurred and national leaders are haggling over details. But for the most part, ambitious deadlines do not prompt sustained heavy lifting. The art of the possible usually has more appeal to political leaders. Getting to zero is a profoundly political process governed by the dictates of national and international security. More progress is likely to result from focusing on pragmatic steps than on picking a date to achieve this ideal end state.

Some reductions can be carried out unilaterally, but unilateral U.S. reductions will not proceed far unless accompanied by steps that provide further confidence in deeper cuts. Will others follow the U.S. lead? The U.S. commitment to and active pursuit of nuclear disarmament is necessary but insufficient to reach this destination. The hardest proliferation cases are likely to proceed whether or not the United States actively pursues the goal of nuclear disarmament—especially if the bomb programs of maverick states are partly driven by the need to deter superior U.S. power. But without U.S. leadership, it is hard to imagine significant progress toward this goal. Besides, if the United States fails to lead wisely, others will be more likely to make poor choices.

The dominant military power is also a dominant standard-bearer, role model, and trendsetter. If, for example, the United States refuses to ratify a treaty banning nuclear tests for all time, its admonitions against nuclear testing by others will ring hollow. Or if Washington insists on loosening the rules of nuclear commerce to benefit a friend, as in the case of India, it will be poorly positioned to hold the line against other nuclear suppliers that seek exceptions for their friends. The adage, "Do as I say, not as I do," doesn't work well in family settings, or in the family of nations. If the United States wants to adopt an a la carte approach to treaties and norms, others are likely to order from this menu. Treaties then become hollowed out, and norms give way to hedging strategies.

Washington's quest for nuclear disarmament would help provide the glue that holds the global nonproliferation system together; its quest for a war-winning nuclear posture acts as a solvent. Policies designed to maintain or extend U.S. nuclear dominance invite the very impulses dominance seeks to prevent. U.S. presidents who seek to maintain nuclear war-winning capabilities and to prevent proliferation also become trapped in contradictions and hypocrisy. Nuclear dominance, unlike conventional military dominance, is not a very usable commodity in the second nuclear age. Conventional military capabilities, for example, can buy time by slowing down or setting back some proliferation programs. The use of conventional firepower to combat proliferation can, however, be exhausting, even for the United States. The best chance of lasting success to prevent proliferation derives from a norms-based system backed up by the threat of collective action. The norm of nonproliferation has the most credibility when it is linked to the norm of nuclear disarmament and when norms apply to everyone, not just to bad actors.

Norms and nuclear requirements are shaped from the top down. The United States, sitting at the top of the nuclear pyramid, has the luxury of choice regarding the size and purposes of its nuclear weapons. Requirements will be determined, in part, by how much of a nuclear advantage Washington seeks. During the first nuclear age, Washington and Moscow adopted all the accoutrements of nuclear war-fighting capabilities while second-tier nuclear powers settled for far more modest requirements. In the second nuclear age, when the U.S. military budget is larger than the next fourteen nations combined,[60] only Washington can afford to possess "high-quality" nuclear deterrence. Russia and China will seek to maintain, at a minimum, the ability to target American cities and will upgrade their capabilities to counter U.S. efforts to escape from nuclear deterrence. China's exertions will, in turn, lend impetus to the nuclear programs of India and Pakistan.

Nuclear requirements are determined by the presumed military and political utility of nuclear weapons. Old arguments on these matters have not been settled, but the weight of these arguments has undeniably shifted. Powerful weapons that have not been used in warfare for six decades have declining military utility, especially for nations that enjoy conventional military advantage against potential foes. The Bomb's military utility for the United States has therefore never been lower. But political considerations relating to the Bomb remain paramount, and this factor comes into play in determining how many—or how few—nuclear weapons to keep.

Complications arise because the political and military utility of nuclear weapons cannot be completely separable, since presumed political value rests on the Bomb's destructive capacity. These calculations reached absurd levels during the cold war. Because the U.S. comparative advantage in the nuclear competition was technical ingenuity, whereas the Soviet Union relied heavily on brute force, there were endless reasons to suspect disadvantage, to stoke anxieties, and to build the next Bomb. Despite arguments to the contrary, there is scant evidence that political leaders in the White House or the Kremlin believed in the war-fighting particulars of the plans they signed off on. But no leaders other than Dwight D. Eisenhower, Nikita Khrushchev, Ronald Reagan, and Mikhail Gorbachev were willing to buck the system.

The Reagan-Gorbachev revolution is ongoing, in the sense that the Bomb's political and military utility continues to decline in relations between major powers. The world's most powerful nation cannot use nuclear weapons except in retaliation. It would be foolhardy for major powers to use nuclear weapons as a deliberate act against one another, and there is growing recognition among them that the manipulation of water or energy resources, trade flows, and currency transactions now has far greater political effect than brandishing nuclear weapons. The days when the United States alone produced fifteen variants of nine warhead designs between 1970 and 1997—an average of one new variant in less than two years—are long over.[61] The average age of a nuclear weapon in the U.S. stockpile now exceeds twenty-two years.[62]

The "mad momentum" of the nuclear arms competition that Secretary of Defense Robert McNamara railed against in 1967 died with the Soviet Union.[63] The "action-reaction" phenomenon that McNamara also warned against[64] has not gone away, but it is far more muted during the second nuclear age. Moscow and Beijing are revaluing the Bomb because of their conventional military inferiority to the United States and to guard against being leveraged by superior U.S. conventional capabilities. But this is not the only reason for Russian and Chinese nuclear requirements. U.S. nuclear offenses and more concerted efforts to deploy missile defenses also affect Moscow's and Beijing's choices.

The relationship between nuclear offense and missile defense has a complex history. A distinct minority view in the formative stages of arms control held that a defensive competition would be far preferable to an offensive competition.[65] This pristine choice was not, however, in the cards. The real-world choice facing the Nixon administration and the Kremlin in the early 1970s was whether the arms competition would proceed unimpeded in both offenses and defenses. Offenses worked and had powerful backers, whereas missile defenses did not work and had powerful opposition in the United States. As a practical matter, the Nixon administration elected to compete on offense while greatly constraining missile defense deployments.

The renewed interest in missile defenses by the George W. Bush administration comes at a time of steep decline in Russian offensive nuclear forces and a renewed embrace in U.S. doctrine of victory in nuclear war. Under these circumstances, even the deployment of limited U.S. missile defenses, especially those situated in what was once the domain of the Soviet Union, will serve to revalue nuclear weapons in Russia and China. Missile defenses do have a role in protecting against worst cases. They also become more necessary as an insurance policy as significant progress is made toward nuclear abolition. In the meantime, missile defenses become an impediment to reaching this destination.

This paradox cannot be resolved unless and until relations between great powers become free of serious contentious issues. In the interim, further nuclear arms reductions can be carried out between Washington and Moscow because legacy nuclear arsenals from the cold war remain so large and because the expense of replacing warheads on a one-for-one basis is so hard to justify. Downsizing excessive nuclear forces in the field would be far more meaningful if accompanied by verifiable nuclear warhead reduction and elimination—a long-sought goal that is worthy of renewed effort.

The permitted deployment of more than 2,000 nuclear weapons in the 2002 Moscow Treaty reflects the preferences of those most heavily invested in their accumulation. A long-term process that produces much deeper cuts requires parallel verifiable steps by the Kremlin. To proceed otherwise would be to invite stoppage and setbacks. Because of the political salience of the Bomb, numbers and verification continue to matter. How far is the Kremlin willing to proceed down this path alongside the United States? Several factors suggest steeper reductions by Moscow, including the block obsolescence of Soviet-era stockpiles and the shrunken size of the Russian military-industrial complex. But old habits are hard to break, especially when the distance between U.S. and Russian military capabilities is so great. The Kremlin's choices will likely depend less on conventional military imbalances than on whether Washington insists on keeping nuclear forces and missile defenses consistent with the goal of prevailing in nuclear exchanges.

Deep, parallel, and verifiable reductions in U.S. and Russian nuclear arsenals are a prerequisite for other countries to join a procession toward nuclear abolition. One crucial determinant will be whether China's leaders become more attached to the Bomb as Beijing's fortunes grow. During the first nuclear age, when China was in the crosshairs of both U.S. and Soviet nuclear targeting plans, Beijing remained remarkably relaxed about its nuclear requirements. The basic necessities of Chinese deterrence appear greater during the second nuclear age, when Beijing faces just one nuclear superpower.

Another crucial determinant for deep cuts in nuclear warheads will be the willingness of states with second-tier nuclear arsenals to accept transparency measures. China has long found safety in opaqueness. This will be a hard habit to break, especially if Washington and Moscow turn their back on intrusive monitoring arrangements negotiated during the cold war. All the other second-tier nuclear weapon states—the United Kingdom, France, India, Pakistan, and Israel—have severe allergies to transparency.

How much can the United States draw down its nuclear arsenal? As low as political and national security conditions permit. The diminishing utility of nuclear weapons and the growing utility of conventional strike capabilities are enduring trends for the United States. Most Americans have fallen out of thrall with nuclear weapons, and the Bush administration's classified endorsement of "decisive" victory in nuclear warfare, which requires large nuclear forces, is not publicly sustainable. If, alternatively, future American presidents accept President Reagan's precept that a nuclear war cannot be won, they can either force the radical revision in nuclear war plans or leave these plans in locked safes and continue the process of incremental reductions.

When the Bomb's military utility is low, then few particulars matter. Having mechanisms designed to prevent accidental detonations and unauthorized use certainly matter. Nuclear laboratories must also be sure that bomb designs and weapons on hand will produce mushroom clouds if, as a last resort, they are needed. Rudimentary bomb designs that never need to be tested can serve this most basic function of deterrence. Of course, the most obvious target for simple bomb designs—the cities on which world civilization has been built—presents a morally reprehensible choice. To avoid this choice, more complex bomb designs have been designed for a long list of targets. In truth, these options have served to provide only more, not fewer, morally reprehensible choices.

During the first nuclear age, the United States and the Soviet Union felt obliged to replace elementary bomb designs with far more powerful thermonuclear weapons, which have subsequently become emblems of status and deterrence for Great Britain, France, and China as well. India has claimed this capability, although its sole test of a thermonuclear weapon design may have been insufficient to warrant this claim. If and when India and Pakistan resume nuclear testing, they will likely be seeking similar capabilities.

All states possessing nuclear weapons are either refurbishing weapons built during the cold war or building new warheads. The United States and, to a lesser extent, Great Britain do not have the luxury of doing so without intense scrutiny. The United States retains many plutonium "pits" from dismantled weapons that could be recycled, as their shelf life may be as long as 100 years.[66] Nonetheless, U.S. deterrence strategists are greatly concerned by the aging cohort of bomb designers and the warheads they built, which are so complex that they might someday fail.[67] These designs were not built to last; they were built to be replaced by newer designs.

The Bush administration has proposed partially replacing cold war–era weapons with "reliable replacement warheads," stressing that they would be easier to maintain and far less likely to require a resumption of underground nuclear testing. Acknowledging that an extensive, high-profile, and expensive swap of old warheads for newer, more reliable designs could be harmful to U.S. global nonproliferation objectives, the Bush administration promised that the swap would facilitate unspecified reductions in warheads held in reserve and that the new designs would not entail new roles or missions for the replacement warheads.[68] The initial reliable replacement warheads were to be fitted atop submarine-based missiles and would carry a yield, like their predecessors, of approximately 100 kilotons—seven times more powerful than the weapon that destroyed Hiroshima. During the cold war, weapons of this kind were planned for use against industrial targets, harbors, and mobile missile launchers.

The Bush administration's initiative was not well received domestically or internationally. Nuclear weapon states under the Nonproliferation Treaty have every right to modernize their stockpiles, but the well-being of the global nonproliferation system mandates that obligations to nuclear nonproliferation and disarmament be taken seriously as well. The Bush administration's enthusiasm for this broader agenda was selective. Supporters of reliable replacement warheads therefore found themselves in the awkward position of arguing that treaties could be discarded as relics of the cold war but that cold war–era warheads needed to be replaced to execute cold war–like targeting plans.

A persuasive case for the reliable replacement warhead program has yet to be made. If such a case is advanced, it will likely be accompanied by far more impressive steps to affirm U.S. commitments to nonproliferation and nuclear disarmament than the Bush administration has been prepared to offer. If the primary rationale for reliable replacement warheads is to affirm deterrence while stockpiles are systematically reduced, their designs could be rudimentary and accompanying diplomatic initiatives could be ambitious. Under these circumstances, reliable replacement warheads could ironically advance the policy preferences of those who are most opposed to them.

THE ROLE OF MISSILE DEFENSES

During the first nuclear age, the primary axis of proliferation was vertical, as U.S. and Soviet nuclear arsenals grew precipitously, even without deploying sophisticated missile defenses. Rationales for missile defenses shifted in the second nuclear age, reflecting concerns over new states seeking nuclear capabilities, especially Iran and North Korea. Although concerns have shifted to horizontal proliferation, the problem of vertical proliferation has not gone away, because the Chinese, Indian, and Pakistani nuclear arsenals are growing. One test of the success of U.S. missile defense deployments in the second nuclear age will therefore be whether they are able to counter horizontal proliferation without encouraging vertical proliferation.

Many obstacles are associated with missile defenses, beginning with their cost and technical feasibility. Predictions of highly effective missile defenses date back to the late 1950s and have yet to be realized, despite U.S. investments of more than $130 billion.[69] Greater returns on investment are now possible. Nonetheless, missile defense purchases require difficult trade-offs. Some states facing proliferation threats might well conclude that expensive missile defense purchases may not be wise investments compared to buying more offensive firepower.

Missile defenses could help dampen horizontal proliferation when they provide assurance of U.S. protection and support against threatening neighbors. At the same time, their deployment could prompt more investments in the very programs that missile defenses are designed to blunt. As ballistic missile defenses mature, investments in cruise missiles—which require different kinds of defenses—are also likely to grow.[70]

The hardest defense is against missiles that travel the longest distances; their warheads arrive at high speeds and are accompanied by decoys designed to fool the defenders. Russia's capabilities to penetrate missile defenses are mature; little has been written publicly about China's capabilities. Very short-range ballistic missiles, such as those deployed by China opposite Taiwan, are also hard to intercept when they are fired en masse. More progress has been made against missiles that travel intermediate distances, such as derivatives of Soviet SCUD missiles, which have been widely copied. Japan and Israel have already deployed "theater" missile defenses, which also accompany U.S. expeditionary forces in regions where SCUD-type missiles are plentiful.

Strong advocates of missile defenses also call for deployments of space-based weapons to intercept missiles in flight. These defenses pose even harder technical and cost challenges, because a large number of interceptors in space would be required to have timely coverage over countries that can threaten missile attacks. If technical and cost challenges can somehow be met, space-based missile defenses would themselves have to be defended against relatively inexpensive countermeasures, such as space mines parked nearby.

Although Moscow and Beijing are particularly sensitive to U.S. missile defenses, they may still help Washington with hard proliferation cases when doing so serves their national security interests—as in the case of North Korea. If, however, U.S. missile defenses appear designed and sized to negate the Chinese nuclear deterrent and to make Russia uneasy about the offense-defense equation, they may generate more problems than they solve. The Bush administration announced plans in 2002 to deploy the first ten missile defense interceptors to deal with the possibility of a North Korean attack. In 2005, the administration requested forty interceptors to be deployed in Alaska and California. In January 2007, it announced plans to deploy an additional ten long-range missile interceptors in Poland along with a new radar facility in the Czech Republic. The stated reason for this decision, which came after minimal prior consultation with Congress, NATO, and Russia, was to intercept missiles launched from Iran. In response, the Kremlin suggested missile defenses closer to the Iranian border, to which the Bush administration responded coolly.

The administration's stated rationales for seeking to deploy more than fifty missile defense interceptors could be a matter of simple prudence. This is, however, a high insurance premium to pay for a low-probability threat. A long-range missile attack by either North Korea or Iran would provide an incontestable return address for American wrath. Besides, both countries have far easier and plausibly deniable ways to attack the United States and its expeditionary forces, friends, and allies.[71]

Another reason to deploy fifty or more missile defense interceptors is to implement a damage-limiting strategy in the event of nuclear exchanges with China or Russia. This threat also seems improbable, but superiority still matters to those who believe in high-quality deterrence. "The victor," as Paul Nitze wrote during the Eisenhower administration, "will be able to issue orders to the loser and the loser will have to obey them or face complete chaos or extinction." The greater the margin of superiority, Nitze wrote, "the less likely it is that a nuclear war will ever occur. The greater that margin, the greater are our chances of seeing to it that nuclear war, if it does come, is fought rationally and that the resulting destruction is kept to the lowest levels feasible."[72] In Nitze's view, there was "no doubt as to the desirability of a war-winning capability, *if feasible.*"[73]

Nitze's views changed, but his old playbook was not thrown away after the dissolution of the Soviet Union—not when the presumed value of high-quality deterrence and the potential for damage limitation were finally so evident. The end of the cold war permitted the retention of superior U.S. nuclear offenses, which could now be supplemented with national missile defenses in sufficient number presumably to ensure dissuasion and victory.

Missile defenses are deployed for many reasons, but the most plausible rationale for fifty long-range interceptors relates more to Russia and China than to North Korea and Iran. If, instead of seeking missile defenses keyed to nuclear war-fighting plans and high-quality deterrence, the United States sought an insurance policy against the Iranian and North Korean missile programs, interceptors would primarily be deployed in regions where threatening missile programs are located. Collaborative missile defense ventures against Iran would be sought with Moscow, but the Kremlin would not be granted veto powers over missile defense deployments. Plans for interceptors based on U.S. soil would be scaled down considerably.

COOPERATIVE THREAT REDUCTION: THE FIFTH ELEMENT

Safe passage in the second nuclear age requires a return to basics and creative adaptation. The basics of containment, deterrence, military strength, and proactive diplomacy have served America well before, and they can do so again. Creative adaptation is needed most in transitioning from arms control to cooperative threat reduction. The best math for dealing with complex nuclear dangers continues to be addition, not subtraction. All five key elements are required for a comprehensive strategy to promote nonproliferation and nuclear disarmament, strengthen norms, build coalitions of the willing, and isolate problem states.

Arms control was a product of the first nuclear age. It played an essential role in reversing vertical proliferation and in building the foundations for a global system to prevent horizontal proliferation. Arms control was state centric, and no state mattered more than the Soviet Union. Cooperative threat reduction has eclipsed traditional arms control because new problems of proliferation and nuclear terrorism are not just state centric. Arms control treaties were central to the first nuclear age because the practice of limiting and then reducing weapons of mass destruction was so novel. Cold war–era treaties that established nonproliferation norms, fostered habits of cooperation, and mandated intrusive monitoring remain essential for preventing new nuclear dangers from arising. But cold war–era bilateral treaties carry less freight, and power differentials in the second nuclear age make complex treaties harder to negotiate.

More adaptive, less formal cooperative threat reduction agreements are now central because the challenges of proliferation and extremism evolve far more rapidly than treaties can be negotiated or amended. This is not an either/ or proposition, however, because flexible practices of cooperative threat reduction work best when they build on and supplement formal agreements. After the sudden shift from the first nuclear age to the second, U.S. nuclear weapon laboratories became the foremost practitioners of cooperative threat reduction, forging novel partnerships with their Russian counterparts to consolidate and protect the sprawling inventories of nuclear weapons in the former Soviet Union. The most important products of U.S. laboratories quickly shifted from highly classified bomb designs to transferable, unclassified technologies to upgrade security at sensitive sites and facilitate safe transits to central storage locations where nuclear weapons could best be secured. Subsequent practices of cooperative threat reduction focused on detecting the movement of dangerous materials across borders and through ports.

These halcyon days are over. Cooperative threat reduction programs have subsequently become sluggish and bureaucratized. U.S.-Russian ties have deteriorated as the Kremlin seeks to reassert its influence around Russia's periphery and as its concerns over the Bush administration's strategic objectives have grown. The extension of cooperative threat reduction programs continues in other regions, but if these practices deteriorate where they began, the entire enterprise will be weakened at its core.

All the central tenets of safe passage during the first nuclear age—deterrence, containment, diplomacy, military strength, and arms control—were severely doubted at one time or another. Skeptics were proven wrong. After the attacks on 9/11, the role of deterrence, containment, diplomacy, and arms control were widely denigrated in dealing with problem states. Wisdom comes with second thoughts and painful experience. Containment, deterrence, and diplomacy, which were treated so dismissively by the Bush administration with respect to Saddam Hussein, appear to have reproved their value in the case of North Korea and may yet prove their worth in the harder case of Iran.

There remains much skepticism concerning the utility of cooperative threat reduction programs, and with good reason: So much work remains to be done, and there is an insufficient sense of urgency to proceed with greater dispatch. And yet there is much upside potential for cooperative threat reduction because all major powers during the second nuclear age face the common enemies of nuclear terrorism and the demise of the global nonproliferation system. There is more of a common basis than ever before for major powers to engage collaboratively on cooperative threat reduction.

The foundations and load-bearing walls of the global system to prevent proliferation need repair, but the structure remains standing and can be strengthened. In truth, there is no other option. If the walls of this structure lose all or most of their load-bearing capacity, many states would seek the Bomb or seek to be a screwdriver's turn away from it. All or most of the key proliferation drivers would be in play, and the potential for acts of nuclear terrorism would be greatly increased. It will be hard to find safety in this nuclear-armed crowd.

The importance of the construction work of the first nuclear age can best be appreciated by imagining the world without the Nonproliferation Treaty. If this treaty were to collapse or become meaningless, it would be extremely difficult to build a solid structure to take its place. Nations that have the Bomb and those that have abstained from acquiring it would be unlikely to negotiate an alternative compact with new rules of nuclear cooperation. And if Washington's actions have much to do with the hollowing out of the Nonproliferation Treaty, U.S. leadership in any new construction project would be suspect.

Many headaches lie ahead, but negotiating treaties during the first nuclear age was far more difficult than implementing cooperative threat reduction initiatives in the second. Much work remains to be done, but there is no secret to success: The techniques and technologies that enable success are readily available. Working in tandem with containment, deterrence, military strength, and proactive diplomacy, cooperative threat reduction initiatives can provide safe passage during the second nuclear age.

PARADOXICAL SAFETY

Nuclear dangers, both familiar and new, have so far been kept in check. Two central paradoxes dominated the first nuclear age. The first was Winston Churchill's "sublime irony," expressed more in hope than in conviction, that "safety will be the sturdy child of terror, and survival the twin brother of annihilation" during the cold war.[74] The other was "the paradoxical fact" identified by Henry Kissinger in 1960 "that there is a certain safety in numbers."[75] These twin paradoxes led to huge superpower arsenals. Additional increments of nuclear "safety" sharpened these paradoxes in extreme ways. Many thousands of nuclear weapons remained poised for use for many decades, but no weapons were used in battle.

Perhaps another paradox will be formulated to deal with widespread concerns over nuclear terrorism in the second nuclear age. An endless number of acts of nuclear terrorism are conceivable, but the first has yet to occur. One protection—so far—has been that the worst acts of nuclear terrorism require the most difficult acquisitions. Producing a nuclear weapon—assuming that an intact, usable bomb has not been purchased on the black market—entails collaboration and diverse skill sets. Terrorist cells typically work in isolation, where they are less susceptible to detection, and if infiltrated or monitored, they do not reveal other cells. These practices make it harder for intelligence agencies and law enforcement officials to uncover plots, but they also make it harder for extremist groups to build nuclear bombs. Illicit acquisitions of dirty-bomb-making material are certainly possible, but these devices are likely to do far less damage than other types of terrorist acts using large batches of conventional explosives; this might explain why dirty bombs have not yet been featured by extremist groups.

Prior efforts to seek safety amid nuclear danger have flirted with catastrophe many times. A bomber on strip alert was engulfed in flames, and others flying H-bombs crashed without producing mushroom clouds. Poorly guarded nuclear weapons on the front lines of the cold war could have been stolen but were not. Security over nuclear weapons somehow remained sufficient during the Cultural Revolution and the breakup of the Soviet Union. Human error and misjudgment repeatedly occurred, including in the midst of severe crisis. U.S. officials presumed that Soviet nuclear weapons were not present during the Cuban missile crisis. They were wrong. U.S. deterrence strategists presumed that a "dead hand" doomsday device for nuclear retaliation was not a part of the Soviet system. They were wrong. The U.S. intelligence community produced overheated threat estimates while profoundly misreading the Soviet Union at key junctures. Lessons of nuclear safety were forgotten, only to be relearned. The Bomb had many thousands of guardians, not all of whom should have passed personnel reliability screening tests. And yet human fallibility did not result in the worst possible consequences. Analogous episodes may well occur in the second nuclear age, but as yet, Murphy's Law has not completely run its course.

Time and again, instinctive human responses have trumped nuclear war-fighting plans. In the depths of the Cuban missile crisis, President Kennedy, Premier Khrushchev, and Vasili Alexandrovich Arkipov—the one officer on board the B-59 submarine who blocked the use of a nuclear-armed torpedo while being depth-charged to the surface by the U.S. Navy—walked up to the abyss and turned back. Nuclear war-fighting plans presumed rationality and human control. These assumptions were heroic, to say the least. Kennedy, Khrushchev, and Arkipov—the apex of the command and control chain and just one link of the chain that could have broken under the severest pressure—knew better.

The quite human instinct of being safe rather than sorry repeatedly worked at cross purposes. Safety led to an excess of caution, and an excess of caution led to excessive nuclear arsenals. George W. Bush and his inner circle took major risks to invade Iraq in order to prevent Saddam Hussein from acquiring nuclear weapons. Their pursuit of safety has produced much sorrow. The human factor invites Murphy's Law, but it also has helped to prevent numerous close calls from resulting in mushroom clouds. If past again becomes prologue, close calls with nuclear terrorism can be expected—especially if cooperative threat reduction efforts lag.

Nuclear history is laden with irony, and more ironies—perhaps deadly, perhaps not—lie ahead. Safe passage during the first nuclear age required steadfastness, good fortune, learning from mistakes, and, above all, wisdom. Safe passage during the second nuclear age will require more of the same.

NOTES

Preface

1. The Natural Resources Defense Council's data indicate that the United States built approximately 70,000 weapons and the USSR another 55,000. See Robert S. Norris and Hans M. Kristensen, "Global Nuclear Stockpiles, 1945–2006," *Bulletin of the Atomic Scientists* 62(4) (July–August 2006): 64–66 (available at http://www.thebulletin.org/article_nn.php?art_ofn=ja06norris).

2. Measured in constant year 1996 dollars. Stephen I. Schwartz, ed., *Atomic Audit: The Costs and Consequences of U.S. Nuclear Weapons Since 1940* (Washington, DC: Brookings Institution Press, 1998), 3.

3. Dan Morgan, "House Passes Massive Farm Bill," *Washington Post*, July 28, 2007 (available at http://www.washingtonpost.com/wp-dyn/content/article/2007/07/27/AR2007072700350.html?wpisrc=newsletter).

4. Amy Belasco, Congressional Research Service, *The Cost of Iraq, Afghanistan, and Other Global War on Terror Operations Since 9/11*, Federation of American Scientists, March 14, 2007, 3 (available at http://www.fas.org/sgp/crs/natsec/RL33110.pdf).

5. Norris and Kristensen, "Global Nuclear Stockpiles," 64–66.

6. Henry L. Stimson, "The Challenge to Americans," *Foreign Affairs* 26(1) (October 1947): 9.

Chapter 1

1. For positive assessments of the Proliferation Security Initiative, see Andrew C. Winner, "The Proliferation Security Initiative: The New Face of Interdiction," *Washington Quarterly* 28(2) (spring 2005): 129–143; and Commander Joel A. Doolin, "The Proliferation Security Initiative: Cornerstone of a New International Norm," *Naval War College Review* 59(2) (spring 2006): 29–57. For a rebuttal, see Mark J. Valencia, "Is

the PSI Really the Cornerstone of a New International Norm?" *Naval War College Review* 59(4) (autumn 2006): 122–130. Also see James A. Russell, "Peering into the Abyss: Non-State Actors and the 2016 Proliferation Environment," *Nonproliferation Review* 13(3) (November 2006): 645–657.

2. United Nations Security Council, "Security Council Decides All States Shall Act to Prevent Proliferation of Mass Destruction Weapons: Resolution 1540 (2004), Adopted Unanimously, Focuses Attention on Non-State Actors," available at http://www .un .org/News/Press/docs/2004/sc8076.doc.htm.

3. Arms Control Association, "International Code of Conduct Against Ballistic Missile Proliferation," available at http://www.armscontrol.org/documents/icoc.asp.

4. The White House, Office of the Press Secretary, "Fact Sheet: The Global Initiative to Combat Nuclear Terrorism, July 15, 2006," available at http://www.whitehouse .gov/news/releases/2006/07/20060715-3.html.

Chapter 2

1. Oliver M. Gale, "Post-Sputnik Washington from an Inside Office," *Cincinnati Historical Society Bulletin* 31 (winter 1973): 226. This wonderful quote was unearthed by Walter A. McDougall, . . . *The Heavens and the Earth: A Political History of the Space Age* (New York: Basic Books, 1985).

2. For examples of apocalyptic warnings, see Fred Charles Iklé, *Annihilation from Within: The Ultimate Threat to Nations* (New York: Columbia University Press, 2006); and Graham Allison, *Nuclear Terrorism: The Ultimate Preventable Catastrophe* (New York: Times Books, 2004).

3. Richard L. Armitage, "Remarks at Educational and Cultural Affairs Exchange Fair," Washington, D.C., November 18, 2003, available at http://www.state.gov/s/d/ former/armitage/remarks/26325.htm.

4. Dean Acheson, *Present at the Creation: My Years in the State Department* (New York: Norton, 1970), 375.

5. Walter Pincus and Dana Milbank, "Bush Reasserts Hussein–Al Qaeda Link," *Washington Post*, June 17, 2004 (available at http://www.washingtonpost.com/wp-dyn/ articles/A48970-2004Jun17.html).

6. Colin L. Powell, "Remarks to the United Nations Security Council," New York, February 5, 2003, available at http://www.state.gov/secretary/former/powell/ remarks/2003/17300.htm.

7. "Interview with Vice President Richard B. Cheney," *Rush Limbaugh Show*, April 5, 2007, available at http://www.rushlimbaugh.com/home/daily/site_040507/ content/01125106.guest.html.

8. The White House, Office of the Press Secretary, "President Bush Discusses War on Terror in South Carolina," July 24, 2007, available at http://www.whitehouse.gov/ news/releases/2007/07/20070724-3.html.

9. George Tenet, *At the Center of the Storm: My Years at the CIA* (New York: Harper Collins, 2007), 341.

10. "Iraq, 9/11, Al Qaeda, and Weapons of Mass Destruction: What the Public Believes Now According to the Latest Harris Poll," Harris Poll 14, February 18, 2005, Harris Interactive, available at http://www.harrisinteractive.com/harris_poll/index.asp?PID=544.

11. "Interview with Condoleezza Rice; Pataki Talks About 9-11; Graham, Shelby Discuss War on Terrorism," *Late Edition with Wolf Blitzer*, CNN, September 8, 2002, available at http://transcripts.cnn.com/TRANSCRIPTS/0209/08/le.00.html.

12. The White House, Office of the Press Secretary, "President Bush Outlines Iraqi Threat," Cincinnati, Ohio, October 7, 2002, available at http://www.whitehouse.gov/news/releases/2002/10/20021007-8.html.

13. Ron Suskind, *The One Percent Doctrine: Deep Inside America's Pursuit of Its Enemies Since 9/11* (New York: Simon & Schuster, 2006), 62.

14. "Interview with Vice President Dick Cheney," *Meet the Press*, NBC, March 16, 2003, available at http://www.mtholyoke.edu/acad/intrel/bush/cheneymeetthepress.htm.

15. See Richard A. Clarke, *Against All Enemies: Inside America's War on Terror* (New York: Free Press, 2004), 264–265.

16. Allison, *Nuclear Terrorism*, 203.

17. Richard G. Lugar, *The Lugar Survey on Proliferation Threats and Responses*, June 2005, available at http://lugar.senate.gov/reports/NPSurvey.pdf.

18. William J. Perry, Ashton B. Carter, and Michael M. May, "After the Bomb," *New York Times*, June 12, 2007 (available at http://www.nytimes.com/2007/06/12/opinion/12carter.html); Sam Nunn, "Statement on Nuclear Weapons Policy," House Committee on Foreign Affairs, May 10, 2007, 2, available at http://www.international-relations.house.gov/110/nun051007.htm.

19. Matthew Brzezinski, *Red Moon Rising: Sputnik and the Hidden Rivalries That Ignited the Space Age* (New York: Henry Holt, 2007), 182.

20. John Mueller, *Overblown: How Politicians and the Terrorism Industry Inflate National Security Threats, and Why We Believe Them* (New York: Free Press, 2006), 2, 34, 142. Also see William M. Arkin, "The Continuing Misuses of Fear," *Bulletin of the Atomic Scientists* 62(5) (September–October 2006): 42–45.

21. Zbigniew Brzezinski, "Terrorized by 'War on Terror': How a Three-Word Mantra Has Undermined America," *Washington Post*, March 25, 2007 (available at http://www.washingtonpost.com/wp-dyn/content/article/2007/03/23/AR2007032301613.html). This argument is elaborated in Zbigniew Brzezinski, *Second Chance: Three Presidents and the Crisis of American Superpower* (New York: Basic Books, 2007).

22. Director of National Intelligence, "Unclassified Report to Congress on the Acquisition of Technology Relating to Weapons of Mass Destruction and Advanced Conventional Munitions: 1 January–31 December 2004," available at http://dni.gov/

reports/2004_unclass_report_to_NIC_DO_16Nov04.pdf; and U.S. Department of State Department, *International Narcotics Control Strategy Report*, v. 2, *Money Laundering and Financial Crimes*, prepared by the Bureau for International Narcotics and Law Enforcement Affairs, March 2007, available at http://www.state.gov/documents/organization/81447.pdf.

23. Strobe Talbott, *The Master of the Game: Paul Nitze and the Nuclear Peace* (New York: Knopf, 1988), 15.

24. See Sheldon M. Stern, *The Week the World Stood Still: Inside the Secret Cuban Missile Crisis* (Stanford, CA: Stanford University Press, 2005); Ernest R. May and Philip D. Zelikow (eds.), *The Kennedy Tapes: Inside the White House During the Cuban Missile Crisis* (Cambridge, MA: Belknap Press, 1997); and Raymond L. Garthoff, *Reflections on the Cuban Missile Crisis* (Washington, DC: Brookings Institution Press, 1989).

25. National Security Council, *NSC 68: United States Objectives and Programs for National Security*, Federation of American Scientists, available at http://www.fas.org/irp/offdocs/nsc-hst/nsc-68.htm. For more on NSC 68, see, for example, Ernest R. May, *American Cold War Strategy: Interpreting NSC 68* (New York: Bedford Books in American History, 1993); and S. Nelson Drew (ed.), *NSC-68: Forging the Strategy of Containment* (Washington, DC: National Defense University, 1994).

26. The Gaither Committee report can be accessed at http://www.gwu.edu/~nsarchiv/NSAEBB/NSAEBB139/nitze02.pdf: Security Resources Panel of the Science Advisory Committee, *Deterrence and Survival in the Nuclear Age*, National Security Archive, George Washington University, November 7, 1957. For more on the Gaither Committee, see, for example, David L. Snead, *The Gaither Committee, Eisenhower, and the Cold War* (Columbus: Ohio State University Press, 1999); and Peter J. Roman, *Eisenhower and the Missile Gap* (Ithaca, NY: Cornell University Press, 1995).

27. Eisenhower's exact words were, "In the councils of government, we must guard against the acquisition of unwarranted influence, whether sought or unsought, by the military-industrial complex. The potential for the disastrous rise of misplaced power exists and will persist." Dwight D. Eisenhower, "Farewell Address," Eisenhower Center, January 17, 1961, available at http://www.eisenhower.archives.gov/speeches/farewell_address.html.

28. National Resources Defense Council, "Table of Global Nuclear Weapons Stockpiles, 1945–2002," November 25, 2002, available at http://www.nrdc.org/nuclear/nudb/datab19.asp.

29. Chalmers M. Roberts, "Enormous Arms Outlay Is Held Vital to Survival: U.S. in Gravest Danger, Gaither Report Holds," *Washington Post*, December 20, 1957.

30. NIE 11-8-59, "Soviet Capabilities for Strategic Attack Through Mid-1964," in Donald P. Steury (ed.), *Intentions and Capabilities: Estimates on Soviet Strategic Forces, 1950–1983* (Washington, DC: Center for the Study of Intelligence, 1996), 73.

31. "The National Intelligence Estimates A-B Team Episode Concerning Soviet Strategic Capability and Objectives," Report of the Senate Select Committee on Intelligence, Subcommittee on Collection, Production, and Quality, United States Senate, Together with Separate Views, 95th Congress, 2nd session, February 16, 1978, 4, accessible at http://www.mtholyoke.edu/acad/intrel/afp/Team%20B.htm.

32. Central Intelligence Agency, "Intelligence Community Experiment in Competitive Analysis: Soviet Strategic Objectives an Alternate View (Report of Team 'B')," December 1976, accessible at http://www.gwu.edu/~nsarchiv/NSAEBB/NSAEBB139/nitze10.pdf. Also see Richard B. Pipes, "Team B: The Reality Behind the Myth," *Commentary* 82 (October 1986): 25–40. For a book-length critique of the Team B exercise, see Anne Hessing Cahn, *Killing Detente: The Right Attacks the CIA* (University Park: Pennsylvania State University Press, 1998).

33. Bernard Gwertzman, "Kissinger Says Idea of Supremacy Makes No Sense in a Nuclear Age," *New York Times*, January 11, 1977.

34. William Beecher, "High-Level Study Says CIA Understates Extent of Soviet Threat," *Boston Globe*, December 17, 1976.

35. For a book-length assessment of the Committee on the Present Danger and its antecedents, see Jerry W. Sanders, *Peddlers of Crisis: The Committee on the Present Danger and the Politics of Containment* (Cambridge, MA: South End Press, 1983).

36. David Binder, "Group Warns on Soviet Expansion," *New York Times*, April 4, 1977.

37. Defense Intelligence Agency, *Soviet Military Power, 1983*, ch. 2, "Strategic Forces," Federation of American Scientists, available at http://www.fas.org/irp/dia/product/smp_index.htm.

38. Director of Central Intelligence, "Soviet Capabilities for Strategic Nuclear Conflict, 1982–92 (NIE 11-3/8-82), Volume I: Key Judgments and Summary," February 15, 1983, in Donald P. Steury (compiler), *(Declassified) Estimates on Soviet Military Power, 1954 to 1984: A Selection* (Washington, DC: Center for the Study of Intelligence, Central Intelligence Agency, 1994), 5.

39. Director of Central Intelligence, "Soviet Capabilities for Strategic Nuclear Conflict," 5.

40. Director of Central Intelligence, "Soviet Capabilities for Strategic Nuclear Conflict," 29.

41. A balanced account of the war scare and the U.S. intelligence community's performance during this period can be found in Benjamin B. Fischer, *A Cold War Conundrum: 1983 Cold War Scare* (Washington, DC: Center for the Study of Intelligence, Central Intelligence Agency, 1997).

42. Christopher Andrew and Oleg Gordievsky, *KGB: The Inside Story of Its Foreign Operations from Lenin to Gorbachev* (London: Hodder and Stoughton, 1990), 70.

43. One of the authors of the Iraqi estimate, Lawrence K. Gershwin, was also

a key figure in the most worrisome Soviet estimates. To read the declassified key judgments of the prewar estimate, see Central Intelligence Agency, *Iraq's Continuing Programs for Weapons of Mass Destruction*, NIE 2002-16HC, October 2002, Federation of American Scientists, available at http://www.fas.org/irp/cia/product/iraq-wmd-nie.pdf.

44. The White House, National Security Council, *The National Security Strategy of the United States of America*, The White House, September 2002, available at http://www.whitehouse.gov/nsc/nss.pdf.

Chapter 3

1. Robert S. Norris and Hans M. Kristensen, "Global Nuclear Stockpiles, 1945–2006," *Bulletin of the Atomic Scientists* 62 (4) (July–August 2006): 64–66 (data provided by the Natural Resources Defense Council).

2. See Michael Krepon, *Strategic Stalemate: Nuclear Weapons and Arms Control in American Politics* (New York: St. Martin's Press, 1984).

3. See McGeorge Bundy, *Danger and Survival: Choices About the Bomb in the First Fifty Years* (New York: Random House, 1988).

4. See, for example, Sherry Sontag, Christopher Drew, and Annette Lawrence Drew, *Blind Man's Bluff: The Untold Story of American Submarine Espionage* (New York: Public Affairs, 1998); and Seymour Hersh, *The Target Is Destroyed* (New York: Random House, 1986). Hans Kristensen has documented "Chrome Dome" B-52 missions carrying nuclear weapons over the Arctic. See Hans Kristensen, "The Airborne Alert Program over Greenland," Nuclear Information Project, available at http://www.nukestrat.com/dk/alert.htm. For more on the U.S. Army's early embrace of tactical nuclear weapons, see A. J. Bacevich, *The Pentomic Era: The U.S. Army Between Korea and Vietnam* (Washington, DC: National Defense University Press, 1986); and John J. Midgley Jr., *Deadly Illusions: Army Policy for the Nuclear Battlefield* (Boulder, CO: Westview Press, 1986).

5. The Pentagon has published a bare-bones treatment of some nuclear accidents. See Department of Defense, *Narrative Summaries of Accidents Involving U.S. Nuclear Weapons 1950–1980*, May 1981, available at http://www.dod.mil/pubs/foi/reading_room/635.pdf. For more on close calls, see Scott D. Sagan, *The Limits of Safety: Organizations, Accidents, and Nuclear Weapons* (Princeton, NJ: Princeton University Press, 1993), 156–203; Defense Nuclear Agency, *Project Crested Ice: USAF B-52 Accident at Thule, Greenland*, Washington, DC, 1968, available at http://handle.dtic.mil/100.2/ADA283578; Andrew Hudgins, "A Sense of Service," *Washington Post Magazine*, January 2, 2000, W12; and Jaya Tiwari and Cleve J. Gray, *U.S. Nuclear Weapons Accidents*, Center for Defense Information, available at http://www.cdi.org/Issues/NukeAccidents/accidents.htm.

6. Interview with General William Burns by author, January 24, 2007. Burns,

then a full colonel, was the commander at the site at the time of attack. He later became the head of the U.S. Arms Control and Disarmament Agency under President George H. W. Bush and later still helped to launch the Nunn-Lugar cooperative threat reduction programs in Russia. For a somewhat embellished account of this incident, see Andrew Cockburn and Leslie Cockburn, *One Point Safe* (New York: Anchor, 1997), 1–6.

7. See Oleg Gordievsky, *Next Stop Execution: The Autobiography of Oleg Gordievsky* (London: Macmillan, 1995); Christopher Andrew and Oleg Gorgievsky, *KGB: The Inside Story of Its Foreign Operations from Lenin to Gorbachev* (London: Hodder and Stoughton, 1990); and Christopher Andrew and Oleg Gordievsky, *Instructions from the Centre: Top Secret Files on KGB Foreign Operations, 1975–1985* (London: Hodder and Stoughton, 1991).

8. Kevin Sullivan, "One Word from Nuclear War," *International Herald Tribune*, October 14, 2002. For more on the unheralded decision that prevented catastrophe, see William Burr and Thomas S. Blanton (eds.), *The Submarines of October: U.S. and Soviet Naval Encounters During the Cuban Missile Crisis*, National Security Archive, George Washington University, National Security Archive Electronic Briefing Book 75, October 31, 2002, available at http://www.gwu.edu/~nsarchiv/NSAEBB/ NSAEBB75/index2.htm; and Vadim Orlov, "Recollections of Vadim Orlov (USSR Submarine B-59): We Will Sink Them All, But We Will Not Disgrace Our Navy," National Security Archive, George Washington University, available at http://www.gwu .edu/~nsarchiv/NSAEBB/NSAEBB75/asw-II-16.pdf.

9. Natural Resources Defense Council, "Table of Global Nuclear Weapons Stockpiles, 1945–2002," November 25, 2002, available at http://www.nrdc.org/nuclear/nudb/ datab19.asp; and Natural Resources Defense Council, "Table of Known Nuclear Tests Worldwide, 1945–1996," November 25, 2002, available at http://www.nrdc.org/nuclear/ nudb/datab15.asp.

10. See Michael Howard, "Reassurance and Deterrence: Western Defense in the 1980s," *Foreign Affairs* 61(2) (winter 1982–1983): 309–324.

11. Thomas C. Schelling and Morton H. Halperin, *Strategy and Arms Control* (New York: Twentieth Century Fund, 1961), 1.

12. Cited in Curtis E. LeMay, *America Is in Danger* (New York: Funk and Wagnalls, 1968), 275.

13. Bernard Brodie (ed.), *The Absolute Weapon: Atomic Power and World Order* (New York: Harcourt, Brace, 1946), 76.

14. Albert Einstein, "The Way Out," in Dexter Masters (ed.), *One World or None* (New York: McGraw-Hill, 1946), 76.

15. Brodie, *Absolute Weapon*, 23.

16. Kai Bird and Martin J. Sherwin, *American Prometheus: The Triumph and Tragedy of J. Robert Oppenheimer* (New York: Vintage Books, 2005), 348.

17. See McGeorge Bundy, "The Missed Chance to Stop the H-Bomb," *New York Review of Books* 29(8) (May 13, 1982): 13–22. Also see Bundy's *Danger and Survival*, 197–236.

18. See Herbert York, *The Advisors: Oppenheimer, Teller, and the Superbomb* (San Francisco: W. H. Freeman, 1975).

19. Henry Kissinger, *Nuclear Weapons and Foreign Policy* (New York: Harper & Row, 1957).

20. For a review of Kissinger's book, see William W. Kaufmann, "The Crisis in Military Affairs," *World Politics* 10(4) (July 1958): 579–603.

21. Known today as the International Institute for Strategic Studies.

22. Hedley Bull, *The Control of the Arms Race: Disarmament and Arms Control in the Missile Age* (London: Institute for Strategic Studies, 1961), vii, 9, 11, 27, 29.

23. Donald G. Brennan, "Setting and Goals of Arms Control," in Donald G. Brennan (ed.), *Arms Control, Disarmament, and National Security* (New York: George Braziller, 1961), 10, 30.

24. Robert R. Bowie, "Basic Requirements of Arms Control," in Donald G. Brennan (ed.), *Arms Control, Disarmament, and National Security* (New York: George Braziller, 1961), 43.

25. Schelling and Halperin, *Strategy and Arms Control*, 1, 2, 4.

26. Schelling and Halperin, *Strategy and Arms Control*, 141–143.

27. See, for example, Glenn T. Seaborg with Benjamin S. Loeb, *Kennedy, Khrushchev, and the Test Ban* (Berkeley: University of California Press, 1981); and Robert A. Divine, *Blowing on the Wind: The Nuclear Test Ban Debate, 1954–1960* (New York: Oxford University Press, 1978).

28. The Gilpatric committee report was finally declassified in 1996, thirty-one years after it was written. It can be accessed at http://www.gwu.edu/~nsarchiv/NSAEBB/NSAEBB1/nhch7_1.htm: *A Report to the President by the Committee on Nuclear Proliferation*, National Security Archive, George Washington University.

29. Avner Cohen believes that Israel "cobbled together" two deliverable devices during the 1967 war. Avner Cohen, *Israel and the Bomb* (New York: Columbia University Press, 1998), 237. Michael Karpin dates Israel's nuclear capability to the latter half of 1966. Michael Karpin, *The Bomb in the Basement: How Israel Went Nuclear and What That Means for the World* (New York: Simon & Schuster, 2006), 268.

30. Waldo Stumpf, the CEO of South Africa's state-controlled Atomic Energy Corporation, has written that "South Africa had a completed nuclear device in November 1979 with HEU [highly enriched uranium] of a relatively low enrichment of about 80% U-235" (Waldo Stumpf, "Birth and Death of the South African Nuclear Weapons Programme," presentation at the "50 Years After Hiroshima Conference," Castiglioncello, Italy, October 1995).

31. George Perkovich, *India's Nuclear Bomb: The Impact on Global Proliferation*

(Berkeley: University of California Press, 2002), 293. Also see Raj Chengappa, *Weapons of Peace* (New Delhi: Harper Collins, 2000), 333.

32. India's most respected strategic analyst, K. Subrahmanyam, has dated completed weaponization in the 1992–1994 time frame. India, however, could have deployed improvised nuclear devices by the late 1980s, if absolutely necessary. See Kargil Review Committee, *From Surprise to Reckoning: The Kargil Review Committee Report* (New Delhi: Sage, 2000), 206; and Perkovich, *India's Nuclear Bomb*, 293.

33. Scott D. Sagan and Kenneth N. Waltz, *The Spread of Nuclear Weapons: A Debate Renewed* (New York: W. W. Norton, 2003), 6.

34. J. Robert Oppenheimer, "Atomic Weapons and American Policy," *Foreign Affairs* 31(4) (July 1953): 529.

35. See Bruce Blair, *Strategic Command and Control: Redefining the Nuclear Threat* (Washington, DC: Brookings Institution Press, 1985); Peter Douglas Feaver, *Guarding the Guardians: Civilian Control of Nuclear Weapons in the United States* (Ithaca, NY: Cornell University Press, 1992); Bruce Blair, *The Logic of Accidental Nuclear War* (Washington, DC: Brookings Institution Press, 1993); and Sagan, *Limits of Safety*.

36. Albert Carnesale, Paul Doty, Stanley Hoffmann, Samuel Huntington, Joseph Nye, Scott Sagan, and Derek Bok, *Living with Nuclear Weapons: A Report by the Harvard Nuclear Study Group* (Cambridge, MA: Harvard University Press, 1983).

37. The B61 gravity bomb appears to have come in second place in this regard, with no less than 5,919 parts. See Stephen I. Schwartz (ed.), *U.S. Nuclear Weapons Cost Study Project* (Washington, DC: Brookings Institution Press, 1998), available at http://www.brook.edu/fp/projects/nucwcost/b61.htm.

38. See Hans M. Kristensen, Matthew G. McKinzie, and Robert S. Norris, "The Protection Paradox," *Bulletin of the Atomic Scientists* 60(2) (March–April 2004): 68–77 (available at http://thebulletin.metapress.com/content/c520186p76821x57/fulltext.pdf).

39. United States Atomic Energy Commission, General Advisory Committee, *General Advisory Committee's Majority and Minority Reports on Building the H-Bomb*, October 30, 1949, available at http://www.pbs.org/wgbh/amex/bomb/filmmore/reference/primary/extractsofgeneral.html.

40. See Bird and Sherwin, *American Prometheus*.

41. NSC 162/2, "Basic National Security Policy, October 20, 1953," in *Foreign Relations of the United States, 1952–1954* (Washington, DC: Government Printing Office, 1954), v. 2, 593.

42. This quote and characterization come from Strobe Talbott's part memoir, part negotiating narrative, *The Master of the Game: Paul Nitze and the Nuclear Peace* (New York: Alfred A. Knopf, 1988), 37. Also see Paul Nitze's biography, *From Hiroshima to Glasnost: At the Center of Decision* (New York: Grove Weidenfeld, 1989).

43. Paul H. Nitze, "Atoms, Strategy, and Policy," *Foreign Affairs* 35(2) (January 1956): 187–191.

44. Nitze, "Atoms, Strategy, and Policy."

45. This either meant a "shortfall" of nuclear weapons or that multiple targets could be covered with singular detonations. William Burr, "Looking Back: The Limits of Limited Nuclear War," *Arms Control Today* 36(1) (January–February 2006): 41–44.

46. Russell delivered these remarks during a Senate debate on missile defenses on October 2, 1968. *Congressional Record*, v. 114, 29,175.

47. This account is drawn from Dean W. Kohlhoff, *Amchitka and the Bomb: Nuclear Testing in Alaska* (Seattle: University of Washington Press, 2002).

48. This was one reason among many that LeMay opposed President Kennedy's 1963 Limited Test Ban Treaty, which prevented further nuclear tests in the atmosphere. Senator Jackson swallowed his reservations and voted in favor after attaching conditions to the treaty mandating continued vigilance in the form of underground testing. For a flavor of the LeMay-Jackson repartee on this issue, see the United States Senate, Senate Armed Services Committee, *Military Aspects and Implications of Nuclear Test Ban Proposals and Related Matters: Hearing Before the Preparedness Investigating Subcommittee of the Committee on Armed Services*, 88th Congr., 1st sess., June 27, 1963, pt. 1, 366–367.

49. A blowup of this image figures prominently in the Hiroshima Peace Memorial Museum.

50. See Robert Scheer, *With Enough Shovels: Reagan, Bush, and Nuclear War* (New York: Random House, 1982), 18. Also see Kenneth D. Rose, *One Nation Underground: The Fallout Shelter in American Culture* (New York: New York University Press, 2001).

51. Herman Kahn, *On Escalation, Metaphors, and Scenarios* (New York: Praeger, 1968), 4. Also see Herman Kahn, *Thinking the Unthinkable* (New York: Horizon Press, 1962).

52. For the *New York Times* movie review of *Dr. Strangelove*, see Bosley Crowther, "Kubrick Film Presents Sellers in 3 Roles," *New York Times*, January 30, 1964 (available at http://www.nytimes.com/1964/01/30/movies/013064strangelove.html).

53. For the deliberations of the Executive Committee, see *The Cuban Missile Crisis, 1962: The 40th Anniversary*, National Security Archive, George Washington University, available at http://www.gwu.edu/~nsarchiv/nsa/cuba_mis_cri/. See also Department of Defense, "Notes Taken from Transcripts of Meetings of the Joint Chiefs of Staff, October–November 1962, Dealing with the Cuban Missile Crisis," National Security Archive, George Washington University, available at http://www.gwu.edu/~nsarchiv/nsa/cuba_mis_cri/621000%20Notes%20Taken%20from%20Transcripts.pdf; also see Sheldon M. Stern, *The Week the World Stood Still: Inside The Secret Cuban Missile Crisis* (Stanford, CA: Stanford University Press, 2005); Ernest R. May and Philip D. Zelikow (eds.), *The Kennedy Tapes: Inside the White House During the Cuban Missile Crisis* (Cambridge, MA: Belknap Press, 1997); and Raymond L. Garthoff, *Reflections on the Cuban Missile Crisis* (Washington, DC: Brookings Institution Press, 1989).

54. See Valery E. Yarynich, *C3: Nuclear Command, Control, Cooperation* (Washington, DC: Center for Defense Information, 2003), 144–159, 215–248.

55. Soviet nuclear war-fighting plans remain classified, but documents released from the East German, Czech, and Polish archives provide important evidence of how Soviet military planners viewed escalation dominance. See, for example, Parallel History Project on NATO and the Warsaw Pact, "Plan of the Easterners' First Massive Nuclear Strike, June 1965," November 2001, available at http://se2.isn.ch/serviceengine/FileContent?serviceID=PHP&fileid=4E3027D1-0500-FB80-C0BE-DBA6ED31604E&lng=en. The Parallel History Project can be found at http://www.php.isn.ethz.ch/collections/colltopic.cfm?lng=en&id=16606. Also see "Inside the Warsaw Pact," *Cold War International History Project Bulletin* 2 (fall 1992), available at http://www.wilsoncenter.org/topics/pubs/ACF1C1.pdf.

56. See Helen Caldicott, *Missile Envy: The Arms Race and Nuclear War* (New York: William Morrow, 1984).

57. Office of Declassification, Department of Energy, *Draft Public Guidelines to Department of Energy Classification of Information*, app. 1, *Glossary*, June 27, 1994, available at https://www.osti.gov/opennet/forms.jsp?formurl=document/guidline/pubg.html.

58. McGeorge Bundy, "To Cap the Volcano," *Foreign Affairs* 48(1) (October 1969): 9–10.

59. See Richard Pipes, "Why the Soviet Union Thinks It Could Fight and Win a Nuclear War," *Commentary* 74(1) (July 1977): 21–34.

60. See Paul C. Warnke, "Apes on a Treadmill," *Foreign Policy* 18 (spring 1975): 12–29.

61. Gerard Smith, *Doubletalk: The Story of SALT I* (New York: Doubleday, 1980), 20. Also see John Newhouse, *Cold Dawn: The Story of SALT* (New York: Holt, Rinehart and Winston, 1973). Also see Raymond Garthoff's two-volume diplomatic history, *Détente and Confrontation: American-Soviet Relations from Nixon to Reagan* (Washington, DC: Brookings Institution Press, 1985) and *The Great Transition: American-Soviet Relations and the End of the Cold War* (Washington, DC: Brookings Institution Press, 1994).

62. See Anatoly Dobrynin, *In Confidence: Moscow's Ambassador to America's Six Cold War Presidents* (New York: Random House, 1995), 150.

63. Edward Ifft, a U.S. arms control negotiator, coined this aphorism in a talk at the Soviet Mission in Geneva in November 1989 to celebrate the twentieth anniversary of the beginning of SALT: "The two sides have the same positions, but never at the same time."

64. See William Hyland, *Mortal Rivals* (New York: Random House, 1987), 45.

65. Henry Kissinger, "A New Approach to Arms Control," *Time*, March 21, 1983, 25.

66. Arkady N. Shevchenko, *Breaking with Moscow* (New York: Knopf, 1985), 202.

67. See Robert G. Kaufman, *Henry M. Jackson: A Life in Politics* (Seattle: University of Washington Press, 2000).

68. In 1972, the United States carried approximately 8,600 warheads on its ocean-spanning land- and sea-based missiles as well as on its strategic bombers. The Soviet Union carried approximately 2,550 warheads on its "strategic nuclear delivery vehicles." See Natural Resources Defense Council, "Table of U.S. Strategic Offensive Force Loadings," available at http://www.nrdc.org/nuclear/nudb/datab1 .asp; and Natural Resources Defense Council, "Table of USSR/Russian Strategic Offensive Force Loadings," available at http://www.nrdc.org/nuclear/nudb/datab2 .asp.

69. See *Congressional Record*, 92nd Congr., 2nd sess., August 3, 1972–September 14, 1972.

70. United States Senate, Committee on Armed Services, *Military Implications of the Treaty on the Limitations of Anti-Ballistic Missile Systems and the Interim Agreement on Limitation of Strategic Offensive Arms: Hearing Before the Committee on Armed Services*, 92nd Congr., 2nd sess., 1972, 3.

71. Richard Nixon, "Address to a Joint Session of the Congress on Return from Austria, the Soviet Union, Iran, and Poland," June 1, 1972, Richard Nixon Library and Birthplace Foundation, available at http://www.nixonfoundation.org/clientuploads/ directory/archive/1972_pdf_files/1972_0188.pdf.

72. United States Senate, Committee on Armed Services, *Military Implications of the Treaty on the Limitations of Anti-Ballistic Missile Systems*, 121.

73. Committee on Foreign Affairs, *Agreement on Limitation of Strategic Offensive Weapons: Hearings*, 92nd Congr., 2nd sess., July 20, 1972, 9.

74. United States Senate, Committee on Armed Services, *Military Implications of the Treaty on the Limitations of Anti-Ballistic Missile Systems*, 148.

75. Henry Kissinger, "Arms Control, Inspection, and Surprise Attack," *Foreign Affairs* 38(4) (July 1960): 559.

76. Henry Kissinger, *The Necessity for Choice* (New York: Harper & Brothers, 1961), 185–186.

77. Paul H. Nitze, "Assuring Strategic Stability in an Era of Détente," *Foreign Affairs* 54(2) (January 1976): 207.

78. Jimmy Carter, "Inaugural Address of Jimmy Carter, Thursday, January 20, 1977," Avalon Project at Yale Law School, available at http://www.yale.edu/lawweb/ avalon/presiden/inaug/carter.htm.

79. James Buckley and Paul C. Warnke, *Strategic Sufficiency: Fact or Fiction?* (Washington, DC: American Enterprise Institute for Public Policy Research, 1972), 21.

80. These quotes are taken from Warnke, "Apes on a Treadmill," 12–29.

81. See United States Senate, Committee on Armed Services, *Consideration of Mr. Paul C. Warnke to Be Director of the U.S. Arms Control and Disarmament Agency and Ambassador: Hearings Together with Individual Views*, 95th Congr., 1st sess., 1977.

82. United States Senate, *The SALT II Treaty: Hearings Before the Committee on*

Foreign Relations, 96th Congr., 1st sess., pt. 2, 20.

83. Nitze wrote this in one of the committee's early pamphlets: Committee on the Present Danger, "Is SALT II a Fair Deal for the United States?" (Washington, DC: Committee on the Present Danger, May 16, 1979), 12.

84. Mimeo text of Jackson's speech, June 13, 1979.

85. United States Senate, *The SALT II Treaty: Hearings Before the Committee on Foreign Relations*, 96th Congr., 1st sess., pt. 4, 1979, 2.

86. Office of the Joint Chiefs of Staff, *United States Military Posture for Fiscal Year 1982: A Supplement to the Chairman's Overview* (Washington, DC: Government Printing Office, 1981), 1.

87. United States Senate, *The SALT II Treaty: Hearings Before the Committee on Foreign Relations*, 96th Congr., 1st sess., pt. 1, 1979, 88–97.

88. United States Senate, Committee on Armed Services, *Military Implications of the Proposed SALT II Treaty Relating to the National Defense: Report of the Hearings on the Military Aspects and Implications of the Proposed SALT II Treaty, Together with Additional Views* (Washington, DC: Government Printing Office, 1980).

89. This commentary appeared in *Trialogue*, published by the Trilateral Commission, and was reprinted in the *Washington Post* on February 25, 1979.

90. For a trenchant analysis of this impasse, see Lawrence Freedman, "Time for a Reappraisal," *Survival* 21(5) (September–October 1979): 198–201.

91. *Foreign Relations of the United States, 1929* (Washington, DC: Government Printing Office, 1943), v. 1, 241.

92. Committee on the Present Danger, "Is SALT II a Fair Deal?" 6.

93. United States Senate, Committee on Foreign Relations, *The SALT II Treaty: Hearings*, 96th Congr., 1st sess., pt. 2, 31.

94. Ronald Reagan, "The President's News Conference," January 29, 1981, Ronald Reagan Presidential Library, available at http://www.reagan.utexas.edu/archives/speeches/1981/12981b.htm.

95. Pipes, "Why the Soviet Union Thinks It Could Fight."

96. Strobe Talbott, *Deadly Gambits: The Reagan Administration and the Stalemate in Nuclear Arms Control* (New York: Knopf, 1984), 348.

97. Roy Gutman, "The Nay-Sayer of Arms Control," *Newsday*, February 18, 1983.

98. Richard Halloran, "Pentagon Draws up First Strategy for Fighting a Long Nuclear War," *New York Times*, June 30, 1982.

99. Richard Halloran, "Weinberger Angered by Reports on War Strategy," *New York Times*, August 24, 1982. Also see Richard Halloran, "Weinberger Confirms New Strategy on Atom War," *New York Times*, July 4, 1982.

100. NSC-NSDD-75, *U.S. Relations with the USSR*, January 17, 1983, Federation of American Scientists Intelligence Resource Program, available at http://www.fas.org/irp/offdocs/nsdd/nsdd-075.htm.

101. Francis X. Clines, "Reagan Denounces Ideology of Soviet as 'Focus of Evil,'" *New York Times*, March 9, 1983.

102. Ronald Reagan, "Address to the Nation on Defense and National Security, March 23, 1983," Ronald Reagan Presidential Library, available at http://www.reagan .utexas.edu/archives/speeches/1983/32383d.htm.

103. John Burns, "Andropov Says U.S. Is Spurring a Race in Strategic Arms; Excerpts from Interview," *New York Times*, March 27, 1983.

104. "Transcript of Shultz News Conference on the Korean Airliner," *New York Times*, September 2, 1983 (available at http://select.nytimes.com/search/restricted/ article?res=F20F11F63E5C0C718CDDA00894DB484D81).

105. Two book-length analyses of this event worth consulting are Alexander Dallin, *Black Box KAL 007* (Berkeley: University of California Press, 1985); and Hersh, *Target Is Destroyed*.

106. See Garthoff, *Great Transition*, 124–125.

107. Dobrynin, *In Confidence*, 537–539.

108. Garthoff, *Great Transition*, 138–140.

109. N. Ogarkov, "A Reliable Defense for Peace," *Krasnaya Zvezda*, September 23, 1983, cited in Garthoff, *Great Transition*, 137–138.

110. "Timeline," *Bulletin of the Atomic Scientists*, available at http://www.the bulletin.org/minutes-to-midnight/timeline.html.

111. George P. Shultz, *Turmoil and Triumph: My Years as Secretary of State* (New York: Charles Scribner's Sons, 1993), 512.

112. Margaret Thatcher, TV Interview with John Cole, BBC, December 17, 1984. Also see Margaret Thatcher, *The Downing Street Years* (New York: Harper Collins, 1993), 459.

113. David Hoffman, "Gorbachev 'Gambits' Challenged; White House Doubts Claim He Has Ended Nicaraguan Arms Aid," *Washington Post*, May 17, 1989.

114. Shultz, *Turmoil and Triumph*, 490, 507.

115. Interview with George Shultz by author, June 11, 2007.

116. Robert C. Macfarlane, *Special Trust* (New York: Cadell & Davies, 1994), 228.

117. Lou Cannon, *President Reagan: The Role of a Lifetime* (New York: Public Affairs, 1991), 248–249.

118. See Gordievsky, *Next Stop Execution*; Andrew and Gorgievsky, *KGB*; and Andrew and Gordievsky, *Instructions from the Centre*.

119. Don Oberdorfer, *The Turn: From the Cold War to a New Era—The United States and the Soviet Union, 1983–1990* (New York: Simon & Schuster, 1991), 65–67; and Garthoff, *Great Transition*, 138.

120. Douglas G. Brinkley (ed.), *The Reagan Diaries* (New York: Harper Collins, 2007), 199.

121. Oberdorfer, *The Turn*, 65–67.

122. Ronald Reagan, *An American Life* (New York: Simon and Schuster, 1990), 588.

123. Robert S. Dudney, "Is U.S. Really No. 2?" *U.S. News and World Report*, January 10, 1983, 16.

124. Reagan, *American Life*, 588–590.

125. Talbott, *Master of the Game*, 168.

126. Kenneth L. Adelman, *The Great Universal Embrace: Arms Summitry—A Skeptic's Account* (New York: Simon and Schuster, 1989), 27.

127. Shultz, *Turmoil and Triumph*, 254.

128. Caspar W. Weinberger, *Fighting for Peace: Seven Critical Years in the Pentagon* (New York: Warner Books, 1990), 307.

129. Shultz, *Turmoil and Triumph*, 264.

130. For a refreshing insider's account of how this game was played, see Adelman, *Great Universal Embrace*, esp. 17–62.

131. This is Frances Fitzgerald's phraseology. Her account of the saga of SDI, *Way Out There in the Blue: Reagan, Star Wars, and the End of the Cold War* (New York: Simon & Schuster, 2000) is well worth reading but gives little credit to Reagan for the surprisingly positive outcomes of the negotiations on his watch.

132. This characterization comes from Shultz, *Turmoil and Triumph*, 701.

133. Gregory F. Treverton, *Europe and America Beyond 2000* (New York: Council on Foreign Relations Press, 1990), 118–119.

134. Adelman, *Great Universal Embrace*, 150.

135. Shultz, *Turmoil and Triumph*, 601.

136. "Cold War: Thatcher-Reagan Meeting at Camp David (Account of Conversation) [memoirs extract]," Margaret Thatcher Foundation, available at http://www.margaretthatcher.org/commentary/displaydocument.asp?docid=109394.

137. Paul Nitze, "Address by the Special Adviser to the President and the Secretary of State on Arms Control Matters (Nitze): Strategic Defense Initiative," in *Documents on Disarmament: 1985*, Arms Control and Disarmament Agency Publication 130 (Washington, DC: Government Printing Office, 1989), 83–88.

138. Nitze, "Address of the Special Adviser."

139. This phraseology is borrowed from Talbott, *Master of the Game*, 214.

140. William Beecher, "Reagan Sent Andropov Secret Letter on Arms," *Boston Globe*, February 12, 1984.

141. David Hoffman, "President's Address at UN Conciliatory Toward Soviets," *Washington Post*, September 25, 1984. Those who wish to learn more about the thaw midway into the Reagan administration could not do better than to read Oberdorfer's journalistic account, *The Turn*, and Garthoff's *Great Transition*.

142. Seth Mydans, "Gorbachev Ready for Reagan Talks; Freezes Missiles," *New York Times*, April 8, 1985.

143. Joint Soviet–United States Statement on the Summit Meeting in Geneva, November 21, 1985. For the origin of this phraseology, see Dobrynin, *In Confidence*, 586.

144. David Hoffman, "Iceland Talks: One World Chills Hope," *Washington Post*, October 19, 1986.

145. "Gorbachev Addresses News Conference on Outcome," *Foreign Broadcast Information Service Daily Report: Soviet Union*, FBIS-SOV-14 (Washington, DC: Foreign Broadcast Information Service, October 1986), DD26.

146. Henry Kissinger, "A Dangerous Rush for Agreement," *Washington Post*, April 24, 1988. Also see Jeane Kirkpatrick, "Nixon the Heavyweight Weighs In," *Washington Post*, March 21, 1988.

147. Dobrynin, *In Confidence*, 637, 632.

148. McGeorge Bundy, George F. Kennan, Robert S. McNamara, and Gerard Smith, "The President's Choice: Star Wars or Arms Control," *Foreign Affairs* 64(4) (winter 1984–1985): 276.

149. James Schlesinger, "The Eagle and the Bear," *Foreign Affairs* 63(5) (summer 1985): 959.

150. Fitzgerald, *Way Out There in the Blue*, 38.

151. Talbott, *Deadly Gambits*, 209.

152. Talbott, *Master of the Game*, 18.

153. Talbott, *Deadly Gambits*, 18.

154. Dobrynin, *In Confidence*, 607.

155. Thomas C. Schelling, "The Thirtieth Year," *Daedalus* 120(1) (winter 1991): 31.

156. Talbott, *Master of the Game*, 15.

157. For a book-length treatment on this subject, see Nina Tannenwald, *The Nuclear Taboo: The United States and the Non-Use of Nuclear Weapons Since 1945* (New York: Cambridge University Press, 2007).

158. Thomas C. Schelling, "From an Airport Bench," *Bulletin of the Atomic Scientists* 45(4) (May 1989): 30.

Chapter 4

1. One of the first—if not the first—identifiers of the second nuclear age is Paul Bracken. See Paul Bracken, "The Structure of the Second Nuclear Age," *Orbis* 47(3) (summer 2003): 399–413.

2. Central Intelligence Agency, *Comprehensive Report of the Special Adviser to the DCI on Iraq's WMD*, report prepared by Charles Duelfer, September 30, 2004, available at https://www.cia.gov/library/reports/general-reports-1/iraq_wmd_2004/index .html.

3. As yet there are no well-researched accounts of Pakistan's nuclear quest. Bhutto's famous quote can be found in Hamid Jalal and Khalid Hasan, *Awakening the People: Speeches of Zulfiqar Ali Bhutto 1966–69* (Rawalpindi: Pakistan Publications, 1970), 21. Also see George Perkovich, *India's Nuclear Bomb: The Impact of Global Proliferation* (Berkeley: University of California Press, 1999), 108.

4. John Lewis and Xue Li-tai, *China Builds the Bomb* (Stanford, CA: Stanford University Press, 1988), 130 (an excellent account of the Chinese nuclear quest).

5. See, for example, Adrian Levy and Catherine Scott-Clark, *Deception: Pakistan, the United States, and the Secret Trade in Nuclear Weapons* (New York: Walker, 2007).

6. According to Thomas Perry Thornton, Pakistan assigned two combat divisions to Saudi Arabia in 1979, after Sunni Islamic dissidents seized control of the Grand Mosque in Mecca. This unofficial arrangement ended in 1987, reportedly when Pakistan refused a Saudi demand to withdraw all Shia troops. Some 500 advisers, however, remained behind. Federal Research Division, Library of Congress, *A Country Study: Pakistan*, ch. 5, "National Security: Foreign Security Relationships," April 1994, available at http://lcweb2.loc.gov/frd/cs/pktoc.html.

7. See Hans M. Kristensen, Robert S. Norris, and Matthew McKinzie, *Chinese Nuclear Forces and U.S. Nuclear War Planning* (Washington, DC: Federation of American Scientists and Natural Resources Defense Council, November 2006); and Jeffrey Lewis, *The Minimum Means of Reprisal: China's Search for Security in the Nuclear Age* (Cambridge, MA: MIT Press, 2007).

8. George Perkovich identified the unwelcome correlation between democracy and the Bomb in his *India's Nuclear Bomb*, 445.

9. David A. Rosenburg, "A Smoking Ruin at the End of Two Hours," *International Security* 6(3) (winter 1981–1982): 27.

10. See William Burr and Jeffrey T. Richelson, "Whether to 'Strangle the Baby in the Cradle': The United States and the Chinese Nuclear Program, 1960–64," *International Security* 25(3) (winter, 2000–2001): 54–99; Lewis and Xue, *China Builds the Bomb*, 64–72; and Gordon H. Chang, *Friends and Enemies* (Stanford, CA: Stanford University Press, 1990), 242–250.

11. Robert Dallek, *Nixon and Kissinger: Partners in Power* (New York: Harper Collins, 2007), 479. The meticulous cold war historian Raymond L. Garthoff found no evidence of this exchange in his *Detente and Confrontation: American-Soviet Relations— From Nixon to Reagan* (Washington, DC: Brookings Institution Press, 1985), 238.

12. *People of the World, Unite, for the Complete, Thorough, Total, and Resolute Prohibition, and Destruction of Nuclear Weapons!* (Beijing, 1963), 85, cited in Lewis and Xue, *China Builds the Bomb*, 36.

13. Lewis and Xue, *China Builds the Bomb*, 214.

14. For a circumspect rendering of this conversation, see Zbigniew Brzezinski, *Power and Principle: Memoirs of the National Security Adviser, 1977–1981* (New York: Farrar, Straus, Giroux, 1985), 409; interview with Robert Oakley by author, February 8, 2007.

15. The U.S. intelligence community has repeatedly overestimated the projected pace of China's nuclear modernization programs. See Kristensen et al., *Chinese Nuclear Forces*, 35–136; and Lewis, *Minimum Means of Reprisal*, 51.

16. Department of Defense, Office of the Secretary of Defense, *Military Power of the People's Republic of China, 2007*, May 25, 2007, 3, available at http://www.defenselink .mil/pubs/pdfs/070523-China-Military-Power-final.pdf.

17. International Institute for Strategic Studies, *Nuclear Black Markets: Pakistan, A. Q. Khan, and the Rise of Proliferation Networks—A Net Assessment* (London: IISS, 2007), 26; William J. Broad and David E. Sanger, "As Nuclear Secrets Emerge, More Are Suspected," *New York Times*, December 26, 2004 (available at http://www.nytimes .com/2004/12/26/international/asia/26nuke.html); and Gordon Corera, *Shopping for Bombs: Nuclear Proliferation, Global Insecurity, and the Rise and Fall of the A. Q. Khan Network* (New York: Oxford University Press, 2006), 44.

18. For more on India's nuclear posture, see Rajesh M. Basrur, *Minimum Deterrence and India's Nuclear Security* (Stanford, CA: Stanford University Press, 2006); and Ashley J. Tellis, *India's Emerging Nuclear Posture: Between Recessed Deterrent and Ready Arsenal* (Santa Monica, CA: RAND Corp., 2001).

19. India's national security adviser publicly released a draft nuclear doctrine written by a group of advisers. In the absence of an official document, this draft serves as the closest approximation of India's nuclear doctrine. The relevant passage reads: "Any adversary must know that India can and will retaliate with sufficient nuclear weapons to inflict destruction and punishment that the aggressor will find unacceptable if nuclear weapons are used against India and its forces." On January 4, 2003, the Cabinet Committee on Security issued a press release. One of its eight points summarizing India's nuclear doctrine was "Nuclear retaliation to a first strike will be massive and designed to inflict unacceptable damage." See Embassy of India, *Draft Report of National Security Advisory Board on Indian Nuclear Doctrine*, August 17, 1999, available at http://www.indianembassy.org/policy/CTBT/nuclear_doctrine_aug_17_1999.html; and Prime Minister's Office, *Cabinet Committee on Security Reviews Progress in Operationalizing India's Nuclear Doctrine*, Indian Press Information Bureau, January 4, 2003, available at http://pib.nic.in/archieve/lreleng/lyr2003/rjan2003/04012003/r040120033.html.

20. Lewis and Xue, *China Builds the Bomb*, 204. Nie Rongzhen's memoirs have references to the destructive impact of the Cultural Revolution on China's science programs but make no mention of the difficulties he encountered in making the Bomb. Jung-chen Nieh (trans.), *Inside the Red Star: The Memoirs of Marshal Nie Rongzhen* (Beijing: New World Press, 1988), 729, 752.

21. See U.S. Department of State, *Chinese MRBM Deployment Delayed*, Intelligence Note 323, prepared by U.S. Department of State Director of Intelligence and Research, May 3, 1968, available at http://www.gwu.edu/~nsarchiv/NSAEBB/NSAEBB26/10-01.htm. Also see Chong-Pin Lin, *China's Nuclear Weapons Strategy* (Lexington, MA: Lexington Books, 1988), 65.

22. Kurt M. Campbell, Ashton B. Carter, Steven E. Miller, and Charles A. Zraket, *Soviet Nuclear Fission: Control of the Nuclear Arsenal in a Disintegrating Soviet Union*,

CSIA Studies in International Security 1 (Cambridge, MA: Center for Science and International Affairs, Harvard University, 1990), 1; Graham Allison, Ashton B. Carter, Steven E. Miller, and Philip Zelikow, *Cooperative Denuclearization: From Pledges to Deeds*, CSIA Studies in International Security 2 (Cambridge, MA: Center for Science and International Affairs, Harvard University, 1993), 117–118.

23. Remarks for Ambassador Eileen Malloy, Department of Energy, *The Proliferation of Weapons of Mass Destruction: How Much of a Challenge?* Center for Nonproliferation Studies, December 12, 1999, available at http://www.cns.miis.edu/cns/projects/nisnp/research/ctrconf/spch02.htm; and William Walker, "Nuclear Weapons and the Former Soviet Republics," *International Affairs* 68(2) (April 1992): 258.

24. See Nuclear Energy Agency, OECD, *Chernobyl: Assessment of Radiological and Health Impacts—2002 Update of* Chernobyl: Ten Years On, available at http://www.nea.fr/html/rp/reports/2003/nea3508-chernobyl.pdf.

25. For a photojournalism perspective of the genetic damage done by nuclear testing at the Soviet test site in what is now Kazakhstan, see Lewis M. Simmons and Glenn Hodges, "Weapons of Mass Destruction," *National Geographic* 2(5) (November 2002): 3–35.

26. For more on this success story, see Strobe Talbott, *The Russia Hand: A Memoir of Presidential Diplomacy* (New York: Random House, 2002); and Gary Bertsch, *Dangerous Weapons, Desperate States: Russia, Belarus, Kazakstan, and Ukraine* (New York: Routledge, 1999).

27. Jacek Rostowski, "Comparing Two Great Depressions: 1929–33 to 1989–93," in Salvatore Zecchini (ed.), *Lessons from the Economic Transition: Central and Eastern Europe in the 1990s* (Boston: Kluwer Academic and OECD Publishing, 1997), 226–227.

28. Mark Hibbs, "Chechen Separatists Take Credit for Moscow Cesium-137 Threat," *Nuclear Fuel* 20(25) (December 4, 1995): 5. A computer simulation developed for the Stimson Center using 17 grams of cesium-137 dusted five city blocks with radiological material. See Kishore Kuchibhotla and Matthew McKinzie, "Nuclear Terrorism and Nuclear Accidents in South Asia," in Michael Krepon and Ziad Haider (eds.), *Reducing Nuclear Dangers in South Asia*, Stimson Center Report 50 (Washington, DC: Henry L. Stimson Center, January 2004): 17–44.

29. Michael Specter, "Russians Assert Radioactive Box Found in Park Posed No Danger," *New York Times*, November 25, 1995 (available at http://query.nytimes.com/gst/fullpage.html?res=9A06EFDF1039F936A15752C1A963958260); Steven Lee Myers, "Explosion Kills Chechen Rebel Tied to Carnage," *New York Times*, July 11, 2006 (available at http://www.nytimes.com/2006/07/11/world/europe/11russia.html).

30. "Loose Nukes: Podolsk, Russia," PBS's *Frontline*, available at http://www.pbs.org/wgbh/pages/frontline/shows/nukes/timeline/tl01.html; and "Loose Nukes: Interview with Yuri Smirnov," PBS's *Frontline*, available at http://www.pbs.org/wgbh/pages/frontline/shows/nukes/interviews/smirnov.html.

31. Gregory Katz, "Uranium Smuggling Raises Fear; Russia's Nuclear Supply at Risk, U.S. Contends," *Dallas Morning News*, May 26, 1996.

32. Matt Bivens and Leonid Bershidsky, "Petersburg Arrests 3 for Trying to Sell Uranium," *Moscow Times*, June 9, 1994.

33. Lawrence Scott Sheets and William Broad, "Smuggler's Plot Highlights Fear over Uranium," *New York Times*, January 25, 2007; and "Moscow Lashes Out at Georgia As Uranium Sale Plot Thickens," *New York Times*, January 27, 2007.

34. "Georgia Halts Plutonium at Border," *Boston Globe*, June 20, 2007 (available at http://www.boston.com/news/world/europe/articles/2007/06/20/georgia_halts_plutonium_at_border/).

35. International Atomic Energy Agency, *Trafficking in Nuclear and Radioactive Material in 2005: IAEA Releases Latest Illicit Trafficking Database Statistics*, August 21, 2006, available at http://www.iaea.org/NewsCenter/News/2006/traffickingstats2005.html#. For the International Atomic Energy Agency's database on troubling incidents, see *Illicit Trafficking and Other Unauthorized Activities Involving Nuclear and Radioactive Materials*, available at http://www.iaea.org/NewsCenter/Features/RadSources/PDF/fact_figures2005.pdf. See *High-Impact Terrorism: Proceedings of a Russian-American Workshop* (Washington, DC: National Academy Press, 2002); Charles D. Ferguson and William C. Potter, *The Four Faces of Nuclear Terrorism* (Monterey, CA: Center for Nonproliferation Studies, 2004); Graham Allison (ed.), "Confronting the Specter of Nuclear Terrorism," special issue of *Annals of the American Academy of Political and Social Science* 607 (2006); and Russell Howard and James Forest, *Weapons of Mass Destruction and Terrorism* (New York: McGraw-Hill, 2007). Also see Charles Ferguson, Tasheen Kazi, and Judith Perera, *Commercial Radioactive Sources: Surveying the Security Risks* (Washington, DC: Center for Nonproliferation Studies, 2003).

36. See Brian D. Finlay and Elizabeth Turpen, *Cooperative Nonproliferation: Getting Further, Faster* (Washington, DC: Henry L. Stimson Center, 2007), 11–26.

37. Brian D. Finlay and Elizabeth Turpen, *25 Steps to Prevent Nuclear Terror: A Guide For Policymakers*, Report 59 (Washington, DC: Henry L. Stimson Center, 2007).

38. See, for example, United States Government Accountability Office, *Nuclear Proliferation: Progress Made in Improving Security at Russian Nuclear Sites, But the Long-term Sustainability of U.S. Funded Security Upgrades Is Uncertain*, Report GAO-07-404, February 2007, available at http://www.gao.gov/new.items/d07404.pdf; and United States Government Accountability Office, *Nuclear Nonproliferation: DOE's International Radiological Threat Reduction Program Needs to Focus Future Efforts on Securing the Highest Priority Radiological Sources*, Report GAO-07-282, January 2007, available at http://www.gao.gov/new.items/d07282.pdf.

39. Anne E. Kornblut, "Bush Signs Major Transportation Measure," *New York Times*, August 11, 2005; also see Taxpayers for Common Sense, "Database of Earmarks in Conference Agreement to the Transportation Bill: State by State Comparison," Au-

gust 12, 2005, available at http://www.taxpayer.net/Transportation/safetealu/states
.htm.

40. This open secret was not stated in unclassified testimony by U.S. intelligence
community officials until January 2007, perhaps in deference to Pakistan's president
Pervez Musharraf, the Bush administration's troubled ally in the war on terror. See
John D. Negroponte, *Annual Threat Assessment of the Director of National Intelligence*,
January 11, 2007, 2, available at http://intelligence.senate.gov/070111/negroponte.pdf;
and Michael D. Maples, *Current and Projected National Security Threat to the United
States*, January 11, 2007, 6, available at http://www.dia.mil/publicaffairs/Testimonies/
statement26.html.

41. See George Tenet with Bill Harlow, *At the Center of the Storm: My Years at CIA*
(New York: Harper Collins, 2007), 281–297.

42. For more on A. Q. Khan, see International Institute for Strategic Studies,
Nuclear Black Markets; Corera, *Shopping for Bombs*; Tenet, *At the Center of the Storm*,
281–297; and William Langewiesche, *The Atomic Bazaar: The Rise of the Nuclear Poor*
(New York: Farrar Straus Giroux, 2007), 70–179.

43. See International Institute for Strategic Studies, *Nuclear Black Markets*.

44. International Institute for Strategic Studies, *Nuclear Black Markets*, 76.

45. Khan's house arrest was relaxed in 2007. See Munir Ahmad, "Pakistan Eases
Curbs on Atomic Scientist," *Washington Post*, July 2, 2007.

46. International Institute for Strategic Studies, *Nuclear Black Markets*, 96.

47. Tenet, *At the Center of the Storm*, 282–283.

48. International Institute for Strategic Studies, *Nuclear Black Markets*, 117.

49. This information comes from my own confidential interviews.

50. See Peter L. Bergen, *Holy War Inc.: Inside the Secret World of Osama bin Laden*
(New York: Simon & Schuster, 2002); and Steve Coll, "Young Osama; Letter from
Jedda," *New Yorker*, December 12, 2005.

51. Steve Coll, *Ghost Wars: The Secret History of the CIA, Afghanistan, and bin
Laden from the Soviet Invasion to September 10, 2001* (New York: Penguin Press, 2004),
367; Peter D. Zimmerman and Jeffrey G. Lewis, "The Bomb in the Backyard," *Foreign
Policy*, 157 (November–December 2006): 32–39.

52. National Commission on Terrorist Attacks, *The 9/11 Commission Report*
(Washington, DC: National Commission on Terrorist Attacks Upon the United States,
July 22, 2004), 126, available at http://www.9-11commission.gov/report/911Report.pdf.

53. National Commission on Terrorist Attacks, *The 9/11 Commission Report*, 380.

54. International Institute for Strategic Studies, *Nuclear Black Markets*, 99.

55. Peter L. Bergen, *The Osama bin Laden I Know: An Oral History of al Qaeda's
Leader* (New York: Free Press, 2006), 341.

56. Nuclear Threat Initiative, "Uzbekistan Overview," July 2005, available at
http://www.nti.org/e_research/profiles/Uzbekistan_overview/1633.html.

57. David Albright and Holly Higgins, *Pakistani Nuclear Scientists: How Much Nuclear Assistance to Al Qaeda?* Institute for Science and International Security, August 30, 2002, available at http://www.exportcontrols.org/pakscientists.html; John Burns, "A Nation Challenged: Nuclear Fears; Pakistan Atom Experts Held Amid Fear of Leaked Secrets," *New York Times*, November 1, 2001 (available at http://query.nytimes.com/gst/fullpage.html?res=9A0DE4D81030F932A35752C1A9679C8B63); Kamran Khan and Molly Moore, "2 Nuclear Experts Briefed Bin Laden, Pakistanis Say," *Washington Post*, December 12, 2001; Jack Kelley, "Terrorists Courted Nuclear Scientists," *USA Today*, November 12, 2001 (available at http://www.usatoday.com/news/sept11/2001/11/12/lede.htm); Bob Woodward, Robert G. Kaiser, and David B. Ottaway, "U.S. Fears Bin Laden Made Nuclear Strides," *Washington Post*, December 4, 2001 (available at http://www.washingtonpost.com/ac2/wp-dyn?pagename=article&node=&contentId=A52369-2001Dec3).

58. Bergen, *Holy War Inc.*, 85.

59. See Michael Krepon, "Dominators Rule," *Bulletin of the Atomic Scientists* 51(1) (January–February 2003): 55–60.

60. This example of the misuse and nonuse of congressional oversight comes from Norman J. Ornstein and Thomas E. Mann, "When Congress Checks Out," *Foreign Affairs* 85(6) (November–December 2006): 67–82. Also see the reporting of Susan Milligan in the *Boston Globe*, especially "Congress Reduces Its Oversight Role: Since Clinton, a Change in Focus," *Boston Globe*, November 20, 2005 (available at http://www.boston.com/news/nation/washington/articles/2005/11/20/congress_reduces_its_oversight_role/).

61. Charles Krauthammer, "The Unipolar Moment," *Foreign Affairs* 70(1) (winter 1990–1991): 25.

62. For an additional sampling of Krauthammer's powerful prose, see Charles Krauthammer, "The Unipolar Moment Revisited," *National Interest* 70 (winter 2002–2003): 5–17; Charles Krauthammer, "In Defense of Democratic Realism," *National Interest* 77 (fall 2004): 1–12; and Charles Krauthammer, "Democratic Realism: An American Foreign Policy for a Unipolar World," 2004 Irving Kristol Lecture at the American Enterprise Institute Annual Dinner, Washington, DC, February 10, 2004, available at http://www.aei.org/publications/pubID.19912,filter.all/pub_detail.asp.

63. President Bush referred to himself as the decider in stating his intention to keep Donald Rumsfeld as secretary of defense, and the characterization stuck. President Bush declared, "I'm the decider, and I decide what's best." David S. Cloud, "Here's Donny! In His Defense, a Show Is Born," *New York Times*, April 19, 2006.

64. David E. Sanger, "The 2000 Campaign: World Views," *New York Times*, October 30, 2000.

65. George W. Bush, "Governor Bush VFW Speech," Milwaukee, August 21, 2000,

available at http://web.archive.org/web/20010305034813/www.georgewbush.com/News/speeches/082100_vfw.html.

66. See James Mann, *Rise of the Vulcans: The History of Bush's War Cabinet* (New York: Viking Adult, 2004).

67. Condoleezza Rice, "Campaign 2000: Promoting the National Interest," *Foreign Affairs* 79(1) (January–February 2000): 46–53.

68. Henry Cabot Lodge, *The Senate and the League of Nations* (New York: Scribner's, 1925), 213.

69. Bernard Brodie, *Strategy in the Missile Age* (Princeton, NJ: Princeton University Press, 1959), 239, 237.

70. This document, *The National Security Strategy of the United States of America*, White House, September 2002, can be accessed at http://www.whitehouse.gov/nsc/nss.pdf; for the Bush administration's companion strategy document for combating weapons of mass destruction, see *National Strategy to Combat Weapons of Mass Destruction*, White House, December 2002, available at http://www.whitehouse.gov/news/releases/2002/12/WMDStrategy.pdf. A more chastened National Security Strategy released by the White House, *The National Security Strategy*, was issued in March 2006 (available at http://www.whitehouse.gov/nsc/nss/2006/).

71. Niccolo Machiavelli, *The Prince* (New York: W. W. Norton, 1992), 17.

72. See Robert Jervis, "The Remaking of a Unipolar World," *Washington Quarterly* 29(3) (summer 2006): 7–19. Jeffrey Legro has suggested to me a variation on Jervis's observation: that the Bush administration would go to great lengths to maintain the status quo.

73. "Video Surfaces of Cheney, in 1994, Warning That an Invasion of Iraq Would Lead to 'Quagmire,'" *Editor and Publisher*, August 13, 2007, available at http://www .infowars .com/articles/iraq/cheney_video_1994_warning_of_iraq_invasion_quagmire.htm.

74. For first drafts of this history, see Bob Woodward, *Bush at War* (New York: Simon & Schuster, November 2002); Bob Woodward, *Plan of Attack* (New York: Simon & Schuster, October 2004); Bob Woodward, *State of Denial: Bush at War, Part III* (New York: Simon & Schuster, September 2006); Tenet, *At the Center of the Storm*; Karen DeYoung, *Soldier: The Life of Colin Powell* (New York: Knopf, October 2006); Ron Suskind, *The One Percent Doctrine: Deep Inside America's Pursuit of Its Enemies Since 9/11* (New York: Simon & Schuster, 2006); Thomas E. Ricks, *Fiasco: The American Military Adventure in Iraq* (New York: Penguin Press HC, July 2006); and Lawrence Wright, *The Looming Tower: Al-Qaeda and the Road to 9/11* (New York: Knopf, 2006).

75. Tenet, *At the Center of the Storm.*

76. United States Senate, Senate Select Committee on Intelligence, *Report of the Select Committee on Intelligence on the U.S. Intelligence Community's Prewar Intelligence Assessments on Iraq Together with Additional Views*, Senate Report 108-301, 108th Congr., 2nd sess., July 9, 2004, 3–4.

77. Scott Shane, "Senate Democrats Say Bush Ignored Spy Agencies' Prewar Warnings of Iraq Perils," *New York Times*, May 26, 2007 (available at http://www.nytimes.com/2007/05/26/washington/26intel.html); and Walter Pincus, "Assessments Made in 2003 Foretold Situation in Iraq," *Washington Post*, May 20, 2007 (available at http://www.washingtonpost.com/wp-dyn/content/article/2007/05/19/AR2007051900843.html).

78. The National Intelligence Estimate on Iraqi weapons of mass destruction programs was requested in letters from senators on September 9, 2002, September 10, 2002, September 13, 2002, and September 17, 2002. The NIE was approved by the National Foreign Intelligence Board and printed on October 1, 2002: Senate Select Committee on Intelligence, *Report of the Select Committee on Intelligence on the U.S. Intelligence Community's Prewar Intelligence Assessments on Iraq Together with Additional Views*, Senate Report 108–301, 108th Congr., 2nd sess., July 9, 2004, 13 (available at http://intelligence.senate.gov/108301.pdf).

79. See "Buying the War," *Bill Moyers Journal*, PBS, April 25, 2007, available at http://www.pbs.org/moyers/journal/btw/watch.html.

80. The most searing indictment to date of multiple derelictions of duty is Ricks, *Fiasco*.

81. Powell made this comment on *Face the Nation*, CBS, December 17, 2006. See Peter Baker, "President Plans to Expand Army, Marine Corps to Cope with Strain of Multiple Deployments," *Washington Post*, December 20, 2006.

82. A total of $532 billion was appropriated and requested for Operation Iraqi Freedom from 2001 to 2008. Funding projections through 2017, assuming U.S. troops would be reduced to 30,000, are estimated by the Congressional Budget Office to be $801 billion. Assuming that the remaining U.S. troops in Iraq after a drawdown are 75,000, the estimated costs through 2017 are $1.265 trillion. Letter to Senator Kent Conrad from Peter R. Orszag, Director, Congressional Budget Office, February 7, 2007, available at http://www.cbo.gov/ftpdocs/77xx/doc7793/02-07-CostOfWar.pdf.

83. For an even-keeled assessment of the prospects of and constraints on acts of nuclear terrorism, see Ferguson and Potter, *Four Faces of Nuclear Terrorism*, esp. 14–45.

84. Matthew Bunn and Anthony Wier, *Securing the Bomb 2006* (Cambridge, MA: Project on Managing the Atom, 2006), 13. For other assessments of cooperative threat reduction efforts, see Finlay and Turpen, *Cooperative Nonproliferation*; Bunn and Wier, *Securing the Bomb*; and General Accountability Office, *Nuclear Nonproliferation: Security of Russia's Nuclear Material Improving; Further Enhancements Needed*, 2001, available at http://www.gao.gov/new.items/d01312.pdf.

85. Strengthening the Global Partnership Project, *Assessing the G8 Global Partnership: From Kananaskis to St. Petersburg*, Center for Strategic and International Studies, July 2006, 3–4, available at http://www.sgpproject.org/publications/SGPAssessment2006.pdf.

86. Brian D. Finlay and Andrew J. Grotto, *The Race to Secure Russia's Loose Nukes: Progress Since 9/11* (Washington, DC: Henry L. Stimson Center and Center for American Progress, September 2005), 1.

87. Amy Belasco, *The Cost of Iraq, Afghanistan, and Other Global War on Terror Operations Since 9/11*, Congressional Research Service, March 14, 2007, 3, available at http://www.fas.org/sgp/crs/natsec/RL33110.pdf.

88. Secretary of Energy Advisory Board, *A Report Card on the Department of Energy's Nonproliferation Programs with Russia* (Washington, DC: U.S. Department of Energy, 2001), iii, available at http://www.seab.energy.gov/publications/rusrpt.pdf.

Chapter 5

1. For more on nuclear-tinged crises in South Asia, see P. R. Chari, Pervaiz Iqbal Cheema, and Stephen P. Cohen, *Four Crises and a Peace Process: American Engagement in South Asia* (Washington, DC: Brookings Institution Press, 2007); Kanti P. Bajpai, P. R. Chari, Pervaiz Iqbal Cheema, Stephen P. Cohen, and Sumit Ganguly, *Brasstacks and Beyond: Perception and Management of Crisis in South Asia* (New Delhi: Manohar, 1995); P. R. Chari, Pervaiz Iqbal Cheema, and Stephen Philip Cohen, *Perception, Politics, and Security in South Asia: The Compound Crisis of 1990* (Oxford: Routledge Curzon, 2003); Michael Krepon and Mishi Faruqee (eds.), *Conflict Prevention and Confidence-Building Measures in South Asia: The 1990 Crisis*, Occasional Paper 17 (Washington, DC: Henry L. Stimson Center, April 1994); Kargil Review Committee, *From Surprise to Reckoning: The Kargil Review Committee Report* (New Delhi: Sage, 2000); Ashley J. Tellis, *Limited Conflicts Under the Nuclear Umbrella* (Santa Monica, CA: RAND Corp., 2001); Bruce Riedel, *American Diplomacy and the 1999 Kargil Summit at Blair House*, Center for the Advanced Study of India, Policy Paper Series, May 2002, available at http://www.ccc.nps.navy.mil/research/kargil/reidel.pdf; Strobe Talbott, *Engaging India: Diplomacy, Democracy, and the Bomb* (Washington, DC: Brookings Institution Press, 2004); Michael Krepon, Rodney W. Jones, and Ziad Haider (eds.), *Escalation Control and the Nuclear Option in South Asia* (Washington, DC: Henry L. Stimson Center, 2004); Michael Krepon (ed.), *Nuclear Risk Reduction in South Asia* (New York: Palgrave Macmillan, 2004); Polly Nayak and Michael Krepon, *U.S. Crisis Management in South Asia's Twin Peaks Crisis*, Report 57 (Washington, DC: Henry L. Stimson Center, September 2006), available at http://www.stimson.org/pub.cfm?id=327; Sumit Ganguly and Devin T. Hagerty, *Fearful Symmetry: India-Pakistan Crises in the Shadow of Nuclear Weapons* (Seattle: University of Washington Press, 2006); and Michael Krepon and Amit Sevak (eds.), *Crisis Prevention, Confidence Building, and Reconciliation in South Asia* (New York: St. Martin's Press, 1995).

2. Bernard Brodie, "Some Notes on the Evolution of Air Doctrine," *World Politics* 7(3) (April 1955): 359.

3. Bernard Brodie, "War in the Atomic Age," in Bernard Brodie (ed.), *The Absolute Weapon: Atomic Power and World Order* (New York: Harcourt, Brace, 1946), 28.

4. Scott D. Sagan and Kenneth N. Waltz, *The Spread of Nuclear Weapons: A Debate Renewed*, 2nd ed. (New York: W. W. Norton, 2002), 119.

5. Natural Resources Defense Council, "Table of Known Nuclear Tests World Wide: 1945–69 and 1970–96," November 25, 2002, available at http://www.nrdc.org/nuclear/nudb/datab15.asp.

6. One indicator of this trend was the test of a powerful new conventional weapon by the Russian Federation in September 2007. See Dmitry Solovyov, "Russia Tests Superstrength Bomb: Military," Reuters, September 11, 2007, available at http://www.reuters.com/article/worldNews/idUSL1155952320070911.

7. Center for Nonproliferation Studies, *Chronology of State Use and Biological and Chemical Weapons Control*, October 2001, available at http://cns.miis.edu/research/cbw/pastuse.htm. For a history of chemical warfare, see Jonathan B. Tucker, *War of Nerves: Chemical Warfare from World War I to Al Qaeda* (New York: Pantheon Books, 2006).

8. In 2002, Assistant Secretary of State for Intelligence and Research Carl W. Ford Jr. testified before the Senate Foreign Relations Committee that Iraq and Libya were also presumed to have covert chemical weapon stockpiles. The Iraq claim proved to be incorrect, and Libya renounced its weapons of mass destruction programs in 2003. Carl W. Ford Jr., "Statement by Carl W. Ford Jr., Assistant Secretary of State for Intelligence and Research, Before the Senate Committee on Foreign Relations, Hearing on Reducing the Threat of Chemical and Biological Weapons," March 19, 2002, Avalon Project, Yale Law School, available at http://www.yale.edu/lawweb/avalon/sept_11/ford_002.htm.

9. See Dilip Hiro, *The Longest War: The Iran-Iraq Military Conflict* (London: Routledge, 1991).

10. For a history of biological weapons, see Erhard Geissler and John Ellis van Courtland Moon (eds.), *Biological and Toxin Weapons: Research, Development, and Use from the Middle Ages to 1945* (Oxford: Oxford University Press, 1999); and Mark Wheelis, Lajos Rozsa, and Malcolm Dando (eds.), *Deadly Cultures: Biological Weapons Since 1945* (Cambridge, MA: Harvard University Press, 2006). For an inside view of the Soviet biological weapons establishment, see Ken Alibek with Stephen Handelman, *Biohazard: The Chilling True Story of the Largest Covert Biological Weapons Program in the World—Told from the Inside by the Man Who Ran It* (New York: Delta, 2000). For policy prescriptions, see Joshua Lederberg (ed.), *Biological Weapons: Limiting the Threat* (Cambridge, MA: MIT Press, 2000); Richard A. Falkenrath, Robert D. Newman, and Bradley A. Thayer, *America's Achilles' Heel: Nuclear, Biological, and Chemical Terrorism and Covert Attack* (Cambridge, MA: MIT Press, 1999); and Jonathan B. Tucker (ed.), *Toxic Terror: Assessing Terrorist Use of Chemical and Biological Weapons* (Cambridge, MA: MIT Press, 2000).

11. See Krepon et al., *Escalation Control*.

12. See George H. Quester, *Nuclear First Strike: Consequences of a Broken Taboo* (Baltimore: Johns Hopkins University Press, 2006); and Nina Tannenwald, *The Nuclear Taboo: The United States and the Non-Use of Nuclear Weapons Since 1945* (Cambridge, U.K.: Cambridge University Press, 2007).

13. The first scientific studies of the vast climate change and environmental consequences of major nuclear exchanges did not occur until nearly four decades after Hiroshima and Nagasaki. See R. P. Turco, O. B. Toon, T. P. Ackerman, J. B. Pollack, and Carl Sagan, "Nuclear Winter: Global Consequences of Multiple Nuclear Explosions," *Science* 222(4630) (December 23, 1983): 1283–1293. More sophisticated models of climate change and the environmental consequences of "limited" India-Pakistan nuclear exchanges were published in 2006. See Owen B. Toon, Richard P. Turco, Alan Robock, Charles Bardeen, Luke Oman, and Georgiy L. Stenchikov, "Atmospheric Effects and Societal Consequences of Regional Scale Nuclear Conflicts and Acts of Individual Nuclear Terrorism," *Atmospheric Chemistry and Physics Discussions* 6 (November 22, 2006): 11,745–11,816; and Alan Robock, Luke Oman, Georgiy L. Stenchikov, Owen B. Toon, Charles Bardeen, and Richard P. Turco, "Climatic Consequences of Regional Nuclear Conflicts," *Atmospheric Chemistry and Physics Discussions* 6 (November 22, 2006): 11,817–11,843.

14. Office of the Director of National Intelligence, *Iran: Nuclear Intentions and Capabilities*, November 2007, available at http://www.dni.gov/press_releases/20071203_release.pdf.

15. See Richard Beeston, "Nuclear Steps Put Region on Brink of Most Fearful Era Yet," *Times of London*, November 4, 2006 (available at http://www.timesonline.co.uk/tol/news/world/middle_east/article624831.ece).

16. Quester, *Nuclear First Strike*, 139.

17. See Sagan and Waltz, *Spread of Nuclear Weapons*.

18. For the application of the stability-instability paradox in South Asia, see Michael Krepon, "Is Cold War Experience Applicable to Southern Asia?" in Michael Krepon (ed.), *Nuclear Risk Reduction in South Asia* (New York: Palgrave Macmillan, 2004), 7–19; and Michael Krepon, "The Stability-Instability Paradox, Misperception, and Escalation Control in South Asia," in Rafiq Dossani and Henry S. Rowen (eds.), *Prospects for Peace in South Asia* (Stanford, CA: Stanford University Press, 2005), 261–280. For a multiregional analysis, see Lyle J. Goldstein, *Preventive Attack and Weapons of Mass Destruction: A Comparative Analysis* (Stanford, CA: Stanford University Press, 2006).

19. See Stephen P. Cohen, *The Idea of Pakistan* (Washington, DC: Brookings Institution Press, 2004); Husain Haqqani, *Pakistan: Between Mosque and Military* (Washington, DC: Carnegie Endowment for International Peace, 2005); and Owen Bennett Jones, *Pakistan: Eye of the Storm* (New Haven: Yale University Press, 2002).

20. See Doug Brugge, Timothy Benally, and Esther Yazzie-Lewis, *The Navajo People and Uranium Mining* (Albuquerque: University of New Mexico Press, 2006).

21. See, for example, "Rogue Regulator: Mohamed ElBaradei Pursues a Separate Peace with Iran," *Washington Post*, September 5, 2007 (available at http://www.washing tonpost.com/wp-dyn/content/article/2007/09/04/AR2007090401810.html); and Elaine Sciolino and William J. Broad, "An Indispensable Irritant to Iran and Its Foes," *New York Times*, September 17, 2007 (available at http://www.nytimes.com/2007/09/17/world/middleeast/17elbaradei.html).

22. Shri Pranab Mukherjee, "Suo Moto Statement by the Minister of External Affairs, Mr. Pranab Mukherjee, on Indo-U.S. Civil Nuclear Co-Operation in Lok Sabha on December 12, 2006," December 12, 2006, available at http://www.indianembassy .org/newsite/press_release/2006/Dec/6.asp.

23. See Peter Baker, "Pakistani Scientist Who Met bin Laden Failed Polygraphs, Renewing Suspicions," *Washington Post*, March 3, 2002, A1 (available at http://www .washingtonpost.com/ac2/wp-dyn/A29790-2002Mar2?language=printer).

24. The 2002 National Intelligence Estimate concluded that "Saddam, if sufficiently desperate, might decide that only an organization such as al-Qa'ida—with worldwide reach and extensive terrorist infrastructure, and already engaged in a life-or-death struggle against the United States—could perpetrate the type of terrorist attack that he would hope to conduct. In such circumstances, he might decide that the extreme step of assisting the Islamist terrorists in conducting a CBW [chemical or biological weapon] attack against the United States would be his last chance to exact vengeance by taking a large number of victims with him." See National Intelligence Council, *Iraq's Continuing Programs for Weapons of Mass Destruction*, National Intelligence Estimate 2002-16HC, Federation of American Scientists, October 2002, 7–8, available at http://www.fas.org/irp/cia/product/iraq-wmd-nie.pdf.

25. See International Institute for Strategic Studies, *Nuclear Black Markets: Pakistan, A. Q. Khan, and the Rise of Proliferation Networks* (London: IISS, 2007), 108.

26. Confidential interviews with the author.

27. See Krepon, *Nuclear Risk Reduction in South Asia*; and Krepon et al., *Escalation Control*.

28. See Glenn T. Seaborg, *Kennedy, Khrushchev, and the Test Ban* (Berkeley: University of California Press, 1981); and Steve Fetter, *Toward a Comprehensive Test Ban* (Cambridge, MA: Ballinger, 1988). For a sense of the arguments used against limits on nuclear tests, see James H. McBride, *The Test Ban Treaty: Military, Technological, and Political Implications* (Chicago: Henry Regnery, 1967).

29. "Soviets OK Limited On-Site Inspections Offer on Troop Moves Seen as Breakthrough in East-West Talks," *Los Angeles Times*, August 20, 1986.

30. Don Oberdorfer, *The Turn: From the Cold War to a New Era—The United States and the Soviet Union, 1983–1990* (New York: Poseidon Press, 1991), 234.

31. For the text of this agreement, see Conference on Security and Co-operation in Europe, "Document of the Stockholm Conference," September 19, 1986, Federa-

tion of American Scientists, available at http://www.fas.org/nuke/control/osce/text/ STOCK86E.htm.

32. See Raymond L. Garthoff, *Détente and Confrontation: American-Soviet Relations from Nixon to Reagan* (Washington, DC: Brookings Institution Press, 2001); and Oberdorfer, *The Turn*. For a detailed account of the Intermediate-Range Nuclear Forces Treaty inspection provisions and their implementation, see Joseph P. Harahan, *On-Site Inspections Under the INF Treaty: A History of the On-Site Inspection Agency and INF Treaty Implementation, 1988–1991* (Washington, DC: On-Site Inspection Agency, United States Department of Defense, 1993); and Steven E. Steiner, "Remarks by Ambassador Steven E. Steinert: INF Commemoration, Moscow" U.S. Embassy at Canberra, Australia, May 21, 2001, available at http://canberra.usembassy.gov/hyper/2001/0521/epf101.htm.

33. See Joseph P. Harahan and John C. Cuhn III, *On-Site Inspections Under the CFE Treaty: A History of the On-Site Inspection Agency and CFE Treaty Implementation, 1990–1996* (Washington, DC: On-Site Inspection Agency, U.S. Department of Defense, 1996).

34. See Mark M. Lowenthal, *The CFE Treaty: Verification and Compliance Issues*, Congressional Research Service, September 1, 1992, available at http://www.fas.org/nuke/control/cfe/congress/22b1.htm#verification_regime; and Wade Boese, "The Conventional Armed Forces in Europe (CFE) Treaty at a Glance," Arms Control Association, January 2002, available at http://www.armscontrol.org/subject/caec/cfeback2.asp.

35. The text of the START I accord (U.S. Department of State, *Treaty Between the United States of America and the Union of Soviet Socialist Republics on the Reduction and Limitation of Strategic Offensive Arms*) can be accessed at http://www.state.gov/www/global/arms/starthtm/start/start1.html. On START verification, see Defense Threat Reduction Agency, *Strategic Arms Reduction Treaty (START) Inspection and Monitoring Sites in the Former Soviet Union*, available at http://www.dtra.mil/newsservices/fact_sheets/display.cfm?fs=start-fsu. Also see Defense Threat Reduction Agency, *Strategic Arms Reduction Treaty (START) Inspection and Monitoring Sites in the United States*, available at http://www.dtra.mil/newsservices/fact_sheets/display.cfm?fs=start-us; and Office of Technology Assessment, *Verification Technologies: Measures for Monitoring Compliance with the START Treaty*, OTA-ISC-479, December 1990, available at http://www.princeton.edu/~ota/ns20/alpha_f.html.

36. See John Borowski, *From the Atlantic to the Urals: Negotiating Arms Control at the Stockholm Conference* (Washington, DC: Pergamon-Brassey, 1988); and James Goodby, "The Stockholm Conference: Negotiating a Cooperative Security System for Europe," in Alexander L. George, Philip J. Farley, and Alexander Dallin (eds.), *U.S.-Soviet Security Cooperation: Achievements, Failures, Lessons* (New York: Oxford University Press, 1988), 144–172.

37. International Atomic Energy Agency, *Annual Report 2005*, vi, available at http://www.iaea.org/Publications/Reports/Anrep2005/anrep2005_full.pdf.

38. International Atomic Energy Agency, *Strengthened Safeguards System: Status of Additional Protocols*, June 13, 2007, available at http://www.iaea.org/OurWork/SV/Safeguards/sg_protocol.html.

39. Organization for the Prohibition of Chemical Weapons, *The Chemical Weapons Ban: Facts and Figures*, June 27, 2007, available at http://www.opcw.org/factsandfigures/index.html#DeclarationsInspections.

40. See Organization for the Prohibition of Chemical Weapons, *The Chemical Weapons Ban: Facts and Figures*, June 20, 2007, available at http://www.opcw.org/factsandfigures/index.html.

41. Concerns over the inability of the global seismic network established by the Comprehensive Test Ban Treaty to monitor low-yield tests figured prominently in the arguments of skeptics. This monitoring system now appears to be able to identify a test twenty times smaller than the one carried out by North Korea. See Won-Young Kim and Paul G. Richards, "North Korean Nuclear Test: Seismic Discrimination at Low Yield," *Eos* 88(14) (April 3, 2007): 157–161. Also see Office of the Director of National Intelligence, Public Affairs Office, "Statement by the Office of the Director of National Intelligence on the North Korea Nuclear Test," October 16, 2006, available at http://www.dni.gov/announcements/20061016_release.pdf.

42. Andrew E. Kramer and Thom Shanker, "Russia Suspends Arms Agreement over U.S. Shield," *New York Times*, July 15, 2007 (available at http://www.nytimes.com/2007/07/15/world/europe/15russia.html).

43. Assistant Secretary of State Paula DeSutter, quoted by Carol Giacomo, "U.S. to Let START Nuclear Treaty Expire," Reuters, May 22, 2007 (available at http://www.reuters.com/article/topNews/idUSN2242996020070522).

44. White House, "Press Conference by President Bush and Russian Federation President Putin," June 16, 2001, available at http://www.whitehouse.gov/news/releases/2001/06/20010618.html.

45. Verbatim excerpt from the Bush administration's *Nuclear Posture Review* submitted to the U.S. Congress on December 31, 2001. U.S. Department of Defense, *Nuclear Posture Review Report*, available at http://www.globalsecurity.org/wmd/library/policy/dod/npr.htm.

46. See National Resource Defense Council, "Table of Known Nuclear Tests Worldwide, 1945–2002," available at http://www.nrdc.org/nuclear/nudb/datab15.asp.

47. Nongovernmental researchers David Wright and Lisbeth Gronlund have concluded that Beijing ceased plutonium production for military uses around 1990. See David Wright and Lisbeth Gronlund, "A History of China's Plutonium Production," *Science and Global Security* 11(1) (2003): 61–80.

48. Two surveys that cover all prescriptive bases are George Perkovich, Jessica T.

Mathews, Joseph Cirincione, Rose Gottemoeller, and Jon B. Wolfsthal, *Universal Compliance: A Strategy for Nuclear Security* (Washington, DC: Carnegie Endowment for International Peace, March 2005), available at http://www.carnegieendowment .org/files/uC2.FINAL3.pdf; and Weapons of Mass Destruction Commission, *Weapons of Terror: Freeing the World of Nuclear, Biological, and Chemical Arms* (Stockholm: Weapons of Mass Destruction Commission, 2006), available at http://www .wmdcommission.org/files/Weapons_of_Terror.pdf. Also see Jeffrey Laurenti and Carl Robichaud (eds.), *Breaking the Nuclear Impasse: New Prospects for Security Against Weapons Threats* (New York: Century Foundation Press, 2007); and Graham Allison (ed.), "Confronting the Specter of Nuclear Terrorism," special issue of *Annals of the American Academy of Political and Social Science* 607 (September 2006).

49. See Navnita Chadha Behera, *Demystifying Kashmir* (Washington, DC: Brookings Institution Press, 2006); and Sumantra Bose, *Kashmir: Roots of Conflict, Paths to Peace* (Cambridge, MA: Harvard University Press, 2003).

50. See, for example, Michael D. Swaine and Tuosheng Zhang (eds.), *Managing Sino-American Crises: Case Studies and Analysis* (Washington, DC: Carnegie Endowment for International Peace, 2006); and Nancy Bernkopf Tucker (ed.), *Dangerous Strait: The U.S.-Taiwan-China Crises* (New York: Columbia University Press, 2005).

51. For suggestions on future steps, see, for example, Alexei Arbatov and Vladimir Dvorkin, *Beyond Nuclear Deterrence: Transforming the U.S.-Russian Equation* (Washington, DC: Carnegie Endowment for International Peace, 2006); and Sidney D. Drell and James E. Goodby, *The Gravest Danger: Nuclear Weapons* (Stanford, CA: Hoover Institution Press, 2003).

52. Of particular value are the series of publications on cooperative threat reduction programs released by the Managing the Atom Project at the Belfer Center at Harvard University (see http://www.belfercenter.org/project/3/managing_the_atom .html), the website of the Nuclear Threat Initiative (http://www.NTI.org), and the publications of the Partnership for Global Security (see http://www.partnership forglobalsecurity.org/).

53. For analysis and policy prescriptions dealing with Iran, see Henry Sokolski and Patrick Clawson (eds.), *Getting Ready for a Nuclear-Ready Iran* (Carlisle, PA: Strategic Studies Institute, October 2005), available at http://www.strategicstudiesinstitute .army.mil/pdffiles/pub629.pdf; and Patrick Clawson and Michael Eisenstadt, *Forcing Hard Choices on Tehran: Raising the Costs of Iran's Nuclear Program* (Washington, DC: Washington Institute for Near East Policy, 2006), available at http://www .washingtoninstitute.org/templateC04.php?CID=257. For background on the North Korean nuclear program, see Joel Wit, Daniel B. Poneman, and Robert L. Gallucci, *Going Critical: The First North Korean Nuclear Crisis* (Washington, DC: Brookings Institution Press, 2004). Also see Charles L. Pritchard, *Failed Diplomacy: The Tragic Story of How North Korea Got the Bomb* (Washington, DC: Brookings Institution Press, 2007).

54. Parts of this section appeared in Michael Krepon, "Ban the Bomb. Really," *American Interest* 3(3) (winter 2008): 89–93.

55. U.S. Department of State, *A Report on the International Control of Atomic Energy*, prepared by David E. Lilienthal (Washington, DC: U.S. Government Printing Office, 1946). Online versions of the Acheson-Lilienthal plan can be found at http://www.learnworld.com/ZNW/LWText.Acheson-Lilienthal.html#text and http://www.honors.umd.edu/HONR269J/archive/AchesonLilienthal.html.

56. See Turco et al., "Nuclear Winter."

57. See Jonathan Schell, *Fate of the Earth* (New York: Knopf, 1982); and Jonathan Schell, *The Abolition* (New York: Knopf, 1984).

58. Henry L. Stimson Center, *An Evolving U.S. Nuclear Posture*, Second Report of the Steering Committee, Project on Eliminating Weapons of Mass Destruction, Report 19 (Washington, DC: Henry L. Stimson Center, December 1995), 39. Also see Henry L. Stimson Center, *An American Legacy: Building a Nuclear-Weapon-Free World*, Final Report of the Steering Committee Project on Eliminating Weapons of Mass Destruction, Report 22 (Washington, DC: Henry L. Stimson Center, March 1997); and Henry L. Stimson Center, *Beyond the Nuclear Peril: The Year in Review and the Years Ahead*, Report 15 (Washington, DC: Henry L. Stimson Center, January 1995).

59. See, for example, Canberra Commission, *The Canberra Commission on the Elimination of Nuclear Weapons: Executive Summary*, NuclearFiles.org, available at http://www.nuclearfiles.org/menu/key-issues/nuclear-weapons/issues/civil-society/canberra-commission-executive-summary_1996-08-00.htm; and Ministry of Foreign Affairs of Japan, *Facing Nuclear Dangers: An Action Plan for the 21st Century—The Report of the Tokyo Forum for Nuclear Non-Proliferation and Disarmament*, July 25, 1999, available at http://www.mofa.go.jp/policy/un/disarmament/forum/tokyo9907/index.html.

60. Henry L. Stimson, "The Challenge to Americans," *Foreign Affairs* 26(1) (October 1947): 12.

61. See Paul H. Nitze, "A Threat Mostly to Ourselves," *New York Times*, October 28, 1999 (available at http://query.nytimes.com/gst/fullpage.html?res=950DE2DC1038F93BA15753C1A96F958260). Also see Paul H. Nitze, "Is It Time to Junk Our Nukes? The New World Disorder Makes Them Obsolete," *Washington Post*, January 16, 1994.

62. George P. Shultz, William J. Perry, Henry A. Kissinger, and Sam Nunn, "A World Free of Nuclear Weapons," *Wall Street Journal*, January 4, 2007.

63. Interview broadcast on the *CBS Evening News*, March 29, 1979.

64. See, for example, Charles L. Glaser, "The Flawed Case for Nuclear Disarmament," *Survival* 40(1) (spring 1998): 112–128; and Brent Scowcroft and Arnold Kanter, "Which Nuke Policy," *Washington Times*, March 24, 1997.

65. See Michael J. Mazarr (ed.), *Nuclear Weapons in a Transformed World: The Challenge of Virtual Nuclear Arsenals* (Washington, DC: Center for Strategic and In-

ternational Studies, 1997); and Jonathan Schell, *The Gift of Time: The Case for Abolishing Nuclear Weapons Now* (New York: Metropolitan Books, 1998).

66. For an authoritative first-person account of these deliberations, see Jayantha Dhanapala with Randy Rydell, *Multilateral Diplomacy and the NPT: An Insider's Account* (Geneva: UNIDIR, 2005).

67. See Kenneth N. Waltz, *The Spread of Nuclear Weapons: More May Be Better*, Adelphi Paper 171 (London: International Institute for Strategic Studies, 1981).

68. Sagan and Waltz, *Spread of Nuclear Weapons*, 29–43.

69. See Kurt M. Campbell, Robert J. Einhorn, and Mitchell B. Reiss (eds.), *Nuclear Tipping Point: Why States Reconsider Their Nuclear Choices* (Washington, DC: Brookings Institution Press, 2004). The editors express differing perspectives, but they conclude on an optimistic note: "Whatever path countries may take toward the tipping point, we are almost certainly not there yet—in fact, we do not appear to be close" (p. 328). Also see Mitchell Reiss, *Bridled Ambition: Why Countries Constrain Their Nuclear Capabilities* (Washington, DC: Woodrow Wilson Center Press, 1995).

70. Devin Hagerty, *The Consequences of Nuclear Proliferation: Lessons from South Asia* (Cambridge, MA: MIT Press, 1998); and Ganguly and Hagerty, *Fearful Symmetry*. Ganguly and Hagerty downplay other factors that might have led to the absence of war on the subcontinent and, notwithstanding their thesis, argue with some urgency for more concerted U.S. conflict resolution efforts on Kashmir.

71. See Krepon, "Is Cold War Experience Applicable to Southern Asia?"; and Krepon, "The Stability-Instability Paradox." For a multiregional analysis, see Goldstein, *Preventive Attack*.

72. Glenn Snyder, *Deterrence and Defense* (Princeton, NJ: Princeton University Press, 1961), 226.

73. Robert Jervis, *The Illogic of American Nuclear Strategy* (Ithaca, NY: Cornell University Press, 1984), 31.

74. Sagan and Waltz, *Spread of Nuclear Weapons*, 150.

75. See Emanuel Adler, "Arms Control, Disarmament, and National Security: A Thirty Year Retrospective and a New Set of Anticipations," *Daedalus* 120(1) (winter 1991): 3.

76. See Michael Krepon, *Strategic Stalemate, Nuclear Weapons, and Arms Control in American Politics* (New York: St. Martin's Press, 1984); and Michael Krepon, *Cooperative Threat Reduction, Missile Defense, and the Nuclear Future* (New York: Palgrave Macmillan, 2003), 165–187.

77. Winston S. Churchill, *Never Give In! The Best of Winston Churchill's Speeches* (New York: Hyperion, 2003), 491.

78. Thomas C. Schelling, "The Thirtieth Year," *Daedalus* 120(1) (winter 1991): 21, 24.

79. See "News Conference Styles of Four Presidents," *New York Times*, January 28, 1969, 12.

80. Paul H. Nitze, "Atoms, Strategy, and Foreign Policy," *Foreign Affairs* 35(2) (January 1956): 187–198.

81. Paul H. Nitze, "Assuring Strategic Stability in an Era of Détente," *Foreign Affairs* 54(2) (January 1976): 232.

82. See Richard Pipes, "Why the Soviet Union Thinks It Could Fight and Win a Nuclear War," *Commentary* 74(1) (July 1977): 21–34.

83. McGeorge Bundy, "To Cap the Volcano," *Foreign Affairs* 48(1) (October 1969): 11.

84. Dean Rusk, Robert McNamara, George Ball, Roswell Gilpatric, Theodore Sorenson, and McGeorge Bundy, "The Lessons of the Cuban Missile Crisis," *Time*, September 27, 1982.

85. See, for example, Henry A. Kissinger, "Arms Control, Inspections, and Surprise Attack," *Foreign Affairs* 38(4) (July 1960): 557–575; Henry A. Kissinger, *The Necessity for Choice* (New York: Harper & Brothers, 1960); Nitze, "Atoms, Strategy, and Foreign Policy"; and Nitze, "Assuring Strategic Stability."

86. See, for example, Colin S. Gray and Keith Payne, "Victory Is Possible," *Foreign Policy* 39 (summer 1980): 14–27. Payne was a principal contributor to the George W. Bush administration's nuclear posture statement.

87. See Keir A. Lieber and Daryl G. Press, "The Rise of U.S. Nuclear Primacy," *Foreign Affairs* 85(2) (March–April 2006): 42–54 (available at http://www.foreign affairs.org/20060301faessay85204/keir-a-lieber-daryl-g-press/the-rise-of-u-s-nuclear-primacy.html).

88. See U.S. Department of Defense, *Nuclear Posture Review Report.*

89. White House, National Security Council, "Transform America's National Security Institutions to Meet the Challenges and Opportunities of the Twenty-First Century," in *The National Security Strategy*, September 2002, available at http://www .whitehouse.gov/nsc/nss/2002/nss9.html.

90. See David E. Mosher, Lowell H. Schwartz, David R. Howell, and Lynn E. Davis, *Beyond the Nuclear Shadow: A Phased Approach for Improving Nuclear Safety and U.S.-Russian Relations* (Santa Monica, CA: RAND Corp., 2003).

91. One reminder of the potential for mishap was the mistaken carriage of nuclear-armed cruise missiles from North Dakota to Louisiana in 2007. See Joby Warrick and Walter Pincus, "Missteps in the Bunker," *Washington Post*, September 23, 2007, 1 (available at http://www.washingtonpost.com/wp-dyn/content/article/2007/09/22/AR2007092201447.html).

92. Bundy, "To Cap the Volcano," 10.

Chapter 6

1. "Excerpts from Two Wilson Hearings Before Senate Committees on Defense Appointment; Senators Get Wilson's Answers on His G.M. Stock Holdings," *New York Times*, January 24, 1953.

2. X [George Kennan], "The Sources of Soviet Conduct," *Foreign Affairs* 25(4) (1946–1947): 582.

3. Dick Cheney, "Vice President Speaks at VFW 103rd National Convention: Remarks by the Vice President to the Veterans of Foreign Wars 103rd National Convention," White House, Office of the Press Secretary, August 26, 2002, available at http://www.whitehouse.gov/news/releases/2002/08/20020826.html.

4. George W. Bush, "President Says Saddam Hussein Must Leave Iraq Within 48 Hours: Remarks by the President in Address to the Nation," White House, Office of the Press Secretary, March 17, 2003, available at http://www.whitehouse.gov/news/releases/2003/03/20030317-7.html.

5. National Security Council, *The National Security Strategy*, pt. 9, *Transform America's National Security Institutions to Meet the Challenges and Opportunities of the Twenty-First Century*, White House, September 2002, available at http://www.whitehouse.gov/nsc/nss/2002/nss9.html.

6. Harry S. Truman, *Memoirs: Years of Trial and Hope 1946–1952* (New York: Doubleday, 1955), v. 2, 383, 359.

7. John F. Kennedy, "Special Message to the Congress on the Defense Budget," March 28, 1961, available at http://www.jfklink.com/speeches/jfk/publicpapers/1961/jfk99_61.html.

8. Charles Krauthammer, "The Unipolar Moment," *Foreign Affairs* 70(1) (winter 1990–1991): 32.

9. For a book-length exposition of this argument, see Robert Strausz-Hupé, William R. Kintner, and Stefan T. Possony, *A Forward Strategy for America* (New York: Harper & Brothers, 1961).

10. For an elaboration of this argument, see David Holloway, "Deterrence, Preventive War, and Preemption," in George Bunn and Christopher F. Chyba (eds.), *U.S. Nuclear Weapons Policy: Confronting Today's Threats* (Washington, DC: Brookings Institution Press, 2006), 34–74.

11. Charles Krauthammer, "The Unipolar Moment Revisited," *National Interest* 70 (winter 2002–2003): 10.

12. George W. Bush, "Bush Addresses VFW National Convention, Milwaukee," August 21, 2000, available at http://transcripts.cnn.com/TRANSCRIPTS/0008/21/se.01.html.

13. Helene Cooper, "North Koreans Agree to Disable Nuclear Facilities," *New York Times*, October 4, 2007 (available at http://www.nytimes.com/2007/10/04/world/asia/04diplo.html?pagewanted=print).

14. The evolution and extension of these techniques is traced in some of my previous writing. See Michael Krepon and Mary Umberger (eds.), *Verification and Compliance: A Problem-Solving Approach* (Cambridge, MA: Ballinger Books, 1988); Michael Krepon, Peter D. Zimmerman, Leonard S. Spector, and Mary Umberger

(eds.), *Commercial Observation Satellites and International Security* (New York: St. Martin's Press, 1990); Michael Krepon and Amy Smithson (eds.), *Open Skies, Arms Control, and Cooperative Security* (New York: St. Martin's Press, 1992); Michael Krepon and Amit Sevak (eds.), *Crisis Prevention, Confidence Building, and Reconciliation in South Asia* (New York: St. Martin's Press, 1995); Michael Krepon, Khurshed Khoja, Michael Newbill, and Jenny S. Drezin (eds.), *Global Confidence Building: New Tools for Troubled Regions* (New York: St. Martin's Press, 1999); and Michael Krepon, *Nuclear Risk Reduction in South Asia* (New York: Palgrave Macmillan, 2004).

15. I believe that the first person to suggest this term to me was General William Burns.

16. This phraseology is borrowed from Charles Krauthammer's writings. See Krauthammer, "Unipolar Moment Revisited."

17. National Security Council, "National Security Strategy."

18. George W. Bush, "President Bush Delivers Graduation Speech at West Point," White House, Office of the Press Secretary, June 1, 2002, available at http://www .whitehouse.gov/news/releases/2002/06/20020601-3.html.

19. See, for example, Raymond Ibrahim (ed.), *The Al Qaeda Reader* (New York: Doubleday, 2007).

20. See George Perkovich, "Giving Justice Its Due," *Foreign Affairs* 84(4) (July–August 2005): 79–93.

21. Don Rumsfeld, "Rumsfeld Memo: Global War on Terrorism," October 16, 2003, available at http://www.globalsecurity.org/military/library/policy/dod/ rumsfeld-d20031016sdmemo.htm.

22. In 2000, the State Department recorded 423 international terrorist attacks, resulting in 405 people killed and 791 wounded. In 2006, the State Department's tally was 14,338 incidents of terrorism worldwide, resulting in 20,498 people killed and 38,191 injured. U.S. Department of State, "National Counter-Terrorism Center Statistical Annex Supplement on Terrorism Deaths, Injuries, Kidnappings of Private U.S. Citizens," in *Country Reports on Terrorism*, prepared by U.S. Department of State, Office of the Coordinator for Counterterrorism, April 30, 2007, available at http://www.state.gov/s/ ct/rls/crt/2006/82739.htm; and U.S. Department of State, *Country Reports on Terrorism 2006*, prepared by U.S. Department of State, Office of the Coordinator for Counterterrorism, April 30, 2007, available at http://www.state.gov/s/ct/rls/crt/2006/.

23. Bernard I. Finel and Holly Crystal Gell, *Are We Winning: Measuring Progress in the Struggle Against Violent Jihadism* (Washington, DC: American Security Project, September 2007), 6 (available at http://www.americansecurityproject.org/files/ ASP_RPTWeb_0.pdf).

24. Walter A. McDougall, . . . *The Heavens and the Earth: A Political History of the Space Age* (New York: Basic Books, 1985), 177.

25. Karl von Clausewitz, *On War,* J. J. Graham (trans.) (New York: Barnes and

Noble, 1956), bk. 8, 127. For an elaboration of this dictum, see Raymond Aron, "Strategy and Diplomacy, or On the Unity of Foreign Policy," in his *Peace and War: A Theory of International Relations* (New York: Doubleday, 1966), 21–46.

26. The clearest example of this double standard occurred during the Senate's consideration of the Chemical Weapons Convention, when Republicans passed a condition expressly permitting the president to block treaty-mandated inspections if they could reveal national security secrets and another curtailing the scope of inspections if they might compromise U.S. copyrights. Only one bilateral treaty with Russia remains in effect mandating inspections, and the Bush administration has declared this inspection regime to be onerous. See Carol Giacomo, "U.S. to Let START Nuclear Treaty Expire," Reuters, May 22, 2007 (available at http://www.reuters.com/article/topNews/idUSN2242996020070522). The Bush administration has opposed ratification of the Comprehensive Test Ban Treaty as an infringement on U.S. nuclear options that might include a need to resume testing.

27. U.S. Air Force Space Command, *Strategic Master Plan FY06 and Beyond*, Center for Defense Information, October 1, 2003, available at http://www.cdi.org/news/space-security/afspc-strategic-master-plan-06-beyond.pdf.

28. The George W. Bush administration's National Space Policy can be found at Office of Science and Technology Policy, *U.S. National Space Policy*, Executive Office of the President, August 31, 2006, available at http://www.licensing.noaa.gov/USNationalSpacePolicy_083106.pdf.

29. "Detection of Debris from Chinese ASAT Test Increases; One Minor Fragmentation Event in Second Quarter of 2007," *Orbital Debris Quarterly News* 11(3) (July 2007): 1 (available at http://orbitaldebris.jsc.nasa.gov/newsletter/pdfs/ODQNv11i3.pdf).

30. William J. Broad and David E. Sanger, "China Tests Anti-Satellite Weapon, Unnerving U.S.," *New York Times*, January 18, 2007 (available at http://www.nytimes.com/2007/01/18/world/asia/18cnd-china.html?ex=1184904000&en=d4cfd4978bcfa96b&ei=5070).

31. Defense Intelligence Agency, *The Decades Ahead: 1999–2020—A Primer on the Future Threat*, July 1999. Reprinted in Rowan Scarborough, *Rumsfeld's War: The Untold Story of America's Anti-Terrorist Commander* (Washington, DC: Regnery, 2004), 203.

32. Verbatim excerpts of the Nuclear Posture Review submitted to the U.S. Congress on December 31, 2001, were leaked and can be found at U.S. Department of Defense, *Nuclear Posture Review Report*, GlobalSecurity.org, January 8, 2002, available at http://www.globalsecurity.org/wmd/library/policy/dod/npr.htm. This excerpt is from pages 12–13 of the original document.

33. National Intelligence Council, *Foreign Missile Developments and the Ballistic Missile Threat Through 2015*, prepared under the auspices of the National Intelligence Officer for Strategic and Nuclear Programs, December 2001, Federation of American Scientists, available at http://www.fas.org/irp/nic/bmthreat-2015.htm.

34. See Hans M. Kristensen, Robert S. Norris, and Matthew McKinzie, *Chinese Nuclear Forces and U.S. Nuclear War Planning* (Washington, DC: Federation of American Scientists and Natural Resources Defense Council, November 2006), 35–136. The extent of official U.S. overestimates of Chinese nuclear capabilities has, however, shrunk over time.

35. Keith B. Payne, "Post–Cold War Deterrence and a Taiwan Crisis," *China Brief* 1(5) (September 12, 2001), available at http://www.jamestown.org/publications_details.php?volume_id=17&issue_id=633&article_id=4569.

36. Colin S. Gray and Keith Payne, "Victory Is Possible," *Foreign Policy* 39 (summer 1980): 14–27.

37. Much is in the public domain about older nuclear war plans, and newer plans have been leaked shortly after they were issued. For excerpts of the George W. Bush administration's nuclear posture, see U.S. Department of Defense, *Nuclear Posture Review Report.*

38. Donald H. Rumsfeld, "Remarks as Delivered by Secretary of Defense Donald H. Rumsfeld, Shangri-La Hotel, Singapore, Saturday, June 04, 2005," U.S. Department of Defense, available at http://www.defenselink.mil/speeches/2005/sp20050604-secdef1561.html.

39. Andrew E. Kramer, "Putin Cites Third Reich in Veiled Criticism of U.S.," *New York Times*, May 9, 2007 (available at http://www.nytimes.com/2007/05/09/world/europe/10cnd-russia.html?ex=1182398400&en=fa9cb71c388ba67e&ei=5070).

40. Joseph S. Nye Jr., *Soft Power: The Means to Success in World Politics* (New York: Public Affairs, 2004), x.

41. National Security Council, *United States Objectives and Programs for National Security*, Federation of American Scientists, April 14, 1950, available at http://www.fas.org/irp/offdocs/nsc-hst/nsc-68.htm. See in particular "U.S. Intentions and Capabilities: Actual and Potential."

42. The Pentagon's usage of "counterproliferation" began in the Clinton administration and subsequently gained considerable traction in the Bush administration.

43. Cooper, "North Koreans Agree to Disable Nuclear Facilities."

44. For a book-length exposition of this thesis, see Ian Shapiro, *Containment: Rebuilding a Strategy Against Global Terror* (Princeton, NJ: Princeton University Press, 2007).

45. David E. Sanger and Mark Mazzetti, "Israel Struck Syrian Nuclear Project, Analysts Say," *New York Times*, October 14, 2007.

46. A spoonful of dirt collected by a clandestine source outside the plant gates at al Shifa showed traces of elements of one of the compounds used in making VX, a nerve gas. This particular compound can also be used to make pesticides. According to CIA director George Tenet, "You can still get a debate within the intelligence community on how good a target al-Shifa was" (George Tenet with Bill Harlow, *At the*

Center of the Storm: My Years at the CIA [New York: Harper Collins, 2007], 117). President Clinton's memoirs include the passage, "I still believe we did the right thing" (*My Life* [New York: Knopf, 2004], 805). An independent, nongovernmental assessment in 1998 concluded, "On balance, the evidence available to date indicates that it is more probable that the Shifa plant had no role whatsoever in chemical weapons production" (Michael Barletta, "Chemical Weapons in the Sudan: Allegations and Evidence," *Nonproliferation Review* 6[1] [fall 1998]: 130).

47. For accounts of the Clinton administration's dealings with North Korea, see Charles L. Pritchard, *Failed Diplomacy: The Tragic Story of How North Korea Got the Bomb* (Washington, DC: Brookings Institution Press, 2007); and Joel Wit, Daniel B. Poneman, and Robert L. Gallucci, *Going Critical: The First North Korean Nuclear Crisis* (Washington, DC: Brookings Institution Press, 2004).

48. The Joint Chiefs of Staff's doctrinal statement for nuclear operations includes the following passage: "Deterrence assumes an opposing actor's leadership proceeds according to the logic of self-interest, although this self-interest is viewed from differing cultural perspectives and the dictates of given situations. This will be particularly difficult with nonstate actors who employ or attempt to gain use of WMD [weapons of mass destruction]. Here deterrence may be directed at states that support their efforts as well as the terrorist organization itself. However, the continuing proliferation of WMD along with the means to deliver them increases the probability that someday a state/nonstate actor nation/terrorist may, through miscalculation or by deliberate choice, use those weapons. In such cases, deterrence, even based on the threat of massive destruction, may fail and the United States must be prepared to use nuclear weapons if necessary. A major challenge of deterrence is therefore to convincingly convey both will and capability to the opposing actor." U.S. Department of Defense, *Doctrine for Joint Nuclear Operations*, Joint Chiefs of Staff, Joint Publication 3-12, Final Coordination (2), March 15, 2005, available at http://www.globalsecurity.org/wmd/library/policy/dod/jp3_12fc2_15mar2005.htm.

49. On October 21, 2007, Vice President Dick Cheney said in prepared remarks that "the Iranian regime needs to know that if it stays on its present course, the international community is prepared to impose serious consequences. The United States joins other nations in sending a clear message: We will not allow Iran to have a nuclear weapon." Richard Cheney, "Vice President's Remarks to the Washington Institute for Near East Policy," Office of the Vice President, October 21, 2007, available at http://www.whitehouse.gov/news/releases/2007/10/20071021.html. Four days earlier, President George W. Bush warned of a possible "World War III" if Iran succeeded in obtaining the Bomb. See White House, Office of the Press Secretary, "Press Conference by the President," October 17, 2007, available at http://www.whitehouse .gov/news/releases/2007/10/20071017.html. Also see William Kristol, "And Now Iran," *Weekly Standard* 11(18) (January 23, 2006), available at http://www.weeklystandard .com/Content/Public/Articles/000/000/006/585tdlqf.asp; Norman Podhoretz, "The

Case for Bombing Iran," *Wall Street Journal*, May 30, 2007 (available at http://www
.opinionjournal.com/federation/feature/?id=110010139); Alan Dershowitz, "Amend
International Law to Allow Preemptive Strike on Iran," *Forward* 108(31,511) (August
20, 2004): 9; and Charles Krauthammer, "The Tehran Calculus," *Washington Post*,
September 15, 2006 (available at http://www.washingtonpost.com/wp-dyn/content/
article/2006/09/14/AR2006091401413.html).

50. See Ashton B. Carter and William J. Perry, *Plan B for Iran: What If Nuclear
Diplomacy Fails?* Preventive Defense Project, Harvard and Stanford Universities, September 10, 2006, available at http://belfercenter.ksg.harvard.edu/publication/2127/
plan_b_for_iran.html. Carter and Perry did not advocate preemption: "While it is
important to explore and analyze various versions of Plan B, it would be premature to
abandon the diplomatic path. There is still time, since Iran is years away from making
its first bomb" (p. 1).

51. One example: "As the Imam [Ayatollah Khomeini] said, Israel must be wiped
off the map." "Ahmadinejad: Wipe Israel Off Map," *Al-Jazeera*, October 28, 2005,
available at http://english.aljazeera.net/English/archive/archive?ArchiveId=15816.

52. Donald H. Rumsfeld, "Nuclear Posture Review," Foreword, submitted to
Congress on December 31, 2001. U.S. Department of Defense, *Nuclear Posture Review
Report*.

53. For Hans M. Kristensen's accounting of the likely size of the U.S. nuclear reserve, see Hans M. Kristensen. "Estimates of the U.S. Nuclear Stockpile, 2007 and 2012,"
Federation of American Scientists, available at http://www.fas.org/blog/ssp/2007/05/
estimates_of_us_nuclear_weapon.php. Also see Robert S. Norris, Hans M. Kristensen, and Christopher E. Paine, *Nuclear Insecurity: A Critique of the Bush Administration's Nuclear Weapons Policies*, National Resources Defense Council, September 2004,
available at http://www.nrdc.org/nuclear/insecurity/critique.pdf.

54. White House, Office of the Press Secretary, "Remarks by Samuel R. Berger,
Assistant to the President for National Security Affairs, to the Annual Washington Forum of Business Executives for National Security," Clinton Presidential Library, National Archives and Records Administration, May 5, 1998, available at http://clinton2
.nara.gov/WH/EOP/NSC/html/speeches/19980519-2612.html.

55. Paul H. Nitze, "A Threat Mostly to Ourselves," *New York Times*, October 28,
1999.

56. George P. Shultz, William J. Perry, Henry A. Kissinger, and Sam Nunn. "A
World Free of Nuclear Weapons," *Wall Street Journal*, January 4, 2007.

57. John Mueller would extend this analysis backward to include the first nuclear
age. See John Mueller, "The Essential Irrelevance of Nuclear Weapons," *International
Security* 13(2) (fall 1988): 3–27.

58. Henry L. Stimson and McGeorge Bundy, *On Active Service in Peace and War*
(New York: Harper and Brothers, 1947), 633.

59. Project on Eliminating Weapons of Mass Destruction, *An Evolving U.S. Nuclear Posture*, Henry L. Stimson Center, Second Report of the Steering Committee, Report 19, December 1995, 38.

60. P. Stålenheim, C. Perdomo, and E. Sköns, *SIPRI Yearbook 2007* (Oxford: Oxford University Press, 2007), 270.

61. E-mail communication from Hans M. Kristensen, August 22, 2007.

62. "The Next Generation of Nuclear Weapons," *Bulletin of the Atomic Scientists* 83(4) (July–August 2007): 30.

63. Robert S. McNamara, "The Dynamics of Nuclear Strategy," *Department of State Bulletin* 57 (October 9, 1967), 450.

64. McNamara, "Dynamics of Nuclear Strategy," 448.

65. One key figure present at the creation of arms control, Donald G. Brennan, left the fold over this issue. See, for example, D. G. Brennan, "The Case for Missile Defense," *Foreign Affairs* 47(3) (April 1969): 434–448. For a comprehensive treatment of defense-oriented deterrence, see David Goldfischer, *The Best Defense: Policy Alternatives for U.S. Nuclear Security from the 1950s to the 1990s* (Ithaca, NY: Cornell University Press, 1993).

66. The shelf life of plutonium pits was estimated by an independent panel of government experts and then relayed to Congress. See Linton F. Brooks, "Letter to The Honorable John Warner, Chairman, Committee on Armed Services," Department of Energy, National Nuclear Security Administration, November 28, 2006, available at http://www.nukewatch.org/facts/nwd/JASON_ReportPuAging.pdf.

67. See, for example, Office of Defense Programs, "Complex 2030: An Infrastructure Planning Scenario for a Nuclear Weapons Complex Able to Meet the Threats of the 21st Century," National Nuclear Security Administration, U.S. Department of Energy, October 23, 2006.

68. For a series of articles making the case for and against the reliable replacement warhead program, see *Bulletin of the Atomic Scientists* 63(4) (July–August, 2007): 24–49, especially John R. Harvey, "Nonproliferation's New Soldier," *Bulletin of the Atomic Scientists*: 63(4) (July–August 2007): 32–33.

69. See, for example, Brennan, "Case for Missile Defense." For missile defense costs, see Steven A. Hildreth, *Ballistic Missile Defense: Historical Overview*, Congressional Research Service, CRS Report Code RS22120, July 9, 2007, available at http://www.fas.org/sgp/crs/weapons/RS22120.pdf.

70. See Dennis R. Gormley, *Dealing with the Threat of Cruise Missiles*, Adelphi Paper 339 (London: International Institute of Strategic Studies, 2005).

71. In a September 1999 assessment, the National Intelligence Council downplayed the possibility as well as the likelihood of this threat. An updated report issued in December 2001 concluded otherwise: "Most Intelligence Community agencies project that before 2015 the United States most likely will face ICBM threats from North Korea

and Iran, and possibly from Iraq." More ominous judgments on presumed Iraqi weapons of mass destruction followed. See National Intelligence Council, *Foreign Missile Developments*.

72. Paul H. Nitze, "Atoms, Strategy, and Policy," *Foreign Affairs* 35(2) (January 1956): 190–191.

73. Emphasis in the original. This reference was to the Soviet Union, but the conclusion applied just as well to the United States. Paul H. Nitze, "Assuring Strategic Stability in an Era of Détente," *Foreign Affairs* 54(2) (January 1976): 216.

74. This version of Churchill's famous dictum appeared in "Defense by Deterrents," *Time*, March 14, 1955 (available at http://www.time.com/time/printout/0,8816, 807084,00.html).

75. Henry A. Kissinger, "Arms Control, Inspection, and Surprise Attack," *Foreign Affairs* 38(4) (July 1960): 561.

INDEX